THAT
IRISHMAN

My friend, John O'Connor Power, once famous as 'the Member for Mayo' gave me, shortly before his death in February, 1919, the papers he had collected in the course of his unique political career – commencing as an Irish Fenian and ending as a British Liberal. 'Make what use you like of them,' he says in his letter to me, 'subject to one condition – they must not be made the basis of an attack on any Irishman'.

Michael MacDonagh, preface to *The Home Rule Movement*

THAT IRISHMAN

THE LIFE AND TIMES OF JOHN O'CONNOR POWER

JANE STANFORD

In memory of Russell and Anne Stanford and for Síle, Anne, Nóra and Lucy Jane

First published 2011

The History Press Ireland
119 Lower Baggot Street
Dublin 2
Ireland
www.thehistorypress.ie

© Jane Stanford, 2011

The right of Jane Stanford to be identified as the Author
of this work has been asserted in accordance with the
Copyrights, Designs and Patents Act 1988.

British Library Cataloguing in Publication Data.
A catalogue record for this book is available from the British Library.

ISBN 978 1 84588 698 1

Typesetting and origination by The History Press
Printed in Great Britain

Contents

Acknowledgments

I would like to thank Dr Rosemary Power for generously sharing her family history.

The Dun Laoghaire librarians were enormously helpful and located books and articles for me in Irish and British libraries.

Brian Casey arranged an invitation to speak at the Ballinasloe Historical and Archaeological and Historical Society. A local photographer, Evelyn Donellan, was unstinting with her help and advice and introduced me to Jimmy Howley, a well-informed cousin. We toured Ballinasloe, Ballygill and Creagh graveyard. Evelyn assembled an impressive Power family tree. The Ballinasloe librarians, Mary Dillon and Colette Hanrahan, were welcoming. I was introduced to many descendants of the Power family and stayed with fourth cousins, Anne and Kieran Kenny, in Ballygill. They were generous in their hospitality and friendship and made me feel at home.

I must pay tribute to the scholarship of Professor T.M. Moody, Professor R.V. Comerford, Dr Donald Jordan, Dr John Cunningham, Dr Gerard P. Moran and many others. Without their published research, this story would not have been told.

I must thank Liam Byrne for posting my essay on the Roscommon History website. Thanks are also due to Dr Paddy Buckley, James Conran, Dr Helen Conrad O'Briain, Eileen Ó Dúill CG, Dr Tom Stanford, Dr Michael Stanford, Sally Corcoran, Maureen McDonnell, Mary McDaid and Peter Edwards, biographer of Henri Le Caron.

The National Library of Ireland, Director of the National Archives of Ireland, Special Collections, Boole Library, University College Cork, Kilmainham Gaol Museum, the Parliamentary Archives UK, the National Portrait Gallery, London, The British Library, the John Rylands Library, the University of Manchester, Indiana State University Library, findmypast.co.uk, Abney Park Trust, St Jarlath's College, Tuam, County Galway, Middle Temple Library, St Bartholomew's Hospital Archives and Museum.

Pen Portraits

So was John O'Connor Power, who was shortly after to be Member for Mayo, and was at that time a chief potentate in the Supreme Council's mysterious sphere of influence; a man of great resolution, with a merciless underjaw, a furious temper governed by a carefully studied urbanity of manner, and a calm strong voice, that made the most common-place observation impressive; resolute enough in the ways of revolution to have himself headed raids for arms, and walked for years under the shadow of the gallows, but gifted also with a common-sense keen enough and fearless enough to guide him in the evolution from the impracticable to a wise and patriotic possibilism.

He would not be a follower of any man.

William O'Brien MP, *Recollections* (1905)

… Mr O'Connor Power, who had been notoriously a Fenian and member of the higher authorities of the conspiracy, but who was universally recognised as an able and conscientious worker in all English and Irish reforms, besides being the possessor of an oratorical gift with hardly any superior in the Parliaments in which he sat. But for the accident of not having been discovered while repression was in progress, Mr O'Connor Power, M.P., was everything wicked and incorrigible which Disraeli had castigated in the helpless and silent men at Portland and Dartmoor.

F. Hugh O'Donnell, *A History of the Irish Parliamentary Party* (1910)

He had all the qualities that make a leader of the people – a good presence, tall, muscular, and resolute looking; sincerity, belief in his cause, unbending determination, a cultivated mind, and oratorical gifts of the highest order. The matter of his speeches was always good. But if oratory is to weave its spells it demands in the speaker fine action as well as high thoughts and beautiful diction. O'Connor Power had a deep sonorous voice, which, used as it was, with fine modulation, was most impressive and appealing.

O'Connor Power was above the suspicion of interested motives.

Michael MacDonagh, *The Home Rule Movement* (1920)

He had very great gifts of speech, and I never knew a member of our party who had a more perfect and instinctive knowledge of what was called 'the tone of the House of Commons'. Not by a demi-semi-quaver did he ever depart from the regular gamut of appropriate Parliamentary speech. In addition, he was a man of great courage, great self-confidence, and great force of character; but he had the tremendous defect of a very irritable and fierce temper.

T.P. O'Connor, *Memoirs of an Old Parliamentarian* (1928)

Abbreviations

AFIL	All-for-Ireland-League
CT	*Connaught Telegraph*
FJ	*Freeman's Journal*
HR	Home Rule
HRCGB	Home Rule Confederation of Great Britain
II	*Irish Independent*
IGTWU	Irish and General Transport Workers Union
IPP	Irish Parliamentary Party
IRB	Irish Republican Brotherhood
IT	*Irish Times*
MG	*Manchester Guardian*
MP	Member of Parliament, UK

NBSP   National Brotherhood of Saint Patrick

NLC   National Liberal Club

NLI   National Library of Ireland

NYT   *New York Times*

PM   Prime Minister

RIC   Royal Irish Constabulary

 SC   Supreme Council

UIL   United Irish League

UVF   Ulster Volunteer Force

Part One

The Home Place

A drift of men gone over the sea
A drift of the dead where men should be.[1]

We have no weapons, except patience and sufferance, and talk about tomorrow.[2]

It was the very worst of times. John O'Connor Power was born on 13 February 1846, in the first cruel winter of the Irish Famine, often called the Great Hunger and sometimes the Irish Holocaust. He lived with poverty, survived smallpox, and spent some time in the workhouse. Yet he rose to make a name for himself in the Fenian ranks, Westminster, radical journalism, and in later life, as a successful author, teacher and barrister-at-law. For over fifty years he would challenge the boundaries of a powerful Empire and build the connective bonds of a far-flung diaspora. One of the outstanding orators of the late-nineteenth century, he was ranked with Gladstone and Disraeli.

O'Connor Power was the youngest of three sons. Patrick Power, his father, was from a farming family in the Ballinasloe townland of Ballygill, in the parish of Creagh. Mary, his mother, was the daughter of P. O'Connor from Roscommon. His uncle, John Power, a tenant farmer with a small holding, has a place in Griffith's Valuation, a property record of the time.[3] Thomas Power farmed beside him.[4] It was an extended family and there were aunts, uncles and many cousins to visit.

A stout, stone bridge, across a broad, full-flowing river, stands close to 'Power's Garden', home to several generations of the family. A gentle, soothing view over lush meadows and sparse hedgerows directs the eye to a townscape, dominated by St Michael's spire and the clock tower of St John's. The Power homestead is no longer standing, but the vista remains unchanged.

Ballinasloe, on the border of counties Galway and Roscommon, and positioned on the River Suck, a tributary of the Shannon, was a thriving boom town. Strategically placed as the gateway to the west of Ireland and the Atlantic Ocean, its location was further enhanced by the expansion in 1828 of the Grand Canal and, later, in 1853, by the advent of the railway. The town provided a meeting ground for farmers, with access to the markets of Britain and Europe. It was the centre of Ireland's inland trade and was bolstered by a productive hinterland.

The Earls of Clancarty dominated Ballinasloe life. They were progressive and enlightened landlords, and under their benign patronage, the town, countryside and local businesses prospered. The flour mill, the three oatmeal mills, the breweries, coach factory, bacon-curing factory and tan yards gave extensive employment. There was also a felt-hat making establishment. A limestone quarry, opened in the early part of the nineteenth century, employed over 150 stone cutters. Many of the main buildings in the town were built of cut stone. Limestone was used for statuary and memorials, and there was a steady export to England and the United States.

The Clancartys were of Huguenot descent. Richard, the second earl, was a former chairman of the Board of Trade and had been ambassador to The Hague. He initiated improvements from the 1810s, which were continued by his son, the third earl, who acceded to the title in 1837.

The Great October Fair, one of Europe's oldest horse fairs and a sheep and cattle mart, was a major agricultural event in the trade calendar, and its wellbeing, it was said, mirrored the state of the national economy. The parkland of Garbally, the seat of the Clancartys, was thrown open to the public for the occasion.

The Ballinasloe Agricultural Society was established in 1841, and a model farm and an agricultural instructor provided training for local farmers. Grants for improvement and development were arranged, and tenants who excelled were rewarded with medals. The Horticultural Society for the Province of Connacht held three shows annually in the town, and these were always well attended.

Ballinasloe '(thanks to the Earl of Clancarty) is neatly built, clean and orderly … the streets are now paved and the town lighted by gas'.[5] Many houses were whitewashed annually, a practice which was believed to be hygienic as well as cosmetic. The principal shops and hotels were illuminated at dusk. The two large inns were always thronged with customers. Steady transactions of commerce were dealt with by Bank of Ireland, the National Bank and the Agriculture and Commercial Bank.

The surrounding countryside was fertile. Rich pastureland served sheep and cattle farming, and graziers had an increasing significance in the economy of the province.

In good years there was food on the table and access to education for the children of farmers and local workers in the national school[6] or in privately run establishments. Gaelic was the language at home, and English was the medium of education. The youngsters ran barefoot, but received a sound formation in reading, writing and arithmetic.

Ireland's teeming population depended on the potato as the main food source. Inheritance traditions, a legacy of the savage penal laws, when land was subdivided between children, spawned small holdings, where a potato crop might just sustain a family. Seasonal migrant labour to England and to Scotland helped to stretch the budget during the lean months before the new harvest. Those who emigrated sent regular remittances home.

Potatoes and buttermilk supported families, at a meagre subsistence level, in a mild climate. A natural source of vitamin C, the potato built strong bones. It was a nutritious if monotonous diet, and the Irish, noted for their vitality, hospitality and good humour, made do in grim conditions. Turf, the local fuel, was plentiful, and its sale provided additional income.

On the old Dublin road, the state-of-the-art asylum St Brigid's opened in 1833 and gave shelter to the disturbed souls of the province. The x-shaped building, crowned with a cupola, is built of local stone. On his tour of Connacht, William Makepeace Thackeray described it as 'magnificent … as handsome and stately as a palace'.[7] Not far from the Power farm, St Brigid's was a steady customer for turf, milk and potatoes and gave employment, direct and indirect, to many families in the locality.

The winter of 1846 was the most severe in living memory. Bad weather had been responsible for poor harvests all over Europe. Ireland was a net exporter of food but, due to Britain's *laissez faire*, non-intervention policy, allegedly adopted to promote self-reliance and discourage idleness, no equitable distribution methods were put in place.

> … no, the Irish ports were left wide open for every kind of *exportation* and trade, while on the other hand they enforced the laws that laid an embargo upon the *importation* of foreign corn; these were enforced with cruel severity until the famine had decimated the population of whole villages and towns.[8]

Markets were glutted with produce, but the hungry had no money to pay even the lowest prices. A dependence on the potato made the Irish predicament impossible.

Famine was inevitable. When the blight struck the crop there was no fall-back position. Over night, in field after field throughout the country, the leaves turned black and gave off an all-pervasive sickly stench. The potatoes, when lifted, had rotted in the ground.

The harvest failed dramatically, and the skills needed to grow alternative crops, or even to prepare other food, were lacking. Poaching game and freshwater fish was harshly punished. A bounteous sea did not provide an answer. Fishing was seasonal. The waters were dangerous, the weather unpredictable, and the boats inadequate for commercial fishing. The absence of refrigeration meant that a good catch could not be stored and sent on to the markets of large towns. Fish, viewed as a poor man's food, was not sufficiently valued. For centuries, when the Catholic Church forbade meat on Fridays, its consumption was penitential. Now migration westward signalled an urgent interest in shellfish, seaweed, and the fruits of a long shoreline.

The workhouses[9] of the country were inundated with victims of famine and disease. Road, bridge and pier building programmes were put in place to provide employment, but it was an inadequate intervention – too little, too late. One million were destitute, in workhouses or on relief. A coveted place in the workhouse was a step away from a slow and agonising death. A lane that led from one was called the pathway of death, *casan na marhb*: failure to gain entry meant all hope was gone.

Ballinasloe workhouse was built to shelter and accommodate 400 inmates. In the late forties it struggled to give food and medical attention to thousands of refugees crowding in from surrounding villages. Fourteen auxiliary shelters were provided to deal with the overwhelming numbers.

Fever followed famine and workhouses doubled as hospitals. Typhus, spread by lice, may have claimed more victims than starvation, taking the lives of close to 3,000 workhouse inmates in Ballinasloe alone. The disease thrived in overcrowded and filthy conditions, and was often referred to as 'jail' or 'ship' fever. Typhus was no respecter of persons. Masters of the workhouses, doctors and clergymen, had little immunity and were most at risk. During Napoleon's retreat from Moscow, the deadly fever decimated the ranks of his soldiers more efficiently than the Russian army.

Livestock was infected; cattle and poultry died. Trade was disastrous, and the famous horse fair, reflecting the crisis, was a total failure. For decades, few reconstruction or agricultural improvements were put in place, and the country went into an irreversible decline. The population dropped dramatically. County Roscommon was devastated and lost almost a third of its people.

The Earl of Clancarty and the Quakers, the Society of Friends, established outdoor relief centres. There were thousands in distress, and the tools for the task were not adequate to the gravity of their plight. Soup kitchens, set up to feed the hungry, did not provide suitable fare for starving people. Thin gruel was distributed but caused dysentery in severely weakened digestive systems. Imported Indian meal, used as a substitute stirabout, had little nutritional value. The potato had provided vitamin C in the Irish diet, and now, in its absence, scurvy was rampant.

Catholic clergy ministered to a terrified flock, attempting to maintain some form of social cohesion. Funds poured in from parishes around the world. Religious groups worked shoulder to shoulder, but there was a barely subtle struggle for the hearts and minds of those they helped.

The Clancartys were active proselytisers, and Ballinasloe's Irish Missionary College supplied Irish speakers for the Anglican ministry. The Famine was an occasion to weaken the hold of the Church of Rome, and 'soupers', 'jumpers' and 'perverts' were names given to those who changed religion for a bowl of soup and other favours. Proselytism, which went hand-in-hand with colonial settlement, had a bitter history:

> Under the penal laws, in force in the last century, an apostate Catholic son was able to dispossess his father, and a younger son, by adopting the new religion, could destroy the heritable right of his eldest brother and procure the devolution of the estate on himself.[10]

Estates, with waves of evictions, were cleared in the years that followed. With picks and crowbars, the bailiffs' men tumbled cottages and levelled cabins with battering rams. Some tenants took refuge in the bogs and mountains, competing 'with the snipe and the curlew for such scanty sustenance as their dreary haunts afford'.[11]

Families fled to towns and cities across the English-speaking world. Liverpool, city of stone, was the first port of call and it became a magnet for the dispossessed. Some stayed in England, others, sick and emaciated, continued their journey. Many died during the long, arduous voyages to America. Vessels, aptly named 'coffin ships', were often unseaworthy, hulks, which sank on the Atlantic crossing.

Sixteen landlords were murdered in 1847, and the British government responded with soldiers rather than food. Queen Victoria and Prince Albert's four-day visit to Dublin and Cobh in 1849, a public relations exercise, was received with apparent enthusiasm, large crowds greeting them at every stage of their journey. The disaffected talked of kidnap, but it went no further. There was no stomach for rebellion.

Young Irelander William Smith O'Brien despaired of an uprising. The Irish were exhausted, rendered torpid by disaster, 'the people preferred to die of starvation at home, or to flee to other lands, rather than to fight for their lives and liberty'. Rebels faced penal servitude and transportation to Australia.

Survival was the priority. Food, clothing, shelter, the basics of life, took precedence over the political questions of Repeal of the Union and land reform. Mastering the language of a new country would be a daunting hurdle for the many whose mother tongue was Gaelic.

In earlier and better times, to leave home had been regarded as the worst of fates. The Irish had been driven out by unjust laws, proscriptions and confiscations. Now there was a mass exodus. What had once been a banishment was now a release, and those who could fled the country. Once established abroad, they sent money home to help their families to join them. A substantial brain drain of native talent, fostering the achievements of the Irish around the world, enriched the host countries. A self-confidence fuelled by the belief in a common descent from the High Kings of Ireland flourished in foreign climes. Money in Gaelic Ireland had not been a necessary adjunct of status, and few emigrants had a sense of inferiority. They carried with them their identity and self-respect.

In 1853 Queen Victoria visited Dublin to open an exhibition of Irish industry and art at Leinster House. The show promoted trade links, and a million people visited over a six-month period. However, countrywide reconstruction efforts moved slowly.

Many villages stood deserted. But Ballinasloe emerged from those years with its infrastructure intact and in a less perilous state than many other Irish towns. Local people had known prosperity and understood the mechanisms to restore and maintain a viable way of life.

A highlight of the Power boys' young lives would have been the visit of Cardinal Wiseman, Archbishop of Westminster, in the autumn of 1858, to consecrate St Michael's Church. From an Anglo-Irish family, the Cardinal had spent his boyhood years in Waterford. In earlier times, he had worked closely with Daniel O'Connell. His nationwide tour was an important gesture of support.

His Eminence, the first Cardinal to set foot on Irish soil for over two centuries, received a rapturous welcome from the crowds, who streamed into Ballinasloe from all over the west. The occasion was as significant and uplifting as the Papal visit to Ireland more than a century later. The faithful had dragged themselves out of the clutches of those terrible, dark years. The Church had sustained its people, taking a strong leadership role in the post-famine era. It was committed to an extensive building programme, and St Michael's construction, begun in 1852 using limestone from the local quarries, had given employment to hundreds. The church could accommodate over 1,000 parishioners.

An estimated one million people died in the years 1846-9. Many children were orphaned. It is not known when and how O'Connor Power's parents, Patrick and Mary Power, died. Was it the typhus epidemic of 'Black '47' or the outbreak of cholera, which depleted the population of Ireland, in 1849? There are few records. In St Michael's parish register, 13 April 1846, they are present at the christening of their niece Ellenora Power, daughter of John and Catherine.[12] Possibly they were buried, uncoffined, in a mass plot, a famine graveyard. The urgencies of the national disaster destroyed the evidence and there remain few sources to inform us.

Nor is it known who cared for the three orphaned boys, but they were fortunate in their extended family, the Powers of Ballygill. Uncle John and Uncle Thomas stayed on the land. Their evangelical landlord, the reforming Dudley Persse, was of an ancient Galway family. He was the father of Lady Augusta Gregory, writer, patron of the arts and founding member of the Abbey Theatre.

The boys received a thorough, if elementary, education in a time when almost a third of the Gaelic-speaking population of Roscommon was illiterate. Standards were high and, in later life, O'Connor Power makes a reference to his early education, 'My recollection of the *pons asinorum* at school is that of a passage on a scientific frontier, which having been once crossed the way was smooth and clear ever afterwards.'[13]

The young Powers survived the devastation and went on to lead extraordinary lives in an era that would be defined by the British Empire. Remaining close throughout their lives, they looked out for each other, maintaining bonds of affection. Family ties survived through the generations.

The second part of the nineteenth century offered exciting prospects for young men with ability and energy. New communication systems – a railway network, steamboats, mail and telegraphic service – in the era of the Industrial Revolution opened up endless possibilities. Inventions multiplied exponentially and changed the working and environmental landscapes, promising prosperity for those willing and able to seize the opportunities.

Centuries-old entrenched class and religious distinctions became blurred. Foreign travel in the service of the Crown was commonplace and the borders of Empire stretched into apparent infinity. The world opened its arms to men of no property or standing, who had the courage to embrace the challenges of a dawning, democratic age. *The Times* predicted that a 'tremendous crash must come in which all interests and all classes will be swept away'.[14]

The eldest Power boy moved to Lancashire in the late 1850s, following the route struck by a million famine exiles. He worked his passage on the Liverpool–Charleston line and then joined the Confederate army, fighting with distinction in the American Civil War.

The cotton trade with the southern states was vital for the mills of the north of England, and the new livelihoods of the Irish depended on this connection. A cotton famine threatened an urban disaster. The mill hands knew the reasons for grim unemployment, and more Confederate flags flew from the rooftops of Liverpool than those of Charleston.

According to family history, the young Power fought bravely and, when the war was over, remained in North America. Towards the end of his life he journeyed home to Galway, by way of Australia. He had many tales to tell and must have told them well as he was fondly remembered by his nephews and nieces.

The economic depression of the early 1860s saw more young men leaving the country. Thomas, the second brother, joined the British army, enlisting with the 59th Regiment of Foot, 2nd Nottinghamshire Brigade.[15] When he was posted to India he met and married Elizabeth (Gabby) Deveay Quinn. Six of their children lived to adulthood. Thomas's service record shows he rose steadily through the non-commissioned ranks to become a Sergeant-Major in the Army Service Corps, provisioning in Ceylon and Afghanistan. In the last years of the century he made his home in Galway City.

In 1860, the summer was the wettest and coldest in living memory. The harvest failed and agricultural prices dropped. Sheep rot and foot and mouth destroyed the pastoral economy. O'Connor Power, the youngest, another link in the chain of emigration, followed his brothers to England, to seek his fortune and make his mark on the world.

Liberty, Equality, Fraternity

John O'Connor Power, 1846-1919: A Forgotten Irish Leader.[16]

It is in Lancashire, England, that we find O'Connor Power embarking on a career in the Irish Republican Brotherhood. At the age of fifteen, moving to Rochdale to live with relatives, he worked by day as a house painter and decorator in the family business, and, in the winter months, in a flannel mill.[17] By night, he became part of the immigrant Irish community, studying in the Mechanics Institute, with its classes, library, and access to books, newspapers and periodicals.

The Mechanics in Rochdale, among the first established in Britain, introduced him to like-minded men, striving to improve their lot in life. He met factory workers, artisans, small traders: Irishmen and Englishmen, who believed that all men are created equal, a novel idea at this time.

A working man, without property, financial security or status, was seen as an inferior, of no consequence. But class prejudice – exclusivity and arrogance were the defining characteristics – had been challenged by the egalitarian constitution of a fledgling American democracy and the violence of the French Revolution. The idea that all men are equal questioned the centuries-old belief in the Divine Right of Kings and in the existing, non-negotiable social hierarchy of the Empire.

As he battled for Catholic Emancipation and Repeal of the Union, Daniel O'Connell had argued for an end to slavery and serfdom. In Britain, the abolition of slavery was only a few decades distant and the pace of change was slow. The Great Exhibition of 1851 displayed chains, fetters, manacles and shackles designed by Birmingham manufacturers for the American slave market.

The north of England, the wheel of the Industrial Revolution, with Manchester as its hub, attracted and nurtured radical thinkers. Egalitarianism was the driving force of the prominent social reformers, John Stuart Mill and John Bright, men who had great sympathy with the Irish fight for justice:

> Why John Stuart Mill's extraordinary proposition – that the Irish tenant is the only human being in existence who has nothing to gain by increased industry and nothing to lose by increased idleness – is not more extraordinary than true.[18]

Mill was a bible for Irish land reformers; he recommended giving the Irish control of their own land, a conversion of tenants into peasant proprietors. Bright, a Quaker who had been imprisoned for Chartist activities, worked alongside Irishmen for decades. Chartists fought for the Repeal of the Corn Laws, which kept the price of wheat, and therefore bread, artificially high. The poor starved. 'It is a pantry question,' said Bright.

Chartists held many aims in common with Irish Nationalists: a belief in universal education, and an end to the restrictive property qualification for the right to vote and seek election. The People's Charter of 1837, at a time of great unemployment and political unrest, proposed a secret ballot, payment for MPs, electoral districts and annual parliaments. An enlarged franchise would give a voice to the English working class and a powerful voting bloc for the Irish in Britain.[19]

Darwinism strengthened the new republicanism, with *On the Origin of Species* reducing mankind to an evolutionary experiment. Karl Marx's *The Communist Manifesto* appeared even earlier. Marx and his daughters worked for the Irish cause, believing the class war, the struggle to free men from economic slavery and political bondage, must be first fought in Ireland. Marx's eldest daughter, Jenny, using the *nom de plume*, J. Williams, exposed the horrendous conditions of life in an English jail. Writing in *La Marsaillaise*, she demanded that the Fenian Jeremiah O'Donovan Rossa be released immediately.

Friedrich Engel's partner was a Fenian, and the Engels entertained and sheltered dissidents in their home in Manchester. A dynamic to rearrange the social order propelled the zeitgeist.

Champions of equality, guided by the tenets of republicanism in America and France, were to the fore in revolutionary activity, in the war on rigid, discriminatory and demeaning class structures. Irish Nationalism and British democracy were different aspects of the same struggle. Industrialisation created prosperity, putting money into the pockets of the poor, creating the desire for a better life, a fairer future. The fight for the rights of workers was at its strongest in the north of England. The Mechanics Institute, a university for the workingman, was the practical response, providing the building blocks and the builders for a just society.

O'Connor Power belonged to the Irish Catholic world, involved in the many activities which bound and sustained the community. Immigrants lived in overcrowded tenements, without the modern comforts of running water and electricity, sheltered from the sky by the towering smoke stacks of new factories, the poet William Blake's 'dark satanic mills'. Open sewers in a 'new Hades' posed a constant threat of cholera. The Irish had exchanged the servitude of the fields for that of the new industrialism. It was a long way from the many shades of green and the changing skies of a mellow Irish landscape:

> Poor, half-clad, half-starved women, sober, honest and virtuous, work twenty hours out of the twenty-four, in order to keep body and soul together, out of a pittance grudgingly paid by the capitalist. Themselves and their families are huddled together in crowded rooms, where, in the hot months, they gasp for one breath of the fresh air, which never visits their pale and haggard faces.[20]

Most of the exiled were unskilled, 'They were obliged, therefore, to accept the very lowest and hardest kind of work, such as railroad working, quarrying, loading and unloading ships, digging foundations, boring tunnels, and excavating mines.'[21]

An enthusiastic teacher, O'Connor Power passed on the knowledge he acquired at the Mechanics Institute to Irish men and women, who were often illiterate, spoke little English and had no training or relevant experience. Language and strong regional accents were barriers to interaction with English workers. It is likely he would have read newspaper articles aloud, translating and explaining when necessary. Writing letters home for those unable to put pen to paper must have been one of the many demands on his time.

Rapid industrial growth increased demand for labour, and the flood of Irish newcomers supplied it. In the late 1860s a third of the population of Manchester was Irish born and they had to deal with the resentment of locals. Englishmen believed they were taking their jobs, working for less, or were brought in by mill owners to break strikes, to block the burgeoning trade union movement. For the most part they were excellent workers. Factory hands had to be quick-witted, 'the only thing to strike a passer-by was an acuteness and intelligence of countenance, which has often been noticed in the manufacturing population'.[22]

Scattered around the world, the Irish took with them an unquenchable hatred of England. They blamed the English parliament for inadequate intervention in the Famine years:

> When a people die in large numbers of starvation in their own country, or fly from it because they cannot get enough to eat out of the food which that country has produced, and which is more than sufficient to sustain them, that people are denied the right to live; and if a people have not a right to live in their own land while it is rich enough to support them, they are deprived of liberty and the pursuit of happiness.
>
> This is what took place in Ireland during the famine of 1846 and 1847. The people perished in the midst of food twice sufficient to sustain them, because the food they produced had to be exported in immense quantities to pay the exorbitant rents of the landlords.[23]

Irish writer George Moore grimly juxtaposes the Dublin Castle social scene with the dire circumstances of the poor, 'Never were poverty and wealth brought into plainer proximity.'[24] Many in the political establishment viewed the Famine as an act of God, and an Irish solution to an overcrowded country. Depopulation would restore equilibrium to a nation in turmoil.

Anthony Trollope's Lord Tulla, a character in the novel *Phineas Finn*, recommends disenfranchising the Irish and establishing a military governor. Irish members of parliament were powerless; Westminster was a talking shop; Ireland was effectively ruled from Dublin Castle, a military barracks which answered to an ill-informed and indifferent cabinet and not the legislative body.

Heathcliffe, the romantic anti-hero of Emily Brontë's *Wuthering Heights*, is a street waif, who, speaking 'some gibberish that nobody could understand', is taken into a Yorkshire home from the back streets of Liverpool. Is he a Gaelic speaker, driven from his homeland? Heathcliffe portrays an Irish state of mind; angry, bitter, black of countenance, he is determined to survive at whatever cost to those who care for him and give him shelter. He reflects the Irish threat within the structured confines of the Empire.[25]

Emily's father, the Revd Patrick Brontë, was born in Ireland and worked tirelessly to raise awareness and funds for famine victims. It is probable that there was at least one Irish stray brought into the household, providing Emily with fuel for her pen.

The new arrivals met with a pervasive anti-Irish, anti-Catholic prejudice, 'no Irish need apply.' In response to the naked hostility of a host nation, they developed a fortress mentality, proudly retaining their religious practices and patterns of life. The words of 'Faith of Our Fathers', the anthem of embattled Catholics in England and in Ireland, were a call to arms, 'in spite of dungeon, fire and sword … we will be true to thee to death'. Religion was 'hallowed by persecution and sanctified by suffering'. Catholics prayed for the conversion of England.

For centuries, the Vatican, in retreat after the Reformation, dealt with England as if it were a missionary outpost. Senior clergy were Vicars Apostolic and took their titles from foreign sees. In the autumn of 1850, Pius IX re-established a Roman Catholic Episcopal hierarchy. Henceforth, there would be one Archbishop and twelve bishops in England and Wales. Described by many as the 'Papal Aggression', the move was controversial. But for the Irish the Church was a bulwark in a foreign land, a haven in an alien culture. Its supranational organisation strengthened ties across oceans and continents, conserving and enriching the collective memory.

New churches were built by Irish parishioners all over Lancashire, an encroachment on the territory of the English. The Scarlet Lady of the Vatican was viewed as a serious threat to the security of the British State. With the cry of 'No Popery!', demonstrations and riots, attacks on Catholic churches and communities, were orchestrated by an Orange demagogue, William Murphy. The Irish, in response, defended their property.

On St Patrick's Day 1872, Murphy, the author of *The Confessional Unmasked*, an attack on the sacrament of penance, met a violent death in Workington, Cumberland, at the hands of Irish miners.

After the unimaginable horrors of the Famine years, only independence would satisfy the Nationalist spirit. Fenianism was a defiant response, and a call to insurrection. The name came from Fianna Éireann, the legendary warriors of Celtic mythology; it was an invocation, reflecting a blossoming of Gaelic revivalism, with pride in race and in the language.

Fenians were the natural successors to Whiteboys, who wore white shirts, and Ribbonmen, identified by green ribbons, secret societies which had sprung up in reaction to an oppressive land system. Irish tenants saw themselves paying rent for land which rightly belonged to them. Landlords – the landocracy, a term coined in the Famine years – were thieves. The native population had been dispossessed by centuries of occupation and were regrouping to reclaim their birthright.

Fenianism promoted the common man. Unlike the Young Irelanders of a previous generation, its members were almost all working or lower middle class. A humble background earned early promotion within the movement's hierarchy. National school teachers were in the ranks, as were commercial travellers. Members were predominantly Catholic, while seeking to be non-sectarian.

Resolute, they held their heads high, challenging authority with newfound confidence. Maddeningly insouciant, they did not defer. Beards were sported, eye contact was maintained. Cloth caps and open shirts might complete the picture. A nonchalant insubordination, imported from the levelling culture of America, identified them. They met regularly to prepare for action, to right Ireland's wrongs. On Sundays they gathered after Mass to march and drill in disciplined formation. Participation had a social as well as a military purpose, and sporting events were encouraged to build morale and consolidate operating strengths.

Coursing, the race track and hurling matches were occasions for clandestine gatherings. Music and dancing, jigs and reels, were part of the entertainment. Stirring national airs were sung with great gusto. The rosary might be told in Irish at the end of the day.

Union with Britain underwrote the comfortable lifestyles of the well-to-do, and many middle-class Catholics, with much to lose, were alarmed. They feared the Government would introduce draconian laws to counter the threat of terrorism. A Catholic bourgeoisie wanted parity of esteem, equality of status within the Empire, and were wary of change, fearing a breakdown of public order.

The Irish Republican Brotherhood was founded in 1858. From the beginning it was a secret oath-based organisation, and there are few records. Absolute secrecy ensured a powerful and secure control centre. The IRB wanted an independent Irish Republic. Independence would be achieved through force of arms. The oath of allegiance was binding unto death:

> In the presence of God, I … do solemnly swear that I will do my utmost to establish the national independence of Ireland, and that I will bear true allegiance to the Supreme Council of the Irish Republican Brotherhood and Government of the Irish Republic and implicitly obey the constitution of the Irish Republican Brotherhood and all my superior officers and that I will preserve inviolable the secrets of the organisation.[26]

Organised in 'Circles', on a cellular principle, members were led by an officer who was known as the 'Centre'. Each Circle numbered 820 men. The Centre was known as A or the colonel. Nine captains (Bs) answered to the Centre. Nine sergeants (Cs) answered to the captain. Nine privates (Ds) were under a sergeant. In the mid-sixties there were Circles in all the major cities in England.

More than a quarter of the Empire's armed forces was Irish-born, and more again of Irish descent. For centuries Ireland had provided a steady supply of troops and some magnificent military tacticians. Fifth columns in British garrisons at home and abroad gave tacit, often active, support to the Fenians. Members of the Royal Irish Constabulary might be fellow travellers. Rebel priests validated the movement and gave comfort.

Almost 200,000 Irishmen fought in the American Civil War and many were Fenians. The conflict was over in 1865 and, trained in guerrilla warfare, veterans arrived home, ready for action, adventure and revenge. They brought with them aspirations to equality, the inalienable right of every man to the pursuit of his own happiness, his own land. Irish Republic bonds, resembling American dollars, were sold in Irish communities to raise money for an army which would free their native land.

The legendary Jesse James was of Irish descent. A Confederate soldier, he fought on after the war had ended and left a mixed legacy. Was he a desperado or a Fenian freedom fighter? The parish priest of Asdee, County Kerry, celebrated a Requiem Mass for Jesse every year on the anniversary of his death and kept a small museum to his memory. Canon Ferris, a Sinn Féin sympathiser, felt there must be a special place in heaven for those poor souls who never had a chance.[27]

The relationship between Britain and America was tense. Britain, with its cotton trade, was perceived to side with the Confederacy. There was always a possibility of a conflict between the Empire and its ex-colony. Militant Irish-America looked forward to an Anglo-American war, when England's danger would be Ireland's opportunity.

A British Canada, with a large Irish population, might prove disloyal. In public places, an image of a fighting Fenian, sword in one hand, a green flag with golden harp in the other, was frequently displayed next to a portrait of Queen Victoria. A glass was often raised to 'the Irish Republic, now virtually established'. This was a very uncomfortable situation for the British government.

Future Prime Minister Benjamin Disraeli was well versed on the Irish Question:

A dense population, in extreme distress, inhabit an island where there is an Established Church, which is not their Church, and a territorial aristocracy the richest of whom live in foreign capitals. Thus you have a starving population, an absentee aristocracy, and an alien Church; and in addition the weakest executive in the world. That is the Irish Question.[28]

He introduces a Fenian element to his 1870 novel, *Lothair*, complete with Head Centre. The Irish are in a state of 'chronic insurrection'. The political situation is fragile:

> Now that the civil war in America is over, the Irish soldiery are resolved to employ their experience and their weapons in their own land …

> … the Irish people were organised and ready to rise: that they had sent their deputies to New York; all they wanted were arms and officers; that the American brethren had agreed to supply them with both, and amply; and that considerable subscriptions were raised for other purposes. What they now required was a commander-in-chief equal to the occasion …

> The movement is not sectarian; it pervades all classes and all creeds.

> … in an Irish business there is always a priest at the bottom of it.[29]

Lothair details the inroads made by the Catholic Church into the upper strata of British society. Disraeli's cardinal has a strong resemblance to Henry Edward Manning, Archbishop of Westminster, who was not only 'highly efficient as a gleaner of souls' but 'of souls who moved in the best society'.[30]

The proximity of the French Republic was threatening. The Irish had always found a generous welcome in France – my enemy's enemy is my friend – and there was an established community of exiles. The French influence – liberty, equality and fraternity – was reinforcing, and IRB leaders met and plotted in a vibrant, recreated Paris. In fashionable café society, revolutionaries learnt the ways of secret brotherhoods: intrigue, subterfuge, sedition.

Fenians infiltrated every sector of communication across the Empire: the railroads, transatlantic steamboats, telegraph and post offices. The Gaelic language served them well, disabling interception.

In the 1860s, the IRB control centre was in Lancashire. John O'Connor Power was an organiser, moving around England and Scotland, recruiting members, addressing meetings and spreading the message. There was no money for train fares and he travelled mostly on foot. Husbanding his meagre rations, he often walked on an empty stomach.[31] He was a young man of some ingenuity; perhaps he 'borrowed' a horse or hitched a ride on a passing barge or train.

He was a natural leader and already a gifted speaker and a skilled and disciplined strategist. His 'dogged tenacity of purpose' was attractive and recruitment drives were highly successful, 'and there are scores of Irishmen today, who can tell how they were, in years gone by, led into the National fold by his teaching'.[32]

Until the early nineteenth century, platform oratory was suppressed. There was fear of rabble rousing and demagoguery, challenges to authority:

> The platform, which now exercises so great an influence in the formation of opinion, is quite a modern institution.[33]

> The public platform is the breath of the nostrils of the ordinary Irish agitator. He loves it.[34]

A mass meeting was the most powerful medium for the transmission of important information, and the skills of a platform speaker were indispensable to a political career. Oratory was a performance art. At large gatherings, names and stirring phrases were repeated and relayed from mouth to mouth, in participatory roundels, building up to a crescendo. Familiarity of sentiment and sonorous, captivating tones were the tools of the practised orator. A spiritual quality in the physical voice, a hypnotic intonation strengthened the message: word power was resonant and persuasive.

In *The Making of an Orator* (1906), O'Connor Power recommends reading aloud as a sound preparation for a public speaker. His near-fatal illness, with a long period of recuperation, may have been turned to great advantage. Many a convalescent child, confined to bed, explores the world of literature, furnishing his mind with new characters, new ideas and new horizons. An able youngster, perhaps he read to patients, developing his voice and his gift for capturing and holding an audience.

He had his early childhood beginnings in the old world of storytellers and myth makers, the amusements of the hearth. Imagination was kindled in a preliterate oral tradition, which fostered memory and exceptional recall. Travelling poets and seanchaí encouraged a sharp aural attentiveness.

Audiences were familiar with the oft-repeated stories. Legends and historical narratives were transmitted through the generations. The spoken word was treasured. It was only in the twentieth century, with widespread literacy, that the supremacy of the voice as the potent medium of communication would diminish.

Dissident groups met under cover of innocuous-sounding Irish societies, teaching republican ideals and raising money for the cause. Green tickets were issued for social events. In 1861, the National Brotherhood of St Patrick was founded in Dublin and it spread rapidly across Britain. It established political clubs and reading rooms for the disenfranchised classes and allowed young Irishmen to socialise, providing alternative venues to the Mechanics Institutes and Church-sponsored functions. Identified with the Fenian movement, it became a training ground, a front for their activities, allowing the IRB to mark its territory in a new bottom-up society.

The NBSP was condemned by the Catholic hierarchy, who had not forgotten the French Revolution's rout of clerical authority. Politics had always been the province of the Church and the gentry, 'the proper order', but Fenians demanded a social and political revolution, an equal say in how society should be structured. Republicanism was a moral imperative.

Advanced communication networks opened up opportunities for the newspaper industry, which expanded dramatically in the second half of the nineteenth century. Publications multiplied. The spread of literacy fed circulation numbers. The need for men who could write and had opinions became pressing. The ability to access a large audience, to influence and shape political opinion, gave the spur to radical journalism: the printed word was an indispensable tool of revolution.

In his Dublin Castle file, O'Connor Power's occupation is given as newspaper reporter. Journalism was a profession he engaged in at an early stage of his career, and, throughout his life, he wrote for newspapers and periodicals in Ireland, England and North America. His writing provided him with a medium to articulate his philosophy, an income to follow his star, and a cover for his political activities, 'For when the Irish agitator is not speaking he is writing, and in Ireland much was done with tongue and pen.'[35] In 'The Irish in England' he writes:

> I know not what would become of the daily press of the country, if the Irishmen employed upon it were suddenly to fling down their pens. Fleet Street is largely Irish, and a good deal of what passes for English opinion in the London morning papers is the product of Irish talent.[36]

And Never Feared Danger

The noblest and most terrible manifestation of this unconquered nation.[37]

O'Connor Power met Michael Davitt soon after his arrival in Lancashire, 'Mr O'Connor Power I knew when I was a boy; we were brought up together.'[38] It is probable that he recruited Davitt, who joined the IRB at the age of nineteen. O'Connor Power was his commanding officer on the raid on the military arsenal in Chester Castle in February 1867. The *Manchester Guardian* wrote in his obituary, 'In his youth he was connected with the revolutionary movement, and is credited with organising the daring Fenian plot to seize Chester Castle.'[39]

Organised with the encouragement of ex-Confederate soldiers, a band of a thousand Irishmen from the north of England, marched on the walled city and converged in large groups in the centre of Chester. They arrived from Manchester, Liverpool and other towns where the Irish were numerous, ostensibly to attend a prize fight.

The success of the raid depended on the Fenian Trojan horse, a sympathetic Irish soldiery within the garrison walls. The plan was to seize arms and ammunition in the castle armoury. They intended to cut telegraph wires and tear up railway lines, creating confusion and preventing pursuit. Commandeering the mail train *en route* to the boat at Holyhead, they would sail to Wicklow to prepare for the planned insurrection.

A police informer, John Joseph Corydon, gave the warning, and the authorities, alerted, were poised to intercept the rebels. News of the betrayal reached the Fenians, and an orderly and speedy withdrawal was set in place. The men dispersed and were heard singing the American Civil War march 'When Johnny Comes Marching Home', as they wended their way to their bases, the 'little Irelands' of Britain. No shots were fired. The attempted raid was aborted without loss of life. O'Connor Power travelled home by train in a second-class carriage. Arriving ahead of his comrades, he greeted them with a welcoming party in Watson's public house in Marybone, Liverpool.[40]

The following month, the planned rising in Ireland failed for lack of men and arms. Bishop Moriarty of Kerry famously declared that 'eternity is not long enough, nor hell hot enough to punish these miscreants'. He condemned the rebels with 'God's heaviest curse, his withering, blasting, blighting curse'.[41]

That summer, the Head Centres met in Manchester to reassess the position. They condemned the ill-conceived rising in the spring and blamed certain members of the American Brotherhood for the misadventure.

O'Connor Power was in Manchester in September for the dramatic rescue of two Fenian officers, late of the American army, on their way to Salford Jail. The police van in which they travelled was ambushed. In broad daylight, on a main thoroughfare in 'a great English city', a band of thirty men emerged from under the railway arch, seized the horses' reins and released the handcuffed prisoners. A bullet fired to force the lock on the van's door accidentally killed the police officer in charge. Several raiders who failed to make good their escape were arrested.

At the trial, Chartist lawyer Ernest Jones led the defence, but the prisoners stood convicted by public opinion and a prejudiced jury. Inflamed by fear and hatred, England was baying for vengeance, 'The truth is that, at a time of panic, a technical point of law was strained against them, and a terrified Manchester jury sacrificed them to political prejudice and national excitement, and convicted them on evidence of the flimsiest description.'[42]

John Bright approached the Home Office for a reprieve, 'to hang these men will embitter the Irish Question'. The Tory government did not yield. Three men have a place in history as the Manchester Martyrs. From the dock, the condemned shouted defiantly, 'God Save Ireland'. These words became the hook in a rousing song, the anthem of the rebels, and sung, significantly, to the tune of the American Civil War march 'Tramp, Tramp, Tramp, the Boys are Marching'.

On a cold, foggy morning in November, the men were taken out and executed. The hangings were botched and the agony cruelly prolonged. Denied a Christian burial, the bodies were consigned to quicklime, adding fury to the flames of outrage. Masses were said in Irish communities throughout the north of England and Scotland. Processions and demonstrations took place in Ireland and across the world. A mock funeral was held in Cork and a Requiem Mass was celebrated in Cong, County Mayo and on subsequent anniversaries. The faithful wore green defiantly. These men were martyrs to the Irish cause – blood sacrifices. In death they acquired iconic status and brought new impetus to nationalist aspirations.

Several others involved in the rescue were imprisoned for life. Eight years later, at Westminster, O'Connor Power did not offer an eyewitness account when rehearsing the events of that day, 'Now, this is, as well as I can recollect from the newspaper reports at the time, an accurate description of what took place.'[43]

In December, while O'Connor Power was in America, an attempt to free Fenian officers from Clerkenwell Prison caused death and serious injury to innocent bystanders. The thick prison wall was blown apart with gunpowder, leaving a very large gap. The explosives had been inexpertly placed, and several hundred neighbouring houses were shattered by the blast. Collateral damage was not part of the plan, and the perpetrators were as horrified as the authorities. Gladstone urged that the violent attack not 'deter the doing of justice to Ireland', and, the following spring, a newly inaugurated IRB Supreme Council would forcefully condemn it: 'This dreadful and deplorable event … was the work of persons … without authority,' and the council saw it not only with horror but also with indignation, 'were the perpetrators within our control … their punishment would be commensurate with our sense of justice'.[44]

The police had received information in advance from a well-placed informer, but no attempt was made to derail the plot, 'Persons in England who deal in statecraft have seized upon this unhappy event, which, in all probability, they foresaw and foreknew, as a circumstance well calculated to afford a temporary apology for their most guilty practice towards Ireland.'[45]

The extent of the destruction panicked the public, and the swell of sympathy brought about by the execution of the Manchester Martyrs ebbed fast. The Fenians' base support, the working class and the trade union movement, was alienated, and the credibility of the rebels' purpose was undermined. Subsequent legal proceedings were weighted against the offenders. John Bright asked for a retrial.

One fifth of the population of Canada was of Irish birth or descent. Here, the Irish integrated with more ease than their fellow countrymen in Boston and New York, who met with the prejudice of an ensconced establishment. The French-speaking community in Canada was Catholic, and the Irishman's faith was not seen as a badge of inferiority, but rather a calling card. Assimilation was less troubled, and the Irish excelled in a country where there were few restraints on their native abilities. Gaelic was spoken so extensively that it might well have been declared a national language.

Over a five-year period, the United Brotherhood in America organised several raids into Canada. It planned to take control of the newly created British Dominion of Canada and exchange the territory for Irish independence. The United States gave covert support to the raiders, who had a long, unguarded border to aid their efforts. Again, the British Secret Service infiltrated the lines of command and the incursions were not successful.

Of the many who escaped to Ireland after the raid on Chester Castle, most were later arrested. O'Connor Power hid out in Manchester and, in the autumn, as 'accredited agent', travelled to America to discuss reorganisation with the United Brotherhood. He returned in the New Year to set up the structures of a revitalised IRB. Its governing body, the Supreme Council, met in Dublin for the first time on 13, 14 February.[46] The organisation continued to enrol, drill and arm in secret, awaiting its chance – England's difficulty.

A few days after his twenty-second birthday, O'Connor Power was arrested on suspicion in Dublin and held under the Habeas Corpus Suspension Act, a law which allowed detention without trial or evidence, in Kilmainham and Mountjoy. The harsh application of this law in Ireland expedited the transference of operations to England, where the deracinated Irish, with intimate knowledge of the foe, were deeply politicised.

The police file and photograph give us a great deal of information.[47] O'Connor Power had dark brown hair and grey eyes. He was well built, 5ft 9in, and had a fresh complexion, with the pits of smallpox evident. He was a newspaper reporter, living in Rochdale, or Bolton, Lancashire. His birthplace was County Roscommon. He glowers fiercely at us from the photograph taken in custody. It was a sedentary life; prison food was stodgy, a common complaint, and he has put on weight.

John Webster was his alias of the day. Had O'Connor Power already developed a great interest in the playhouse? And had he recently seen the Jacobean, bloodthirsty revenge plays of John Webster? But the adjective websterian was current, an allusion to Webster's dictionary. Phrenology was fashionable, and a websterian head spoke of great knowledge and prodigious memory.

He became seriously ill in prison and was offered his freedom if he would take a ticket of leave and go to America. He refused, 'I would rather die on the floor of my cell than make such a bargain with the British Government.' He was the last of the Fenians arrested on suspicion to be released.[48]

Ten years later, at Westminster, he made a reference to the contemporary report of the medical superintendent in Mountjoy:

> The untried prisoners committed to this prison during the last twelve months have undergone a discipline in some respects more stringent than the convict during the eight months of his probationary period … the length of their confinement makes the case of these prisoners unlike that of ordinary untried prisoners awaiting trial … some have shown signs of mental disturbance … I must recommend, on medical grounds, that some relaxation of this discipline be introduced.[49]

At large again, he became one of the most influential members of the IRB Supreme Council, which severed its ties with Irish America. The four Irish provinces, Connacht, Leinster, Ulster and Munster, Scotland, the north of England and the south of England, which included London, had representatives. Later, four honorary members were co-opted. The Council elected three members to the executive: the President, the Treasurer and the Secretary. The President was chairperson, the Treasurer managed recruitment and finance and the Secretary, a key figure, was director of operations and the Treasurer managed recruitment and finance. The Council met twice a year, usually in spring and summer.

The command structure was hierarchical, secret and secure. Few leading members were imprisoned and very little documentation was intercepted by Dublin Castle or British intelligence. The Irish Republican Brotherhood recognised the Supreme Council as the provisional government of the Irish Republic. The fraternity was laying the foundations of an Irish State. The British had no legal or moral claim to govern Ireland.

O'Connor Power was known by many aliases to the police in Britain and in Dublin Castle: John Webster, Charles Fleming, Charles Ferguson and John Delaney. He was an Irish pimpernel and, most probably, a master of disguise – many of his family were gifted actors.

In the correspondence of American activists, he was known for a time as Mr Shields. A Mr S— appears in an IRB Address:

> In view of the probable embarrassment of the enemy in its foreign relations it was deemed wise to cast about for a suitable party to put our case in a proper light before foreign powers. And Mr S— whose long and great services are well known to us all was pitched upon for that purpose, and a resolution was come to opening the way to the appointment of Mr S— as foreign representative of the S.C.[50]

Dublin Castle ran a squad of detectives. The menace of trade unionism and the insolence and defiance of Fenians, fearsome threats to the middle-class comfort zone, were noted and filled police reports. Any gatherings of urban workers or rural labourers were viewed as subversive. Republicanism was a threat to the British connection and prosperity. In April 1868, the Prince and Princess of Wales visited Ireland for a week and received an even more enthusiastic welcome than Victoria and Albert a decade earlier.

Special legislation, not in force anywhere else in the United Kingdom, denied Irishmen the right to bear arms. Without a gun, the Irishman, vulnerable, could not defend his person or his liberty, a basic right of citizenship. The restriction of the right to vote was seen as less humiliating than the embargo on the right to bear arms. Were the Irish slaves or citizens of Empire? The law sharply distinguished the rulers from the ruled. The Irish were a subject nation, with a 'degradation of wives and daughters … Speaking a language that is despised, professing a religion that is abhorred, and being disarmed, the poor find themselves in many cases slaves even in the bosom of a written liberty.'[51]

With the end of the American Civil War, there was a slump in the armaments market and guns were competitively priced. In 1869, the IRB, independent of the American supply chain, set up a subscription scheme to import arms. Its recruitment and fundraising strategy was to acquire and supply weapons to its swelling ranks. In rural areas a strong desire to possess a gun ensured a rapidly rising membership.

A New Departure

Thanks to the remedial policy begun sixteen years ago.[52]

George Henry Moore, whose family claimed descent from St Thomas More, was a Catholic landlord and member of parliament for Mayo. His ancestors owned a fleet of ships and made a home in Alicante in southern Spain. They acquired a fortune in the wine and brandy trade. Traditional Irish hospitality, the convivial welcome of the 'open house', ensured a sound market and prosperity. From the shores of Ireland's western seaboard, they exported seaweed to Europe for the manufacture of iodine, candles and soap.

Moore Hall, 'a great grey barrack of a home,' was built on the shore of Lough Carra in east Mayo. The lake shore abuts on an avenue, once lined with 'tall firs and graceful larches' leading to a 'gravel sweep in front of the square Georgian house with the great flight of steps and big pillars supporting a balcony. On these steps a couple of redsetters were always waiting.'[53]

In former times, it was the final stage of a water thoroughfare from Galway, carrying guests and provisions to the hall. A nearby track accommodated carriages arriving by road to the rural fastness. Visitors and trades people would pass through a tunnel to the rear of the house with access to stables, storehouses and the paddock. The walled potager, the orchard and greenhouse provided fine fare for the table. Racing stables, a deer park and flower garden completed the idyll.

During the 1798 Rising, Moore's uncle John had been, for a short time, President of Connacht. The Declaration of the Rights of Man and the Jacobin Convention of 1793 rekindled the desire for freedom from British rule, and the Rising, aided by French forces led by General Humbert, defeated English troops at the Battle of Castlebar. Humbert proclaimed Connacht a Republic and John Moore, its President. The insurrection failed abruptly, and the British took swift revenge, dismantling the Irish parliament with the Act of Union. Henceforth, the Irish would be ruled with an iron grip from Westminster and the threat of a French invasion, launched from Ireland's shores, would be forever stalled, 'Pitt's object in promoting the Union in 1800 was not so much to make Ireland tranquil as to make England secure; nor was it so much his hatred of Irish liberty as his fear of French hostility and intrigue.'[54]

Moore's brother Augustus had died in the saddle riding in the Grand National. George Henry, who had been a famous steeplechaser in his youth, had inherited two abiding passions – his country and his race horses. A man 'of sterling patriotism', he defended the rights of his fellow Irishmen throughout his life. During the Famine years it was said nobody starved on the Moore estate, and no family was evicted. No one was turned from his gate empty handed. Elected first to parliament in 1847, Moore fought for immediate famine relief. Deploying his expert knowledge and harnessing his lifelong passion, he bet on his horse *Corunna* to win the Cheshire Cup. With the proceeds from bets and winnings, he collected £17,000, a substantial sum at the time.

Together with sympathetic local landlords, he devised a scheme to feed the destitute. A ship, the *Martha Washington*, was charted in New Orleans and, in July 1847, it sailed into Westport harbour with a cargo of 1,000 tons of flour.[55] Moore wrote to his mother 'the horses will gallop all the faster with the blessings of the poor'. Soon he would have to sell land in nearby Ballintubber to pay his debts.

In 1851, with twenty-four Irish Liberals, he formed the Catholic Defence Association to oppose the Ecclesiastical Titles Bill, legislation intended to stem the Vatican's incursions on British territory.[56] In the election, the following year, the 'Irish Brigade' joined forces with the Tenant League, becoming the Independent Irish Party. Michael MacDonagh writes that Moore had 'a combative and determined disposition, and an impatience of all bars and restraints to the advancement of his cause'. He supported the rights of tenants and, with an even hand, the rights of landlords.

He retired from active politics, but ten years later he was persuaded by his friend Archbishop McHale and the Nationalist clerics Fr Patrick Lavelle and Fr Ulick Bourke, both Mayo men, to run again for parliament in 1868, 'He [Moore] was induced to stand again for the constituency in 1868, when Fr Ulick Burke got about a dozen of the students, myself included, to write out a number of appeals to prominent and influential people on behalf of Moore.'[57]

He would campaign on the amnesty issue, land reform and the disestablishment of the Anglican Church. Over four million Catholics were paying tithes for the upkeep of a minority Protestant religion. Calls for home government would wait until after the election.

On his release from prison at the end of July, O'Connor Power travelled to Mayo to set up Fenian units. Uniformed in white jackets of báinín tweed and black Spanish hats, they campaigned across the county for Moore's election. They trusted Moore, regarding him as an important ally. His would be the voice to promote Ireland's interests and defend the rights of prisoners. Fr Bourke named him 'a Fenian sympathiser and tenant right supporter', and it was widely believed that he took the IRB oath:

'I am in favour,' said he to O'Connor Power, 'of whatever is practicable in the struggle against English rule in Ireland.'

He was the one man of the gentry class who had joined the Irish Republican Brotherhood.[58]

Not initially a friend to the Fenians, he was horrified by prison conditions and became actively involved in the amnesty movement. Fenians were treated with brutality in Irish and British jails, and some died or committed suicide. Others lost their sanity or lived in constant fear of a descent into madness.

The execution of the Manchester Martyrs, a blunder on the part of the British, created a blood sacrifice, reconciling strands of the Catholic Church to Fenianism. High Masses were said for the souls of the three hanged men, and sympathy, by association, was extended to prisoners held under barbarous conditions.

In 1866, John Bright visited Dublin and held discussions with Cardinal Cullen in Eccles Street. Bright was based in Rochdale and met with Fenian groups in the aftermath of the Manchester Martyrs debacle. In his diary he notes, 'Power lived in Rochdale at one time.'

Bright, who had a strong dislike of Tory landlords, had been fighting for Irish causes for over a quarter of a century. He advised the British Liberal leader, William Gladstone, that if there was no change in the government's approach, Ireland would be ripe for revolution.

Gladstone, a Liverpool man born and bred, had a lifelong interest in the affairs of Ireland. Fenianism had taught him 'the intensity of Irish disaffection', and he now spoke of 'Irish ideas' in an overture to Irish voters, 'the intensity of Fenianism' had acted as a chapel bell to rouse the conscience of England to 'the vast importance of the Irish controversy'.[59]

An Irish Liberal alliance was forged. Gladstone's much quoted pronouncement to a hostile Queen Victoria, 'My mission is to pacify Ireland,' marked the Liberal party's statement of intent.

With the 1867 enlargement of the franchise, parliamentary parties had to court a new electorate. Over forty Fenian prisoners were released, and concessions to Ireland's demands were expected from a Liberal administration. With an improvement in Anglo-Vatican relations, Gladstone, in consultation with Archbishop Manning, undertook to deal with the disestablishment of the Anglican Church in Ireland. To register their disapproval, Orangemen torched effigies of the Premier on Ulster's 12 July bonfires.

John Bright's 1870 Land Bill was seriously flawed but it was a step in the right direction, the first time the land question was seriously addressed. The tenant farmer was to be given compensation for improvements to his property, establishing the principle of dual ownership. Denominational education continued to be a sticking point with hostile nonconformists in the Liberal party ranks.

That winter, George Moore met with O'Connor Power. They discussed the possibility of an alliance between the physical force nationalists and parliamentarians, a way to bring Fenians into the political process:

In 1870, Moore had in contemplation the starting of a nationalist movement, part revolutionary and part constitutional. The plan was laid before him in the winter of 1868/9 by its author, O'Connor Power, and two other representative Fenians, James O'Connor of *The Irishman*, and Edmund O'Donovan.[60]

James O'Connor, IRB treasurer, was at the meetings in Moore Hall and in the House of Commons. Edmond O'Donovan, son of the famous Gaelic scholar Professor John O'Donovan, was also present at the discussions and toured Irish communities in England and Scotland with O'Connor Power during the autumn of 1869.[61] The strategy was a course of parallel action, revolutionary and constitutional politics to run in tandem. MacDonagh writes of O'Connor Power:

> He, more than any other man, had induced the Fenians to give the Home Rule movement a chance. It was he who originated the idea of a Nationalist movement with two wings, the one carrying out extreme action in Parliament, and the second pursuing revolutionary methods in Ireland, each acting independently of the other in its separate field, but both working in harmony towards one common end — the realisation of the completest measure of self-government that was possible, as circumstances changed from time to time.[62]

An assembly of IRB delegates, representatives from all over Ireland, met in Cork, the Irish headquarters. The up-and-coming William O'Brien was 'Clerk of this revolutionary Parliament' and 'the medium of communication between the County Centres', 'In January 1870 an assembly of delegates of the organisation, representatives of all Ireland and convened by O'Connor Power, met secretly in Cork.'[63]

The Poor Law, an 'instrument of degrading proselytism', was to be a target. Activists were encouraged to run for election to Union Boards of Guardians, and to nominate prisoners for parliamentary elections. If successful, they would not be eligible to take office, but they would have given significant publicity to their plight. The Supreme Council directed, 'persistent efforts should be made to obtain control of all local bodies such as corporations, town commissioners as a means of increasing the power and influence of the Irish Republic'.[64]

The Amnesty Association, uniting Fenians and constitutional Nationalists, was formed in June 1869. At Westminster, Moore's speech to mark the occasion was a *tour de force*. He asked for a pardon for the Fenian prisoner O'Donovan Rossa, and demanded an inquiry, 'It is the duty of the Government to institute a public inquiry into the penal discipline of our prisons … The people of Ireland for years had been misled, deluded, deceived, betrayed, disappointed by successive governments.'[65]

A petition was organised and signed by more that 1,400 priests. In November, O'Donovan Rossa, from his prison cell, won a seat in a Tipperary by-election. Three months later the decision was reversed; as a convicted felon he might not take his place in the House of Commons. At a meeting in Manchester, it was arranged that when O'Connor Power was speaking, he would make a reference to 'the lion-hearted O'Donovan Rossa'. Mark Ryan would then stand up and lead the crowds with three rousing cheers.[66]

Moore and O'Connor Power joined forces. They were both fervent Nationalists, men of action, who shared a vision of a strong, independent Ireland. Moore heartily disliked Cardinal Cullen, who had spent thirty years in Rome and had no patience with the revolutionaries. The Mayo landlord was a man the Fenian could trust.

O'Connor Power's experience of the landlord class had not been a thoroughly negative one. Landlords may have been landowners by conquest, the English garrison in Ireland, but the Ballinasloe Earls of Clancarty showed a practical, if patriarchal concern for their tenants. Dudley Persse, the Powers' landlord, was active in promoting trade links by rail and sea. During the Great Famine, the Hamiltons of Brown Hall, County Donegal and the Gore Booths of Lissadell in County Sligo sacrificed their fortunes to protect the local tenantry.

Moore and O'Connor Power cherished a mutual love of Edmund Burke's life and works. Moore's son read Edmund Burke's speeches aloud to his father at a very early age. O'Connor Power quoted Burke frequently in his speeches. His article to mark the centenary of Burke's death, 'Edmund Burke and His Abiding Influence', reveals a great deal: Edmund Burke was the giant at his shoulder.

He probably shared with Moore an understanding and love of horses. Certainly O'Connor Power was badly shaken by the latter's sudden death in April 1870. Moore was in London defending the rights of prisoners and, simultaneously, found himself in dispute over rents with his tenants in Ballintubber. 'Obstinate and impetuous', he abruptly decided to make the long journey back to Mayo. A few hours after his arrival at Moore Hall, he died of a heart attack. His son and heir, the author and art critic George Moore, wrote emphatically of his father's death, 'He died killed by his tenants, that is certain, he died of a broken heart.'[67]

Moore supported the Land Bill, believing that the 'alienation and hostility of the Irish to the British' was a fact of history. At the time of his death, a notice was before the House to move a resolution on the state of Ireland under the Union.[68] It was to be the beginning of a new campaign for home government.

A month later, a private conference was held in Dublin. Michael MacDonagh opens his account, 'The curtain rose on the movement for Home Rule in the Bilton Hotel, Upper Sackville Street, Dublin, on Thursday, May 19, 1870.' Isaac Butt convened the meeting. Admired, loved and trusted, he had delivered the eulogy at Moore's funeral and signalled new beginnings, 'All thoughtful men feel and know that the cause of Irish nationality is entering a new phase; new influences are silently moving which before many months will produce results'.[69]

Butt, a brilliant lawyer, held the Fenian brief and defended prisoners *pro bono* at their trials for high treason, berating informers and bullying juries. He was not, at this time, a member of parliament, but he had been central to the launch of the amnesty campaign. On the eve of the meeting he met with Fenian leaders and an understanding was reached that they would 'assume an attitude of benevolent neutrality towards the "open movement".'[70]

At the Bilton Hotel, there were sixty men present, constitutionalists and revolutionaries. There were Catholics and Protestants, Conservatives and Liberals. Apart from Fr Lavelle, Catholic priests were conspicuous by their absence.[71] Butt promised Repeal of the Union within three years and the restoration of an Irish parliament. At the end of the discussions he proposed, 'That it is the opinion of this meeting that the true remedy for the evils of Ireland is the establishment of an Irish parliament with full control over our domestic affairs.'[72] The motion was carried without a dissenting voice.

The Home Government Association was officially formed in July and was better known as Home Rule. It replaced Repeal of the Union and, as a term, Home Rule was acceptable to a broad spectrum of Nationalist opinion.

Federalism was the preferred option; it was an unwieldy Americanism, and did not roll off the tongue, but as an unfamiliar, nebulous term, it might be interpreted sympathetically and variously by proponents of self-government. Federalism would maintain the ties with twelve million Irishmen across the world living under British rule, the Irish garrison within the Empire. Irishmen would not forfeit the advantages of a colonial system, which they had helped build. The Protestant minority would not be isolated from the mainland. Daniel O'Connell had suggested a federative arrangement.

In a stratified society, O'Connor Power, a man of no property, without means or formal education, had little hope of taking his struggle to a wider public. The discussions with Moore and Moore's unexpected death gave him pause. The Amnesty Association had lost its voice at Westminster. Who would take Moore's place?

The Anglican Church had been disestablished, a notable concession from the British. The main beneficiary was the Catholic Church, which had waited 300 years for restitution, 'the Anglicans have only a lease on our property'.[73] The Land Act had attempted some corrective measures, with a wedge power shift from landlords to tenants.

In a *quid pro quo*, Pius IX condemned the Fenian movement, undermining their militant stance. IRB members were automatically excommunicated. Old grudges are rarely laid to rest, and objections to Pius's beatification were raised in recent times by an Irish-American group in Washington DC.

But while Irish bishops were meeting in Rome, a large number of their clergy signed a petition asking the British government to grant amnesty to the imprisoned rebels. The Irish Catholic Church had some autonomy, and Nationalist clerics, led by Archbishop McHale, sympathised with the Fenians and their goals. However, the unsuccessful Rising in Ireland, the ill-fated invasions of Canada, and the public fury at the carnage at Clerkenwell Prison, showed flaws in the armed conflict strategy.

O'Connor Power was at a crossroads. His guiding light, Edmund Burke, had not been 'swaddled and rocked and dandled into a legislator'. Burke had entered parliament 'without rank or wealth or hereditary prestige – the three great instruments of political power of his day.' The Ballot Act, with secret voting, had opened up the political landscape. The die was cast.

The Long Game

The Fenians were the best men in Irish politics.[74]

In January 1871, a month before his twenty-fifth birthday, O'Connor Power enrolled at St Jarlath's Diocesan College in Tuam, County Galway.[75] With a third-level education from a recognised and respected establishment, he would gain admission to the corridors of power and influence – where the decisions were made.

St Jarlath's was founded to educate Catholic priests after centuries of persecution, to provide soldiers for the Counter-Reformation. Lay students were welcome. Affluent Catholics, descended from the merchant classes of Galway, would be sure of a good education for their sons. The atmosphere was liberal and, in later life, O'Connor Power would speak of his college days with pride and affection.

The previous year, Fr Ulick Bourke, President of the college, prepared to extend the facilities and appealed for money from Irish Catholics at home and abroad. He planned to accommodate an increasing number of students and provide secular education at third level. The prospectus invited applications from abroad:

> In consequence of some fathers and friends in America and in the Colonies, having expressed a wish to have their sons or relatives trained in an Irish College, the President is happy to announce that he can now receive from those countries any number who may wish to study at St Jarlath's.[76]

His intention was to broaden the scope of the curriculum and establish a well-stocked library. The worldwide fundraising campaign attracted great attention, and many students from overseas, sons of emigrants, often Fenians, came home for further studies. Several veterans of the American Civil War enrolled. Ecclesiastical students paid reduced fees.

Latin and Greek were the foundation of a good education. But President Bourke, like his cousin and patron Archbishop McHale, was a leading Gaelic scholar, with a strong interest and pride in Irish language, literature, history and archaeology. These subjects had an important place in the curriculum. Irish studies were not taught in the British school system, and at Westminster O'Connor Power would introduce an amendment to an education Bill, proposing that 'Irish language, literature and archaeology' be examination subjects.

For three years his college fees, £24 per annum, and expenses were paid for by lecture tours in Britain and America. In August 1871, he was at a meeting near Durham, which was attended by many exiles, aggressively decorated with green rosettes. He was to lecture on 'Ireland: Her Past Struggles and Present Hopes', with a concert to follow the talk. The police arrived but refrained from interfering.[77] In July 1873 he gave a lecture in Liverpool on 'The Martyrs of Irish Liberty':

> Mr J O'Connor Power of St Jarlath's College, Tuam, referring to the execution of the three Fenians in Manchester in 1867 characterised it as a lesson in the very highest self-sacrifice. On that day, he said, Irishmen laid down their lives for their own and their country's friends. He would not attempt to give expression to the eternal gratitude and the stern resolve that took root in millions of Irish hearts in the solemn moment when the martyred three gave their bodies to the executioner and their souls to heaven, but he could never forget how Ireland marked her appreciation of that act of British vindictiveness, by which these three young men were sacrificed on a public scaffold.[78]

On other occasions he spoke less controversially on 'Irish Wit and Humour' and 'Ireland and the Irish'. In his third and final year he was an assistant lecturer of Irish history at St Jarlath's.

He was active in college dramatics, and plays were often chosen with patriotic themes. Early on, he earned praise for his part in *Lord Edward*: 'the grace and fitness of his gestures … a finished elocutionist … achieves the highest flights of oratory', reported the *Tuam News*.

In his second year, he took the leading role in a production of James Sheridan Knowles's *William Tell*, the story of Switzerland's national icon. In this particular version, a second arrow in the hero's belt is reserved for the oppressor's black heart.

O'Connor Power was already a skilled debater:

> On one remarkable occasion, in the presence of the archbishop and several dozen of the diocesan clergy, he 'brought the broadside of his arguments and the power of his elocution to bear' in a debate entitled 'Was the Inquisition justified in condemning Gallileo?'
>
> There was no sickly palliation of the acts of what is often called an ecclesiastical tribunal; there was no glossing over inquisitorial misdeeds by command, or not intentionally weakened defence of [Galileo].[79]

He was not alone at St Jarlath's. The college, at one time referred to as 'a nursery of Fenianism', admitted other revolutionaries to its precincts. O'Donovan Rossa's sons and a son of one of the Manchester Martyrs were students there. Mark Ryan writes that O'Connor Power had visited Tuam as a Fenian organiser some years earlier and 'from fifteen to twenty of the students joined the movement'. Ryan's time at the college overlapped with O'Connor Power's first months.

A mature student, he did not take a break from his extra-curricular activities. As the representative for Connacht on the Supreme Council, he lectured for the Amnesty Association in America and Britain, simultaneously building the IRB network. He continued to oversee arms importation and distribution. Dublin Castle kept a watchful eye on his movements and his mail bag. British intelligence noted that he signed himself John Delaney in letters intercepted during these years.

A Rebel's Progress

'We shall fight England,' one of them said, 'not with bullets, but with the ballot-boxes.'[80]

There were over 100 centres in Britain. In January 1873, the Home Rule Confederation of Great Britain, organised by O'Connor Power and two mainland-based Fenians, John Barry and John Ferguson, was established in the Free Trade Hall in Manchester. The Irish in England were persuaded to formally support Home Rule and to invite Isaac Butt to be President. The electoral power of the Irish would be harnessed. An Irishman who did not join the Home Rule

Association was an enemy of Ireland and its fight for freedom. The IRB discontinued its importation of arms.

O'Connor Power, as X, was Barry O'Brien's source for an account of the difficulties persuading Isaac Butt and many reluctant Fenians to support the HRCGB:

> We need not give up our principles by joining the Home Rulers. They go part of the way in our direction; why not help them so far? In addition we will stiffen their backs by joining them. Here are the Irish in England – a great force; but absolutely lost at present. It is our policy to make the English feel the presence of the Irish everywhere. They don't know what a power the Irish can be in their midst. The English only recognise power. We must make ourselves troublesome. We can make ourselves troublesome by organising the Irish vote in Great Britain, and forcing the English candidates to take the Home Rule pledge. We can control the parliamentary movement if we go into it. At all events let us try.[81]

Butt was uneasy and wrote to X:

> On the eve of the meeting to say that he was afraid he could not attend. X wired back a telegram of nearly 1,000 words, urging him not to fail, saying that the meeting had been got up on the strength of his promise to attend, that delegates had been summoned from all parts of Great Britain and his absence would be nothing short of an insult.

Butt's reply was to the point, 'Shall be with you if I am alive.' He later told X that he had received the telegram in a busy court room and, interrupting the proceedings, immediately read the voluminous message, 'But it was not your arguments that made an impression on me – it was the length of the telegram. "The man," I said, "who has sent me this telegram of 1,000 words must be terribly in earnest, and the men behind him must be terribly in earnest too." Barry O'Brien asked X, 'Was the Confederation always under the control of Fenians?', '"Always," he answered. "They were well represented on the council; our best workers and best organisers were Fenians. Of course, there were plenty of members who were not Fenians. But the Fenians were the masters of the situation."' O'Brien continues:

> The Irish vote was perfectly organised; the Irish voter was made formidable. Every candidate who stood for a constituency where the Irish vote was strong had the following pledge submitted to him:

'To vote for the appointment of a select committee, to inquire into and report upon the motive, extent and the grounds of the demand made by a large proportion of the Irish people for the restoration to Ireland of an Irish Parliament with power to control the internal affairs of the country.'[82]

In Ireland 24,000 men of influence signed a petition calling for a conference. The 1800 Act of Union had weakened the social and political advantages of the ruling class in Ireland. Only a few had done well – earldoms in exchange for compliance. Mere parvenus in Debretts, these were Union peers, agents of English hegemony.

At the 'Solemn Convention of the Irish Republic' on St Patrick's Day in Dublin, leading Fenians met and agreed to support Isaac Butt's movement for a limited period. Subsequently, the IRB introduced a revision into its constitution, which included the following section:

The IRB shall await the decision of the Irish nation, as expressed by a majority of the Irish people, as to the fit hour of inaugurating a war against England, and shall, pending such an emergency, lend its support to every movement calculated to advance the cause of Irish independence consistently with the preservation of its own integrity.[83]

In September, Archbishop McHale came out in support of Home Rule. A few weeks later, at the conference in the Round Room in the Rotunda, Isaac Butt recommended a federal solution for Ireland with its own parliament in the Old House in College Green. He spoke of the conciliation of revolutionary elements:

Mr Gladstone said that Fenianism taught him the intensity of Irish disaffection. It taught me more and better things. It taught me the depth, the breadth, the sincerity of that love of fatherland which misgovernment had tortured into disaffection, and, driving men to despair, had aggravated into revolt …

They were men who were run down by obloquy. They had been branded the enemies of religion and the social order. I saw them manfully bear up against all. I saw the unflinching firmness by which they testified the sincerity of their faith in their own cause, their deep convictions of its righteousness and truth, and I saw them meet their fate with a fanaticism that made them martyrs.[84]

The conference lasted four days. The delegate from Tuam pledged qualified support for Butt and the Home Rule League:

Mr O'Connor Power rose from the midst of the Extreme Left to speak his message
of toleration and encouragement, a quiver of delight went through the Conference,
and many of the shakier Members of Parliament, who had been waiting to see how
far it would be safe to stand aloof from this irksome new movement, promptly
made up their minds that Butt's flag was going to sweep the country.[85]

Members of parliament were to be answerable to all their constituents.
O'Connor Power seconded a resolution, 'It is recommended by this conference
that at the close of each session of parliament the representatives should render
to their constituents an account of their stewardship.'[86] He believed 'Ireland has
been powerless because she has not been able to watch her representatives'.[87]
A Member of parliament should report to constituents, not just electors, those
few eligible to vote. Edmund Burke believed that an MP should live 'in the
strictest union, the closest correspondence and the most unreserved communication with his constituents'.[88] Close consultation with the constituency would
prevent corruption by English influences, the 'Anglicization' or 'prostitution' of
Irishmen.

The IRB acknowledged that armed insurrection was not feasible at this time, and
that co-operation with Home Rulers would further the objectives of land reform
and self-government. It was agreed that there should be an appeal to Irishmen
across the world to support the alliance.

Utterly Changed

By the 1870s Mayo was, in the opinion of New York-based Fenian leader John
Devoy, the 'best' organised county in Ireland and was believed by police authorities to contain one of the most fully armed Fenian organisations in the country.[89]

In January 1874, after consultation with his mentor, Canon Bourke, and with
private encouragement from Archbishop McHale, O'Connor Power threw his
hat into the ring, declaring his intention to contest the Mayo election. He visited all the main towns in Mayo, addressing mass meetings: he was standing 'in
response to the call of the Nationalists of your noble county, and in accordance
with the expressed wishes of many of the leaders of the Home Rule movement'.
He stated his intention to take the oath of allegiance to the Queen, contradicting
traditional Fenian principles, and cloaking a parallel approach. He renewed his
promise to make annual tours of his constituency as recommended at the Home
Rule conference.

Members of parliament received no salary, and he would be dependent on earnings from lectures, journalism and on finance from his supporters. In the run up to the election, he toured the Irish communities of Britain, delivering radical speeches to Home Rule branches, raising awareness and funding. Almost a third of Mayo's able-bodied men worked for three to six months at harvest time in Britain. Money flowed in from his Manchester base, the north of England province of the IRB. O'Connor Power was 'high in the councils of the Fenians' in that city.[90]

Canon Bourke's public support was crucial to his successful candidacy, and he hoped this would ensure backing from the clergy, who, in general, feared the free-thinking Fenian spirit rather more than they disliked the imperial yoke.

The Catholic Church in Ireland was not monolithic, and Gallicanism was the Irish solution to an Irish problem, allowing priests to take a strong, partisan role in national politics. By contrast, ultramontanes, led by Cardinal Cullen, took their line from the Vatican and fought to control and suppress the popular movement. Cullen, the first Irish cardinal, had spent many years in Rome and was determined to assert his authority; any organisation not authorised by the gentry or the Church must, he believed, be in the hands of subversives. On the other side, McHale, the first bishop for centuries to have been wholly educated in Ireland, remained silent on Vatican condemnation of Fenianism.

There was widespread opposition to O'Connor Power's candidacy, led vociferously by the contentious Fr Lavelle, the parish priest of Cong. Lavelle considered him to be an upstart, an interloper, trespassing on his territory. At the Home Rule convention in 1873, he had opposed O'Connor Power's proposal that MPs should keep constituents, not just electors entitled to vote, abreast of parliamentary activities.

O'Connor Power had the support of prominent Home Rulers, and Canon Bourke agreed to nominate him. Archbishop McHale was to bring his influence to bear at the clerical selection committee which took place 4 February in Castlebar. They were outmanoeuvred by Fr Lavelle; arriving a little late, they discovered that he had pre-empted the vote, and his preferred candidates were in place.[91] McHale never forgave Lavelle, a reputed loose canon, for his sleight of hand.

There was a violent reaction. Galway's Bishop MacEvilly, the Vatican's listening post in the west wrote to Cardinal Cullen, 'things took a dreadful turn in Mayo, Dr McHale and the priests were *hooted* because they did not support a Mr O'Connor Power, a *student* at St Jarlath's, the recognised head of the Fenians in this country'. He quoted a Mayo priest, '"Please observe that the Archbishop came from Tuam accompanied by his cousin Revd U Burke to promote the candidature of madman Power the Fenian."'[92]

The Fenians were denounced from the pulpits. Priests controlled institutional property, making it difficult to find accommodation for meetings. Clerical hostility was well organised, and in face of widespread intimidation and victimisation, O'Connor Power withdrew his name.

His followers in Mayo, disappointed and thwarted, threatened to withhold clerical dues and demonstrated in large numbers, denouncing the priests and the bishops. Mayo erupted:

> The roughs and all the phalanxes of Fenians paraded the town, round and round with banners, fife and drum, shouting and hurraing for Power. Fr Lavelle was mobbed and hooted, priest and Bishops denounced as traitors … The mob passed backwards and forwards where the Archbishop was, hooting and shouting and groaning …[93]

Years of secret drilling throughout the county delivered a highly disciplined force, 'The Fenian demonstration in support of O'Connor Power had a patent military format.'[94]

Lavelle used every ploy to destroy O'Connor Power's standing and wrote to the Home Rule leader, Isaac Butt, with an unfounded, but potentially damaging, allegation of illegitimacy. He accused O'Connor Power of being a 'communist' and an 'internationale member'.[95]

The Irish in England, who had once stood wholeheartedly behind Lavelle and his estimable work for Irish causes, turned against him. Twenty Home Rule associations condemned his attacks on O'Connor Power, who declared: 'Sensible men are heartily sick of him and all his electioneering wire-pulling. They do not share his love of contention, and they will henceforth regard his affirmation or denial of anything with the most perfect indifference.'[96]

For technical reasons, the election result was declared invalid. O'Connor Power, despite growing clerical hostility, stood in the subsequent by-election in May:

> When I last addressed you as a parliamentary candidate, I was bound by a pledge, which made my candidature conditional on my adoption by his grace the archbishop of Tuam and the bishops and clergy of Mayo; and when their decision was against me I retired from the contest, though it appeared that my return was certain had I gone to the poll. Before, however, my committee accepted my resignation, they in the name of the Nationalists of Mayo, extracted a promise from me that I would again become a candidate for the county if, at any ensuing election, they should still be dissatisfied with the candidates then in the field.

Sooner, many years sooner than I could have anticipated, I am now called upon by a numerously-signed requisition of the electors to fulfil that promise. I kept my word on the last occasion, I am determined not to break it on this; and hence I again offer myself as a candidate.[97]

Hundreds of Fenians, in disciplined formation, gathered to back their candidate. O'Connor Power explained why he withdrew earlier, and declared his intention to stand 'with a reputation on which calumny has vainly endeavoured to fix a stain'. He was 'prepared to strike a blow for the independence of Mayo and the freedom of their native land' and declared himself in favour of denominational education, security of tenure and an extension of the franchise. He pledged to prioritise the fight for amnesty, 'Having been a sharer in the sufferings of political prisoners, I am not likely to grow lukewarm in my efforts to procure their release.'

Seasoned campaigners, with experience of the earlier Moore campaign and a controversial by-election in Galway in 1872, were back in play. Matt Harris of Ballinasloe, a friend of the Power family, was chairman of the O'Connor Power election committee, and Mark Ryan, who first met O'Connor Power in Lancashire, was treasurer and secretary. Thomas Brennan, P.W. Nally, local men and close comrades, were on the team. Electioneering units covered Mayo, 'All the Fenian forces were unloosed over the county, and the priests were not idle. The supporters of O'Connor Power complained of the language and actions of some of the clergymen, and Fr Lavelle complained of speeches made in reference to himself.'[98]

James Daly, a prosperous grazier farmer, played a prominent role in local politics and backed O'Connor Power's candidacy. Influential and law abiding, Daly was a town councillor and Poor Law guardian. He was not a Fenian, but believed in the necessity of a strong voice at Westminster to represent Mayo's interests. He brought to O'Connor Power's campaign the support of anti-landlord farmers, merchants and artisans who were eager for change.

The county's landowners were, on the whole, absentees, with little or no interest in their tenantry. Their properties were under the supervision of agents, who collected rents to be sent out of the country. Landlords, who stripped Ireland of its wealth, were a focus for the grievances of Mayo, a county on the brink of rebellion.

An emerging middle class filled a vacuum; the new men threw down the gauntlet to an absent landed elite and a hostile clerical establishment, determined to break their political and economic power. Ten Castlebar merchants, including Daly, signed O'Connor Power's nomination papers. The candidate 'symbolised both the vitality and ambiguity of the Nationalist alliance'.[99]

Sustained by the 'vastness of his organisation', O'Connor Power campaigned across the county:

> Mr O'Connor Power is ... more prominently before the electors than perhaps either of the other candidates. He has already visited all the principal towns of the county and has delivered stirring addresses in each. He is without doubt the 'popular' man – the favourite with the populace. His eloquence and his advanced political opinions have secured him this honour.[100]

Bishop McEvilly wrote to Cullen, 'a bad business. O'CP is a Fenian and swore in as Fenians some alumni of the college he was in ... it would be most humiliating if he was returned'.[101] A sceptical Mayo priest wrote to Mitchell Henry, Home Rule MP for Galway:

> As you see by the papers, Mr O'Connor Power has created great excitement in the places he visited, but you will find that it will cool down before the day of polling ... I very much fear that he does not know Mayo well. I was there for the last ten years and as far as I can give an opinion there is no county in Ireland so much in the hands of the priests as Mayo ... One word from the altar next Sunday, or even a word privately to the electors before the polling day, will set the electors at ease and turn the scales for *the selected one*.[102]

The controversy was now a national issue, and the public followed the campaign closely. *The Times* reported that the Cullenites 'were leaving no means untried to influence popular feeling ... the power of the mobs was not left in abeyance'. The *Irishman* wrote of O'Connor Power's 'desperate struggle against the combined influence of the whole priesthood of the county' and believed, if he lost, the election result would be invalidated on grounds of clerical intimidation.[103]

The introduction of secret voting, a move denounced as 'underhand' by its opponents, meant careful preparation on the canvass: voters were to be instructed in the valid use of the ballot sheet in the new system. It was a show of X, at this point the mark of the illiterate. Twenty years later O'Connor Power recalls the difficulties, 'I remember very well the difficulty which we had then to make the voter understand the secrecy of the ballot, and how to mark his voting paper, without rendering it null and void in the operation.'[104]

At close of poll, 29 May, George Browne, a local landlord, was just eleven votes ahead of O'Connor Power who 'stirred the people of Mayo as they had not been stirred since the days of George Henry Moore. In those days, however, the franchise was confined to the freeholder and the £12 rated occupiers, which accounts for the fact that he was only second in the poll.' Mark Ryan would write in his memoirs, 'The return of O'Connor Power was regarded by us as a great victory, in view of the formidable forces which had been arrayed against him.' [105]

O'Connor Power was the first man of no property to represent Mayo at Westminster. He had defied the vested interests of the establishment and the Catholic Church. Deference to a ruling class, clerical or secular, was fast drawing to a close. Concerted action on land reform would follow.

Part Two

Confessors of Irish Nationality

The Felons of our Land

The franchise was severely restricted but it was the first election where the votes were cast within the privacy of a ballot box. Previously a voter had publicly named his choice of candidate, and a perceived miscast vote jeopardised his standing with agent and landlord. A secret ballot and an increase in the number of polling stations ensured that no pressure could be applied, and a decisive majority of Irish representatives elected to Westminster were Home Rulers, many of whom were Catholic. Just over a decade later, a large number of Ireland's MPs would be selected from outside the landowning class. The edifice of ascendancy was slowly crumbling.

In England, the Home Rule Confederation played Liberal against Tory, and a number of English Liberals took the Home Rule pledge and, on the back of the Irish vote, were elected.[106]

Dod's *Parliamentary Companion*, providing biographical details of members, shows that most of the Home Rule party described themselves as Liberals, 'in favour of the system called Home Rule for Ireland'. At Westminster they took their seats below the gangway on the Opposition side, in what came to be known as the 'Irish Quarter'. A party apart, they signalled their independence.

But Gladstone, who had called a snap election, had misjudged the mood of the British electorate and the Tories had swept back into power.

O'Connor Power was well prepared and adapted rapidly to the ways of the House of Commons. On his travels across the United States, he had closely observed the political system of the New World. Democracy, federalism, anti-imperialism, the pursuit of happiness – said to have been written in pencil as the 'pursuit of property' in the first draft of the American Declaration of Independence – these were the way forward.

He hit the ground running. The Home Rule debate, scheduled for 30 June and 2 July, attracted a crowded House and packed galleries. In his maiden speech, O'Connor Power pinned the Home Rule colours to the mast. He regarded 'federalism as the most logical base on which a perfect union between Great Britain and Ireland could be secured'. A federal solution would accommodate Orangemen and Fenians. It would strengthen and confirm the ties of the Irish dispersed throughout the Empire.

All did not run to plan. The script of his speech, issued to the press, was printed in full in the *Freeman's Journal*, but he 'failed to catch the Speaker's eye', and it was not delivered. The newspapers reported that Mr O'Connor Power had supported the motion, but it was a Mr Richard Power of Waterford who had spoken. 'Over zealous', O'Connor Power had performed 'a superhuman feat', having a speech reported before it was delivered:

> Power argued that should England ever become involved in a European War, it was in the contentment of the Irish people – a race of soldiers – that her best security lay.

> Though your ships of war have ploughed every sea, though your soldiers have planted the Flag of England on every spot of that wide dominion over which the sun never ceases to shine, you have yet to achieve the noblest victory of all – a victory over your own prejudices against the Irish race.[107]

The error created its own momentum and was widely commented upon in the House and in society in general, a hilarious instance of 'all publicity is good publicity'.

Many years later, in an after-dinner toast, he spoke of the incident, 'I learned in the House of Commons that the cheapest and easiest way of gaining a reputation for eloquence was to keep generally silent'.

At his next attempt, the second night of the Home Rule debate, he rose to cries of 'spoke, spoke,' and asserted: '[Home Rule] had a substantial existence in Ireland, and the people of Ireland were determined that she should no longer be treated as a trampled Province, but should take an important part in the management of the world's affairs.' Exchanges with The O'Donoghue, a Catholic landowner from Kerry, marked him as a man who could survive the cut and thrust of parliamentary debate. The O'Donoghue quoted scathingly from the undelivered script.

In response and with impressive versatility, O'Connor Power turned the tables on The O'Donoghue, quoting a speech he had made decades earlier. Timothy Healy, who joined him in the House seven years later, remarked on his performance, 'Power's dexterity in thus extricating himself proclaimed him a coming man.'[108]

The party's leader, Isaac Butt, made his case and his speech was well received. But the Premier, Disraeli, with withering condescension, spoke against Home Rule, declaring that it would 'bring about the disintegration of the Kingdom and the destruction of the Empire'. 'Yes,' he said scathingly, to roars of laughter, 'I will not deny that Oliver Cromwell conquered Ireland, but it was after he had conquered England. William III could not have succeeded in conquering Ireland if he had not previously conquered England.' The motion was defeated by an overwhelming majority.

Ten days later, O'Connor Power launched the parliamentary campaign for amnesty – Professor T. W. Moody described him as its 'moving spirit' – with an Address for Returns of 'the names of the prisoners who had died or become insane during the last ten years in consequence of the severity of the treatment'.[109]

'John O'Connor Power asks for amnesty for the "Manchester murderers" and for "soldiers false to their oath",' reported *Punch*'s column 'The Essence of Parliament'.[110] Fenians, he argued, were political prisoners, not murderers, not felons. They should be treated 'as men not brutes'. In subsequent years, inside and outside of parliament, he battled long and hard for amnesty. Making constant demands for improvements in prison conditions, he persisted after others had lost heart, refusing to give up the fight. His sympathy for the prisoners and their families was hands-on. He had personal experience of the treatment meted out and understood their plight, 'In our days men have endured, with heroic, silent fortitude, sufferings I dare not trust myself to mention.'[111]

At Westminster, he recalled the speeches of his predecessor, the former member for Mayo, George Henry Moore, who, in 1870, had fought in parliament for the rights of O'Donovan Rossa. The recommendation of the Devon Commission (1845), that political prisoners be housed separately from convicts, had not been implemented.

Fenians, imprisoned for the Manchester Rescue, were held as accessories to the murder of Sergeant Brett. O'Connor Power argued:

If a similar daring exploit were perpetrated in Paris under the rule of Napoleon, in Madrid under Isabella, in Rome under the Pope, or in Warsaw under the rule of the Muscovite, the actors in it would not be called murderers, but heroes. The English Press would be loud in their praise, and would tell the world that courage and fidelity like theirs should be recorded on one of the brightest pages of history.[112]

Michael Davitt, O'Connor Power's close friend from the Lancashire years, and formerly chief arms agent in England, was held in Dartmoor, for the importation of guns into Ireland. Convicted on the false testimony of John Joseph Corydon, for treason-felony, he was sentenced to fifteen years' penal servitude. Corydon, an American army officer, had come back to fight for Ireland's freedom but, turning spy, betrayed the men who planned to breach Chester Castle's defences, 'The testimony of a perjured informer named Corydon was accepted against him [Davitt], but an English jury could hardly have been acquainted with the character of their infamous witness, or they would have hesitated before convicting anyone on his evidence.'

O'Connor Power spoke of Davitt's character from personal knowledge, 'He was one of the most disinterested men I ever met – upright and honourable in every relation of life. I say he was for the tomb could not more effectually separate him from life, all that makes life worth having.' He described how Davitt reached out compassionately to the Englishman who, unwittingly, had sold him guns illegally. After hearing his own devastating sentence, he spoke eloquently in defence of John Wilson, the Birmingham gunsmith:

> I declare to your lordship this Englishman beside me is innocent. He never knew the purpose for which those arms were intended. He has a wife and a helpless family of young children depending upon him. I implore your Lordship to discharge him, and I shall cheerfully undergo his punishment in addition to my own.

Davitt, who left Ireland as a small child, had a strong Lancashire accent and presented as an Englishman. The Amnesty Association supported John Wilson on his release and provided for him until his death.

O'Connor Power excoriated the British justice system and spoke of his many applications to the Home Office for permission to visit prisoners and how he was refused private interviews at every turn. Colour Sergeant Charles McCarthy and Corporal Thomas Chambers were sentenced, for breaches of the Articles of War, to imprisonment for the term of their natural lives. Soldiers, they had broken their oaths and 'abandoned the standard of the Queen'. He praised McCarthy's character. One of the most upright of men, a brave man, he had earned several medals from engagements in the service of the Queen.

Corporal Thomas Chambers, held under the Articles of War, had sent many memorials for clemency from Dartmoor. O'Connor Power insisted that non-commissioned Irish soldiers, who, at an early age, joined the British army out of economic necessity, could not be judged harshly. In their defence, he cited the example of John Churchill, who took an oath to King James II in Whitehall and defected, opportunistically, twenty-four hours later, to William of Orange. John Churchill was 'embraced with royal affection' and rewarded with the Dukedom of Marlborough for his defection. The comparison of the treachery of a Marlborough to the dual allegiance and sentiment of an Irish soldier became a talking point at Westminster and in the press, attracting wide attention and energetic debate.

John Churchill's descendants numbered the Duke of Marlborough, Lord Lieutenant of Ireland, and his son Lord Randolph Churchill, a Tory MP. Randolph was a flamboyant figure, and the ensuing exchanges in the House were lively. Provoked, Randolph asserted (mistakenly) that the dukedom had been granted in gratitude for the General's victory at Blenheim. The argument continued.

In 1906, the insult, which had hit its mark – the Marlborough pride – still vexed. Winston Churchill writes in his biography of his father, *Lord Randolph Churchill*, of 'an unkind comparison drawn by Mr O'Connor Power between the soldiers who had become Fenians' and his ancestor, the first duke.[113]

O'Connor Power took aim at Irishmen on the government benches, 'My country-men who sit opposite revere the "pious, glorious and immortal" name of William, but I ask them did that prince refuse the proffered services of Churchill because he was a soldier who had broken his oath?' He spoke of soldiers sentenced by military tribunals:

> They believed the obligations to patriotism were more binding than the obli-gations of a military oath. You may denounce their conduct as illegal and revolutionary, but there is nothing sordid or mean about it. It is conduct, which you are accustomed to applaud in foreign countries, and which you regard as courageous, magnanimous and disinterested everywhere but in Ireland.
>
> The principle of allegiance is not founded in public office. It must spring from a higher source to be binding on the conscience of the subject.

All classes in Ireland were in favour of amnesty for these prisoners, who had come to symbolise the searing resentments of the nation. Mass meetings were held in every considerable town and city in Britain and Ireland. Boards of Guardians, town councils, petitioned for clemency. The Irish around the world spoke and wrote of British injustice.

An application to the Home Office for permission to visit Davitt was refused in October 1871, and again in September 1874. In January 1872, John Francis Maguire, MP for Cork and owner of the *Cork Examiner*, asked that O'Connor Power might meet with Davitt. The head of the prison service, Colonel Edmund Du Cane, refused. He would not allow convicts to receive visits and communica-tions from those suspected of 'being connected with them in crime'.[114]

Suspected Fenians, under the Suspension of Habeas Corpus Act, were arrested and held for up to two years without trial. Many of the detained were there because of the work of paid informers, and might eventually be convicted by perjurers, forged testimony, entrapment or rigged juries. Proof of guilt was commonly manufactured by agents of the State, and convictions were obtained on insufficient or tainted evidence. Informers were 'carefully drilled for the witness-box'.

On 1 August 1876, the amnesty question was reopened. The signatures of 138 MPs were appended to a declaration in favour of a speedy release. This memorial was presented to Disraeli, and to no avail. O'Connor Power had reminded him that in his *roman à thèse, Sybil, The Two Nations*, he lays down the principle that political offenders must not be treated like common criminals.[115]

In the House, he repeatedly urged clemency, appealing to Queen Victoria to mark the occasion of the creation of the title, Empress of India, with a full pardon:

> … the time has come when Her Majesty's gracious pardon may be advanta-
> geously extended to the prisoners, whether convicted before the civil tribunals or
> by court-martial, who are and have been for many years undergoing punishment
> for offences arising out of insurrectionary movements connected with Ireland.

He brought forward a motion for the release of prisoners and read aloud his correspondence with the Home Secretary and Whitehall civil servants. John Bright took part in the debate and, speaking of the Manchester Martyrs, declared that it was hardly condign punishment to hang three men for the death of one. He condemned the official practice of calling the three dead men 'murderers' and the crime 'murder'.

The *Catalpa* whaling boat and its daring crew freed six Fenian prisoners from a penal settlement in Western Australia in the late spring of 1876. The sensational rescue was publicised around the world, a great propaganda coup. In Dublin, an effigy of Disraeli was burnt on a bonfire in a frenzy of celebration. O'Connor Power warned the House:

> It reflects no honour on the Government of the Empire that while you were declar-
> ing here that public safety demanded the retention of the Fenian prisoners, an
> expedition should have made its way to Western Australia, and have torn from the
> strongest prison six of the men whom you most desired to keep in the gaoler's grasp.

The incarceration of Irish prisoners was impolitic as well as unjust, O'Connor Power persisted. The government's policy bred disaffection. The Irish across the world would rise up against the oppressors and eventually undermine and destroy the British Empire. Had it not become more difficult to rule Ireland than to govern the rest of England's vast territory?

He invoked the American dimension:

> You are fomenting a hostile spirit in the breasts of millions beyond the Atlantic. Whenever an Irish Bill is unjustly thrown out of this House the fact is noted by the Irish-American papers … You are prepared, I suppose, to meet all this with the resources of the Secret Service Fund; you will send the spy and the informer on the track of your enemies in America as you have done in Ireland; but you cannot take the rifle out of a single Irish hand in the American continent. The millions of Irish there are beyond the reach of your power. I have been amongst them, and I know how they are animated by the glorious passion of patriotism. I am not delivering a menace, but expressing my solemn conviction, when I say that unless you adopt and carry out a policy of conciliation and complete justice to Ireland you will be responsible for invoking a spirit and erecting a power among the exiled Irish race that may yet lay the empire of England in the dust.

The following day the motion was rejected, but seventeen English Liberal members, including John Bright and Charles Henry Hopwood, voted for the immediate release of the Fenians. None of the Liberal leaders voted against the motion. Mr Playfair, a Scot, voted for it.[116] Davitt, over twenty years later, reminded the House of the occasion, describing Mr O'Connor Power as an 'ornament of debate'.

There were repercussions. Prison security intensified. Military prisoner John Patrick O'Brien's failed bid for freedom increased the tight precautionary measures. The *Freeman's Journal* reported, 'For an attempt to pick a hole through his cell wall, O'Brien was kept in a dark cell for some six months in chains.'

The prison regime became yet harsher. A special watch was put on the cells of Irish prisoners, with frequent disturbance of sleep. Charles McCarthy was moved to an end cell, without an outside wall. It was secure but lacked ventilation; the only air vent was close to the water closets in the hall, and the stench was poisonous. A murmur of complaint was met with a vengeful response: lives would be more onerous and cells would be routinely searched and trashed. Sleep deprivation, and frequent and regular interruptions at night, increased disorientation.

In vindication, the authorities asserted that there were 'emissaries in England for the purpose of aiding their escape'. The memory of the attack on Clerkenwell

Prison, with the deaths of innocent bystanders and the destruction of neighbourhood homes, was still raw.

In 1876 Lord Derby, the British Foreign Secretary, made representations to the Peruvian government. English sailors on board the *Talisman* had been captured and detained for many months 'in a filthy hole' without trial. The dispute dragged on. An analogy was employed to great effect, 'Mr O'Connor Power aptly instanced the American Fenians who had been kept for long periods in jail without a trial as suspects, and the matter dropped.'[117]

Disraeli's Bill to reform and nationalise the prison system provided opportunities to renew the case for amnesty. On 5 June 1877, O'Connor Power detailed a catalogue of the prisoners' ill-treatment. In the House he read aloud letters from Davitt and from Colour Sergeant McCarthy, which described the horrendous conditions of their lives. He argued that to deny them the status of political prisoners, a position not taken by any other country, was 'rolling back the tide of civilisation'. He read out his own correspondence with Whitehall civil servants: his requests for visitation rights and the cold, bureaucratic refusals. Visits would not, in fact, yield satisfaction, as the inmates were under supervision on these occasions and forbidden to speak of the degrading cruelties of the regime.

Solitary confinement, deliberately demeaning strip searches, foul quarters, food deemed unfit for fodder, and constant humiliations, were among the many tribulations endured by the 'men of the Moor'. Young boys were at the mercy of 'old gaol birds'. Self mutilation was common. Cold, hunger and restraint, in dark, wet and dirty cells, with a cacophony of 'the ravings of madmen and the howling of flogged wretches', were daily hardships, but solitary was the harshest punishment, and many never recovered from the terrors of social isolation.

Wardens, often ex-servicemen, under orders and with bias and prejudice, treated Irish political prisoners with more contempt and brutality than convicted English murderers. Corporal Chambers asserted, 'The whole object of the prison officers was to break our spirit … and many of those prisoners, confined without an appeal to either judge or jury, were tortured to death or driven to madness by the barbarous treatment they received.'

McCarthy wrote from his cell, 'The melancholy conclusion has forced itself upon us that nothing less than our lives are aimed at, and that too in a cowardly and assassin-like manner.' The inquests' verdicts: 'Death resulted from natural causes', or, in one instance, the 'unkind treatment of the assistant surgeon'.

Writing to Gladstone, O'Connor Power asked him to break his silence and promote an early release for the remaining Fenian prisoners. He retained a copy of the letter, composed in the Prince of Wales hostelry. Among Michael MacDonagh's papers, it is now in the National Library of Ireland:

23, Ebury St S.W.
July 18 1877

Dear Sir,

History will I believe assign you a high place among the champions of humanity for the just indignation against Turkish oppression which you have excited in the breasts of Englishmen and to which you have given expression in soul-stirring language that has rung around the world.

Since, therefore, you have pleaded the cause of political offenders in the Turkish dominions thereby following up your previous action on behalf of the Neapolitan rebels, and I point out to you that there are still lingering in English prisons Irish political prisoners well deserving of your sympathy and solicit your influential support of the motion in favour of their liberation which I intend to move in the House of Commons on 20th inst.

Had you remained in the position of Her Majesty's principal adviser I feel convinced that you would before now have completed the work of amnesty which you partially carried out in 1874 and enabled your country to boast that her gaols contained not a single political prisoner.

The additional punishment of the last six years which these prisoners have undergone, have I am sure affected, and I would hope entirely removed, the objections to their release which you felt when you were in office, but I am afraid that your silence on the subject may have led Her Majesty's present advisers to a different conclusion.

I would rejoice at all events it you could see your way to such support of my motion as would deprive the governing of any excuse to be fortified by your example for the further incarceration of political prisoners.

Although a very humble member of the House of Commons I make this appeal to you with a large degree of confidence because the object I have in view has already received the support of 141 members of the House including two Right Hon. Gentlemen who were distinguished members of your Cabinet, Mr Bright and Dr Lyon Playfair [postmaster general] and I venture in conclusion to express my belief that you would show the possession of a noble magnanimity and greater moral power in recognising the merits of patriots who have incurred the displeasure of a government for whose shortcomings you as an Englishman may be responsible than by the warmest manifestation of your sympathy, with the effort of the patriots in foreign lands against whom I presume your country has done no wrong.

I have the honour to remain,
Dear Sir,
Your obedient servant,
John O'Connor Power

Two days later he again appealed to the House and spoke of the *Catalpa* Rescue:

If those rescued men were not political prisoners, why did not her Majesty's Government demand their extradition from the American government? ... England could not demand the extradition of those men without disgracing herself before the civilised world. She, the professed champion of political offenders abroad, would stand before the nations a self-convicted hypocrite, were she to make so preposterous a demand.

He warned that each indignity visited on the prisoners only increased the love and esteem in which they were held by the Irish around the world. They may be felons under your law, but are regarded in Ireland as 'the confessors of Irish nationality – the martyrs of Irish freedom'. He recited all the verses of the most popular Irish marching song of the day, 'The Felons of Our Land'. The last reads:

> Let Cowards swear and tyrants frown
> Oh! little do we care –
> Such 'Felon's' cap's the noblest crown
> An Irish head can wear:
> And every Gael in Innisfail
> Who scorns the serf's vile brand,
> From Lee to Foyne will gladly join
> The Felons of our Land.

He continued:

Is it vain to hope that now, after eleven long years of penal servitude have passed over those imprisoned Irish patriots, an English Minister will be found who will drop one flower of sympathy on the altar of Irish patriotism, and recognising the purity of their motives and the courage and endurance with which they have met their fate, open the prison doors and set the prisoners free? I trust, Sir, that such a hope is not vain, and that the answer of the right hon. gentleman will leave no room for the reflection:

> Forgiveness to the injured doth belong,
> They never do forgive, who do the wrong.

Gladstone made a significant intervention, and, as early as August, the release of the Fenians was expected.[118] In the autumn he visited Ireland, staying with his family on the Kilruddery estate in County Wicklow. He paid a visit to St Patrick's College, Maynooth and later met informally with Cardinal Cullen.

Disraeli never set foot on Irish soil.

Charles McCarthy's Death

… the perils of Irish patriotism.

In early December, O'Connor Power was in Mayo for the unveiling of a monument commemorating the French soldiers who had died near Castlebar during the 1798 Rising. He was expecting good news, and, a week before Christmas, Michael Davitt, who had spent seven and a half years in jail, was granted a ticket of leave (parole).

Charles McCarthy, Thomas Chambers and John Patrick O'Brien were released from Chatham two weeks later. They travelled with Davitt to Dublin and were greeted with a tremendous reception as they disembarked in Kingstown (now Dún Laoghaire) Harbour on 13 January 1878. Another large crowd met them off the train in Westland Row. The following day they visited O'Connor Power in his lodgings in Doran's in Molesworth Street and 'thanked him for his unceasing exertions on their behalf'.[119]

That night, a visit was arranged to see Dion Boucicault's *The Shaughraun* at the Gaiety Theatre, which they enjoyed enormously. Boucicault's plays show English audiences how Irishmen view the world and, aptly, *The Shaughraun* deals with the formation of the Fenian Brotherhood and the climate of political unrest.

It was the last night of Charles McCarthy's life. The following morning, at a widely publicised and well-attended breakfast in Morrison's hotel, he collapsed and died. The Home Rule Conference was taking place in Dublin, and over eighty prominent politicians and newspaper men were in the city and witnessed his dramatic death.

A few weeks later, Davitt, in a sworn statement, described Charles McCarthy's state of mind, 'I accompanied him to the theatre the eve of his death, and heard him express himself as highly pleased after returning therefrom.'

The next day, a jury ruled that his death had been hastened by the regime in Chatham. Inhumane treatment had destroyed his health and was the direct cause of death. The post-mortem doctors gave evidence under oath. Dr O'Leary testified that McCarthy had been 'utterly unfit to undergo prison discipline for over two years'. Dr Egan confirmed that his heart disease had been progressive.

Charles McCarthy was forty-four years old when he died and had spent twelve years in British jails. He was waked in the Carmelite church in Clarendon Street and buried in Glasnevin Cemetery, and the funeral procession was the longest in Ireland since that of Daniel O'Connell.

At a meeting in Liverpool, it was proposed that the remaining prisoners be released immediately. In the House of Commons, O'Connor Power demanded an official enquiry.[120] Davitt, Chambers and O'Brien travelled back to England.

O'Connor Power collated and published the findings of this enquiry into McCarthy's treatment and cause of death. 'The following documents have been sent to you for publication' prefaces the statements and letters. There was his own letter, sent on 22 February 1878, to Sir James Ingham, the Chief Magistrate of the Police Courts of the Metropolis, on the procedures of the enquiry. He demanded that prison staff be questioned under oath and the proceedings, held in the Chatham Convict Prison, be made public. Relatives and next of kin were to be present with their counsel, and an independent medical man was to be in attendance. These requests were not allowed. O'Connor Power was present as an observer but, as his conditions were not met, he did not participate.

Despite poor health, McCarthy had been employed in the tailor's room and in the laundry, which involved carrying very heavy bags up several flights of stairs. As an orderly, he took out the slops – emptying the waste buckets of the other prisoners – a job which everyone loathed because of the foul smells. Frequent requests for a transfer to an invalid prison had been refused. Several stays in hospital were cut short, with no time for recovery or a full investigation of his condition.

The statements of the official witnesses at the enquiry were inconsistent. The prison doctors – Davitt argued in his statement that 'the class of medical men' are not well qualified and only there through patronage – contradicted each other and created imaginary scenarios in their accounts. One even asserted that if McCarthy had not been freed, he would still be alive. He believed the welcome reception and celebrations in Dublin were injurious to his health and accelerated his death. His heart disease was the result of an earlier attack of rheumatic fever and not a consequence of ill treatment. McCarthy had, on several occasions, told medical officers that he had never had rheumatic fever.

O'Connor Power publicly denounced the conclusions and insisted it was an attempt to whitewash the prison authorities. He understood very well the importance of continuous agitation and publicity for the plight of the men still behind bars. Public opinion must be informed and formed. Publishing the statements of the released men gave them a voice at last, the meagre solace of a victim statement.

In full stride, he arranged to have Davitt's account of his prison treatment and his recommendations published with a collection of his own speeches on amnesty,[121] including the letters from Davitt and McCarthy, which he had read aloud to the House.

Devoy's Post Bag contains a letter from Thomas Chambers, writing to John B. O'Reilly that O'Connor Power will denounce the whole enquiry as 'a humbug', '[O'Connor Power] has some failings (who has not) but his goodness – his exertions for us – *publicly and privately*, has earned *my* gratitude. His private kindnesses to Mr Davitt and I were of a nature that it would not be prudent to explain on paper.' Devoy regarded 'Chambers as the most intelligent and the best educated of the Fenian soldiers … absolutely faithful to an ideal'.[122]

In November 1878 there is a letter from John O'Leary in Paris to John Devoy in New York:

> I suppose I need not inform you that Davitt like *your* friend Mr Kelly (if he still be your friend) is a thick and thin friend of Mr O'C.P., whom by the way, he seemed to hold up in that speech of his as the model of what an MP should be.

A series of public meetings was planned. The first was held in St James Hall, Piccadilly in early March. There were over 2,500 present, mainly Irish Londoners. Messages of support arrived from Home Rule associations. Groups gathered with bands and banners. O'Connor Power presided and twelve MPs, ten Home Rulers and two English Liberals, joined him on the platform. Davitt, Chambers and O'Brien sat with them. The following resolutions were passed: unconditional release of the remaining Fenian prisoners; condemnation of the treatment of political prisoners, and a demand that they should have first-class misdemeanant status. These resolutions were to be conveyed to the Home Secretary and the Irish Chief Secretary.

On 28 April, at the Adelphi Theatre in Liverpool, O'Connor Power, in 'an eloquent address', presented Davitt to a large public meeting.[123] Still in a 'precarious state of health',[124] Davitt was speedily instated as a member of the Supreme Council, the representative for the North of England. He travelled extensively through–

out Ireland, Scotland and England, addressing public gatherings in Nationalist strongholds. O'Connor Power had requested the Home Secretary not to rigorously enforce the conditions of his parole, and his movements were not restricted. A trip to Mayo was the first since he had left as a small child. He was received with turf bonfires blazing on the hillsides and a fanfare of introductions to local leaders. James Daly arranged torchlight parades, cheering crowds and a magnificent reception. Davitt had a platform and a role.[125]

In July, Sir James Ingham's Report was reviewed in the House of Commons. Mitchell Henry, member for Galway, requested that ladies be excluded from their gallery, such were 'the shocking details which he had to produce … When Mr Mitchell Henry sat down his motion was seconded without a word by Mr O'Connor Power.'[126]

The battle for the release of Edward Meagher Condon (of the Manchester Rescue), Patrick Melady, Thomas Ahern and several others continued. The following December they were free. O'Connor Power accompanied Clancy and Ahearne to the welcome reception given by the Irish Political Visiting Committee at the Cambridge Hall in London and moved a resolution:

> … expressing indignation at the application of the silent system to political prisoners, and said that 11 golden years had passed since he stood side by side with men like Mr Clancy and his colleagues ready to share all the perils of Irish patriotism, and the remembrance that he was associated with such men as O'Donovan Rossa and Clancy was to him a prouder recollection and a higher honour than that of being a member of the British parliament …

He added he had received assurances that the remaining prisoner, Edward O'Kelly, would be released before Christmas and that 'he had represented in the proper quarter the passionate desire of the prisoner that he might not be compelled to go into exile'.[127]

A New Career

O'Connor Power is eating his dinners for the Bar.[128]

On his thirty-second birthday, O'Connor Power, writing on House of Commons notepaper, thanked the Knights of St Patrick in St Louis for their invitation to attend their twelfth anniversary celebrations. He wrote of the 'Saxon oppressor' and the 'Saxon House of Commons':

You know I have been accused of a desire to obstruct the progress of legislation and throw the parliamentary steam engine off the rails, but really all that Parnell, Biggar and O'Donnell and a few others of us have done so far, has been to put the brake on occasionally, just to prevent accidents.[129]

Obstructive tactics were designed to draw attention to Ireland's demands for self-government, land reform and the immediate release of Fenian prisoners.

The following morning, a month to the day after the dramatic death of Charles McCarthy, O'Connor Power enrolled at the Middle Temple, one of the Inns of Court, to read for the Bar. An abiding concern for the rights of prisoners must have been an impulse behind his decision; as a lawyer, he would have the authority of the profession to pursue his campaign for prison reform.

And like Anthony Trollope's Irish MP Phineas Finn, earning nothing from politics, presumably, he hoped to make a living as a barrister, a supplement to his earnings from journalism and lectures. MPs did not receive salaries, and his funds for campaigning, parliamentary expenses and accommodation had initially been subsidised.

Three years later, he was admitted to the Bar. His calling would provide the legal training vital for work on land legislation and proposals for Home Rule. The barrister who signed his papers was Charles Henry Hopwood MP, a leading liberal crusader, a noted penal reformer and founder of the Romilly Society.[130] Hopwood's mother was born in Dublin. His headmaster, Phelim Mullens, was an Irishman. The sympathetic Hopwood, champion of the working man and tireless advocate for social justice, had an intimate understanding of the Irish Question and favoured Home Rule.

'A Towering Figure'[131]

… the darling of the advanced Nationalist press and of the Irish in Britain. In the opening months of 1875 two pages of each issue of the *Irishman* were devoted to the Mayo MPs engagements, including his speeches to Irish communities in Britain and letters on a large number of Irish topics.[132]

These were stormy times. On 6 August 1875, bitter rows stalled the Dublin parade celebrating the centennial of Daniel O'Connell's birth. The route, lined with an estimated 500,000, was five miles long, finishing in Sackville (now O'Connell) Street. Shops were closed and streets were cleared of carriages. The city was in festive mood.

The Dublin organisers wished to exclude Fenians and the Amnesty Association. In response, the 'advanced' men said they represented the Home Rule

Confederation of Great Britain and joined the parade with the amnesty car. Their banners were emblazoned 'Liverpool Home Rule Branch, Manchester Home Rule Branch, Freedom for Political Prisoners', and were hung with rattling chains. Flags were draped with black crepe, in token of mourning. They sang 'God Save Ireland' and other Fenian anthems.

Angered by this intrusion, the Dublin men overwhelmed the car and its crew, cutting the traces and driving off the horses, 'But the confederates and the amnesty men were not the stuff to be balked … And immediately seized the traces and pulled the car themselves along the route … The stern columns of our contingents, converging to their appointed stations.'[133]

Amid roars of protest, the 'advanced' men hoisted a black flag and took their places on the speakers' platform, a site now host to O'Connell's statue. O'Connor Power went in search of Isaac Butt and returned triumphantly with the Home Rule leader.

The Lord Mayor's oration was subjected to loud heckling, 'Down with whiggery!' O'Connor Power intervened saying that the interruptions were 'unworthy of Nationalists'. Every man was entitled to speak freely.[134] F. Hugh O'Donnell believed it was one of his finest speeches.

Two days later, on 8 August, the Supreme Council met in the Imperial Hotel. There was a good turnout. Nine members were present, and O'Connor Power chaired the meeting. He was shortly to leave for America, and 'it was decided to give him a discretionary power to treat with all parties friendly to the family interests'.[135]

Cardinal Cullen was watchful, and the Pastoral address of the archbishops and bishops of Ireland on 20 September did not mention the IRB by name but advised, 'Avoid all secret societies, all illegal combinations.'

O'Connor Power made good his promise to maintain close contact with the home base and visited his Mayo constituency before he set sail. In early September he arrived in New York, and in October he took up residence at the Fifth Avenue Hotel.[136] Invited to deliver a series of lectures, he spoke on 'The Condition of Ireland Politically, Socially, and Industrially', at the Cooper Institute. He was there:

> … to express the objects and principles of the New National Movement which has agitated the country for the last five years, this is precisely the task which, because a better man has yet not found time to discharge it, has fallen to my lot … no matter how many lectures or speeches it requires, I shall continue my humble efforts while an American town remains to be visited, and while one friend of freedom remains to be enlisted in the cause of Irish independence.

.

He spoke of Home Rule and the parallel approach, 'I am a member of that Parliament simply in order to do my best to restrain its power for evil and to assert the right of my country to manage its own affairs'.[137] His detractors saw it differently, 'if a man conspires against English rule in private, and in public preaches up Home Rule, that I consider public and private dishonesty of the blackest dye'.[138]

He was invited to Philadelphia for a Clan gathering and Thomas Luby's lecture on 'The Regeneration of Ireland'. In November he lectured on 'The Ireland of Today' in the Trement Temple in Boston and in December he spoke in Chicago on 'English Rule in Ireland'.[139]

From modest beginnings, O'Connor Power understood only too well the class system's impenetrable ceiling. The first Home Rule Conference in Dublin was represented by every strand of Irish society except the working man. To be without means in nineteenth-century Britain was to have no voice, to be invisible. A man of no property had no solid stake in a country and was not to be trusted. O'Connor Power, an Irishman without property, was not a gentleman and might not be taken seriously in the political echelons. The New World accepted him. *The New York Times* described him as 'a self-made man'. Westminster was another matter. On one occasion he berated the House of Commons, saying its founders had 'not intended it to be a House of snobs'.[140]

Isaac Butt was a fearless courtroom champion of political suspects. In 1848 he had successfully defended Young Irelander William Smith O'Brien against charges of sedition. Butt was an extremely popular figure, but advancing age and an excessive lifestyle had taken a toll on his health. Patrick Egan and O'Connor Power, both executive members of the Supreme Council, despaired of the effectiveness of his faltering leadership, and chose to approach Charles Stuart Parnell.[141]

Parnell's first biographer, Barry O'Brien, relates that he had a limited knowledge of Irish affairs at this time but had shown an interest in entering politics. He makes enquiries:

'Did Parnell,' I asked one who was familiar with Irish politics, 'ever meet any Fenians about this time?' 'Yes' was the answer, 'I sometimes saw him with —. They used to talk about the amnesty movement, so far as Parnell ever talked at all, but he was a better listener than he was a talker. He knew nothing about Home Rule but he was interested in Fenianism. For that matter,' my friend added, 'so was Butt … when the question of the Wicklow candidature was practically decided, — was present and supported Parnell, though a leading Constitutional-Nationalist said "he would never do".'[142]

Patrick Egan was probably '—'. Parnell was asked to stand as a Home Rule candidate. The Protestant Wicklow landlord was a man of pedigree and property, and the Westminster establishment would trust him. O'Connor Power advised him to build up popular support and a public profile by promoting amnesty and working with the Home Rule Confederation. The enlargement of the franchise had increased Irish voting power, and he emphasised that an organised electorate of the Irish in England would greatly strengthen the party's influence.

Michael MacDonagh writes of Parnell, 'Of the past of Ireland he was very ignorant.'[143] F. Hugh O'Donnell lamented his 'chaotic ignorance'. Barry O'Brien recounts:

'I met Parnell,' says Mr O'Connor Power, 'in 1874, the time of the Dublin election. He seemed to me a nice gentlemanly fellow, but he was hopelessly ignorant, and seemed to me to have no political capacity whatever. He could not speak at all. He was hardly able to get up and say, "Gentlemen, I am a candidate for the representation of the county of Dublin." We all listened to him with pain while he was on his legs, and felt immensely relieved when he sat down. No one ever thought he would cut a figure in politics. We thought he would be a respectable mediocrity.'[144]

In February 1876, O'Connor Power was combative. At a meeting in Liverpool he said he would 'not hesitate to form an Irish army for the protection of national interests'.[145] In July, maintaining his contacts in north-east England, he was a guest speaker at the Durham Miners' Gala.[146] Local MP Joseph Cowen of Newcastle, worked for Home Rule and 'was thoroughly Irish in feeling'.

The following month, in London, O'Connor Power was laid low with a recurrent fever, 'Mr O'Connor Power is, I hear, seriously ill. He has been in failing health for several days, and his participation in the amnesty debate has rendered him very much worse, causing considerable anxiety to his friends.'[147]

On 20 August he was still not well enough to attend the Supreme Council 'meeting of friends' in the Imperial Hotel, 'Power was sick.'[148] In his absence, the council voted, by a majority of one, to withdraw its support for the alliance with parliamentarians. Members were given six months to dissociate themselves from Home Rulers.

O'Connor Power protested to the Secretary that a two-thirds majority of the Council was necessary to carry the resolution, and that his 'severe illness' would not have prevented him from attending the meeting if he had known about the vote. His attempt to invalidate the decision was not successful, and rejecting a course of abstentionism, he continued his parliamentary activities. Withdrawal from

Westminster would be an abandonment of the Home Rule party to those who favoured conciliation rather than confrontation. The House of Commons was the best platform to plead Ireland's case.[149]

On 18 September, restored to health, he was in Mayo to address his constituents in Castlebar. There were no men of rank, no clergymen present. It was the third year he appeared, as agreed, to give an account of his work for the county, and he received a unanimous vote of confidence.[150] Two days later he was in Manchester. His lecture on 'Irish Wit and Humour' was disrupted by Limerick man John Daly and his followers. Chairs were smashed and benches used as battering rams.

The following day O'Connor Power sailed to the United States. He was on a mission to present an illuminated framed parchment to President Ulysses Grant, congratulating the United States on the centenary of American Independence. His arrival in New York harbour on the SS *Britannic* received a great deal of publicity.[151] There was an informal meeting with the President in New York, but the planned presentation in Washington was frustrated by hostile British diplomacy. The British government insisted that the address was to be presented through the British Minister Sir Edward Thornton or not at all.

But why, O'Connor Power wondered, should congratulations be delivered through the British legation to a people who had flung off the British yoke, from a people who were still struggling to free themselves? Writing from the Arlington Hotel in Washington, he asked that the address be returned:

> … may we ask you to be good enough to deliver the address, which we left at the Executive Mansion, to the bearer of this note?[152]

The President was believed to be sympathetic to the Irish cause and had greeted Fenians on the steps of the White House.[153] There were over three million Irish-born naturalised citizens in the United States, a not insignificant voting bloc. Later, on his retirement from office, Grant spent time in Ireland. A contemporary account has the crowds pursuing his carriage on his visit to Cork, the Rebel County, and Irish home of the IRB, 'Why did ye not receive O'Connor Power?'[154] 'O'Connor Power' became an incantation.

The Centennial International Exhibition, the first official World Fair, was held in Philadelphia, and O'Connor Power was in the city in early November. Dr William Carroll wrote to John Devoy, 'O'C.P. called here on Sunday night in company with Fr Barry, for whom he is to lecture next Sunday night, and with whom he is sojourning, I being out missed the call.'[155]

It was decided to prepare a new address and present it to the House of Representatives, and, with the help of the well-connected celebrity Dion Boucicault, he made the necessary contacts in Washington DC. Boucicault, from a Dublin Huguenot family, was a dramatist, actor and theatre manager. His box office triumph, *The Shaughraun*, was first produced a year earlier. Associated with the Young Ireland movement in his youth, he championed Home Rule.

The House of Representatives, with its prerogative 'as to Foreign Relations', recorded in the Congressional Record that the address and the illuminated manuscript were presented and formally accepted on 20 December 1876,[156] 'Whereas it has been announced to this House by the Speaker that Mr John O'Connor Power MP, has been deputed to present to the people of the United States the congratulations of the Irish nation on the centenary of American Independence.'

He asked that the United States recognise Ireland's claim to independence. An unanimous resolution was passed on 3 March 1877, acknowledging the great contribution made to the United States by Ireland and Irishmen:

> Be it resolved by the House of Representatives – that the people of the United States of America accept the congratulations of the people of Ireland, with a profound acknowledgement and grateful recognition of the cordial sympathy always entertained and manifested toward themselves and their institutions, from the first struggle for freedom of our infant nation to the present time; and we sincerely hope that the example of this Republic will spread its benign influence among the nations of the earth until the principles of self-government shall be firmly established, and descend, as a sacred heritage, to all future generations.

The Times reported that there had been some dispute about the wording. By what authority was O'Connor Power 'deputed'? Was the House's resolution to use the word 'people' or 'nation'? O'Connor Power held to 'nation' against a proposal of 'people'. As we read, a compromise was reached, and he delivered the address before the House's Judiciary Committee.

The Washington visit attracted press coverage in Britain, Australia and New Zealand, as well as in North America, and the furore created far more publicity than the proposed presentation to the President. It was the year Disraeli declared Victoria Empress of India. Was the sacred heritage of self-government among nations a repudiation of England's imperial ambitions?

No opportunities were lost, and O'Connor Power spent six months touring Irish centres. Enlarging his repertoire, he spoke on 'Irish Members in the English Parliament', and at the end of January on 'The Martyrs of Irish Liberty' in Boston.

In French-speaking Canada, he topped the bill, '*en tête apparaît le célèbre homme d'état irlandais, John O'Connor Power, Membre du Parlement Anglais.*'[157]

A decade later, in an after-dinner speech, he mentions a visit to Cyrus Field, an American entrepreneur and pioneer in communications:

> I would have travelled a long distance, if necessary over mountains and across seas, for the purpose of seeing Mr Cyrus Field. It is ten years since I paid one of my visits to America, and I then had the honour of enjoying Mr Field's hospitality in his own home, and whatever might be the differences of opinion between the democracies of the two countries, they did not prevent Mr Field receiving me, an almost unknown Irishman, at his fireside, and making me heartily welcome.[158]

Cyrus Field laid the transatlantic cable in 1858. It was not a success. Eight years later, a cable stretching between Newfoundland and Valencia, County Kerry was operational.

Among some Irish Americans, O'Connor Power was regarded with deep suspicion: a parliamentarian, he had taken the oath to the Queen. The Clan had no patience with gradualism, the step-by-step approach of the Home Rulers, and wanted an Irish State, separate and independent of the Empire, by force of arms if necessary. Undeterred, he renewed attempts to persuade the American wing of the Brotherhood to support the Home Rule movement.

By August 1876, plans for a Directory, a permanent revolutionary committee, had been agreed. The Directory would provide formal links between the Clan and the IRB and establish an arms importation scheme into Ireland. There were to be seven members on the Directory, which was to unite Nationalists worldwide. Three were to be nominated by the executive of the Clan, three by the IRB Supreme Council, and one was to be selected by the Fenian organisation in Australia and New Zealand.[159]

Agreement was reached at the Clan's seventh annual convention in Philadelphia. Ostensibly Clan na Gael and the IRB had equal representation on the Directory but, in effect, control and direction were handed over to Irish Americans.

O'Connor Power was still in America when the Supreme Council met on 5 March 1877, and four members, who were still Home Rulers, were 'compelled to resign'.[160] As X, he told Barry O'Brien:

> I was always opposed by a party on the supreme council who wished to have nothing whatever to do with the Parliamentarians. They wished the Fenians to remain within their own lines, to go on collecting arms, drilling, keeping alive the separatist spirit, watching, waiting, preparing. They believed in a policy of open

warfare. Parliamentarianism, they said, was bound, sooner or later, to undermine the secret movement. I had no objection to the policy of open warfare, but open warfare seemed a long way off, and here was a new field of activity, which might not be neglected. Our great idea was to keep the spirit of nationality alive.[161]

He added, 'This resolution was carried by a majority of one. I immediately resigned. I said that I did not agree with the decision of the council and as I wished to have a free hand I would retire. Biggar agreed with me but refused to resign.' However, Biggar was expelled, 'They expelled Egan and others who voted with me.' The move cost the IRB a significant loss of membership. The north of England province seceded, withdrawing its allegiance to the Council.[162]

X mentioned Kickham, Biggar and Egan. It was an 'open secret' they were members of the Supreme Council but he does not name anyone else, 'The other names have not transpired, and accordingly cannot be published.'[163]

In 1880, Matt Harris and Michael Davitt were expelled from the Supreme Council. It had been decided that 'under no circumstances should Fenians co-operate with the constitutional party'.[164]

The tensions between American and British-based Fenians remained dangerously taut. Acrimonious divisions over tactics and goals made a cohesive strategy difficult. The diverse personalities based in Ireland, Paris, North America and the Empire created strains impossible to reconcile. Conciliation was, in fact, suspect, with the probability of compromise and double-dealing.

The Clan had been infiltrated by British intelligence officers, working as *agents provocateurs*, and its links with the IRB left the network in Britain at risk. The IRB went further underground, rebuilding an impregnable system. Written communications and careless words, were frowned upon. Indiscretion might betray active members and endanger the Brotherhood. Charles Kickham had denounced 'keeping letters in an open drawer', when carelessness had led to the convictions of three activists. *Devoy's Post Bag*, a vast correspondence, has no UK-based equivalence.

On 14 April 1877, the *Adriatic* sailed into Queenstown (Cobh) harbour, and the press announced O'Connor Power's return. Travelling to London, he addressed an amnesty rally of over 100,000 in Hyde Park. Money was collected, as at every public meeting, for the families of prisoners and a legal defence fund.

It was not only the oath of allegiance to the Queen that angered orthodox Fenians; they feared the 'Anglicisation' of their representatives at Westminster. Vindictive accusations against O'Connor Power, who had taken a constitutional route, were aired vigorously in public, with little regard for truth. John Daly, the Limerick Fenian, led the attacks, which continued, unrelenting, for decades. Playing on an anti-intellectual bias in the movement, Daly disparaged 'college' education. In March 1876, heading 'an assaulting party' armed with blackthorn sticks, he had disrupted a Home Rule procession led by Isaac Butt.[165]

In October 1877, the *Freeman's Journal* published an account of 'Mr O'Connor Power and Mr John Daly'.[166] The exchanges were timed to excite maximum attention. The Home Rule League was meeting in Dublin, and Gladstone was visiting Ireland. O'Connor Power wrote that he was unable to accept an invitation to take part in a demonstration in Glasgow as Mr Daly's 'bludgeonmen' promised to disrupt the event. The previous year, Daly had caused chaos at a meeting in Manchester but 'not one of whom [the local Irish] he could get to join in or sanction his violence'.

He recalled the presentation to the House of Representatives, where 'in spite of the great English ambassador I have obtained a hearing for the voice of Irish liberty'.

Daly's accusations were vituperative rather than enlightening. O'Connor Power had been seen enjoying 'a good dinner', and Daly claimed it was paid for with government gold. A Mr McLaughlin sent a follow up letter to the newspaper, '[O'Connor Power thinks] he is a big man now.' During the 1874 election campaign, Fr Lavelle had claimed that O'Connor Power was illegitimate and had given the name Fleming to a putative father. McLaughlin revived the slur, '*Fleming est mort vive O'Connor Power*.' 'Fleming' had worked as a journeyman painter, 'he was only a daub.' House painters, with indoor access, were traditionally to the fore in revolutionary activity.

O'Connor Power defended himself, calling Daly 'a foul mouthed liar', a 'renegade and a traitor', and accused him of attempting to:

> ... destroy that unbroken union and magnificent discipline which have for the last ten years prevailed in the national ranks [that] I proudly claim at least one man's share in the building up of ... We must never forget that the triumph of faction means the defeat of freedom and if we want to raise the temple of Irish liberty on permanent foundations we must make national union the corner stone.[167]

The good dinner was, perhaps, to celebrate the imminent release of the Fenian prisoners.

Thomas Brennan, a Mayo Fenian, came to his defence and wrote to Matt Harris. The letter is dated 20 October 1877 and posted from a sub post office in Russell Street, Dublin:

> I enclose you a letter that appeared in the Freeman of the 18th and as the part I underline evidently refers to you I think that it calls for a reply from you in return.

I know that you are the person to whom it refers. If the first part of this assertion is untrue it is only fair I think that the public should know it and as to the second part I think for the last four years from that Sunday morning on which you, he and I met in Castletown there are few in Ireland who know more of O'Connor Power's thoughts than I do and I assure you that I never heard him mention your name save in terms of the greatest respect. We may differ with him on some questions, I do at least, but that is no reason why we should allow charges against his private life that we know to be untrue to pass unrefuted.

Brennan wrote again four days later:

Yours of the 21st only reached me yesterday. When I wrote you the last time I did so on my own responsibility and without Mr Power's knowledge but when I saw him last night I told him of your suggestion but he is not at present able to consider anything. He is confined to his bed since Sunday last and is very unwell indeed but so soon as he is able he will write you, his address is 10 Molesworth St.

What is to become of the National Cause? Where are those exposures to end or must we who have any self respect separate ourselves from what is going faster and faster to rowdyism.

I every day receive letters from men in the West telling me that they can no longer do anything if a stop is not put to this disgrace. No man knows but his own turn may arrive tomorrow and every act of his private [life] gazetted in the morning papers.

Now what I want to do is this – write a letter to next week's *Irishman* (don't write anything personal in it for I agree with you it is better to let that drop) protesting against these exposures and point out the criminal folly of this Felon setting.

Now if this is carried on it will make the name of the Nationalists hateful to every patriotic and sensible man.

If you do this you will be rendering incalculable service to the National Cause, not only in Connaught but everywhere it exists.

The men in the North of England are already taking steps to put down the madness and I think they will be successful. Meantime I know of no person from whom a letter on the present position would do so much service as from yourself. Believe me I don't say this in any flattering spirit but for reasons you will understand when I say I can't explain here.[168]

There was consternation in America. Dr Carroll had written to Devoy in July that he was 'in daily expectation of a cable dispatch on R.D. [the Revolutionary Directory]' from Shields (O'Connor Power). In August he reported 'Cablegram just received from Shields … R.D. has passed.' Again, at the end of October, he asked Devoy to find him a picture of St Patrick's Cathedral in New York for O'Connor Power. When news of the exchanges between O'Connor Power and Daly reached Carroll in mid–November, he was explosive, 'God help us with such revolutionaries as the leading conspirators.'[169]

O'Connor Power earned money from journalism, 'It is well known that I earn an independent livelihood.' At his lectures he would receive 'testimonials', a hat might be passed among the crowd. A testimonial was arranged by the clansmen of the Robert Emmett Literary Association on a visit to Butte, Montana. He was remembered by his family as a man of great generosity, and his writings confirm that he believed generous dealings to be the hallmark of a true Irishman. Whatever the largesse of a testimonial, it was dispersed freely.

John Daly's fiery attacks highlighted the ambivalence at home. The Irish, by proximity and with mutual interests, were an integral part of the Empire, and many did well in its service. They attained prominence in the army and navy, in the civil service and the professions, particularly law, journalism and medicine:

> Yet it must be borne in mind that many wealthy merchants, able lawyers, clever doctors, artists, actors, and authors to be found in high repute in London and elsewhere in England, come from the Emerald Isle … In recent years Irish men have made their way so rapidly onto English local boards and municipal councils, that some wag has suggested that Home Rule means 'Ireland free with England annexed'.[170]

Irishmen of talent and education, with parity of opportunity, achieved equal citizenship and ease of social movement. Disparities in success rate were arguably a matter of class and religion, not nationality. An easy charm and natural courtesy opened doors, '[Ireland] is about the only country in the world where English is spoken *where the Irish don't rule*'.[171]

The Irish were colonising the Empire, playing a significant role.

Parliamentary Manoeuvres

To work only in Government time.
To aid anybody to spend Government time.
Whenever you see a Bill, block it.
Whenever you see a Raw, rub it[172]

It is not a union of hearts …

Taking a lead from American politics, a system of organised filibustering was devised to block the progress of legislation in the House.[173] The Irish party chose obstruction, a retaliatory stratagem, when Disraeli's government, pursuing imperial, expansionist policies, callously ignored Ireland's concerns. English MPs ridiculed Irish members, blocking Irish Bills. Now the Irish turned on them, becoming 'troublesome'.

On 22 April 1875, Joseph Biggar, delaying the passing of coercion legislation, the Peace Preservation (Ireland) Bill, fired the first salvo and held the House captive for four hours, as he read from dreary parliamentary blue books, administrative publications available in the Common's Library. He was reputed to be inaudible and irrelevant, qualities which furthered his purpose, 'Parnell and Biggar came along with their dull, indomitable genius for being disagreeable.'[174] Obstruction was the policy of exasperation.

The Recess of 1876/1877 was a time of reappraisal. In Mayo, O'Connor Power assured his constituents of his personal loyalty to Butt but condemned his 'timid policy ... in the presence of the enemies of Ireland'.

The parliamentarians were not making progress and a more aggressive approach was required. In former times, Irish representatives had refrained from interfering in the affairs of Britain and the Empire, but now they purposed mayhem.

In 1877 there were major measures under discussion; the Mutiny Bill, the Proposal to Amend the Prison Bill, a unification of the prison code and the South Africa Bill presented opportunities for displays of effective disruption. During the Mutiny Bill, in April, discipline in the army and navy was examined. Flogging was the major issue. John Bright urged that the number of lashes be 'reduced from fifty to twenty-five at the least'. Charles Hopwood suggested 'that the punishment be inflicted by a "cat" with one tail, instead of a "cat" with nine tails'.

O'Connor Power, who had been absent for the first days of the debate, insisted that if a man is insensible after twelve lashes it is foolish to administer fifty, 'Those who had seen soldiers flogged knew how quickly any man subjected to that punishment became insensible.' In the House Isaac Butt reacted angrily to what he felt were undignified scenes. O'Connor Power questioned Butt's behaviour:

> Mr. Butt, in accordance with the views of the London Times, thought proper on Thursday night last to protest in the name of the Irish nation against the policy recently pursued by Mr. Parnell and Mr. Biggar in the House of Commons ... It seems to me that it is the duty of a Home Rule member to give Mr Butt an unqualified support on those great Irish questions upon which the Irish people are unanimous ... But the policy which requires an Irish representative to sur-

render his judgment to the leader of the Home Rule party on other questions strikes at the very principle by which men differing widely on those questions have been united on the question of Home Rule.[175]

At the end of May there was an exchange of peremptory letters between Biggar, Parnell and Butt.[176] The following year Healy commented:

> If [Parnell] could have O'Connor Power at his elbow continually, it would be a good thing as Power understands the necessities of agitation and Parnell does not. I hope he will make a good fist of his answer to Butt, though I have never been persuaded that he shines as a letter writer.[177]

On 2 July 1877, the House was in Committee of Supply and it promised to be a long night. At midnight, O'Connor Power moved to report, 'He declined to vote away the public money at such a late hour.' Obstructionists followed each other in relay to block progress.

The House voted down the 'irrepressible five', but they persisted. The 'small minority' did not yield, and, on a beautiful sunny morning, at 7 a.m., the government surrendered, leaving the Irish victors of the field.[178]

Over the next two years, flogging remained a major issue. O'Connor Power returned to the fight during the reading of the Army Discipline Bill: flogging should be abolished in the armed forces, 'with the object of bringing native solders in India under the operation of the Bill'.[179] If the amendment stood, the word 'fifty' should be removed and 'ten' inserted.

He made several interventions. There was no 'moral stigma' attached to political offences. He deplored the 'inhumanities committed in prison'. Solitary confinement could still be awarded by courts martial, and he proposed that the period, which a prisoner could be confined, be reduced from seven to three successive days.[180]

In June 1879, he said he wished to 'resist the principle that corporal punishment should be inflicted in any circumstances whatsoever'. He moved that a prisoner might have the right to challenge three officers of a general court, two of a district court and one of a regimental court without reason given. A prisoner should have the right to be heard.[181]

Ten days later, Irish MP Philip Callan inspected the pattern cat of nine tails at the Admiralty. O'Connor Power went further and asked the First Lord of the Admiralty to bring the navy cat to the House so members might see exactly what they were voting for, '[O'Connor Power] thought the government ought to save

Hon. Members the trouble of going to the Admiralty, or on board ships by placing the cat to be used in the Library of the House.'[172] In Hibernian style he insisted, 'Mr Speaker, since the government has let the cat out of the bag, there is nothing to be done but to take the bull by the horns.' It was 'The Great "Cat"- Contention'. F. Hugh O'Donnell, in his account, writes:

> Mr O'Connor Power claimed that 'a specimen cat' should be placed in the library. It was a case of produce the 'cat' or 'stop the Bill' ... next day the 'cats' were produced in the cloak room for the inspection of members. And flogging in the army was abolished for ever.[183]

The awesome physical presence of the cat made an indelible impression. Eighty years later, British poet laureate, Ted Hughes, celebrated the occasion and 'A witty profound Irishman' who brought the cat into the House of Commons. Hughes imaginatively re-enacts the event with 'the gentry fingering its stained tails'. The dramatic confrontation is persuasive:

> quietly, unopposed
> The motion was passed.[184]

A week later there was a dramatic turn in the campaign. A stranger, taking notes, was observed in one of the side galleries, reserved for members. O'Connor Power demanded an explanation from the Speaker, who replied that the notes were being taken 'for his own information'. O'Connor Power went on to 'dispute the authority of the chair'. The conduct of the Speaker was 'impugned': 'The proceedings, he had been pleased to order, were unprecedented in the House of Commons.' The Speaker turned to leave and O'Connor Power, protesting, moved as if to stop him:

> His protest, whatever it might have been, was lost amid the roar of contumely from the Ministerialsits, during which the Speaker, gathering his robes about him, turned and left the Chair, O'Connor Power, with passionate gesticulations, protesting dumb show. It seemed that if he had been able to reach the Chair there would have a repetition of an historical scene, and Speaker Brand, like Speaker Lenthall would have been forcibly kept down in his seat. As it was, the length of the table and the space of half the floor intervening, the Speaker escaped, and disappeared from the scene.[185]

The New York Times reported, 'Mr O'Connor Power almost speaks treason, he wholly speaks insult.'[186]

In 1877 the first and second readings of the South Africa Bill (the annexation of the Transvaal) had passed with few interruptions. Obstructionists were biding their time, cards close to the chest. On the third reading, the Irish, led by an indomitable Frank Hugh O'Donnell, came out in force. The ebullient O'Donnell, a newly elected MP, was an experienced foreign correspondent, a talented playwright, and knew how to stage a spectacular show. He was well briefed, 'Paul Kruger, the President of the Republic, and his Attorney-General, were in London on a mission of protest, and as the result of an arrangement come to with them, O'Donnell put down forty hostile amendments to the Bill.'[187]

It was the first public display of support for what became a long-running Irish Pro-Boer movement. The obstruction was relayed by seven Irish MPs. A well-timed rumour circulated that Davitt's promised release was to be rescinded. O'Connor Power gave urgent notice of a question on the subject.

Parliamentary warfare had reached new heights. The Irish were interfering in matters imperial.

The proposal to form a Confederation of the British colonies, including the Boer Republic and the Transvaal was anathema to Home Rulers, determined to set boundaries to the Empire's ambitions. Pulling out all the procedural stops, they held up the business of the House for forty-five hours, breaking existing records.

English members were not well organised and, staying up all night to prove a sturdy physical endurance, were 'hungry, head-achy and sleepy'. One joker declared, 'Home Rule meant not going home all night yourself and keeping as many other people out of their beds as possible.' The Irish napped, returning fresh and cheerful to the fray. O'Donnell alone took no rest and held the field.

Butt, still nominally the party leader, excoriated his junior colleagues. In the early hours of the morning he burst into the House and denounced O'Connor Power and his team – 'a vulgar brawl'. His intervention was brisk, but gave further publicity to the obstruction, which continued on its marathon course. O'Connor Power accused the Government of uniting to crush the Irish opposition. With cries of 'Withdraw', he was asked to immediately retract the charge of 'conspiracy'. A week later in Liverpool:

Mr Power said they had been threatened with 'muzzling' but so long as the tax-paying class claimed the right of revising taxation, six members would retain the power of obstructing bad measures. There were English obstructives of Irish measures for out of one hundred and twelve measures introduced by Irish members not one had yet passed this session.[188]

In September he spoke in Hull, and introducing a note of gravitas, 'strongly denounced the English press for coining the word "obstructionist" in speaking of the Home Rulers'.[189]

There was a final break with Butt. John Dillon wrote in his diary on 1 August, 'This day I mark as the beginning of a new era in the history of Erin. And I wish to have in my room the portraits of the three men who pointed out to Ireland her way to freedom – Parnell, O'Connor Power and Biggar.'[190]

At the end of the parliamentary session, the 'Seven Champions of Obstruction' returned to Dublin. They were declared heroes and given a triumphal reception at a meeting in the Rotundo.

Russia moved its sphere of influence to Afghanistan, and the British responded by sending Anglo-Indian forces into Afghan territories. Unable to attend a St Patrick's Day celebration in St Louis, where he was to be the guest of honour of the Knights of St Patrick, O'Connor Power sent his regrets. He was detained by 'the storm in the East'. A stand-off between Russia and the Empire, England's trouble, was Ireland's opportunity. In his signing off he wrote, 'I shall be with you in spirit and drink a flowing goblet to the dual sentiment – Long live the United States and Erin-go-Bragh.'[191]

The 'dual sentiment' of 'Long live the United States and Erin-go-Bragh' was a response to the protests at his two apparently irreconcilable oaths – fidelity to the Irish Republic and allegiance as an MP to the Queen.

In his other life, the private, cherished space, he was anxious for the welfare of his brother Colour Sergeant Thomas Power and his young family. Thomas was in India, and had married Elizabeth Quinn in 1872. Now his regiment had been transferred to Kandahar. His tour in Afghanistan lasted for the duration of the Afghan Campaigns (1878-80).

The Irish party's obstruction policy attacked parliamentary procedures, delaying legislation; now opposition to the Government's policies abroad was a condemnation of the Empire's very existence. International conflicts, England's difficulties, gave Irishmen occasions to assert their own distinct identity.

Butt had never favoured the disruption of the business of the House. He had helped to obstruct the Coercion Bill in 1875 but that was an Irish matter. Leaning to conciliation rather than provocation, he did not believe it appropriate to block foreign policy legislation. Cheered on by English members, he defended the Empire's Afghan policy and denounced obstruction as parliamentary misconduct.

At the Home Rule Confederation meeting in Liverpool, 1 September 1877, Butt resigned as President. Parnell, who had joined in the disruption of the South Africa Bill, was unanimously elected in his place. Arranging a whistle-stop tour of the cities of England and Scotland, O'Connor Power deployed his extensive network to set up fourteen meetings for the new leader, '"We got Parnell a platform" said the founder of this organisation [HRCGB] – himself a member of the Fenian Brotherhood – to me some years ago; "we made him".'[192]

The crowds no longer thronged to hear Isaac Butt but they came to hear Parnell. The Irish believed they could depend on his hatred of England and his ability to 'twist the tail of the British lion'. On 23 September 1878, Dillon wrote to the *Freeman's Journal*, 'No honest Irish Nationalist can any longer continue to recognise Mr Butt as leader.'

O'Connor Power drew the short straw and was delegated to push Butt aside for the new men and the 'forward' policy. In November, Healy wrote:

> I met O'Connor Power and he was unaware, until I told him, that his name was down to propose one of the resolutions in Dublin. He expressed disgust, and said he told the Dublin people he would not go over, and that it was only another piece of their cowardice in being afraid to face Butt themselves.[193]

In early December O'Connor Power delivered a powerful speech in the Commons. There was no reference to Irish legislation in the Queen's Speech; the claims of the Irish people were ignored. He was more concerned about the Government's intentions in Ireland than its policy in Afghanistan. He repeated his call for the restoration of an Irish Parliament and denounced this 'wicked war':

> We are more concerned about the Government's intentions in our own country than the Government's policy in Afghanistan … Ireland is often regarded as an integral portion of the Empire; but my first duty as an Irish Nationalist is to assert the distinct nationality of Ireland. And why? Because, in ordinary times, Ireland is shut out from the observation of Europe, and her aspirations are judged by the caricatures given in the English Press. It is, therefore, when questions of an inter-national character are before the House, that it becomes the duty of Irishmen to stand forward before Europe and declare that their first consideration is the nationalists of their own country. The Union between Ireland and England is only a union in name. It is not a union of hearts. It is the result of the blackest crime ever perpetrated by one nation against another – the destruction of the Irish Parliament … I object to the Address in answer to the Royal Speech because it is the duty, Sir, of the Representatives of the people to demand the redress of grievances before granting Supplies. I, for one, shall exhaust all the Forms of the House in refusing the Supplies for this wicked war. In the name of my constitu-

ents I denounce it as a base and cowardly aggression on an independent State.
I shall vote against the Address, because the Government has turned a deaf ear
to the cries for justice which have been repeatedly raised on behalf of the Irish
people in this house.[194]

Ireland's sympathies were on the side of 'struggling freemen in every oppressed
land'. Writing on House of Commons notepaper to the *Freeman's Journal*,
6 December, he delivered the *coup de grâce* to Butt:

> Sir, The Address in answer to the Royal Speech, which calls upon us to sanction the
> blood-stained acts of the Royal butchers who have invaded Afghanistan is passing
> through the House without any division representing the protest of the Irish nation,
> without any demand by the Irish Party for the restoration of the Irish Parliament, or
> even redress of grievances. The man, who has brought this disgrace upon our coun-
> try is Isaac Butt. At an informal meeting of the Irish members today, I denounced
> him as a traitor to the Home Rule party and the Irish cause, and I now repeat the
> accusation. At a future time I shall review the steps taken by Mr Butt in his work of
> betrayal, leading up to the supreme treason of the present hour.
>
> Yours truly,
> J. O'Connor Power

Michael MacDonagh relates, 'The ablest and most crushing onslaught made on
Butt, and his policy of moderation and conciliation, was a letter, three columns
long, addressed by O'Connor Power to the Home Rule Confederation of Great
Britain in December 1878.'[195] X tells Barry O'Brien:

> It was very painful. I was very fond of Butt. He was himself the kindest-hearted
> man in the world, and here was I going to do the unkindest thing to him.[196]

> We were all were warmly attached to him; for he was one of the most genial and
> affectionate of men.

The following March, Healy noted, 'O'Connor Power had a letter from Robert
Butt this week, stating his father might recover but his mind was going.'[197] Butt died
two months later.

The imperial predations of Disraeli's administration invited comparison with the
Elizabethan and Cromwellian conquests of Ireland. Zulu assegais were likened to

Irish pikes – both militarily inferior weapons to the gun and bayonet, but, used skilfully, inflicted great damage on the enemy. A significant Zulu victory was received in Ireland with public delight, and empathetic, rousing cheers for King Cetshwayo, the Zulu leader, were delivered at every crossroad.

Conflicts in Afghanistan and South Africa, and the famines in India, stirred the scarred sensibilities of the Irish psyche. An era of high imperialism was denounced. The Empire's wars were offensive. Irishmen serving in the British army kept families informed at the domestic hearth and, in letters home, confirmed the atrocities committed against the invaded peoples.

Increasing literacy and new communication systems made news accessible and immediate. Journalists, often Irish, reported with urgency on current events. Accounts of the barbarities of the conquering forces were detailed, and were read and relayed with deepening repugnance. Anti-war sentiment was fuel to stoke the flames of domestic discontent.

England had abolished slavery in 1807 but the practice continued in the United States for another half century. Serfs were emancipated in Russia in the 1860s. Daniel O'Connell had compared the condition of the Irish peasant to that of a slave or a serf. Analogies continued to be drawn. The birthright of every man to shape his own destiny was at the core of the Fenian gospel.

Hostility to the ambitions of the Empire and its wars, heightened anti-British feelings during the Land War. There was even a suggestion in 1878 to run an Indian Nationalist in an Irish constituency, giving India a voice in the Imperial parliament.

In March 1879, in a strong speech in the Commons, O'Connor Power declared 'his thorough detestation of English policy in South Africa'. The war was 'unprovoked and unpatriotic':

> ... the ultimatum presented to the Zulu king by Sir Bartle Frere was unjustifiable: and that this House condemns the conduct of Her Majesty's Government in not recalling Sir Bartle Frere from the government of the South African colonies, and in declining to take proper measures to terminate the war waged by him against an unoffending people.

He advised the Government:

> ... if they wanted to be on good terms with the black population of South Africa, they must treat them as if they were a white population.

He deplored the 'brutal craving which "Jingoism" had impressed on the English public mind', and 'the evil effects of aggressive imperialism'. He believed he was expressing the 'true feeling of the Irish people on the subject, as well as the views of a large portion of the English nation'.[198]

Boers refused to pay taxes as the Irish refused to pay rent.

In July 1878, O'Connor Power recommended that the Irish language be put on same footing as Latin, Greek and French in the national grammar schools of Ireland:

> Mr O'Connor Power gave notice that on Thursday he would ask the Chief Secretary for Ireland whether he would lay upon the table an influentially signed memorial recently presented in favour of the teaching of the Irish language on the voluntary and results principles in the national grammar schools of Ireland [199]

His interest in education was wholehearted:

> Power's advocacy for tenant societies in 1878, the year before he assisted in founding the Land League, was coupled from the beginning with a demand for the establishment of libraries. In Claremorris County Mayo, in November 1878, O'Connor Power toured the reading rooms of the Sacred Heart Confraternity and insisted that the people 'themselves must be up and doing'.[200]

The only concessions made by Disraeli's administration were the Intermediate Education Act of 1878, giving State support to secondary schools, and the University Education Act of 1879. The new measures would be financed from the Church Surplus Fund, which had accrued after the disestablishment and the disendowment of the Church of Ireland. The legislation, an election pre-emptive strike, was a nod to the *two nations*, and another stepping stone towards equal opportunity for Catholics. By the end of the following decade there were seven Catholic teacher training colleges in Ireland. Catholic representation in the professions increased slowly but steadily. They filled civil service positions in Ireland and worked as administrators in the colonies.

The Irish party claimed the measures as a triumph for obstructive tactics and, not wishing to impede reforms, remained subdued. Many other bills had been introduced to improve conditions in Ireland – poor law reforms, local government legislation, promotion of sea fishing, reclamation of waste lands – but not one was passed.

Ten years later, O'Connor Power supplies an afterword:

If Disraeli had attempted to carry out any of these schemes of popular legislation with which I believe his mind was as full as that of the most radical reformer, he could not be leader of his party nor prime minister of England. Only the judgement is harsh, and may be unjust. I would say that he sacrificed his convictions to his fame.[201]

Worth Working For, Worth Fighting For, Worth Dying For[202]

The campaign of John O'Connor Power, whose election to the House of Commons transformed Mayo politics, establishing alliances that made possible the Land War.[203]

Until the seventies Ireland was feudal.

The IRB had established several platforms, and extra-parliamentary activities took place within the tenant right movement, the Home Rule Associations, the Amnesty Association and the NBSP. These were the channels of action, which gathered momentum and direction in the seventies and eighties. Public meetings, processions, petitions, press campaigns, celebrations of the Fenian dead were opportunities for consolidation. Popular politics encouraged parish reading rooms and temperance associations, and O'Connor Power urged 'the formation of clubs throughout the country as a means of strengthening the hands of their representatives'.[204]

Alongside the amnesty campaign, waging war on many fronts, he was simultaneously progressing tenant rights in parliament. Restating the three Fs – fixity of tenure, fair rents and free sale – he demanded that the Bright clauses of the 1870 Land Act be implemented efficiently. Long-term agitation in Ireland was for a root and branch reform of the land system; an end to evictions, reduction of rents, relief, wasteland reclamation and redistribution of land were priorities. Failure to grant concessions would provoke an insurrection against the landlord class.

Public works should be undertaken to provide employment. Transportation costs kept the price of food very high. Railway extensions would strengthen the communication network, essential to the movement of people, goods and livestock. The inadequacy of postal and telegraphic services must be addressed. The development of manufacturing industries would create jobs and replace reliance on agricultural activity.

A previous generation of Irish parliamentarians had pledged to oppose every administration unless it was prepared to make tenant rights a priority. O'Connor Power's former campaign manager, Matt Harris, built on the traditions of tenant associations and farmers' clubs and, encouraged by James Daly, established a tenant defence association in Ballinasloe. Amnesty and Home Rule had not put land issues on the back burner. A war on landlords was at the heart of the struggle for independence.

Arable land had been given over to grazing and tillage had reverted to pasture, robbing the small farmer of his livelihood. The land-hungry grazier, who displaced the labouring man with cattle and sheep, was a hated figure and regarded with a loathing previously directed at the landlord.

A series of disastrous harvests in the late seventies delivered a devastating blow to the economy. Summers were wetter and winters more severe. There was talk of climate change. Harvests were bad throughout Europe, with little seasonal work for Irish labourers in Scotland or England. Remittances from migrant workers registered a disastrous decline, causing intolerable hardship. Cheap meat imports from the United States further destabilised the market.

Irish MP Edmund Dwyer Grey, editor of the *Freeman's Journal*, estimated that in one year alone, £30 million had been lost due to a bad harvest and foreign competition. Figures dramatically exposed the evil of the existing relationship between landlord and tenant. The land system stopped all progress. O'Connor Power writes:

> It has blasted the hopes, ruined the homes, and destroyed the lives of millions of the Irish race. It has stopped the social, political, and industrial growth of Ireland as effectually as if the country had been in a state of perpetual civil war … 'The worst fed, the worst clothed, and the worst housed people in Europe' – this is the description which every impartial traveller who has seen the Irish people at home has given of them. Behold the result of the system of tenant-at-will and centuries of English rule!

> The struggling farmer whose imagination is haunted by the alternative prospect of the poor-house or the emigrant ship, has certainly a gloomy existence, bereft of comfort, encouragement, and aspiration.[205]

With no security of tenure, the tenant saw no advantage in excessive industry or improvements to a property. On some estates, a tenant could not marry without the permission of the landlord or agent. In his autobiography, *Hail and Farewell, Vale*, George Moore recalls:

> Until the seventies Ireland was feudal, we looked upon our tenants as animals that lived in hovels round the bogs, whence they came twice a year with their rents … And if they failed to pay their rents, the cabins they had built with their own hands were thrown down, for there was no pity for a man who failed to

pay his rent. And if we thought that bullocks would pay us better we ridded our lands of them; cleaned our lands of tenants, is an expression I once heard, and I remember how they used to go away by train from Claremorris in great batches bawling like animals.

In the previous thirty years, millions were forced to emigrate. In the House of Commons, O'Connor Power quoted some lines from Lady Wilde's poem 'The Exodus':

> A million a decade. What does it mean?
> A nation dying of inner decay;
> A churchyard's silence where life has been,
> The base of the pyramid crumbling away;
> A drift of men gone over the sea,
> A drift of the dead where men should be.

There had been no resolute leadership during the Famine years, nor during the great depression in the early sixties. In the 1870s a formidable triumvirate emerged in Mayo. James Daly, the prosperous farmer from Castlebar, an early advocate of an organised all-county land movement, was now owner and editor of the Nationalist newspaper the *Connaught Telegraph*; a fearless Matt Harris, the seasoned tenant-right activist, had intimate knowledge of the people and the terrain; O'Connor Power, fighting for remedial measures at Westminster, raised political awareness during his tours of the constituency. They were unstoppable.

At the founding of the Mayo Tenants Defence Association in Castlebar on 26 October 1878, O'Connor Power attended, representing the advanced faction of the Home Rule movement and its commitment to the land agitation. Tenants wanted an end to evictions and rack-renting and demanded peasant proprietor-ship – ownership of the land. He gave his constituents the annual account of his parliamentary activities. His clarion call, 'The land of Ireland for the people of Ireland' – effectively echoing and reshaping Fintan Lalor's 'The soil of Ireland for the people of Ireland' – would become the battle cry of the Land War. 'Rack-renting and evictions must be stopped at all hazards', but he warned that ownership of the land and the abolition of landlordism would be a gradual proc-ess. Public opinion in Ireland must be mobilised. The land struggle was bound up inextricably with the struggle for independence. Energetic action in the House of Commons must be accompanied by 'a policy of energetic action in Ireland'. He was encouraged by their solidarity: 'When I reflect upon your patriotic enthusiasms, "I can truly say the West's Awake".'

A tour of south Mayo was set in train, and just over a week later, he spoke at a meeting of the Ballinasloe Tenants Defence Association and called for an alliance between tenant farmers and the Irish party.

The following April, James Daly, who was 'the storm centre' of the movement, organised the Irishtown meeting, at the very heart of Connacht. He worked closely with O'Connor Power, and arrangements were put in place to make certain he would be there.

In *The Fall of Feudalism* (1904), Michael Davitt reminds his readers, 'O'C.P. was the only Member of parliament invited to or who attended the historic Irishtown meeting.'[206] He records O'Connor Power's words:

> Whence arises this difference in the conduct of British and Irish landlords? It arises from the fact that we have no organised public opinion in Ireland, and the lords of the soil may do the grossest acts of tyranny with impunity, acts which if committed in Great Britain would bring upon them the well-merited condemnation of the community. Now, if you ask me to state in a brief sentence what is the Irish Land Question, I say it is the restoration of the land of Ireland to the people of Ireland; and if you ask me for a solution of the land question in accordance with philosophy, experience and *common sense*, I shall be equally brief and explicit. Abolish landlordism, and make the man who occupies and cultivates the soil the owner of the soil.[207]

O'Connor Power recommended that, 'Every crossroad, every market place and every chapel yard in Mayo should be dedicated to the formation and manifestation of a sound and honest public opinion.'[208] It was the opening scene of the Land War. Healy's account of 'Power's meeting' is worth recalling:

> Power's presence there gave birth to the Land League and made history ... No reporters attended the meeting. Power called on me when he returned to London to give an account of it. From what he said I realised that a new portent had arisen out of a leaden sky. He related that footmen in legions, and horsemen in squadrons, gathered round him to demand reductions of rents. The horsemen, he declared, were organised like cavalry regiments. The police were powerless, and Power foreshadowed that Ireland was on the verge of a movement which would end a dismal chapter. Yet this meeting was unnoted, save by a local weekly *The Connaught Telegraph*, owned by James Daly.[209]

William O'Brien recollects that O'Connor Power believed the Irishtown meeting would 'make history':

The whole country-side had flocked together, as at a word of command, including horsemen enough to form a regiment of cavalry, and Mr Power, who had sounded all the subterranean depths of Irish disaffection, spoke very solemnly of what was coming. It was the first whisper I heard of the Land League movement, although even the name was not yet invented.[210]

A month later at Westminster O'Connor Power warned of the dire consequences which would follow the Government's failure to deal with the crisis:

The patience of the Irish people was entirely exhausted and if Parliament did not come forward, within a reasonable time, with some measure of legislation calculated to relieve the depression of the present state of agriculture in Ireland, scenes would arise that would be far more dangerous to the rights of property and to the order and tranquillity which should prevail … than any that Ireland had been afflicted with in her long struggle with the ignorance, if not the incompetency, of the English Parliament. If these warnings were unheeded, and Parliament should plead for further delay, the consequences must be fixed on their own shoulders.[211]

As a small child, O'Connor Power had lived through the terrible years of the Great Famine and its horrendous aftermath. He understood only too well the necessities of the emergency. Hunger and disease demanded a swift and radical response. But parliament was otherwise engaged, chiefly concerned with its imperial wars in Afghanistan and South Africa. At the end of June, he launched a full-scale attack, 'one of the most violent scenes ever witnessed in the House of Commons'. He claimed the Government had inaugurated 'a Reign of Terror in the County of Mayo.' It was sending its troops to put down lawful and legitimate meetings. Its policy would lead to revolution, 'conspiracy and assassination':

They had been forewarned of the state of the country by the demands which have been made on behalf of the people of Ireland by their Representatives, who are not now going to see the people robbed of the fruits of their industry on the one hand, and then bayoneted by the police on the other.

He deplored the slur cast on Michael Davitt's character by Chief Secretary Lowther, describing him as 'a man who had suffered long years of penal servitude because he had had the courage to resist inhumane English rule in Ireland'. His pleas were ignored:

From the time when the hon. member stated his intention to move the adjournment of the House, and it appeared probable that a debate was about to be raised, hon. members ceased to pay any attention to the hon. member's remarks, and conversation became so general and so loud that the hon. member could with difficulty be heard.

John Bright rebuked the Irish Chief Secretary and his 'unmannerly followers'. The Irish were a minority party and obstruction was for them the one way to highlight injustice. Mitchell Henry, member for Galway County, intervened, 'The interruptions to which the hon. member for Mayo was subjected were of a kind that if used against any hon. member sitting opposite them would have drawn forth the strongest expressions of disapprobation.'[212]

The fight was on three fronts: the Irish countryside, the law courts and Westminster. The weapons of war were the provincial papers writing aggressively on local issues, mass rallies protesting against evictions and high rents, and the organisational skills of the men on the ground. An effective campaign in Britain's parliament and press and the leverage of an actively sympathetic diaspora gave strong backing to the struggle.

O'Connor Power was not present at the foundation of the Land League but sent a letter of support.[213] The League proposed that tenants should be organised, those threatened with eviction defended, and progress made towards tenant ownership. Michael Davitt was in charge of organisation, Thomas Brennan was responsible for publicity and Patrick Egan managed the finances. The agitation spread throughout the country.

At American wake parties, a feature of Irish life since the Famine years, families bade desolate farewells to young men and women on the eve of their departure for the New World, convinced they would never meet again. Plangent songs of exile illustrate how emigrants were haunted by a life-long loss and longing for the homeland.

But the ties that bind sent succour to the Old Country and irresistibly drew many back. Irish Americans gave money and manpower but, in return, their leaders wanted total control. In *A Drama in Muslin*, George Moore describes 'The Irish Americans with their sinister faces and broad brimmed hats'. Most sported the drooping moustaches and square, steel-tipped shoes of the Civil War veteran. Round-tipped shoes might betray an outsider, a possible British spy. Anthony Trollope notes American demagogues in the west of Ireland with no visible source of income. The dispossessed had come home to claim their rightful inheritance, giving sustenance – arms, money and moral support – to the land agitation. They regarded landlords as predators and in many cases took back land with violence.

Communication and transport networks eased their work, and money flowed in from American donors, 'Five dollars for bread but twenty for lead.'

The Irish now had a strong niche in American society. They had established credentials and formed a constituency, creating an Irish American identity and a power base for their leaders. Three thousand miles distant, they were safe from the repercussions which were visited on the Irish in England. An American Fenian had no first-hand experience of the oppressed in Britain, where poverty and hunger were not solely the condition of the immigrant Irish.

In the late 1870s, Clan na Gael built a strong base in Ireland, and the land movement came swiftly under its direction. In November 1877, the Clan's chairman, Dr William Carroll, travelled to Europe. He was in Dublin at an IRB meeting in March 1878 and then in London to discuss plans with Parnell for the Clan's 'New Departure', a collaboration with parliamentarians. Parnell was a parliamentarian yet not a Fenian: unlike O'Connor Power, he had not perjured himself by taking conflicting oaths. The Clan, dismissive of federalism, wanted total separation. Barry O'Brien related:

We have now seen how X formed the Home Rule Confederation of Great Britain, drew some of the Fenians into it, and made Parnell President. The difficulties which X had to encounter from the beginning in reconciling Fenianism with Parliamentarianism in any shape or form much increased in 1878. I shall, however, let him tell his story in his own way:

'In the spring of 1878, about the time I left the Supreme Council, the American Fenians sent an agent to London to discuss the question of united action with Parnell. But that part of the story belongs to the Clan-na-Gael. I can only speak of what happened between Parnell and the Clan by hearsay.'[214]

O'Connor Power took the diplomatic route, 'force without violence'. Dr Carroll wrote to John Devoy on 16 May 1878, 'Mr Shields in not now in business.'[215]

James O'Kelly, based in New York, persuaded John Devoy to support the constitutional movement. He acted as an intermediary between Parnell and the Clan, in what MacDonagh called the 'voice and sword conference'. The Clan wanted complete separation from Britain, withdrawal from Westminster and a National Convention to be held in Ireland. The meeting was a battleground:

... animosity towards Power within Fenian circles was intense. At the meeting the two principals sat silently while John O'Leary and James J. O'Kelly, two Fenian activists, quarrelled vehemently about Power. It was evident that Power's association with the advanced parliamentarians led by Parnell would be a formidable obstacle to a rapprochement between Parnell and the Fenians.[216]

Davitt agreed to the course of parallel action,[217] and Devoy telegraphed Parnell in October offering the Clan's support. O'Kelly 'was sent to Ireland with $10,000 for the purchase of arms in 1879, but funds were withdrawn when the Supreme Council rejected proposals designed to streamline the IRB'.[218] With trenchant irony, James Daly praised Devoy:

> ... and his friends [for] coming round to the programme before the public for the last seven years. They admit their errors like honest men, and they should give dignity to their admission by joining heartily and unconditionally with those who have been all along working in the way they now so heartily commend.[219]

The Land War swept Devoy's initiative into a period of turbulent and equivocal partnership.

Land Hunger

> ... I do affirm most boldly that in its main character, in its essential objects, in its essential means, this was a movement and a combination which was not only justifiable before God and man, but necessary in the condition of things which existed.[220]

> ... no hope of agricultural peace so long as the landowners are trained to detest the national convictions and aspirations of the cultivators of the soil.[221]

Another famine seemed inevitable. Hunger and hopelessness unleashed desperate forces. Violence was endemic. Blood was shed indiscriminately. Innocent lives were lost. The British government responded with brute force. Matt Harris and Michael Davitt were imprisoned. Fever inevitably followed famine. *The New York Times* reported:

> In the House of Commons tonight, Mr O'Connor Power called attention to the medical reports presented by the Irish Local Government Board in regard to the fever-stricken districts in Mayo and other parts of the west of Ireland, and moved a resolution that it was essential that effective sanitary arrangements be immediately made in view of the spread of contagious diseases.[222]

A third bad harvest left farmers with no money to pay their creditors, and the number of threatened evictions doubled. The marriage rate was at its lowest ever, and the death rate the highest. Emigration figures surged.

The years since 1870 and its Land Act had been a period of prosperity, with excessive borrowing and spending. The boom was over, and an overextension of credit left banks dangerously exposed. Farmers and merchants were faced with debts they could not repay. Banks refused to lend or demanded exorbitant rates of interest. A credit crunch faced the country. James Daly advised farmers to first settle debts with shopkeepers and then pay landlords. If evicted they should repossess their farms.[223]

In early September 1879, on an annual tour of the constituency, O'Connor Power outlined the issues at meetings in Castlebar and Ballyhaunis. Official statistics showed that, as in the terrible years of the Great Famine, and every year since, Ireland produced more food than was required for the support of her population. Agricultural exports would feed the population three times over.

Hunger and disease were not eased by the government's refusal to set up fuel depots throughout the country. Three years of heavy rainfall had flooded the bogs and turf was unfit to burn. The people faced bitter cold, as devastating as hunger.

A handful of 'robbers' took the resources of Ireland to spend in foreign lands 'in the gratification of their luxurious tastes'. Taxing absentee landlords was not the answer. Land should be appropriated with compulsory sale. O'Connor Power dismissed the claim that for the government to assist farmers to buy out land was equivalent to communism. Did not the government purchase land for the railway companies, compensating owners? The reclamation of waste land would accommodate half a million peasant proprietors, and the drainage of marshes throughout the country would improve the climate and the health of the population.

Some of his correspondence with a central figure in the Land War has survived. Fr John O'Malley, former curate to the old adversary Fr Lavelle, was now parish priest of The Neale. An extremely popular figure, he assumed the leadership mantle of his former superior and worked closely with Mayo's MP. O'Connor Power declined an invitation to stay with Fr John at this time but would visit after the Castlebar meeting 'although I might have to rough it'.[224]

In October 1879, four miles from Lough Mask in County Mayo, the Ballinrobe tenant right meeting, with Fr O'Malley as chairman, was the first where priests joined forces with the land warriors. It was the biggest demonstration since the Irishtown meeting. O'Connor Power was invited to speak to over 20,000, gathered under banners proclaiming, 'God Save Ireland'.

At a mass meeting in Balla on 22 November, Thomas Brennan called for the implementation of a boycott policy. He appealed to the large number of troops and local police brought in to restore order, not to be 'the destroyers of your own kith and kin'. If anyone bought a farm from which a tenant had been evicted he should be shunned, 'Let none of you be found to buy with him or sell with him, and watch how the modern Iscariot will prosper.'[225]

Fr O'Malley, the guiding hand behind the initiative, felt strongly that the movement should be non-violent. Passive resistance, civil disobedience, would, in the long term, be more effective than murder and mayhem. Censure was better than 'removal', and ostracism, a potent sanction, was a centuries-old 'act of moral reprehension', punishing those who undermined a community.

Captain Charles Boycott, agent of the landlord Lord Erne, refused to lower rents. Along the shores of Lough Mask, local people refused to trade, deal, work or talk with the shunned Boycott family. Mail and telegraphic services were disrupted. Socially isolated, the Boycotts were in moral Coventry.

The term 'boycott', coined by Fr John, first appeared in print in the American press, and then again, a month later, in a Paris newspaper. Boycotting, as an act of aggression, spread like bushfire, becoming a widespread phenomenon. An example of 'triumphant anarchy', lamented *The Times*.[226]

The tactic was effectively used against tenants reckless enough to take over farms from which the previous occupants had been evicted. Usurpers received the same cold treatment as land-grabbing graziers and offending landowners. Straining the interdependence of rural and urban groups, the boycott interrupted supplies, causing severe difficulties for town and country.

At harvest time, the authorities brought in labourers – emergency men – from Cavan and Monaghan, who were protected by a thousand troops and several hundred police. The heavens, in sympathy, opened, and a torrential rain persisted for weeks. The *Freeman's Journal* reported, 'it is only Mayo that can produce rain in its perfection as an instrument of torture'.

New York Tribune correspondent James Redpath, who first wrote of the boycott in the international press, teased Fr John that he was endeavouring 'to make of The Neale a political Knock'. The first Marian vision was in the Mayo village of Knock in August 1879.

Of Boycotting, Trollope writes in wonder at 'the quickness and perfection of which this scheme was understood'. George Moore reports, 'Like a comet the verb "boycott" appeared.'[227] The practice was used against men unwilling to participate, and violence or threats of violence rendered the reluctant compliant. The men of Connacht were masters of the situation.

O'Connor Power stepped up the war in the press. His widely discussed article 'The Irish Land Agitation', which appeared in the *Nineteenth Century*, draws attention to the irresponsible coverage by English journalists reporting on the Land War:

> The manufacture of fictitious Irish news and fictitious Irish opinion for the English market is an extensive and profitable journalistic industry. People generally like to read what flatters their self-complacency, and nothing could be more agreeable to the self-complacency of Englishmen than to be told that the Irish people whom they have so miserably failed to govern are a turbulent, unmanageable, and unreasonable race.

The British public must be told what was happening in Ireland, 'Never since O'Connell summoned the mighty multitudes to his standard in the struggle for Repeal, has Ireland been so deeply moved or so thoroughly roused to public action, as it has been by the cry for land reform'.[228]

In Hyde Park he addressed a monster rally protesting against the imprisonment of Land League leaders. Representatives of working-class groups were present:

> Mr O'Connor Power, the chairman, said he rejoiced to see present thousands of Irishmen and friends of Ireland who were animated by the passion of patriotism and the love of public liberty. They had assembled in numbers that far exceeded those of any assemblage in Hyde Park, and which included Englishmen as well as Irishmen because they were convinced that the action of Her Majesty's government endangered the liberties of Great Britain and Ireland.[229]

The Chief Secretary for Ireland described the Land League's demands as 'undiluted communism' and a crusade against property. O'Connor Power insists it is the duty of parliament to step in, to provide relief and fund public works:

> *The Times* and other journals are making to parade Ireland in the face of Europe as a beggar at England's door. Ireland wants no alms from the English government or the English nation. She only asks justice, and the freedom to develop her own resources in her own way, and the power to use them for the maintenance of her own people.[230]

A cultivation of the land would add greatly not only to the support of the Irish nation but also to the food security of the British Isles. What was required was a board of commissioners to assess the problems. If Holland could reclaim its wasteland so might Ireland:

What the poorest tenants unaided have accomplished in draining swamps and cultivating bare mountain sides, nothwithstanding the prospective penalty of an increased rent when the soil became richer by their exertions, is truly marvellous, and affords the best proof that the elements of fertility lie hidden in the vast waste tracts of Ireland; and may be called into action by skilful cultivation.[231]

The graziers' cattle fattened on rich pastureland while the 'mountainy men', dispossessed, carried soil and manure up to high ground to create fertile tracts out of wasteland. The iconic figure of the stoic Irish labourer, reclaiming barren tracts, is familiar.

Peasant ownership would ensure political stability and prosperity as evident in many European countries. Cultivators of the soil should be the owners of the soil. It would be far better if money was spent on Ireland's agriculture than thrown away on a war with Russia. The country needed investment and legislation to correct industrial stagnation and prevent social strife. Farmers, without secure tenure, tenants-at-will, must be protected from the rapacity of ruthless landlords, who stole Ireland's wealth and lived in luxury abroad.

The transfer of ownership to tenants would require government loans. O'Connor Power argues that the state should hold the mortgage on properties. A reasonable rate would be fixed and a tenant, with pride in his property and secure in his holding, would be industrious and thrifty in good times in preparation for lean years. A good start would be the purchase of waste ground. Its reclamation would accommodate many families. There should be a tax on absentee landlords.

His article drew acrimonious criticism in the House. Davitt was present in the Visitors' Gallery to hear the debate. Disheartened, he returned to Ireland on 13 February.

Remedial measures were more swift and effective than in the dark days of the Great Famine. Money was raised for relief. There were four main funds: the Irish bishops raised over £830,000; the Mansion House Committee, £180,000; the Duchess of Marlborough's appeal, £135,000, and Parnell and Davitt's tour of the United States, £72,000.[232]

A Change of Government

[Disraeli] published a manifesto to the astonished country, hinting that his adversaries were contemplating the dismemberment of the empire by some tremendous concession to an Ireland in a state of veiled rebellion.[233]

Disraeli, in response to the emergency, called an election and went to the country, warning voters that the Land War and 'pestilential' Home Rule would sever the ties between Ireland and Great Britain.

The Irish vote was organised and Irishmen were asked to vote for Liberal candidates favourable to Home Rule and ensure a change of government:

> No sort of influence will be able to induce Irish electors in English constituencies to vote for a candidate who is not willing to support a motion for a parliamentary inquiry into Home Rule. The executive of the Home Rule Confederation has drawn up a test question to be put to all candidates at English and Scotch elections in constituencies where the Irish are strong, or sufficiently strong to turn the scale between the two English parties, and the answer given to this question will determine, in each case, the action to be taken by the Irish party ... but the Irish elector, who is both a Catholic and a Home Ruler – and there are few exceptions to this description – will vote for Home Rule at all hazards. He will vote for it as a Catholic because it represents freedom for the greater number of Catholics, namely the Catholics of Ireland; and he will vote for it as an Irishman, because he is convinced of the wisdom and necessity of Irish self-government.[234]

A month before the election, a manifesto was issued to branches of the Home Rule Confederation, 'Vote against Benjamin Disraeli as you should vote against the mortal enemy of your country or your race.'[235]

The HRCGB was an efficient and effective electioneering machine, and throughout Britain, the Home Rule Associations and National Clubs rose to the challenge; the Irish in England came out in large numbers and turned the scales in over forty constituencies.

Disraeli acknowledged that Ireland had finally defeated him. In the House of Commons, O'Connor Power claimed victory, 'for the first time in the political history of this country an English Minister has appealed in vain to the anti-Irish prejudices of his countrymen; and his discomfiture affords incontestable proof of the growth of Irish political power and the advance of Irish opinion in England'.[236]

Disraeli died within the year.

Gladstone, the incoming premier, spoke of 'peace, retrenchment and reform'. He had promised support for 'local patriotism', local government, in his Midlothian election address, 'if we can make arrangements under which Ireland, Scotland, and Wales, portions of England, can deal with questions of local and special interest to themselves more efficiently than parliament now can, that I say will be the attainment of a great national good'.[237]

O'Connor Power was an established figure, but in correspondence with Fr John, he detailed his personal difficulties. Parnell, in a bid to oust him, asked Westport lawyer John J. Louden, the Land League's lawyer, to run in Mayo. In a letter marked 'strictly private', he told Fr John O'Malley that Louden and Parnell:

> ... detest the power of the clergy and seek to wrest control from them ... just as much as Louden himself, and he is personally jealous of me, and determined to thwart me covertly. However, in the spirit of your Irish motto, I have declined the contest with Parnell, Louden, etc, and intend to forbear still further, although a system of the most damnable lying has been set up against me. The half dozen gentlemen who have constituted themselves the 'Land League of Mayo' are determined to ride roughshod over the county. They are now urging the people to remain away from the Castlebar meeting because they know the Castlebar people detest them and would not allow them to have everything their own way.[238]

He believed his opponents were attempting to 'embarrass him financially by forcing him into a costly canvass'.[239] Elections were expensive. Returning officers had to be paid. With the introduction of the secret ballot, a voter was not easily intimidated and had to be courted for his preference. The candidate had to hire poll booths, print and distribute literature and provide transport and treats.

Davitt wrote to Matt Harris that O'Connor Power's association with the Land League did not go down well in America but that it would not do to alienate Mayo voters, who continued to support their MP. Nonetheless, on his return from the United States, Davitt was persuaded to be Parnell's election agent in the fight for the Mayo seats.[240] There was even a campaign to discredit James Daly, and accusations of financial improprieties were flung at him by League leaders, who disliked his independent journalism.

Parnell stood nominally against local landlord George Brown but in reality against O'Connor Power, 'on whom he wished to be revenged'.[241] With Fr John's influence and James Daly's strong backing, O'Connor Power, in 'a memorable engagement', thwarted his opponents and 'topped the poll in the hotly contested election'.[242]

Parnell opted to sit for Cork and controversially yielded the Mayo seat to Revd Isaac Nelson, a septuagenarian Presbyterian minister from Belfast. O'Connor Power thanked Fr John in a letter dated 16 April 1880:

> I am surprised to find that I have not written to you since the election. I need not say that I am thoroughly satisfied. Parnell got at least three plumpers [243] for the one I did showing that the 'secret agency' was at work all the time. Let that

pass! I lecture here [Ballyhaunis] for the band on Wednesday. Will go to Ballindine tomorrow afternoon, attend anniversary land meeting at Irishtown on Sunday afternoon, give lecture for Claremorris band on Sunday night and start for Dublin (Imperial Hotel) on Monday morning. I hope to be able to remain a week in Dublin, and I trust that within that time we may give the world some proof that Ireland has elected a united and energetic party. Your action in the barony of Kilmain was the chief cause of placing me at the head of the poll.

It would be futile for me to endeavour to express the full extent of my obligations to you. Accept, however, the expression of my heartfelt thanks and believe me, my dear Fr John, Yours ever sincerely. J. O'Connor Power

Ten days later, his lecture 'The Philosophy of Irish History' in the Rotundo Room received full coverage in the press. His schedule was frenetic. At the end of February 1881, he was at the home of Bernard McAnulty, a feather merchant, in Newcastle upon Tyne. McAnulty, a former Repealer and tenant right activist, attended the Home Rule conference in the Rotundo in 1874 and was an executive of the HRCGB. He was the first Irishman to sit as a Nationalist on an English town council. Known as 'The Grand Old Irishman of the North', he was elected as a Home Ruler and held his council seat between 1874 and 1884, 'His stalwart frame and pleasant, genial face were well known during the whole of the Home Rule movement.'[244]

O'Connor Power sent a registered letter from McAnulty's address, thanking Fr John for his invaluable help and enclosing two cheques to repay his debt:

2 Claremont Place
Newcastle Upon Tyne
28 Feb 1881

My dear Fr John

I enclose the cheques for fifty pounds each. I could not bring myself to write to you until I was able to enclose the money. I return you my very warmest thanks for your great kindness and patience, and I trust you will forgive me for all the annoyance and trouble I have caused you in connection with the last election. Believe me, with kind regards and best wishes for your health and happiness.

Yours sincerely
J. O'Connor Power

The potato harvest in 1880 was a particularly good one, but the land agitation gathered momentum. Tensions were growing between small and substantial farmers. Businesses in town and country suffered significant financial losses. Private vendettas and internecine feuds were the backdrop. Threats and violence were everyday occurrences. Martial law was enforced to contain a dangerous situation.

Connacht gave birth to the Land War, but among Nationalists bitter divisions were ever present. In Paris, IRB President, Charles Kickham believed the land struggle and parliamentarianism diverted attention from the goal of a separatist Ireland. X tells Barry O'Brien, 'Well, Kickham was dead against any alliance with the Parliamentarians. He believed that contact with them was demoralising, and that Parliamentarianism was nothing more nor less than an Anglicising influence.'[245]

In April, the Supreme Council met in Paris. They 'remained officers without an army', and open warfare, on an undefined battlefield, had no realistic hope of success.[246] In Ireland, militant Fenians pursued a physical force response to British tyranny and had no patience with self-serving elements within the Land League. James Daly questioned the workings of the League and the integrity of its members; he criticised the centralisation of the movement, the management of funds and the neglect of local groups. Irish Americans held the purse strings. The divide between the Clan and UK-based Nationalists was not a new phenomenon. In 1848 the Young Irelanders did not defer to the Irish in America.

O'Connor Power, unrestrained, was pushing hard for land reform. Challenging the Queen's speech, the Programme for Government, he asked why there was silence on the Irish Land Question. The programme was 'meagre'. He demanded that legislation be introduced immediately, 'When I talk about Liberalism I mean the genuine article'. Irish poverty was blamed on the Malthusian theory, overpopulation, but:

> These people have been chased out of their ancestral homes where they could well have supported themselves and their families. They have been hunted out of the rich valleys, and obliged to take refuge, like the wild birds, in the bogs and the mountains. They have been driven forth by the avaricious cattle-dealer. If I might parody a well-known couplet, I would say:
>
> Ill fares the land, to graziers greed a prey
> Where beasts accumulate and men decay.[247]

It is not over population but the law of eviction, which produces an unequal distribution of population that is responsible for the mischief; nor is it from want of capital, but from want of a just distribution of capital, that Ireland suffers. I do not mean to convey that the gains of one portion of the community should be periodically divided among the rest who are less fortunate. I cordially repudiate a theory so fatal to individual exertion and individual aspiration ... But we shall be told of another alleged hindrance to Irish prosperity – the land agitation. In the famine of 1846-7 the Irish people were good enough to lie down and die of hunger, without a murmur ... and some people have wondered why they were not equally patient and self-sacrificing during the last twelve months. I do not regret that a little more than a year ago I quitted my duties in this House to attend the first meeting of the land agitation in the county of Mayo, which I have the honour to represent ...[248]

His notice of a motion in the Commons on 20 May 1880, proposed a Bill designed to stop evictions. Compensation should be paid to a tenant in any case of disturbance. A landlord would reconsider eviction if it meant he would be out of pocket. Nine years later Sir Charles Russell would recall the occasion:

That proposition was originally made by one of the members of the Irish Parliamentary Party, Mr O'Connor Power, a member of the English bar. He may be known to some of your Lordships. Mr O'Connor Power would not be ashamed if it were necessary to tell your Lordships, that he is one of those hot-headed and impulsive young men who in 1865-6 saw no hope from constitutional agitation and from Parliamentary effort, and who joined the ranks of the Fenian body. He, nevertheless, afterwards became in Parliament an important ally in the useful discussion of questions directly and intimately affecting Ireland ... It was their [the Land League's] bill taken up by the Government after Mr O'Connor Power, had, as one of the Land League, introduced it.[249]

Chief Secretary Forster felt the Bill went too far, and its introduction was delayed for days. O'Connor Power suggested he consult with Irish MPs on Irish issues:

Mr Forster and the Irish Attorney General are understood to be considering very diligently how they can advance in the direction of Mr. O'Connor Power's Land Bill which is regarded as one of the most important projects of legislation now before Parliament.[250]

Gladstone was on board, 'Am I to shrink from doing what is just and consistent because, as I admit, I shall be told I am doing it at the bidding of O'Connor Power?'[251,252]

It was to be a significant marker in a series of Land Bills, preparing the way for peasant ownership and, eventually, independence. Orthodox Fenians were not happy with the proposals and gathered in Irishtown, the cradle of the land movement, to denounce parliamentarianism. Matt Harris believed that fighting rather than talking would free the country.

On the other hand, the Compensation for Disturbances Bill went several steps too far for the House of Lords and was defeated some weeks later.

A Relief of Distress Bill, cynically called the 'Relief of Landlords', channelled over a £1 million from the surplus Irish Church funds through landowners. Many believed that if the Compensation Bill and the Relief Bill had been presented to the House of Lords in tandem, both would have passed into law. The rejection of the Compensation Bill, destroying confidence in the Liberal administration's good faith, united Ireland. Gladstone visited Dublin at the end of August 1880 but, deeply disillusioned by the inadequate response of Gladstone's government, the foot draggers, particularly the Catholic hierarchy, now backed the land movement. The League set up branches in every village in Ireland, and its power centre shifted from the west to the prosperous farmers of the south and east of the country.

Like many bureaucracies, the League did not function perfectly. Money was not accounted for and was unevenly administered. Outgoings went under a general heading of salaries and expenses. Those most in need were neglected. James Daly accused it of militancy and selfish motives. He believed its executive was avaricious, erratic and ignorant. Condemning physical force and urging calm, he attempted to contain the worst excesses of the boycott.

At a meeting in Bohola in July 1880, Daly threatened to expose members who were abusing the League's finances. He criticised Fenians who attacked O'Connor Power at Mayo meetings and demonstrations and 'asserted that the Mayo MP was the best parliamentary representative in the country and that he represented his constituents well'.[253]

While outsiders 'hijacked' the agitation, O'Connor Power worked with Gladstone on land legislation. Charles Russell had a significant input into the 1881 Land Act, as he proudly wrote to his brother Fr Matthew Russell, 'I had on Saturday a long talk with the Prime Minister *solus cum solo*, which lasted full three hours'. The next day he had another long talk with Gladstone, in which he did not:

> ... lose the opportunity of expressing roundly the strong opinions I entertain ... I also, in particular, ventilated my ideas about the Land Bill, to many of which ideas

effect has since been given. Indeed, I think I am entitled to say that in this matter I have rendered real and substantial service – far more than has met or ever will meet the public eye.[254]

Gladstone and John Bright argued against a policy of coercion but finally yielded to Dublin Castle's advice. Repression was the accepted response to civil unrest, and the Lord Lieutenant and the Chief Secretary both threatened to resign if they did not have their way. In January 1881, the Chief Secretary introduced a bill which would empower the authorities to imprison without trial those 'reasonably suspected' of criminal intent.

In the House of Commons, the Irish were effectively blocking parliamentary business. Gladstone's private secretary lamented, 'The waste of parliamentary time has reached such a pitch that parliamentary machinery has become completely out of gear and we are becoming the laughing stock of the world.'[255] The Irish party resisted the passage of the coercion legislation:

Mr O'Connor Power said that the proposals of the government were a mockery of the wrongs of Ireland, and it would be the duty of every Irish member, who, like himself, had taken no part with the Land League, to expose their imposture to the intelligence of the people of Ireland.[256]

He drew attention to the House of Representative's Resolution in 1877, 'is the Hon. Gentleman aware that Congress passed a resolution in the spirit of the question? [The principles of self-government]'.[257]

In Olympian style, the obstructionists ran a spirited and aggressive relay. When one member of the team rested in an antechamber or went home for a few hours' rest and recuperation, another would speak at great length. The session continued all through Monday, that night, then Tuesday. Irish members spoke for hours, often to empty benches, and effectively prevented an adjournment. Dishevelled, exhausted, they rose in turn until nine o'clock on Wednesday morning, when the Speaker, employing *force majeure*, ended the debate with a 'gagging resolution'. Prior to this *coup d'état*, he had consulted with Gladstone and the Leader of the Opposition, 'The dignity, credit and authority of the House are seriously threatened and it is necessary that they should be vindicated.' The rebels were stymied. O'Connor Power pronounced the division to be illegal:

Then rose the tall form of O'Connor Power, his strong jaw twisted with passion, and having with an uplifting motion of his right arm, brought his colleagues –

twenty in number – to their feet, he started shouting 'Privilege! Privilege!' in a deep, baying voice, in which all joined in a wild chorus.[258]

The Chief Secretary presented the Bill and at half past nine the House adjourned after a non-stop sitting of forty-one and a half hours, which broke all records. O'Connor Power was for abstention, a return to Ireland to consult with the constituencies. He recommended:

> That the irregular and unprecedented course adopted by the Speaker on summarily closing the debate on the Coercion Bill, by which the Irish members had been deprived of the opportunity of protesting against the suspension of constitutional liberty in Ireland, requires to be taken notice of, and that a protest signed by members be forwarded to Mr Speaker and circulated to the public press and that we, the Irish members, now retire from the House pending the result of consultation with our constituents.[259]

Other advice prevailed.

The obstruction took place over three days, from 31 January to 2 February.

The rebellion did not go unpunished. The following day the Home Secretary revoked Michael Davitt's ticket of leave, and he was arrested in Dublin. The move:

> … when almost the entire House, in one of those fits of brute animal passion, that will sometimes carry away even the most civilised assemblies, hailed the announcement with approving yells, did more than a generation of secret conspiracies could have done to associate England in the Irish imagination with a stroke of cowardly and squalid vengeance upon an all too generous adversary.[260]

On Thursday 3 February, the Irish, belligerent, returned to the House, where the police had taken up positions in the building and in the Palace Yard. The Chamber was packed with members, the galleries crowded with visitors, all eager to watch the drama unfold. Parliamentary obstruction resumed, with a refusal to vote and ensuing confusion. The rebels were suspended but declined to leave the House. O'Connor Power accused the government of attempting to crush Irish members, 'I will withdraw only in obedience to the law of force which you have established in place of legality in this assembly … The Speaker directed the Serjeant-at-Arms to remove him from the House.'[261]

Thirty-six Irish members left the House in single file, bowing to the Speaker before quitting the Chamber, and were escorted one by one to the door by the

Sergeant-at-Arms. In the autumn, the session was devoted to the reform of the Rules of Procedure, to ease the dispatch of business. The Irish must never again run riot.

Gladstone's government purposed that coercion would be the stick, and land reform the carrot, to bring closure to the Land War. Gladstone now declared 'Conciliation is to replace coercion', and, 7 April 1881, the Land Law (Ireland) Bill was introduced.

The previous year, James Daly had worked with the Bessborough Commission, collecting and presenting evidence and exposing abuses and exorbitant rents. The commissioners had interviewed tenant farmers, landlords and land agents across Ireland. Their report, signed in early January 1881, recommending that the Three Fs of the 1870 Land Act be implemented, provided a structure for legislation.

Dublin Castle, taking an independent line, believed that by arresting the League leadership they would disable the movement. On 14 April James Daly was arrested. His newspaper articles were considered inflammatory. A few days later, O'Connor Power visited Chief Secretary Forster to intercede. Within a fortnight he forwarded a letter from Daly to Forster, asking that he be given his freedom on the grounds of his wife's ill health. Daly was released. The authorities had been persuaded that Daly at large was a restraining hand on the hard men.

The Compensation for Disturbance Bill acknowledged that the tenant was part owner of the land. The Land Court was established to arbitrate rent based on the rental value of the holding. Parnell attempted to obstruct the working of the courts with test cases but as long as the rent was paid the landlord could not evict the tenant. If the tenant wished to emigrate or move on he was to be allowed to sell his interest on the open market. The Bill restated the Three Fs — fair rent, fixity of tenure and free sale of interest in the holding. Over 11,000 tenants would avail of the legislation to have their rents fixed judicially.

A horrified Randolph Churchill attacked the Bill, stating that it was 'an attempt to raise the masses against the propertied classes'. At a party meeting, Parnell threatened to resign if the party voted for it, but several prominent MPs, among them James O'Kelly, disobeyed. O'Connor Power conferred with his constituents:

Mr O'Connor Power said that after seeking to get at the opinion of his constituents on this matter he felt he should be justified in voting for the second reading without admitting that the Bill constituted a solution of the difficulty.[262]

... that while we reaffirm our convictions that the only final solution of the land question is to be found in legislation enabling the cultivators to become the owners of their own farms, we recommend our parliamentary representatives to support the second reading of the Land Bill and to make strenuous efforts, after its getting into committee, so to improve its provisions that in its passage through parliament it may become a measure of real protection to the tenant farmers of Ireland.[263]

His position was endorsed by Archbishop Croke of Cashel and leading national newspapers.

There was a good harvest that summer. At a land meeting, Canon Ulick Bourke urged the Mayo people to accept the Bill – it was 'seed sown in the soil of Mayo'. James Daly believed it was a step in the right direction and encouraged farmers to make full use of the courts.

Gladstone's private secretary commented, '[Gladstone] has achieved many legislative feats, but none so immense and so difficult as this Land Bill. It is impossible to overrate the mastery of detail which he has shewn, the tact, judgment and good temper'.[264]

In April, O'Connor Power was listed in the 1881 census at the home of English MP Charles Thompson, a vocal opponent of the Coercion Bill. Later that month he visited Jarrow-on-Tyne in north-east England to plead Ireland's case and protest against coercion. In October, he was at a demonstration in Bradford's Mechanics Institute.

For the militant in Paris, fears of a parliamentary compromise were realised, and the belief that the Land War deflected from the fight for independence was confirmed. Disagreements were aired vigorously in public.

Patrick Egan's letter to Thomas Brennan, written on official Land League notepaper and sent from the Brighton Hotel in Paris, was dated 26 May. Egan criticised the conduct of members of the House, and particularly O'Connor Power, in 'gross and vulgar terms', for supporting the Land Bill. His letter was published in the *Freeman's Journal*.

In a public reply, O'Connor Power defended himself and deplored the attacks on Irish MPs. *The New York Times* reported the exchanges:

A Dublin despatch says Mr John O'Connor Power, replying to a letter from Mr Egan to Mr Brennan, wherein Mr Egan abuses Messrs Power and McCoan for voting for the second reading of the Land Bill, taunts Mr Egan with skulking in Paris, and warns his countrymen that if they allow themselves to be goaded into unarmed insurrection by the screaming of hired demagogues who have already shown the white feather they will be abandoned and betrayed in the hour of trial. Mr McCoan also taunts Mr Egan, with hiding in Paris, and hints that Mr Egan's letter was inspired by others.[265]

Mitchell Henry called attention to the Breach of Privilege, a charge made against a member of the House in his capacity as a member of the House. The Land Bill was still under discussion. He revealed that Patrick Egan was in the habit of coming into the Lobby of the House and threatening members. Henry read Egan's letter to the House and came to O'Connor Power's defence: 'whilst he is a man very advanced in his opinions, he is also known as one who has the courage of his opinions.' O'Connor Power disclaimed any appeal for help, 'I do not require any Resolution of this House in vindication either of my public or personal character.'[266] And continued:

> ... if the letter of Mr Patrick Egan were not an official document, stamped with the official sanction of an organisation which is presided over by the hon. Member for the City of Cork [Parnell], it might be ignored ... I am not to be terrified by the resolution of the Land League ... the word has gone round, Sir, from persons high in authority in that organisation, that every man who dares to support any measures introduced by the Government shall be branded as a 'place hunter' ... I challenge any Member of this Assembly to dare to assert that my vote or action has ever been compromised by mercenary considerations. Nay, more, I regret to be obliged to add that gentlemen who are engaging in bringing these accusations against their countrymen, are themselves gentlemen who have within less than 12 months repeatedly applied to me to use my influence to obtain for them situations under Her Majesty's Government ... It is my invariable rule not to interfere in Government patronage in my constituency or anywhere else in Ireland ... Unfortunately, Irish politics are in this position – that it requires greater courage to support a Government when they are right than to oppose them when they are wrong.

Parnell dismissed the Breach of Privilege and spoke of 'my friend, Patrick Egan'. O'Connor Power countered, 'truth has been sacrificed to gratify insane ambition'. O'Connor Power regretted the 'System of terrorism' which the Land League, under Mr Parnell's presidency, carried out against Irish politicians.[267]

In Mayo, James Daly joined in the fray:

> This class of mercenary patriots think they do their duty to Ireland by holding their weekly meetings and lodging the funds they receive abroad, while those who are suffering for the cause of Ireland are allowed to pine or starve on prison fare in Galway and other Irish gaols, while their families are equally shamefully neglected.[268]

Leading Fenian P.W. Nally, a local sports hero, encouraged Mayo's tenant farmers to take advantage of the terms of the Land Act, despite the League's instructions to the contrary. In a letter dated 12 October 1881, Nally accused the League executive of squandering League funds:

> The tenants should avail themselves of the Land Act, not such fools as to trust themselves to the mercy of the landlords or Land Leaguers. Resolutions should be passed expressing confidence in J. Daly and O'C. Power, and calling on Parnell to purge the Executive of such men as Louden and a lot of other greedy vultures.[269]

Mayo tenants applied to the newly established Land Court to secure fixed rents, and the law began to make a difference.

Early in 1882 O'Connor Power defended his reputation:

> On misrepresentation of a speech in a report:

> So far from expressing an enforcement of coercion, I stated, that in my judgement tranquillity would be more rapidly brought about without coercion than with it. My opinions on this subject are so well known that it can hardly be necessary for me to correct a mistake so obvious ...[270]

In March he was again very ill.[271] The attacks continued, 'Mr O'Connor Power's paper the *Connaught Telegraph* states that an overwhelming majority of the people of Mayo have accepted his vindication of his public conduct against "the brutal assault made upon him by the hired organ of the Land League".'[272]

An anonymous columnist in the *Connaught Telegraph* retaliated with *Michael Davitt on the Rampage*:

> We believe that still further good would be done if Mr Davitt had remained subordinate to Mr Parnell and had not assumed to himself the leadership of the Irish party, and vilifier of its oldest, best, tried, trusted, and admittedly most honest and deserving worker in the cause of the country.[273]

O'Connor Power told the Government: 'Things will get even worse before they get better'.[274] In August 1882, the Arrears Act, agreed under the terms of the Kilmainham Treaty, was introduced to help tenants who, due to successive bad harvests, were in difficulties:

To meet this situation the Arrears Act was passed in 1882. It affords an example of the temporary measures to which I have applied the term 'emergency'. No matter how much the tenant owed, by paying the rent for 1881 and one year of the arrears due – the State providing another year of the arrears out of the Church Surplus Fund – he got a clean receipt from the landlord. In these Acts the Imperial Parliament set aside the so-called 'rights of property' which had been regarded as so sacrosanct and, furthermore, did the unheard of thing of applying the moneys of the State to relieving debtors of their obligations.[275]

Security of tenure was addressed, a further step towards peasant ownership. An extended railway network was promised. The Act undertook to reclaim waste land and redistribute grazier pasturage. Irish landlords, eager for payment, rushed the legislation through the House of Lords. The Parnellites' support was perceived as a late endorsement of the 1881 Land Act.

In an interview with Barry O'Brien, John Bright admitted that coercion was a failure, but, without it, there would have been no progress, 'Remember, too, that if we had not passed a Coercion Act we could not have got a Land Bill through. That was a consideration which weighted much with me, and I think with all of us.'[276]

Part Three

At large

Poets with whom I learnt my trade
Companions of the *Cheshire Cheese*.[277]

To keep that memory green.

Ye Old Cheshire Cheese, one of the oldest pubs in London, stands on the site of a thirteenth-century Carmelite guesthouse. Convenient for Fleet Street and the Old Bailey, it has, for centuries, been the haunt of writers, newspapermen and barristers in pursuit of good conversation and stimulating friendships.

In the eighteenth century, the writers Samuel Johnson, Edmund Burke[278] and Oliver Goldsmith, the painter Joshua Reynolds and the actor David Garrick met there in a convivial setting to indulge in *noctes ambrosianae* – long, delicious evenings of good fellowship. Johnson's Literary Club was somewhat exclusive and was reported to have initially blackballed the eminent historian Edward Gibbon.[279] Pedantry was not encouraged. Jollity was an objective. They met once a month in a 'Temple of Mirth and Wine' and certainly, informally, more often, as Goldsmith lived almost opposite the Cheese, and Johnson only a minute's walk away. Johnson's much-rehearsed dicta set the tone:

The chief glory of every people arises from its authors.

If a man does not make new acquaintances as he advances through life he will soon find himself alone. A man, Sir, should keep his friendship in constant repair.

Through the years, the traditions continued unbroken, and the popular novelists Charles Dickens, Wilkie Collins and Arthur Conan Doyle were among some of the distinguished, likeminded *habitués* of the storied tavern, with its warren of low-ceilinged rooms and comforting, dark wooden interiors, discreetly tucked away from the average punter, 'Unless you have Sam Weller[280] at your elbow, you will not very easily find the Cheshire Cheese.' In *A Tale of Two Cities*, Sidney Carton, on leaving the Old Bailey, takes Charles Darney to the nearest tavern:

> 'Let me show you the nearest tavern to dine well at.' Drawing his arm through his own, he took him down Ludgate Hill to Fleet Street, and so, up a covered way, into a tavern. Here they were shown a little room …'[281]

The Cheese remains much as it was 'in the days when Goldsmith used to pass its side door on his way to the dark entry of his club life'. For the poet, who had spent part of his youth in County Roscommon, it was 'club, discussion forum, and even home'. The tavern had certain codes. One did not ask for Irish or Scotch, but for whiskey, for Cork and not gin. One supped, one did not dine.

The pudding served in the snug premises was renowned throughout the islands and celebrated in verse and song by the regular customers, 'It is composed of a fine light crust in a huge basin, and there are entombed therein beef steaks, kidneys, oysters, larks, mushrooms, and wondrous spices and gravies, the secret of which is only known to the compounder'.[282]

On 13 December 1884, the centenary of Samuel Johnson's death, a group reconstituted itself The Johnson Club. The first meeting was in the Cock Tavern in Fleet Street, close to the Middle Temple gateway. Thereafter, it usually met in the Cheese, in a room with mullioned windows, sanded floor, 'firelight dancing', and 'gloomy charm'.[283] Wooden partitions like pews divided the tables, set with white linen, silver service, willow pattern plates and large, thick glasses. In deference to past splendours, the illumination for Johnson suppers was provided by candles. The Club met four times a year.

The members, the brethren, chose a presiding figure, the Prior, who occupied a seat under a portrait of Johnson, 'There on the ground floor we meet our "Prior", sitting on a bench, above which is set in the wall a brass tablet bearing the following inscription: The Favourite Seat of Dr Samuel Johnson. Born September 18 1709; Died December 13 1784.'[284] The picture's frame reprises, 'The glory of a nation are its authors'. Another quote, as defined in Johnson's *Dictionary*, is *à propos*, 'A tavern chair is the throne of human felicity.'

At the quarterly gatherings, the brethren smoked long, churchwarden clay pipes of the sort in use in the eighteenth century and they were served from a claret punch bowl. They were invited to sup 'by swallowing as much beef-steak pudding, punch, and tobacco smoke as the strength of each man's constitution admits'. The Chaplain, a role undertaken by the Scribe, said grace before supper. At the end of the meal, a toast was drunk in solemn, respectful silence to the memory of Dr Johnson. It was, indeed, 'an assembly of good fellows, meeting under certain conditions', the lexicographer's comprehensive definition of a club. The purpose was 'Fellowship and free Exchange of Mind':

Each Brother says his say, and all take sides,
Save one, who through the intellectual scrimmage
Sits still and silent as a graven image.[285]

Papers in prose and verse were presented to the company, 'post-caenatically read'. Francis Bacon was cited and discussed, 'Reading makes a full man, conversation a ready man, and writing an exact man.'[286]

T. Fisher Unwin, the publisher, was the originator of the club and its first Prior. The roll call of Priors is impressive and numbers the leading thinkers of the age and heads of every liberal and scientific profession. Not confined to belletrists, it includes statesmen, lawyers, engineers, abolitionists, men who were highly conspicuous in public life.

Augustine Birrell, author, lawyer and member of parliament, was Prior in 1895. He writes in the *Atlantic Monthly* (1896), 'Our Favourite Haunt is the Old Cheshire Cheese, the only tavern in Fleet Street left unchanged by what Johnson called the "fury of innovation"...'. Birrell was well acquainted with the denizens of Westminster's Irish Quarter and was as committed to Home Rule as any Irishman. Later, a popular Chief Secretary, he attempted to introduce self-government through the back door. In 1907, his Irish Council Bill,[287] a proposed stepping stone to Home Rule, although cautiously welcomed by Padraig Pearse, was dismissed by Nationalists and Unionists alike. He was a member of the government which placed Home Rule on the Statute Book – a development which would have put him out of a job. He ignored the nationalist 'mosquito press', and his benign neglect of the Irish political scene certainly facilitated the Easter Rising. He promptly resigned thereafter.

John O'Connor, affectionately nicknamed 'Long John, six feet six of treason felony', was a former Secretary of the IRB Supreme Council, MP for North Kildare and a distinguished lawyer. In 1911, he read a paper on 'Dr Johnson and

Ireland'.[288] Dr Johnson had many Irish friends, the playwright Richard Brinsley Sheridan among them, but he never visited Ireland, 'It is the last place I should wish to travel.'

O'Connor tells us that Brother Birrell, as Chief Secretary, gave grants for the building and repair of Irish schools and for the teaching of the Irish language. He quotes a sympathetic Johnson on Ireland, 'Still the Irish are in a most unnatural state, for we see the minority prevailing over the majority.' On the Union he says, 'Do not unite with us. We should unite with you only to rob you.'

In October 1918, Irish lawyer Sir Charles Russell read a paper on 'Dr Johnson and the Catholic Church'.[289] The 'old philosopher' was ecumenical in spirit and had many Catholic friends. He was a practical, committed Christian, with 'unfailing goodness of heart'. His manservant, Frank Barber, was treated like one of the family and bequeathed a substantial legacy when the good doctor died, 'Men like Johnson are the champions of faith and morality in their time … His home was a veritable house of charity.'

Herbert Asquith was Liberal PM from 1908 to 1916, and his government introduced the People's Budget, a curb to the power of the House of Lords and Home Rule. He cited Johnson frequently throughout his public career. On 13 December 1922, after stepping down as leader of the opposition, he read a paper before the Club on 'Johnson and Fanny Burney'.[290]

O'Connor Power, bringing the requisite Irish dimension, was most likely a founding member. He was Prior in 1888, the year the Cock Tavern reopened, refurbished, across the road from its original site, and took office at the anniversary dinner in December 1887, in 'that noted city hostelry, the Old Cheshire Cheese', 'The Prior proposed "The Memory of Dr Johnson", and made the customary speech on assuming his new office'.[291]

'Edmund Burke and His Abiding Influence', published on the centennial of Burke's death in *The North America Review*, was perhaps built on a paper read before the club. It was during his tenure as Prior that the rules of the club were laid down. Membership was a selection by competitive ballot and the number, originally thirty, was to be restricted to thirty-one. The thirty-first member, who threw the even number, just happened to be the intrepid and volatile explorer H.M. Stanley, of Dr Livingstone fame. He was elected and included in the toast to 'Absent Friends': '[Brother Stanley] told us that the only books he carried into darkest Africa were the Bible and Boswell's *Life of Johnson*'.[292] It was enacted that members were to 'sup together annually, on or about the 13th of December, if possible at some eighteenth-century tavern, and, also, at least three times more in each year'.[293] Past Priors became Abbots, and 'as becomes a happy club we lived not by rule' but by custom and tradition. Meetings were well attended, with interesting guests to season the evening's pleasure.

In 1938, the members still numbered thirty-one. There was always a waiting list. Augustine Birrell recounts an amusing anecdote – no names are mentioned:

> Not many years ago at our annual gathering on December 13, two of our guests were called upon (the practice is inhospitable) to say something. One was an Irish patriot, who had languished in jail during a now *ancien régime*, who demanding from the chaplain to be provided with some book that was not the Bible, a collection of writings with which he was already, so he assured the chaplain, well acquainted, was supplied with Boswell, a book it so chanced, he had never before read. He straight away, so he told us, forgot both his own and his country's woes. 'How happily the days of Thalaba went by', and now, in the retrospect of his life, his prison days were the hues of enjoyment and delight. He has since ceased to be a patriot, but he remains a Boswellian.[284]

The verse 'At the Cheshire Cheese' sets the mood:

> The town and its taverns, the sound of the street,
> To the genuine Johnsonian are merry and sweet …

> But the place of our pride we have best to remember
> Is *the Cheshire Cheese, Fleet Street, Thirteenth of December*,
> When the Brethren, all eager and and bright, flock together,
> Johnsonianissmi, birds of a feather.
> When the Scribe gives the word for beginning the revel,
> And everything dismal is sent to the Devil.[295]

From time to time, they gathered in Pembroke College, Oxford, Samuel Johnson's *alma mater*. John Betjeman's 'college so polite and shy', was named for the third Earl of Pembroke. Several centuries earlier, Strongbow, the second Earl of Pembroke, was Governor of Ireland. In August 1170, he married Aoife, the daughter of the King of Leinster.

George Birkbeck Hill, Scribe and Oracle of The Johnson Club, compiled *The Johnson Club Papers*, a record of the proceedings. There is an echo in J.R.R. Tolkien's unfinished story, *The Notion Club Papers*, which has a similar title page. Its foreword reports, the 'papers' are 'nothing more than an elaborate minute-book of a club, devoted to conversation, debate …' which were read before the members and discussed.[296]

Fictional dons relate vivid dreams of other times and places and discuss the possibility of travel in space and time. Augustine Birrell's paper, read before the Johnson Club, 'The Transmission of Dr Johnson's Personality', asserts that 'Johnson's, I repeat, is a transmitted personality.'

Tolkien scholars link the characters of his abandoned work, written at the end of the Second World War, to the Inklings, a discussion group which included C.S. Lewis. The Inklings 'the Public House School', like The Johnson Club met in taverns. However, Tolkien was a Fellow of Pembroke College in the 1940s and must have been familiar with *The Johnson Club Papers*. His friend and publisher was Stanley Unwin, the nephew of the club's first Prior.

In 1920, T. Fisher Unwin published Michael MacDonagh's *The Home Rule Movement*, partly based on O'Connor Power's personal papers. MacDonagh was himself a Johnsonian, writing on *Samuel Johnson, Parliamentary Reporter*.[297]

With an irrepressible zest for life, a delight in serious conversation, fine literature and good cheer, O'Connor Power found a home from home with the brethren. As a gifted raconteur, a man of many parts, he was a welcome addition to the company. A public figure with a reputation as a rebel, an orator, and a human rights activist – he had no need of introduction. His versatile repertoire encompassed stirring rhetoric and stand-up comedy; he was a great entertainer, eminently clubbable, and an asset in any convivial setting.

William Butler Yeats, a leading light of the Irish Literary Revival, was a member of the Rhymers Club, which met in the Cheese for a short time. He immortalises the tavern in his poem 'The Grey Rock'. The company of the Cheese recalls Yeats's lines in 'The Fiddler of Dooney':

> For the good are always the merry
> Save by an evil chance
> For the merry love to fiddle
> And the merry love to dance.

There is no record of fiddling or dancing but there were many songs and recitations at the Cheese get-togethers, 'Merry, too, was the night when Arthur Perceval Graves came and sang us his own song, "Father O'Flynn".'[298]

It was Augustine Birrell who arranged for Yeats to receive a Civil List pension. In his reply to Yeats's thank you letter, he writes:

The Prime Minister was at least as eager as I was. I know you don't much care about Dr Johnson but I always think his pension was the money best spent in

England during the whole of my beloved eighteenth century. It is well that the twentieth should follow suit.[299]

On 11 June 1892, the Johnsonians, on one of their occasional out-of-town jaunts, held a dinner at Pembroke and were given facsimiles of the 'Sale Catalogue of Johnson's Library' (1775), courtesy of the Unwin brothers. The finest port was brought from the cellars, '[The Master] drinks claret now but he was built up on port.' In 1896, they gathered again at Pembroke, and each guest was presented with a copy of Johnson's epitaph on Oliver Goldsmith.[300] An Irish poet was quoted, in Jonathan Swift's translation:

> O'Roorke's noble fare
> Will ne'er be forgot,
> By those who were there,
> Or those who were not.

At one gathering, a mock examination paper was set for the revellers, 'Show how a slice of plum-pudding can be made a measure of a man's feelings.' The second question was provocative, 'Prove that the fact that the Irish never speak well of one another shows that they are a fair people.'[301]

The spiritual President, Dr Johnson, professed to 'aspire after righteousness', and there was an underlying seriousness of purpose, 'Our alms must not be sounded before men, so I pass over our contributions to Johnsonian objects.'[302]

In July 1886, Johnsonians and their guests gathered at the National Liberal Club to honour the presiding Prior, F.W. Chesson, a prominent anti-slavery campaigner and promoter of aboriginal rights. O'Connor Power gave the after-dinner toast to 'Cheers', 'Laughter' and 'Applause':

> Then, I have another reason, a selfish reason, founded on that fund of natural
> laziness with which nature has endowed me, in consenting to propose the toast.
> Again, it seems to me such a natural and graceful movement when the head is
> bowed to indicate assent: but, when asked to indicate a negative, the head has to
> be twisted in a most unnatural manner. And so, when I was asked to propose the
> toast, I accepted the easy and natural form of movement, and assented.[303]

As was the wont, he mentioned Boswell, 'How delightful it would be if our honoured guest had some industrious and polite Boswell to record his conversations', and friendship, 'Cicero was the first to say that friendship was one of those things concerning the usefulness of which all men were agreed.'[304]

In the concluding chapter of *The Making of an Orator*, he makes obeisance and inserts the opposing arguments of Dr Johnson and his biographer, James Boswell, "'I asked him," says the biographer, "whether, as a moralist, he did not think that the practice of the law in some degree hurt the nice feeling of honesty." The brief exchange that follows is familiar to all serious jurists. Boswell argues that dissimulation in the defence of a client you know to be in the wrong is immoral, 'Is there not some danger that a lawyer may put on the same mask in common life in the intercourse with his friends?' Johnson replies, 'Why, no, sir. Everybody knows you are paid for affecting warmth for your client: and it is therefore properly no dissimulation. The moment you come from the Bar you resume your usual behaviour.'

Oliver Goldsmith spent the last years of his life at 2 Brick Court, with its view over the Temple Gardens. Here he entertained Johnson and his friends and wrote his best-loved poems, 'The Deserted Village' and 'The Traveller'. O'Connor Power occupied chambers in 2 Brick Court from 1888 to 1896. The house remained much as it was in Goldsmith's time.

From 1888 to 1890, the periodical the *Universal Review, Essays on Life, Art and Science*, was published. It followed in the footsteps of Johnson's *The Literary Magazine* or *Universal Review* of 1756. Articles covered international topics as well as the arts. There were contributions in French from Maupassant and Verlaine. Walt Whitman wrote for the *Review*. Sir John Millais was an illustrator.

O'Connor Power provides a critique of Andrew Carnegie's 'Gospel of Wealth (A Reply to Andrew Carnegie)' in 1890, expounding the arguments in dialogue form. He reports a conversation with a friend, Adam Strong, 'a self-educated artisan, by trade a carpenter', who has 'his *Mills' Political Economy* and his Green's *History of the English People*, as the saying is, at his fingers' ends'. Adam, the primeval man, goes back to basics and deals with the views of the 'social philosopher', Mr Carnegie in 'a somewhat vigorous manner'.

Adam Smith, father of modern economics, was invited to be a member of Samuel Johnson's Literary Club in 1775 and *The Wealth of Nations* was published the following year.

On 13 December 1934, at the 150th anniversary celebration of Johnson's death, 'R. W. Chapman, claimed that the Club had, in its modest way, Johnsonized the land'.

The Artist in Irish Politics

The Fenian is the artist in Irish politics. He is an inspiration, an ornament, a hero.[305]

The literature of one's country is the abiding product of its history, the imperishable reflection of its life and character.[306]

Art reflects a societal landscape, resonating with the language, colours, rhythms and structures of its time and is the most significant resource for evidence of a culture. An artist and his work showcase a nation, its values and preoccupations.

Culture was a weapon of colonisation and O'Connor Power reminded an audience in New York that Britain's literary treasury was a potent tool of Empire, 'although England is not so largely represented here [America] as Ireland is, in point of numbers, she exercises, nevertheless, an influence, by means of her literature, which is fully equal to that exercised by the presence of an Irish nation on American soil'.[307]

A literary critic, he was keenly aware of the artist's role in the formation of national identity and peppered his speeches with quotations from the works of Irish writers. He was never happier than in the company of men and women of letters, and his forays, his cross-channel and transatlantic peregrinations, contributed to several literary creations.

Fiction, mirroring a reality, informs and questions our perceptions. In May Laffan Hartley's *Christy Carew*,[308] published in 1876, O'Connor Power may have supplied some of the traits of the character of Farrell O'Gorman. Madeleine Kelleher Kahn, Hartley's biographer, identifies some qualities of this poll-topping Member for Mayo in her well-researched book, 'I think for the rest, he is thoroughly sincere and honest; in fact, I know he is – an utter visionary.' Nevertheless, in *Hogan MP*, published in 1876, the eponymous Home Rule candidate shares some of O'Connor Power's physical characteristics. Mr John O'Rooney Hogan, the member for Peatstown, with his brown-black hair, was, 'not handsome, but there was nothing insignificant in his expression and bearing; and under the heavy eyebrows was a pair of grey, bright eyes, observant and humorous.' Further on the picture becomes clearer, he had an 'irreproachable accent' and 'bushy brows and large wide white teeth, gleaming in a wide mouth, which seemed almost smiling but could wear a determined look at times'.

Hogan's parents had died young. His father 'had been a tradesman in a little inland country town'. He had absorbed a 'limited stock of knowledge' at a diocesan college but did not want to be a priest. He 'owed everything to his uncle, the bishop', who was possessed of a good library. This seems to be an allusion to O'Connor Power's clerical sponsor, Archbishop McHale, and the new library at St Jarlath's.

The author and art critic George Augustus Moore, son and heir of George Henry Moore, attacks an apparent conflation of Mayo's James Daly and O'Connor Power in his essay 'The Patriot', in *Parnell and His Island* (1887).[309] One of Ireland's most gifted, if jaundiced, writers, Moore, unlike his patriot father, was an absentee landlord. He left Ireland after his father's funeral and spent most of his adult years in Paris and London. Forced to quit a sybaritic life in Paris when the tactics of the Land War dried up the cash flow, he returned home reluctantly to the family seat in Mayo. The Land League's proposed tax on non-resident landlords was galling.

In a leader column in the *Connaught Telegraph*, James Daly described George Augustus as 'the degenerate son of a worthy father'. Moore retaliates in 'The Patriot' and 'the Radical print', the *Connaught Telegraph*, transmutes to the *Clare Telegraph*, the publisher of unpleasant articles.

'The Patriot', using the name James Daly, a man held in such high esteem in Connacht, is a vindictive and libellous piece of writing, and the implications are slanderous. But barbed and scantily veiled attacks and parodies in print were common currency among the writers of the period. Public figures might speak their minds openly and be indiscriminate in their insults.

George Augustus admires 'pale aristocratic faces' and writes with apparent disdain of the Irish peasantry, although his father, with his 'clear blue eyes', was said to have the map of Ireland written on his face.[310] O'Connor Power saw himself as the successor to the Westminster seat of George Henry. The prodigal heir, George Augustus, an outsider in his family and in life, was undoubtedly discommoded by the upstart's exuberance and his ease of social intercourse.

Moore places the composite character at the playhouse in the company of the cast. O'Connor Power had been involved in dramatic productions at St Jarlath's and had even tried his hand at writing plays. He had a close friendship with one of the most popular playwrights of the day, the Dublin-born Dion Boucicault, who would have had a professional appreciation of the performances of an accomplished orator.

Wilkie Collins, who frequented the Cheese, borrows some traits from the most colourful Irishman in London to flesh out the character of his charming but weak protagonist, Lord Harry, in his unfinished last novel, *Blind Love*. It is a love story with a background of Fenian intrigue. Scenes are set in Ireland and Paris. Men are hunted down, are on the run. A secret network threatens, 'Strangers wondered whether Lord Harry was an actor or a Roman Catholic priest … The hot temper of an Irishman, in moments of excitement, is not infrequently a sweet temper in moments of calm.'[311] We learn that his accent slips when overwrought. O'Connor Power had a fierce temper, a passionate nature and the attributes of an actor.

He was a committed and 'vigorous' Catholic.

He ran away when he was a boy, and went to sea: he was a strolling actor after that: he went out to the States and was reported to have been seen in the West: he has been a ship's steward: he has been on the turf. What has he not been?[312]

Did O'Connor Power play the part of ship steward when he made his early transatlantic crossings? Charles Dickens, in his novel *Our Mutual Friend*, has the police inspector declare to Miss Abbey that you can always spot a ship's steward:

Who wouldn't know your brother to be a steward! There is a bright and ready twinkle in his eye, there is a neatness in his action, there is a smartness in his figure, there is an air of reliability about him in case you wanted a basin, which points out the steward …[313]

A steward would be well placed to overhear confidential conversations. With his Ballinasloe roots, O'Connor Power was no doubt a connoisseur of horse flesh. There is no question of his histrionic leanings.

The Lord Harry was the colloquial name for the devil, and Collins's novel was to have originally borne the title of its hero. O'Connor Power's reputation as a revolutionary and his Pimpernel 'seek him here, seek him there', 'now you see him, now you don't' propensities continued to make his acquaintance uneasy.

The Landleaguers, Anthony Trollope's unfinished last novel, is a story of the Land War. Trollope, the inventor of the pillar box, had spent many years in Ireland as a Post Office surveyor and went back to research the book. It is reported that he was extremely distressed by the violence of the conflict. The reader views the disturbances from the perspective of a well-meaning landlord, and the narrative unfolds with upheavals in the lives of the family members of the Big House. Trollope relates the withholding of rents and labour, the boycott, death threats, murders, maiming of cattle, picketing of the hunt and flooding of fields. Old scores are settled under the pose of patriotism. The Irish American Gerald O'Mahoney, the heroine's father, returns to Ireland, the home of his ancestors. 'Hot for Home Rule', he has no apparent source of income and is a frequent platform speaker in Galway and at the Rotundo meeting room in Dublin. He claims he is 'not Irish but Irish at heart'.

The nineteenth-century Post Office network was a principle agent of government, and its services ranged from collecting and delivering the mail, to banking (the Post Office Savings bank was established in 1861) and the transmission of telegrams. Employees signed a confidentiality agreement. A post as surveyor was a desirable Civil Service position.

Over the years Trollope had built up an extensive network of contacts: judges, civil servants, members of the constabulary, local landowners. As a member of the hunting set he mixed with all classes of society and he interviewed many of them for the material for his story.[314]

Phineas Finn and *Phineas Redux*,[315] Trollope's earlier novels, relate the history of an Irishman's progress through the layered structure of English society. They predate O'Connor Power's rise to prominence but give us some background to his journey. Was he, like Phineas, a skilled horseman and sound judge of horse flesh? Hunting is a pastime which requires courage and persistence. For Phineas and Trollope, these traits opened doors and they opened some for O'Connor Power, who blithely ignored rigid social demarcations and, with apparent ease, vaulted, like many another able Irishman, over the class barriers.

Trollope, with his familiarity with the management of mailbags, his knowledge of the Post Office network and its well-informed personnel, appears to pinpoint O'Connor Power's birthplace in *The Landleaguers*. The meet for the hunt is outside Ballinasloe in Ballytowngal (Ballygill, Bellagill) and close to Ahaseragh (Ahascragh), a neighbouring townland. Mr Persse, the Powers' landlord, makes an appearance in the narrative. Persse was the father-in-law of Sir William Gregory, Trollope's lifelong friend.[316] The topography is remarkably familiar.

The boycotted Bodkins (the slim daggers, the pikes) are resident in Ballytowngal. Bodkin was a west of Ireland surname. Trollope chooses names with deliberation and knew his bodkins. He paraphrases *Hamlet* in *Phineas Redux*, 'Doubtless there is a way of riddance. There is the bare bodkin.'[317]

Trollope had a real affection for Ireland and disliked civil servants who ruled through informers, using the techniques of entrapment. He prided himself on his ability to read a letter and analyse it. Was he privy to the contents of the mailbags? Did he know when certain letters were delayed and copied by Dublin Castle and the Home Office? Trollope was, and remains, popular bedtime reading for British mandarins.

Arthur Conan Doyle was a physician, a newspaperman and a successful author. His mother was Irish and his father was of Irish descent. A Catholic, he was educated by the Jesuits at Stonyhurst College in Lancashire. Sherlock Holmes, his fictional detective, became so popular with the public that his creator felt his life was no longer his own. In desperation, he decided to write a short story, *The Final Problem*, in which Holmes would meet his nemesis, the arch-criminal, Professor Moriarty.

The ascetic looking Moriarty was (like Lord Harry) a man of clerical mien, 'He'd have made a grand meenister.'[318] He assumes the name and opposing qualities of the Bishop of Kerry, who had cursed the Fenians, promising them eternal damnation. The fictional professor is the head of a secret, subversive organisation, and at the centre of a worldwide conspiracy. A man 'of mathematical celebrity', he had taught at a small provincial college, before moving to London to work as an army coach. He is a man of mystery and his name and his very existence is known only to Sherlock Holmes and very few others. Holmes tells his friend and confidant Dr Watson that he has been tracking the 'Napoleon of Crime', 'my intellectual equal', for some time. He finally catches up with Moriarty at the Reichenbach Falls, and, locked in mortal combat, they famously plunge to their deaths.

The Final Problem was published in 1893, the year the second Home Rule Bill dominated the Empire's political agenda. Holmes's death was to be the final solution to his author's problem. Ironically, Holmes, due to overwhelming pressure from his admiring public, was found alive in a subsequent story.

Professor Moriarty appears in several other narratives, the timelines of which predate *The Final Problem*. *The Valley of Fear* was published in serial form in the *Strand* magazine in September 1914, the month Home Rule, the Government of Ireland Act, was placed on the Statute Book.

A cryptic Doyle, companion of the Cheese, juggles his ingredients, and there may be a sprinkling of O'Connor Power in his stories with a strong Irish flavour, 'Everything comes in circles – even Professor Moriarty.' Fenians organised in circles, and Moriarty's chief of staff is the Irish Colonel Sebastian Moran, 'the second most dangerous man in London'. Moran was educated at Oxford and Eton and his military rank is also the designation for a Head Centre. There are connections to a Philadelphia manufacturer of shotguns and the brotherhood of the 'Eminent Order of Freemen' in Chicago. The secret society is a 'hidden menace'.

In *The Valley of Fear*, Brother John McMurdo of Chicago's Lodge 29, takes a train journey in early February 1875. He is a familiar figure, about the right age, colouring and build, and personifies the compelling duality of a Holmes/Moriarty creation, genius capable of exerting influence for good or evil:

> It is with this man that we are concerned. Take a good luck at him, for he is worth it. He is a fresh-complexioned, middle-sized young man, not far, one would guess from his thirtieth year. He has large, shrewd, humorous grey eyes which twinkle inquiringly from time to times as he looks round through his

spectacles at the people about him. It is easy to see that he is of a sociable and possibly simple disposition, anxious to be friendly to all. Anyone could pick him at once as gregarious in his habits and communicative in his nature, with a quick wit and ready smile. And yet the man who studied him more closely might discern a certain firmness of jaw and grim tightness about the lips which would warn him that there were depths beyond, and that this pleasant, brown-haired young Irishman might conceivably leave his mark for good or evil upon any society to which he was introduced.[319]

O'Connor Power's article contrasting Gladstone and Disraeli reveals his own gifts, not unlike those of Sherlock Holmes, for reading body language and assessing character and intent:

What first struck me about Gladstone's manner was that there was nothing in it which you could stereotype. It was always graceful, but so free and unconstrained, so energetic and variable that you soon forgot all about it in your overpowering interest in the man … In observing Gladstone's style one hardly ever thought of art at all, for his art disappeared in the intense earnestness of his whole manner, and was always subordinate to the object he had in view.

In Disraeli you admired the artist, in Gladstone the man, though it must be added, Gladstone was not without art, and Disraeli, besides being an artist, was also a man of genius.

Disraeli was calm and cool at all times, and his mind seemed to be quite at ease. Such men, I am convinced, are without approaching foppery, more attentive to dress and personal appearance and manner than those of a warmer nature. They are able to disengage themselves from the serious business of life without much effort and have time to consider its artistic requirements. The only drawback to the effect they are able to produce is that is lacks spontaneity; it is eminently proper, faultlessly conventional, but it does not excite enthusiasm.[320]

In *The Making of an Orator*, O'Connor Power outlines, in the chapter on 'Logic and Debate', the criminal lawyer's examination of circumstantial evidence, and hypotheses, in Holmes-like fashion, on a prisoner's guilt or innocence:

He shows in the first place that, although the prisoner's boots agree with the footmarks in size and shape, there is one peculiar impression missing: those footmarks which they must have received if they had been made by the boots of the prisoner. Both boots have on the outside heel a half-tip, which stands well above the heel sole, the impression of which would be plainly visible if the footmarks really belonged to the prisoner. The footmarks are without this impression, and are perfectly smooth and level.

Comparisons can be odious, portrayals may distort, but parallels in fiction reflect the ambivalence with which he continued to be assessed. Perhaps no longer a 'patriot' in the physical-force mould, he was still observed with some perplexity.

Punch refers to 'Pat-riotism'. In its 'Help for Hibernia', 'More (O'Connor) Power to your elbow',[321] sits awkwardly beside the Head of the Secret Service, Sir Robert Anderson's papers in which O'Connor Power is described as 'having been the associate of a Fenian group in England which at one point plotted to kidnap the Prince of Wales'.[322] He remained an unknown quantity, elusive, yet highly visible, ubiquitous, indefatigable.

O'Connor Power invites F.C. Burnand, editor of *Punch*, to meet 'G.S.'. Burnand replies 3 May (no year) that he will be '75 miles away' and humorously scribbles 'Suspects out! What a muddle!' across the top of the page. As a postscript: '* This is an "inter"'.[323]

Burnand, a barrister, humorist and writer of burlesques, lived much of his life with his large family in Ramsgate. A convert, he compiled and published the *Catholics in England Who's Who* in 1908. He was a friend to Ireland and was responsible for the toning down of the Caliban cartoon simian images of Irishmen in *Punch*, 'not one of his myriad of arrows of wit was ever yet poisoned'.

The National Library of Ireland has O'Connor Power's reply to Lady Wilde, who had requested a copy of his 'lecture on Moore', a talk given in February 1885.[324] Lady Wilde's letter 'containing allusions to current events' is answered but he can not oblige as the talk was 'extempore' and he has no copy.

Among Michael MacDonagh's papers, there is a letter inviting O'Connor Power to dine with Lady Gregory, author and patron of the arts. His friendship with the Gregorys spanned several decades. Lady Gregory, in her autobiography, *Our Irish Theatre*, writes that an Irish audience had been 'trained to listen by its long acquaintance with great oratory … Ireland is the home of ancient idealism'.[325]

He inspires a few lines in James Joyce's *Finnegans Wake*. 'O'Colonel Power' evokes the militarist aspect of his career. The 'scaurs' are noted as is the 'groot big bailey bill'. Joyce connects the O'Colonel Power to the O'Conor Don (O'Connor Dan) a direct descendant of the Kings of Connaught and Catholic MP for County

Roscommon. Power was so 'promonitory' that he was oblivious of 'the headth of the hosth that rose before him'.

Finnegans Wake was written long after O'Connor Power's death, but his legend lived on. Doran's public house in Molesworth Street, his Dublin *pied à terre*, finds a niche in *Ulysses*.

Irish scholar and novelist Eilís Dillon slips him several times into her powerful Fenian saga, *Across the Bitter Sea* (1973). At Irishtown, 'Mr O'Connor-Power said that public opinion must be organized, and that there's nothing tyrants dread so much as exposure. He said evictions must be stopped and no more emigration must be allowed unless the people want to go.'

Sir Leslie Ward was a renowned portrait painter and caricaturist, and his work was regularly published by *Vanity Fair* under the *nom de crayon* 'Spy'. Pictures speak louder than words, and Ward was famous for capturing the personality of his subjects. His portraits chronicle his times. In his 'The Men of the Day' series for the magazine, he included a picture of O'Connor Power, which appeared as a chromolithograph in December 1886.[326] The latter had just published a well-publicised collection of his articles on Home Rule for the *Manchester Guardian*.

In *Vanity Fair*, the cartoon is captioned, 'the brains of Obstruction', and notes he 'furnished the brains of obstruction during the struggles with decency and the Speaker'. In the original watercolour in London's National Portrait Gallery Archive, he steps out against a bright blue background with light-brown border. He is wearing the formal dress of a lawyer: a black frock coat, white wing collar, striped trousers and top hat. One foot forward, hand on hip, he stands engaged, supremely confident. He has an infectious, wide smile, a well-shaped beard, and sparkling, merry eyes. Here is a man who has enormous energy, enthusiasm, a delight in life. The nose, slightly curved, is hawkish. The pitted skin is not evident, but the fine, white teeth, the thick black hair, and the trim, slim figure, breathe purpose, determination, vitality and health. It is inviting to superimpose Michael MacDonagh's portrait:

> In 1884, as in 1874, a distinguished Nationalist member rose in the Irish quarter, below the gangway on the Opposition side – a big loosely jointed man, with a swarthy, pockmarked face a slightly curved nose, firm mouth, and determined jaw, and a moustache and side-whiskers. He suggested not only massive physical strength but intellectuality also – a man of strongly held opinions, and, in disposition, resolute and combative. As he spoke the impressiveness of his deep voice, with its modulated cadences, enamoured the ear of the crowded House, and his words so eloquently argumentative swayed its mind. This was O'Connor Power, member for Mayo.[327]

O'Connor Power resigned from the Irish party on matters of principle and disagreements on strategy. His enemies imagined his decline, but Ward depicts a man, who, with one spring, was free and bounding onward.

Part Four

The Irish in England

The truth is they are in England, not of it.

They are the most active workers in the national cause and have taken part in every national struggle since the days of O'Connell.[328]

In 1880, the Irish in England voted decisively for the Liberal party. Resigning on the steps of 10 Downing Street, Disraeli placed the blame for his defeat squarely on Ireland.

O'Connor Power topped the poll in Mayo and was a serious contender for the leadership of the Irish party, but his individualistic style and his impatience with all those less single-minded did not suit many of his parliamentary colleagues.

In the *Fortnightly Review* he set out his thoughts in a landmark article, 'The Irish in England'. For centuries, the English, believing the Irish to be a naturally inferior race, instigated policies to exterminate an 'ungovernable and troublesome people':

And this supposed natural inferiority of the Irishman, as a political theory, did important State service in its day. It was used to excuse, if not to justify, the most barbarous acts ever perpetrated by one man against another, or by one nation against another ... Lord Deputy Mountjoy reported to Queen Elizabeth that she had nothing to reign over in Ireland but carcases and ashes, had Ireland passed through such horrors as those which surrounded her in the famine years, and spread desolation and death in the homes of her people

Today we would use the terms pogrom, genocide, ethnic cleansing. It was the apocalypse of the Famine years which drove over three million Irish from their homes. Many moved to England, the nearest perceived refuge. They settled in the manufacturing towns of Manchester, Liverpool and Birmingham and in the mining districts of Yorkshire and Northumberland. Rural by birth and tradition, they found themselves in alien, industrial landscapes, with only their 'pluck, energy and endurance' to fall back on.

On arrival, they met with hostility, with strong anti-Irish and anti-Catholic prejudices. They persevered, and by the 1880s, the Irish-born in England numbered over two million. Defiantly, they retained their separateness and their religious fidelity:

> But to a highly imaginative, emotional and sentimental people like the Irish, it [religion] appeals with double force. In the penal days, when the Irish were hunted outlaws in their own land, they found in their persecuted religion the only solace of their affliction; and when their churches were destroyed or converted to profane uses, they were content to worship at its altars under the canopy of heaven, in many a hidden valley and lonely glen. That religion still appeals to the exiled Irishman with all the power of these historical recollections and associations.

Some of the Catholic cloth regarded the Famine as, perhaps, an act of providence. The Celts, driven from their land, scattered the seeds of faith across the world, bringing 'strange peoples into the one true fold'. Wherever they settled, they built churches, schools, convents and colleges, nurturing a great pride in the sacraments, the rituals, the unity and universality of their religion. Their places of worship were thronged, and communal practice was rigorous, heartfelt and constant. An Irishman cherished his faith 'as an unpurchasable inheritance, throughout every vicissitude of fortune'; his distinguishing trait was his 'devotion to faith and freedom'.

In a country where prejudice was longstanding and robust, the Church was a potent protector. Its power was centralised, ultramontane, but, with an unbroken history and a common language (Latin), it was transnational. A worldwide community fostered the Celtic migrants, validating Irish identity and values. The most senior churchman on the islands, Cardinal Manning, was a familiar figure in the corridors of Westminster. He was a man with all the right connections and championed their interests and advised British governments for over two decades on the Irish Question.

The spiritual life of England was reinvigorated by the Oxford Movement, which sought to restore the apostolic link. Many notable Church of England clerics seceded to Rome; a resurgent authority of English Catholicism was strengthened by the acquisition to its ranks of John Henry Newman, Henry Edward Manning and Gerard Manley Hopkins. It was a period in English history when the Catholic Church attracted men of great stature, intellectual giants. Eminent converts, faithful 'Old Catholics', and a ground swell of Irish immigrant stock constituted a significant force. The work on the ground of such men as Canon Johnson in Lancashire and another convert, Fr Lockhart, in London, rebuilt strongholds of the faith. Northumberland had a large indigenous Catholic population, and the Irish flourished there in a familiar clime. York, native city of the Catholic conspirator Guy Fawkes, never burns the traditional 'Guy' on its 5 November bonfires. English Catholics do not choose to 'remember'.

Canon Murnane of Camberwell was active in the Total Abstinence League of the Cross, which led the fight against drunkenness. O'Connor Power described the work done by the League, with over 20,000 members in London and branches throughout the Empire. Abstinence from alcohol was, as always, a thorny issue – the national Achilles heel. Sunday Closing was hotly debated. In 1877 he told parliament: 'In the proportion in which the people were addicted to this vice, the arm of popular freedom was paralysed; and if they were to have a free Irish people they must have a sober Irish people – and if they could not have them sober by suasion, he was prepared to remove the drink from them.'[329] Throughout his career he gave public support to temperance, but he wrote of lifting a goblet to toast St Patrick's Day revellers in St Louis, and the claret bowl was a ritual of The Johnson Club suppers. In Manchester on St Patrick's Day 1880, he gave an 'amusing address on Temperance'.

In 'Fallacies about Home Rule', he indicated there were no Catholic Members from English constituencies at Westminster, 'We see the Catholics of Great Britain, numbering about two millions, without a single representative in the Legislature, although within their ranks are to be found men of the highest social rank and the most distinguished ability.'[330]

Until Catholic Emancipation, no Catholic could be a member of parliament. This meant that Ireland, where four-fifths of the population was Catholic, was not proportionately represented. In 1828, Daniel O'Connell was elected in the historic Clare election but could not take his seat until the subsequent passing of the Catholic Emancipation Act. He was re-elected on 4 February 1830.

Irish Catholic MPs were the Catholic party in British politics, allied with Church interests and paying due respect to the head of the hierarchy, the Cardinal, Archbishop of Westminster.

In the spring of 1875, O'Connor Power was in Rome 'for health reasons' and had an audience with Pius IX.[331] The forceful and influential Manning was also in Rome, and was made a Cardinal on 15 March. In England, fears of Rome Rule surfaced.

At Westminster, Mr Whalley, MP, claimed that Manning's mission was 'to bend and break the Imperial power into submission to the Papacy'. O'Connor Power championed the Cardinal: the Church's mission, he said, was strictly spiritual, its purpose 'to bend to the reception of the true faith the will of the English race'.[332]

The Vatican's intentions remained suspect, Disraeli's character, Monsignore Berwick, illuminates: 'We must all pray, as I pray, every morn and every night, said the Cardinal, for the conversion of England.' – 'Or the conquest,' murmured [Monsignore] Berwick.'[333]

In 1879, with a new Pope in the Vatican, John Henry Newman was elevated to Cardinal. On his appointment, he accepted an address from Irish Catholic MPs, and in his reply told them, 'You are representatives of an ancient and faithful Catholic people.' He recalled the years he had spent in Ireland.

Sir George Bowyer, a convert, was the foremost Catholic MP until his death in 1883. Henry Mathews served as Home Secretary (1887-91) in a Tory government, the first Catholic Cabinet Minister for two centuries, and was remembered for his work for the Westminster Cathedral project. In 1868, Mathews claimed the Fenians were 'misrepresented', but, twenty years later, his hard-line approach made him a hated figure among the Irish.[334]

The clan system of the Gael, with a strong attachment to friends and kindred, survived expatriation:

> The Irish poor are distinguished for their charity and benevolence one to another. They consider it unlucky, and sometimes a sin, to send a poor man away empty from the door when he has asked something for the love of God. They lend each other money and clothes in their necessities, and when some of them fall out of work and have no means, those still employed and earning give freely of what they have to tide their friends over want and misfortune. They live sparingly in order to save money for the purpose of sending assistance to their friends … I have known many instances of equal love and devotion towards kinsfolk in their old land on the part of the Irish in England. The truth is they are in England, not of it.

He wrote of the nostalgia pervading an Irish household:

> If you step into an Irish dwelling, just after the evening meal, you will probably find, if there be nothing in your presence to repel confidence, that the conversation will turn mainly on recollections of the old land, suggested in the simplest way, perhaps by some snatch of an Irish air hummed at the cradle, or by the last

letter home, or by some scrap of local news contained in the Irish penny newspaper which the eldest boy has been reading aloud.

Of the Irishman in England, where a wider franchise prevailed:

[He] finds himself possessed of a political power which he was never permitted to exercise in his own country, and his first thought on becoming conscious of this fact is that it is his duty to utilise this new power for the advancement of Irish rights and Irish interests.

And British misrule:

To suppress the national aspirations of the Irish has been the steady and uniform purpose of succeeding generations of soldiers and statesmen; and in the endeavour to accomplish this task their uninventive minds have never risen above the vulgar expedient of repression. Hence, wholesale extermination, social effacement, commercial and industrial extinction, religious persecution, and educational subjugation have been the distinguishing features of English rule in Ireland.

He believed the 'battle for Irish rights must be fought in England'. The National Clubs and Home Rule Associations formed a persuasive political grouping, and the last annual conference in the Crystal Palace was a show of Irish power, working at maximum efficiency.

The Irish in England have really nothing to gain for themselves by the establishment of Home Rule, or Tenant-Right, or Denominational Education in Ireland … They are the most active workers in the national cause and have taken part in every national struggle since the days of O'Connell … The [Fenian] spirit which animated them in those trying times, when all that was chivalrous, brave and unselfish in the national ranks seemed determined to sacrifice itself in one desperate struggle for liberty, has survived among the Irish in England down to the present day, and although it works now in the more peaceful courses of constitutional action it is not the less earnest, determined, courageous, and self-sacrificing.

Misunderstanding between the two very different races had a long history:

But the Irish differ from the English, not only in race and religion, but in national character, in feeling, in temperament, in modes of thought, in habits and prejudices; and there is, besides, a long-standing national quarrel between them which is yet far from settlement. Taking all these considerations into account, it may be affirmed, with perfect accuracy, that, for all purpose of social unity, the Irish and English people are as alien to each other as they were three hundred years ago.

The Irish are in the mines of Durham and Northumberland, in the factories of Lancashire and Yorkshire, in the farms of Essex and Sussex and Kent, in the market-gardens near London, in the docks of the large seaports, and wherever the strong arm, combined with quick intelligence, can obtain an honest livelihood.

Many Irishmen have, he admitted, done well in England and are well represented in the professions and the intellectual life of the country. He did not favour emigration. The happiness of a people was not to be estimated by worldly wealth alone and was dependent on other considerations. Ireland was capable of supporting double its population. It was 'nothing less than national suicide' that Ireland had not developed her resources. If she were allowed to do so, her people would be happier and better off at home, in the old country.

In a lecture in Dublin he enlarged on the clan system, a double-edged heritage:

…I have pondered many a night and day over the pages of Irish history, and I find that, except at intervals which have been far too rare, we have been a divided people. It was the multiplicity of our clans and petty kings which invited the incursions of the Danes, and which facilitated the work of conquest by the Anglo-Normans, and the same spirit since then has often been the fruitful source of our national weakness and our national misfortune.[335]

A Party Divided

… in Parliament but not of it.

There was a malaise within the parliamentary party. Parnell was rarely at Westminster and seemed distracted. He was absent for crucial meetings in Paris and the House of Commons.[336] Irish members, with little direction or occupation, were negligent in attendance. The party appeared to be in freefall. Its members were unpaid and usually financially strapped. The long journeys from distant counties of Ireland and the cost of London accommodation were prohibitive. Late-night sittings in the House and a hostile environment, added to the strain.

MPs were dependent on outside sources for a livelihood. If they were in a profession or in business, they lost income by long absences in London. The financial costs for a serving member discouraged many good candidates.

O'Connor Power survived on income from legal work, lecturing, newspaper articles and the kindness of fellow travellers. Apart from periods in London when the House was in session, he never seems to have spent more than a night in the same town. His legendary charm ensured a bed and a good dinner and, moving on, he did not outstay his welcome.

Others were not so lucky, nor so energetic. Frequently bachelors, leading irregular, disrupted lives, they spent a great deal of time at Westminster, 'the best club' in London. Impecunious MPs might socialise or slumber in the library and smoking rooms, and the dining room was the best value in the city. Westminster was a gentleman's club. Now the irrepressible Irish invaded the Chamber and, worse, took possession of the comfortable facilities.

Precarious finances made many vulnerable and open to brokerage politics. Party activists and constituents, who sent a representative to parliament, looked for rewards, sinecures and civil service positions. A member had to watch his base and keep his workers and his voters happy. One of the gifts of office was the power of patronage, and a reward system, 'pork barrel' politics, strengthened the constituency seat and the party. It was an opportunity to promote Catholics and Irishmen, giving them access to decision makers, to careers in the home civil service and the colonial administration. Gradually the playing field would be levelled. It was affirmative action.

On the other hand, kleptocratic politics encouraged intrigue. Soliciting favours and jobbery weakened the party and left it open to ridicule.

A generation earlier, Charles Gavan Duffy entered parliament at the same time as his great friend, George Henry Moore. Together with the member for Meath, Mr Lucas, an English Quaker, they formed the Irish Tenant League to protect small farmers threatened by 'great clearances', the post Famine whole scale evictions of 1849-53. The League was made up of Catholics and Protestants from all over Ireland, and its programme introduced the Three Fs (fair rent, fixity of tenure and free sale). The Independent Irish Party represented 'independent opposition' and its MPs took a pledge to oppose all governments and to refuse preferment until their policies were in place. Many were from the wealthier classes, either professional or landowning, and cushioned from the harsher facts of life.

When John Sadleir and William Keogh joined forces with Gavan Duffy and Moore, they pledged not to take government office. Notoriously, Sadleir accepted the post of Lord of the Treasury, and Keogh, the office of Solicitor-General. Keogh later became Attorney-General. Shunned by former colleagues, they both met sorry ends. Sadleir committed suicide and Keogh, some years later, pursued by allegations of mental instability, was reported to have also taken his own life. The names Sadleir and Keogh became synonymous with disloyalty and treachery. These men, 'self-seeking and discreditable', had broken the pledge for personal advancement and were remembered as turncoats, their sad, lonely deaths a warning to all placehunters in Irish parliamentary circles. Thereafter, canvassing for office breached a long-standing principle of Irish nationalism and earned everlasting opprobrium.

However, appointments to the Civil Service were not by examination but on recommendation. Applications were routinely made to a minister, who might take up references in government circles. A Victorian politician spent a great deal of time dispensing patronage, yet many senior politicians made much of Irish members' scramble for positions. Lord Harcourt wrote to Gladstone, '[They will] go for the money, for which they care a great deal more than they do either for Home Rule or the English alliance.'[337]

As Home Secretary, Harcourt was well briefed and familiar with methods of entrapment and the duplicity of *agents provocateurs*. In April 1883, he complained of his workload to Gladstone, 'Fenianism being so rampant and police-work being so heavy.'[338] Lord Richard Grosvenor wrote to Gladstone that 'every Irishman, without a single exception, always jobs'. They were 'completely immersed in the business of securing patronage'.[339] It was impossible to expend all one's energy seeking patronage and preserve integrity. Accepting preferment put one under obligation, a *geasa*.

O'Connor Power endeavoured to stop the rot. In the National Library of Ireland, among the MacDonagh papers, there is a copy of his reply to Lord Richard Grosvenor, Parliamentary Secretary at the Treasury. Grosvenor, an opponent of Home Rule, had written to ask him to name a fit person for appointment as keeper of the post office at Pullathomas in North Mayo. He replied:

Copy

March 4 '82

My Lord,

I am in receipt of your lordship's letter of the 3rd instant, in which you ask me to name a fit person for appointment as Keeper of the Post-Office at Pullathomas.

I have no desire to recommend anyone for that or any other Govt. appointment, but I am much obliged for your Lordship's courtesy in writing to me, as

you have done on the subject, and I hail your letter, I trust not prematurely as
a sign that in appointments to public office in Ireland the Government intend
henceforth to pay due regard to the wishes and feelings of the Irish people.

I remain, My Lord,
Your obedient Servant
J. O'Connor Power

Lord Richard Grosvenor MP
The Treasury
S.W.

Why did he make and retain the copy? Was Grosvenor's invitation to name a suitable candidate a trap?[340] If he had made a recommendation, it would have been
bruited abroad as cronyism.

The party's resentment at his independent stance led to accusations of jobbing
and place-hunting, the pursuit of office. With scant regard for truth, it was an
attempt to deflect internal party scandal:

T.M. Healy MP presided at the fortnightly meeting of the Irish National League
on December 5. The Secretary announced that £1,000 had been received from
America since the last meeting. Biggar referred to J. O'Connor Power MP for
Mayo as the James Carey of Irish politics, and added that no Irishman had choice
of a Government situation who had not first become a traitor to the interests of
Ireland.[341]

In *United Ireland*, O'Connor Power took issue:

Unlike [the party's] leader and paymaster I have not assisted a Cabinet Minister in
filling up government situations, and the blandishments of some paid official of
the Land League could not persuade me to become a place-hunter in the interests of friends. The hypocrisy of some of these people is positively stupendous.
They ask you to approach the government in private to obtain favours for their
friends, and then they denounce you in public for not opposing the very same
government, right or wrong.[342]

In October 1880 the Government, alleging conspiracy to prevent payment of rent
removed Parnell and members of his party from the public scene. Confined in pri-

vate quarters in Kilmainham, as guests of Her Majesty, they would live comfortably apart from other prisoners.

Almost a thousand suspects were held without trial in the prison, but the administration's strong-arm tactics and its rigorous implementation of the Protection of Persons and Property Act only led to further atrocities. 'Captain Moonlight', a reign of terror, was unleashed, and marauders with blackened faces, ran riot across the countryside.

William O'Brien drew up a No Rent Manifesto but the intended impact of a rent strike was weakened by clerical condemnation. Michael Davitt, whose name had been appended to the manifesto, was in Portland Jail and denounced the proposed withholding of rent, believing it would exacerbate an already dangerous situation.

Six months later, Captain O'Shea, an Irish Catholic and husband of Katherine O'Shea, Parnell's mistress, acted as intermediary and successfully negotiated the release of the privileged detainees, in what came to be known as the Kilmainham Treaty, or sometimes, cynically, by its opponents, as the 'Kilmainham Transaction'. Gladstone, to the end of his life, denied there had ever been a 'treaty'.

Parnell allowed the O'Sheas to speak for him and arrange his life. The *ménage à trois*, a kitchen cabinet, was an open secret.[343] With no particular coterie in the Irish party, Parnell often acted on apparent whims and without consultation. He rarely dined out and had few friends. Some have suggested he was shy, others that he was a depressive.

Over a number of years, Captain O'Shea exploited his wife's intimacy with Parnell to further his own political ambitions, and the treaty, which saved Parnell's parliamentary career, accommodated several of his leading supporters with government jobs.

The backlog of unpaid rents was dealt with, and the details of the Arrears Act, amending the 1881 Land Act, were agreed. A letter from Parnell gave an undertaking that 'he and his party would cooperate cordially for the future with the Liberal party in forwarding Liberal principles'.[344] Davitt thought Parnell had taken a wrong turning and, horrified by the conditions of the release, concluded that Parnell 'was only the instrument in her [Katherine O'Shea] hands'.

Gladstone's approach was 'Conciliation to replace Coercion'. In February, he had asked the Irish party to produce a plan for self-government. O'Connor Power noted that the 'open invitation was without precedent in parliamentary history'.[345] The Chief Secretary, Forster, disagreed and resigned. A new Lord Lieutenant and Chief Secretary, Lord Spencer and Lord Cavendish, were despatched to show evidence of goodwill, their appointments to signal a new approach. The Arrears Bill was to be passed in August, and Parnell was to support the Liberals in the House.

But the best laid plans may come to grief, and four days after Parnell's release, and on the same day as Davitt's, the new Chief Secretary for Ireland, Frederick Cavendish and Under Secretary, Thomas Burke, were assassinated in Phoenix Park. Cavendish had arrived in Ireland that very day. Parnell's sister Anna believed that in any other country the much-hated Burke would have been murdered many years earlier. The popular Cavendish had served as Gladstone's private secretary and was married to his wife's niece. He was 'sacrificed to the accident of his being in Burke's company'.

The Dublin-based breakaway group the Invincibles appeared to have acted alone but the public was horrified, and the goodwill enjoyed by Parnell dissipated, despite the insistence that 'crime and outrage is foreign to our organisation'. He was forced to reassess his position. After the humiliation of imprisonment and his concessions to the government, his confidence failed and he never regained his energy. Captain O'Shea, a keen eye on high office, made an unsuccessful bid for the vacant Under Secretary post, but Katherine's efforts to secure Burke's job for her husband were dismissed out of hand.

Davitt, released after fifteen months in Portland, wrote to the *Standard* condemning the crime and all forms of violence. The Fenian dream was one 'of the enfranchisement and fraternisation of peoples'.[346]

Gladstone had no choice but to introduce further repressive legislation and, to show seriousness of intent, the House sat on Derby Day for the first time in forty years. In the following months the number of agrarian murders had doubled. Public figures feared for their lives. The Viceroy only ventured forth with a heavy military escort.

In debt long before he entered politics, Parnell was in serious financial difficulties. The mortgage owed on his house was said to be in the region of £11,000, and in 1883 the Irish people were asked to bail him out. Opposing the 'Parnell Tribute', Archbishop Croke of Cashel called for an audit of national funds. Despite this intervention, £37,000, mainly made up of subscriptions from tenant farmers, was raised and Avondale, the family estate, was saved from the auctioneer's hammer. The Wicklow landlord had a strong sense of *droit de seigneur*, and the residue went to subsidise an aristocratic lifestyle in Eltham, the fashionable home in the south of England. Unimpressed, County Mayo, the cradle of the Land War, contributed a mere £174 4s 6d.

In mid-December 1883, Parnell accepted the substantial cheque and pocketed it, without a word of thanks. Many were aghast, 'The Quaker nationalist, Alfred Webb, complained of Parnell's "autocratic management of "funds"," a style which provoked Webb's resignation from the position of League treasurer.'[347] Randolph Churchill claimed Parnell was 'levying taxes on the Irish people'. In 1888, the acceptance of a large cheque from Empire builder Cecil Rhodes would draw ire.

Healy and Biggar were painfully aware of Parnell's long-standing relationship with the O'Sheas. Parnell campaigned in 1885 for O'Shea, the complaisant husband, when he stood as a Liberal in Liverpool. Perversely, he issued a statement composed by T.P. O'Connor to Irish voters in England asking them to vote for the Tories, the party of property. O'Shea failed to win a seat.

T.P. O'Connor won two seats, one in a Liverpool constituency and another in Galway. Choosing to sit in Liverpool, he opened the way for a by-election. The following February, Parnell selected O'Shea as the Irish party's candidate in Galway. For his lieutenants, Healy and Biggar, it was a step too far and they were incensed to 'the point of insubordination': O'Shea was not a party member and refused to take the party pledge.[348]

Biggar composed a telegram to Parnell, which initially read 'Mrs O'Shea will be your ruin.' Healy persuaded him to rephrase it, 'The O'Sheas will be your ruin.' With a cowed T.P. in tow, Parnell, arrived in Galway, determined to brook no opposition. An ignominious Healy was swiftly brought to heel. The truculent Biggar resisted to the bitter end.

Parnell, imperious, threatened a collapse of the party and all hope of Home Rule, 'I have a Parliament for Ireland within the hollow of my hand. Destroy me and you take away that Parliament.'

William O'Brien rowed in behind him, effectively saving the day. O'Shea was elected, and, in June 1886, he abstained on the second reading of the Home Rule Bill and resigned his seat. Davitt writes in *The Fall of Feudalism* of Parnell's 'dictatorship'. He believed that the Galway election brought 'home to even the intolerant lieutenants what their advocacy of Mr Parnell's pontifical power was leading to'.[349] In touch with Irish landowners, Parnell wanted a home government led by reformed landlords and a 'rehabilitated gentry'. He, himself, would be First Minister in the College Green parliament.

Parnell had prevailed, but it was a pyrrhic victory, sowing the seeds of a bitter resentment leading to his dramatic downfall. In a very few years, he would be hunted down by his erstwhile henchmen. The Galway election was Parnell's last public appearance in Ireland until he spoke at the Rotundo almost five years later; his leadership was under threat and, summoning what little strength remained, he made a last-ditch effort to save his political career. In the last ten years of his life he visited his Avondale estate infrequently and for shorter periods. He had made his home in Eltham. Mrs O'Shea never visited Ireland.

Parnell was believed to be anxious for his personal safety and appeared quieter, more malleable:

Some debilitating influence fell upon Parnell after his release from Kilmainham Jail in 1882. He was a changed man. He withdrew himself from the conspicuous position which he filled in public life. This tendency became more marked after the adoption of Home Rule by the Liberals. He rarely spoke in Parliament, and not at all in Ireland, but when he did speak he was all for moderation and conciliation. His long disappearances had the result of enveloping him still more in a veil of mystery. In those years hardly one of his colleagues can be said to have been intimate with him; and he, on his part, did not know, even by sight, several of his new members returned to fight under his standard at the General Election of 1886.[350]

Among the T.D. Sullivan papers in the NLI are letters from Gavan Duffy in Nice, in which he complained of the Irish party's behaviour. Members are 'tippling in its bars or yawning in the House of Commons'[351] and have lost the confidence of their backers, 'All supporters here have fallen away from a party or people engaged in such bootless brawls.'[352] And later to John O'Leary in 1886, 'I am glad you saw those representative Englishmen. We cannot do without them and they ought to know that there are other Irishmen than those who go to bawl at Westminster.'[353]

In early 1884, Irish MPs were required to sign a pledge, authored by Healy,[354] which effectively denied individual action, 'a pledge to sit, act and vote with the Irish party and to resign one's seat if it should become impossible to carry out such an undertaking'.

They were the only parliamentarians to be given a salary, thus ensuring loyalty. The 'patriot's pay' came from a central fund. Again, Archbishop Croke and Davitt opposed the move, believing MPs should be financed by their constituencies. Both objected to Parnell nominating his own candidates and proposed they should be selected locally. Davitt wished to run radicals and former prisoners.

The backdrop to the Westminster malaise was a bombing campaign financed by Irish America's skirmishing fund. Alexander Sullivan was one of the Triangle, the triumvirate which dominated Clan na Gael, and directed the dynamite war from his base in the United States. Dynamitards planned to reduce London to rubble. A dynamitard, a term coined at the time, was 'a cloaked figure carrying a concealed bomb with clockwork fuse'. Webster's Dictionary definition is 'One that uses dynamite for anarchic or other political acts.' Robert Louis Stevenson objected strongly to the neologism.[355] Dynamite was the new weapon of destruction for dissidents, and in 1881 Tsar Alexander was killed by a bomb in St Petersburg. President Garfield was killed by an assassin's bullet the same year. Dynamite was manufactured in cities in northern England, and police seized the contents of one clandestine factory in Birmingham. Phosphorus had been Greek Fire, now dynamite was Fenian Fire.

Major institutions were targeted: Scotland Yard, the Tower of London, London Bridge and Westminster. Railways and tube stations were difficult to secure and were at greatest risk. Dynamitards took care not to harm the civilian population. Those regarded as legitimate targets, Ministers and senior officials, were protected with heavy security. Apart from three bomb makers who blew themselves up during an attempt on London Bridge, there were no fatalities. This did not go unnoted, and Sir Edward Hamilton, Gladstone's private secretary, recorded in his diary, 'Last night there was another dynamite explosion, this time at Victoria Station. It is remarkable that these explosions are made with an apparent regard to loss of life and likewise levelled at private property instead of Government buildings.' And two days later:

> There have been more attempts at explosions discovered. Dynamitic portmanteaus of evidently American origin have been found at Charing Cross and Paddington Stations. Fortunately the clockwork in both was defective. Otherwise, as the cloak rooms where the luggage had been deposited were under hotels, the destruction might have been horrible. It almost looks as if the fiends had intended their machinations to be false alarms.[356]

Attacks on the Empire were many pronged. The Secret Service, operating with a huge budget for anti-terrorism measures, developed its resources to keep abreast of the Fenian threat, 'Sir W.H. demands unlimited Secret Service money.'[357]

The Clan proposed that the Mahdists in Sudan be supplied with men and arms in their fight against the British. John Holland, an inventor from County Clare, had served in the American navy. Lavishly financed by the Skirmishing Fund, he developed a prototype of an underwater vessel, the *Fenian Ram*, which was to be ready for action in 1881. It would approach British ships by stealth and, at close quarters, blow them to smithereens. British intelligence operatives in America were well aware of the submarine and its purpose, and the *Fenian Ram*, now on display in a New Jersey museum, was never in service. English engineers later adapted Holland's designs.

In 1883, Patrick O'Donnell was sent for trial. He had shot the informer James Carey, whose evidence helped convict the Invincibles. Charles Russell defended him ably, but failed to convince the jury. Russell applied in vain for a reprieve. The execution went ahead on 17 December 1883, and a wave of retaliatory bombings followed, a display of Fenian disapproval.

The relationship between Irish parliamentarians and dynamitards was ambivalent. MPs were perceived to distance themselves only by their silence. Fearing reprisals on Irish communities and the reintroduction of coercion, Nationalists based in England and Scotland did not support the bombings. Campaigns of terror were counterproductive, alienating the middle classes in North America and the colonies. Davitt believed terrorism was a 'war against democracy'. Measures of reform were more effective:

> Surely seven millions of us residing in Ireland and Great Britain are not going to stand this, to see a movement ruined which has been sanctioned by the entire Celtic race, and the lives of our kindred in England jeopardised, because a small group of men are growing tired of the struggle for independence through reform, and are desirous of striking at England for revenge.[358]

The arrest of dynamitards in 1884-5 and the reintroduction of coercion was a crisis point for Nationalists. Gladstone, in a major conciliatory gesture, introduced a Reform Bill which would triple the Irish franchise. The Redistribution Bill, reshaping constituencies, would leave the number of Irish MPs unchanged, and protect the Protestant minority. Ireland was to be advantageously overrepresented. O'Connor Power commented:

> I trust it is not too much to hope that one of the earliest results of the New Reform will be such a thorough change in our legislative system as shall extend the blessings of self-government to every part of the United Kingdom, and free the Imperial Parliament, for ever, from the worry and embarrassment of local business ...[359]

Home Rule would seem to be a certainty as, after the imminent election, the Irish would hold the balance of power in the British parliament.

A Democratic Position

> I will not surrender my convictions to please any body of men living but I will continue to work for Ireland to the best of my ability while she has a single grievance to be redressed, or wrong to be remedied, or a right to be won.[360]

In February 1884, two months after Parnell had accepted the tribute cheque, the *Connaught Telegraph* attacked 'Mr Parnell and his party' for 'pocketing the people's money'. The plight of evicted tenants was neglected, and democratic Nationalists, who represented the interests of constituents, were marginalised.

The *Manchester Guardian* reported that, in a speech in his Mayo constituency, O'Connor Power declared that his opposition 'to the most selfish and mercenary movement' earned him the 'hatred of the clique'.[361] Attacks on him increased in frequency and intensity. He refuted the 'revilings of poisonous tongues', and a final public break with the party became inevitable when he was obliged to reply to accusations made outside the House, 'It seems to have been supposed that I had some private relations with the National Land League, which would enable me to give the House some information respecting that organisation which the House has not already in its possession.' He was not a member of the Land League, 'nor privy to its financial transactions'.

In the House of Commons he criticised Parnell's response to the Queen's speech:

> He practically joins with Her Majesty's Government in informing the country and all interested that there has been a substantial improvement in the condition of Ireland. Now, one would have thought that, having made an admission of the kind the hon. Member would have referred us to some facts or circumstance in the history of Ireland since we last met here that would justify the declaration, and that he would have addressed himself to the important subject involved in that declaration ...[362]

The Irish leader did not condemn sufficiently the policy of stimulating emigration, nor did he make mention of the importance of developing Irish resources and promoting indigenous industries.

He believed Mr Parnell was surrounded and urged on by men, who were hoping to arrive at a similar prominence. He described 'certain lieutenants' with Edmund Burke's words, '[they are] a species of men to whom a state of order would become a sentence of obscurity'.[363] These men prevented him from speaking at meetings of his Mayo constituents.

The Land League and Orange Society factional fights in Ulster during the autumn and winter months had been transferred to the floor of the House of Commons and had distracted from proposed legislation:

> It was said that the beginning of the trouble in Ulster was the Monaghan election but there was not one word in the address of the member for Monaghan [Timothy Healy] to the electors about Irish Nationalisation beginning to end. That was suppressed and in its place was substituted modern socialism, and on the strength of that and an imaginary composition called the Healy clause the votes of the Monaghan electors were obtained.

He hit home with his reference to the 'imaginary composition' in the Land Act called the 'Healy Clause', which had ensured Healy's election in Monaghan.[364] The well-aimed cut earned Healy's 'unfailing antipathy'. He believed Irish members were rendered ineffective, torn apart by factional disputes at the expense of beneficial legislation:

> He objected to the policy which they [the certain lieutenants] pursued in Ireland ever since the introduction of the Land Bill ... it had postponed beneficial legislation for Ireland ... it had subjected the country for the last three years to the most stringent and hateful form of coercion that had ever been imposed on any people.

He condemned sectarian intimidation:

> Is intimidation hateful, odious, disgraceful, or as one writer said, damnable in Ulster; and is it philanthropic, good, delightful, pious in every other province in Ireland? I have waited a long time for my vindication against the policy of intimidation, and it has come at last, and out of the mouths of those who were responsible for denouncing me two years ago, when I denounced intimidation as a brutal and immoral practice. Out of their mouths I read today that vindication of my conduct ... 'An Orangeman has no more right to rob me of freedom of speech than he has to steal my purse out of my pocket'. Good. And I say a Land Leaguer had no more right to rob me of freedom of speech than he has to steal the purse out of my pocket.

The party had been pursuing a policy 'adverse to the interests of Ireland since the Land Act was introduced':

> I believe that, of all England's difficulties, her greatest difficulty is the condition of Ireland ... I say that there are large and influential classes in various parts of Great Britain today, who are willing to make large concessions to Ireland upon that [self-government] and other subjects; but who declare that it is utterly impossible to hint the faintest possible concession, because of the exasperated feeling which has been created by these agitations.

In 1881 the Queen's speech had contained a paragraph intimating that a measure would be submitted in the House for the establishment of county government:

Notwithstanding all that has been done to embitter this struggle, I am convinced that many of us will live to see this strife brought to a close; and we will see it succeeded by a real and permanent union – a union such as Grattan and O'Connell contemplated who, yielding to none in the warmth of their Irish sympathies and in the intensity of their Irish nationalism, were still loyal to the union and integrity of the Empire. I believe that we shall have a union of equal laws and equal liberties, a union based on National right and Imperial integrity, a state of prosperity and tranquillity in Ireland, in which Irish industry that has built up flourishing cities across the waters of the Atlantic shall be fully occupied in the development of Irish resources, in which Irish intellect, that has been so successful in Colonial Governments and Parliaments, shall be devoted to the councils of the Irish nation, and in which Irish courage that has never wavered on any field in the darkest hour of defeat, or the brightest moment of victory, shall be the proud defence of free institutions at home, and the unassailable bulwark of social order without which no civilised community would be either happy or free.[365]

He quoted Thomas Davis's *Anglo-Saxon and Celt*:

What matter though at different times
Our Fathers won the sod.
What matter though at different shrines
We kneel before one God;
In fortune and in fame we're bound
By stronger links than steel
And neither can be sage and sound
But in the others weal.

He was listened to 'in that perfect stillness, which prevails in the House of Commons only on occasions when an orator of the front rank has arrested its attention'.[366] The onslaught caused a sensation, making headlines across the English-speaking world. Once again O'Connor Power was at the centre of a storm.

Timothy Healy, Parnell's former secretary, was the 'lieutenant', the 'disciple' who, in the absence of the leader, gave the party direction and was a recipient of Land League funds. *The Times* referred to 'Mr Healy's rhetorical shillelagh', and in his response, he wielded it with glib brutality. This 'Member for Mayo' speech has been frequently aired. In it, Healy alluded to the salient fact that Mayo supported its MP's position, 'and when did we ever stand between him and his constituents in those places'.

In Castlebar, O'Connor Power spoke at a constituency meeting and gave a detailed account of the new Irish Land Bill. He believed the Liberal programme 'would level every inequality to the dust'. He received a unanimous vote of confidence.[367] The following week he was warmly welcomed in Cork.[368]

Fourteen years later, his centennial tribute, 'Edmund Burke and his Abiding Influence', would be an occasion to explain and justify his decision:

> The passage is indelibly engraved upon my memory, and I confess that I have never ceased to feel the influence it exercised upon me when I first read it many years ago, at the time of my own election to Parliament. Burke said: 'It ought to be the happiness and glory of a representative to live in the strictest union, the closest correspondence, and the most unreserved communication with his constituents. Their wishes ought to have great weight with him, their opinions high respect, their business unremitted attention. It is his duty to sacrifice his repose, his pleasure, his satisfactions to theirs, and, above all, ever, and in all cases, to prefer their interest to his own. But his unbiased opinion, his mature judgement, his enlightened conscience he ought not to sacrifice to you, to any man, or to any set of men living.'[369]

In April, he formally left the IPP and the *Manchester Guardian* reported:

> Mr O'Connor Power yesterday formally dissevered himself from the party of Mr Parnell, taking up his seat at the Liberal side of the House of Commons. The hon. member, we are informed, intends at the general election to offer himself as a candidate for an English constituency.[370]

The New York Times informed its readers on 26 April, 'John O'Connor Power joined the Independent Liberals and will contest an English constituency at the next election.'

Frank Hugh O'Donnell, Vice-President of the HRCGB, educationalist, playwright, historian and human rights activist, has been maligned. Eccentric he undoubtedly was, but his opinions must be recorded:

> [O'Donnell] claimed that Parnellism reduced the popular organisation both in Ireland and America by its schemes for obtaining money; sapped the foundations for self-government by abusing nominees and fostered deceptive confidence by claiming triumphs on the adoption by Parliament of every worthless Irish measure.[371]

In June 1884 O'Connor Power accompanied Charles Russell to a Liberal Conference in Belfast. Their speeches on the extension of the franchise were interrupted by heckling and violence.

Young Irelander Charles Gavan Duffy was back in the frame. After a successful career in Australia, he returned, politically seasoned, to Europe to promote Home Rule. He invited O'Connor Power to dine 'before the House closes'. The letter is headed 11 August (no year) and P.J. Smyth, who resigned his seat in 1882 in protest against the methods of the Land League, was among the guests. Smyth died in January 1885. He, too, was incensed by the party pledge, regarding it as 'a defacement of the rights of conscience'. The majority of the 1880 IIP MPs still described themselves in *Dod* as Liberals in favour of Home Rule.

The proposal to extend the franchise across the United Kingdom was not welcomed by Parnell:

> At the same time it is believed that Parnell in his heart of hearts is not very keen about the Reform Bill in Ireland. He would have preferred a Registration Act with the present franchise, as most likely to secure for him a greater number of votes than an electoral system on an assimilated basis.[372]

Introduced in February, the Third Reform Bill gave the right to vote to agricultural labourers. The government threatened to create new Peers if the Lords rejected it. Ireland (there had been an attempt to exclude her) would finally be granted the same household franchise as England, effectively increasing the Irish electorate from 200,000 to 700,000. The Cabinet believed that the far-reaching measures would not be passed, but Gladstone was sanguine:

> Sir W. Harcourt was very gloomy in my room this afternoon after the 'open Cabinet' held to discuss the details of the Reform Bill. He declares that the Bill has not a chance (in the House of Commons) and that this is the opinion which is shared by all the Cabinet save Mr G. himself, who lives in a fool's paradise. It remains to be seen who is right. The opinion of course is founded on the assumption that the Irishmen will somehow or other oppose the Government; and I cannot see how, much as they like to see the Government beaten, they will dare to do this. But I admit their behaviour is a very broken reed on which to depend.[373]

Much depends on whether there will be a dissolution this year. If the Reform Bill comes to grief somehow or other in the House of Commons, of course a dissolution would be inevitable. But, if it passes with decent majorities, as Mr G. expects it will – (an expectation which his colleagues little share) – it is not likely that Mr G. will dissolve this year, no matter what the House of Lords may do.[374]

On 29 February 1884, Hamilton recorded:

Mr G. is pleased with the reception of his measure last night ... The main bone of contention will doubtless be the inclusion of Ireland in the Bill, on which Mr G. insisted strongly. The Irish were silent but seemed in good humour and can hardly dare not to support the Bill.[375]

The Bill passed into law in December. The Redistribution of Seats Act followed, leaving the number of Irish seats undiminished, despite strong opposition from Liberal and Tory MPs. The representation of the Protestant minority was secured. The Catholic middle class had benefited from the Land League boycott at the expense of Protestants, and was firmly re-established. With an enlarged franchise, many popular local people – shopkeepers and professionals – were to win seats in the 1885 election.

In May, Gladstone prepared a Land Purchase Bill and, in the long term, he had plans for local government for Ireland. His proposals would be 'a legacy' for his successor. His private secretary wrote a summary of Gladstone's letter to Queen Victoria in his diary:

Mr G has written from Hawarden a long letter to the Queen on the Irish Question by way of preparing Her for the proposal to give Ireland some real local Government, which he thinks is as inevitable as it is expedient. He expresses his own strong inclinations in favour of a larger scheme which he regards as a fairly certain solution; but he studiously treats the question as a legacy and as one which he will be unable to deal with himself. He is against any 'coercive' legislation – i.e. anything calculated to infringe the liberty of the subject.[376]

Gladstone had hoped peace and a political settlement in Ireland would be the crowning achievement of his long career. Now in his declining years – he was seventy-six – he thought often of retirement but his Cabinet colleagues, decisively divided on other issues, wanted him to remain until after the election.

The government was defeated on the budget in June 1885, when the Irish party, who had been promised an end to coercion, supported the Tories. Lord Salisbury formed a caretaker government and, using the services of Randolph Churchill, negotiated with Parnell. As part of the deal, the Land Purchase Act, which allowed the tenant to borrow the full price of his land, was speedily enacted. It was a step in the right direction for peasant proprietorship, but Ireland was again deep in agricultural depression and poorer tenants were unable to avail of the terms. Three years later, Chief Secretary Balfour would claim that as a result of the Act, 'Districts showed improvement and new owners were disinclined to join secret societies or take part in agitation.'[377]

Tories, representing the propertied classes, considered ascendancy's hereditary power was threatened by the enlarged franchise. They feared a combination of Irish democratic agitators and English Radicals would overturn class rule and strip away aristocratic privilege. Randolph Churchill, who refused to sit with tradespeople at the Cabinet table, fanned the flames of hostility to Home Rule. He believed a coup was in the offing:

> Inspired chiefly by Randolph Churchill, the upper classes in Britain were afraid that if the Irish democratic agitation were to continue in conjunction with the English radicals, class rule might be overturned altogether. So, to save themselves, they are going to set up a *class* Conservative government in Ireland, with the aid and consent of the Irish democracy or, in other words, with our assistance, having no connection with England …[378]

Ireland was the thin edge of the democratic wedge. Randolph Churchill – Ulster will fight and Ulster will be right – disseminated widespread 'Home Rule Rome Rule' fears. His stand against Home Rule was a defence of the Empire's integrity and its ruling class. He maintained close contact with Parnell and William O'Shea. Randolph had been private secretary to his father, the Duke of Marlborough, during his tenure as Lord Lieutenant, and his fond ambition was to return to Ireland.

At the end of 1885, an election was called, and two days before the poll, Parnell published a manifesto, directing the Irish in England to join forces with Tories and Ulster Conservatives. Healy's name was appended as a signatory, but Healy, who favoured the Liberal alliance, claimed he had first heard of the manifesto in a Dublin newspaper. Under Parnell's directive, the party machine co-operated with the Tories to eliminate Liberal MPs.[379] Irish party candidates stood side by side with Tories on election platforms.

Gavin Duffy was well connected to establishment figures and was not a man to be impressed by Parnell's autocratic mien. He was alarmed by this attack on the Liberals and gave an account of his intervention and its aftermath in a chapter in Barry O'Brien's biography of Parnell:

[Parnell] said the new government was not going to renew Forster's Coercion Bill beyond that he did not know. I said if Parnell abandoned the idea of vengeance on the Liberals, which I considered insensate in a popular leader, and took the ground that he would help the new Government provided they took up the Home Rule question, I would go to Ireland and open up negotiations with Lord Carnavon, which Parnell might confirm later.[380]

Was Parnell vindictive after his six months confinement? 'Parnell's hatred of Gladstone since the Kilmainham imprisonment never died away.'[381]

Or did a fear of Fenian vengeance prevent him from allying himself with the Liberals prior to the election? Did he fall prey to Randolph's persuasive charm? Many thought the abrupt realignment was a disastrous miscalculation and a serious failure of political responsibility. Irish members, who wished to preserve the Liberal alliance, were dismayed. In defiance of Parnell's directive, Davitt campaigned for Radical Liberals.

Gladstone was privately committed to Home Rule, but he walked a fine line between the Radicals and the traditional Whig elements in the party. There were many still to convince, and his plans for Ireland could not be revealed publicly before the election. Nonconformists in the Liberal ranks were resistant to devolution; they believed the Irish were incapable of self-government and feared their subservience to the Church of Rome. A master of practical politics, Gladstone, in a delicate balancing act, had yielded coercion as he negotiated an enlarged electorate and the democratisation of Britain.

A disciplined Irish vote delivered a decisive gift of power in parliament. But after the election and before parliament met, Gladstone's son Herbert 'flew' what was to be remembered as the 'Hawarden Kite' (Hawarden Castle in Wales was the home of William Gladstone). *The Times* published his letter, 'if five-sixths of the Irish people wish to have a parliament in Dublin ... in the name of justice and wisdom, let them have it'.[382]

Over forty years later, the *Manchester Guardian*, in 'Gladstone and the Radicals', commented, 'Gladstone would not disclose his hand before the election.' At the time of the Hawarden Kite, Herbert wrote in his diary of a meeting at Hawarden with O'Connor Power.[383]

Despite the filial intervention, the Tories took office under the leadership of Lord Salisbury. The administration was short-lived. Gladstone combined with the Irish party to defeat Lord Salisbury and on 1 February 1886, he had an audience with the Queen and informed her of his intention to introduce Home Rule.

In vain, a bi-partisan approach was attempted, 'Gladstone invited Arthur Balfour to join a Conference to see if the Irish Question could be settled by consent as the Franchise and Redistribution controversies were disposed of the year before …'[384]

Man of the Day

Let us have peace.

Mitchell Henry, the progressive Galway landowner, left the Irish party and was elected a Liberal in Glasgow. Frank Hugh O'Donnell did not seek re-election and devoted himself to journalism. Ulster Catholic Charles Russell, Liberal member for Dundalk, then chose to run in South Hackney.

In May, O'Connor Power was asked to stand in Greenwich, and Lancaster Division, Lancashire also extended an invitation. He declined both offers and James McCoan, Home Rule MP for Wicklow, stood in Lancaster. With a letter of recommendation from John Bright, he agreed to contest the Kennington Division of Lambeth.[385] Burnand, *Punch's* editor, wrote 'a manifesto in favour of Mr O'Connor Power for Kennington'.[386]

Kennington was viewed as a safe seat but violent gangs disrupted meetings and attacked his supporters. It was not unusual at election time for hired thugs to cause mayhem. Slandering one's opponent was accepted behaviour. Polling days were an excuse for rowdyism and heavy drinking. These disruptions were calculated to destroy O'Connor Power's electoral chances. He would not be forgiven for his independent strategy and would be the scapegoat for Nationalist frustrations.[387] With just under 3,000 votes, he failed to win the seat: (Conservative) 3,351; O'Connor Power (Liberal) 2,991; (Labour) 32.

A petition was organised but was not successful, 'The sudden collapse of the Kennington election petition has caused great astonishment among the Liberals, who thought their case had been well prepared.'[388]

Never a man to be downcast, O'Connor Power continued to practise as a barrister, lecture and write for various newspapers. In the National Liberal Club's Charing Cross quarters, he was a member of a radical group, which met in one of the 'small smoking rooms sacred to a certain clique'. He was present at the laying of the foundation stone for the splendid new premises in Whitehall Place, overlooking the Thames.

As the NLC grew in size and political influence, so did the members of the 'clique', which included Thorold Rogers, Alfred Bennett, Fisher Unwin and F.W. Chesson. Fisher Unwin, publisher, was married to Richard Cobden's daughter, who marked her independence as Mrs Cobden-Unwin. Richard Cobden supplied Davitt with a preface for *The Fall of Feudalism*: 'It is in Ireland that the crash of feudalism will first be heard.'[389] Many of the group were founding members of The Johnson Club.

After 1886 and Gladstone's public declaration for Home Rule, Irish MPs who favoured the Liberal alliance joined the NLC.

O'Connor Power was training new recruits for the party:

> The members of the National Liberal Club living in the provinces will be glad to know that the attempt which has been made to introduce weekly discussions on practical politics has been successful. At the first of these discussions on Wednesday night, under the presidency of Mr J. O'Connor Power ...[390]

As ever, practical and forward thinking, he was building the foundations of a strong and organised opposition. It was never too soon to prepare for the next confrontation with the Tories.

Westminster was not the most likely place to effect change. In an after-dinner speech in 1886, O'Connor Power made a point:

> On the question of foreign policy I can only venture to repeat what I have often said in the House of Commons. I wish to say it with special emphasis on the present occasion, that little indeed is the influence of the people of England, and little indeed is the influence our representatives in the House of Commons can exercise, owing to our system of government, on the conduct of foreign affairs. (Cheers)
>
> Under this system the executive could involve the country in a thousand ways before the House of Commons knew what was going on.[391]

His series of articles on Home Rule, written for the *Manchester Guardian*, was revised and published by the National Press Agency as *The Anglo-Irish Quarrel, A Plea for Peace*. It was well received, and a second edition was printed.

Setting out the stall for Home Rule, he selected his title with care. 'Anglo-Irish Quarrel' replaced the patronising, rather tired 'Irish Question'. Anglo-Irish denoted equal interests were at stake. 'Quarrel' signalled a familial dispute between neighbouring countries, closely allied by propinquity, common interests and ties of kinship. He acknowledged that moves had been made to achieve an accommodation. When the disagreement was between the Empire, on which the sun never set, and a hostile neighbour with an infinite capacity for disruption of imperial business, the quarrel was of international concern.

David Ayerst, in his history of the *Guardian*, commented:

He analysed closely the governmental system of Ireland and showed that the key positions were regularly in the hands of Englishmen. His articles discussed the grievances of the Roman Catholic majority in some of the Ulster counties. He looked across the Atlantic and concluded that 'the influence of Irish America on our domestic politics is at the present moment one of the greatest dangers'.[392]

Gladstone had shown his hand and the principle of Home Rule was accepted by a major British party. It was now obvious that Parnell and his followers regretted their 'zealous efforts' to reduce the Liberal majority. Lord Salisbury was 'commanding' the House of Lords, which 'can and will veto any proposed Home Rule legislation'. Home Rule involved many issues, and whatever was decided upon had to be legal and binding. There should be open agreement and a consensus settlement.

Under the present administration, the five senior government posts were usually filled by men who knew nothing of Ireland. One of the five, the Commander of the Forces, had a considerable role, and Ireland was effectively ruled from a military barracks, Dublin Castle.

The struggle had been for civil and religious liberties. Scotland had religious liberties and a large measure of self-government:

But, considering the age in which we live, the progress of civilisation, and the spirit of free institutions everywhere, the injustice which Ireland suffers at the present time in being deprived of a native Administration may be as galling to her and as intolerable as were the wrongs of the past in their own evil time.

With her 'greater capacities for freedom', Ireland now had 'enlarged ambitions', and an impatience with English rule. At the same time, 'immense forces are in operation towards a closer union'.

And if the settlement of the Anglo-Irish quarrel is necessary for England's peace, it is equally necessary for Ireland's progress.

Thanks to the remedial policy begun sixteen years ago by Mr Gladstone, and since resolutely pursued in the face of enormous difficulties by the Liberal party, and without which Irish effort must have been fruitless, they are now in possession of a Parliamentary force which enables them to treat on something like equal terms with the strongest of their opponents.

The advantage to Britain was that an Irish parliament with a native government party and opposition would deprive them of the power of annoyance. Irish representatives in the Westminster parliament would still be in a position to disturb the proceedings of the legislature but would have no reason to do so. The Irish parliament would be sending representatives from both Irish government and Irish opposition parties. Both legislatures would be more efficient.

Many versions of Home Rule had been proposed. Parnell favoured a Grattan's parliament, T.P. O'Connor was promoting Dominion status like Canada, and Justin McCarthy inclined to the system in the United States of America:

> There is no subject about which Mr Parnell is so indifferent as that of Irish history, and his contempt for books is strikingly shown in his reference to Grattan's Parliament. Mr Parnell deceives himself, through sheer indifference to history and a dislike of the trouble of inquiring into facts, when he tells us he wants Grattan's Parliament. Does Mr Parnell want a Parliament in Dublin controlled by a few nominees of the British Cabinet, who, under the Viceroy, constitute an Irish Government in no way responsible to the Irish House of Commons? ... Under Grattan's Parliament there was no Irish Administration responsible to Irish opinion. The Irish Government consisted of the Viceroy and his Secretary and their subordinates.
>
> He finds comparison with Canada unrealistic and impracticable. Ireland is only a few hours distant from England, and its interests are bound up with the United Kingdom.

Justin McCarthy's advocacy of a federal solution, where Ireland would have control over her internal affairs was his preferred option. Westminster would be rid of the burden of Irish business. Federalism was the favoured solution at the 1873 Home Rule Conference, and the following year fifty-nine members were returned to support it.

An Irish government would be responsible for the enforcement of law and order and would guarantee the rights of property. The Royal Irish Constabulary would come under the control of the new county authorities. Freedom of conscience and worship would be inviolable. In the counties of Ireland, Catholic magistrates were vastly outnumbered by Protestants, even in areas where the population was predominantly Catholic. In an independent Ireland, the minority would be protected and integrated into the community, and would come to rely on its own courage and resolution. Accommodation and conciliation are the answers, as with every minority group who wish to live in harmony within a nation.

The landlord system had broken down irretrievably in Ireland and was in decline in the United Kingdom. If the Irish landlord was not able to sell his land, an Irish government, where rents were not paid, would buy the interest of the land at a price determined by the Land Commission or a court protecting the landowners' rights.

The Protestant minority, thanks to the 1885 Redistribution Act, would have a proportionately larger representation in the Irish parliament than the Catholics of Great Britain have at Westminster. O'Connell used to say that he would take his theology from Rome but not his politics.

A Supreme Court of Appeal would be established for the settlement of all disputed questions arising between the local and imperial authority. The 'terrible alternative' to a settlement would be civil war, with the destruction of the Irish minority in Great Britain and the destruction of the English minority in Ireland:

> It means the immediate enrolment of hundreds of thousands of disaffected Irishmen in the United States and the colonies in one vast confederation, combined for the purpose of crippling English commerce, attacking English power, and thwarting English policy as far as possible in every part of the world.

It is a time for action:

> This is not a time for dissolution but for action, not hasty or precipitate, but measured, just and firm action: action based on wise statesmanship and experienced counsel. Pausing for a moment at one of the turning points of history and in the march of the nations, we have now to decide whether we shall go backward in the ways of coercion and despotism, or forward on the road of constitutional reform and national freedom.
>
> Millions in England and in Ireland are waiting for the kindly light and the generous leading, and if they could make themselves heard they would send up from their inmost hearts one universal cry – 'Let us have peace'.

Taking a Stand

The mules of politics, without pride of ancestry, or hope of posterity.[393]

Gladstone's cabinet found it difficult to agree on any issue, and finally the leadership split on Ireland. Liberals who opposed devolution regrouped as Liberal Unionists under the leadership of Lord Hartington, brother of the assassinated Cavendish. Hartington had raised objections to the Redistribution Act, and Gladstone believed his 'estimate of Irish affairs' was coloured by the murder of his brother. Deeply disillusioned, John Bright, long-time champion of Irish causes, joined them.

In 1883, Bright, in failing health, had attacked the Irish party, 'whose oath of allegiance is broken by association with its enemies … The main portion of whose funds for the purpose of agitation come from the avowed enemies of England'.[394] In an obituary, 'In Memoriam John Bright', published in the *Universal Review*, Thorold Rogers felt his change of heart was puzzling:

> Many of us thought him to be in error in his attitude on the Irish Question; not a few found it difficult to reconcile that attitude with his avowed principles. But the belief in his integrity was so strong that his name and reputation alone were the explanations of the reverses of 1886 … He was alienated from a cause by what he thought was intemperance, the impolicy – he used stronger words about them of its principle advocates.[395]

Gladstone believed that the argument that Irishmen could not be trusted to run their own country was mischievous. Earl Spencer, the Lord-Lieutenant, had a hand in drafting the Home Rule Bill and was ostracised by his class for his views. He wrote to O'Connor Power that he had read his paper on Home Rule with interest: 'I shall be glad if I will see you.'[396] Irish Under-Secretary, Sir Robert Hamilton, was also a strong proponent of devolution.

Liberal Unionists, who remained on the opposition benches, pushed for local government reforms, a National Councils scheme, hoping to weaken the arguments for Home Rule. A Central Board, with a limited area of responsibilities, was suggested and for a time had the backing of the Catholic hierarchy.

Cardinal Manning had misgivings. He believed local government would provide training for political responsibility. Extremists threatened stability. Republicans separated State and Church, undermining the Church's dominant position. In certain quarters, it was suspected that Manning was more interested in his crusade for the Conversion of England than Home Rule. George Moore writes in *Hail and Farewell, Vale*, 'an English duke is more to Rome that the entire province of Connacht'.

The threat of Home Rule led to a resurgence of the Orange Order. Ulster wanted no truck with a down-at-heel Catholic State. The province was industrialised and prosperous, and the Unionist party was the richest political organisation in Britain. Belfast was a modern Victorian city, not steeped in a Georgian past like Dublin. Shipbuilding was a major source of wealth, and the linen industry had taken a lead during the cotton shortage in the American Civil War years. Growing flax for the manufacture of linen was notoriously difficult, and agriculture in Ulster had to be modern and efficient.

Landowners, manufacturers and merchants anticipated mismanagement in a united Ireland. With fears of Rome Rule, the province erupted and sectarian riots signalled Orangemen's intransigence. They were ready to defend their way of life to the death.

Gladstone's introduction of the Home Rule Bill drew a great deal of attention. The Prince of Wales was in the House, and the Strangers' gallery was occupied by prominent men from every walk of life. Extra seating was brought into the Chamber to accommodate the overflow. Large crowds gathered in the Lobby and in the Palace Yard. The opposition cheered dissidents, John Bright and Lord Hartington. Liberals and Nationalists responded with loud cheers, waving of hats and handkerchiefs, for Mr Gladstone.

In June 1886, the second reading of the Bill was defeated in a full House by 343 to 313 votes. The Liberal government fell shortly afterwards, and Ireland was again the central issue of an election campaign.

The Tories swept back into power, and in the first Unionist government, Lord Salisbury promised, 'Twenty years of resolute government for Ireland'. He recommended the removal of the Irish of the overpopulated districts to Manitoba. The stark approach was condemned by John Morley as 'manacles and Manitoba'. The atmosphere at Westminster changed dramatically, and for the worse.

Ireland was again in a deep agricultural depression and emigration figures were soaring. At the end of October, William O'Brien launched the Plan of Campaign, 'No Reduction, No Rent', a revival of the land agitation. Threatened evictions were to be met with demands for rent negotiation, accompanied by rent strikes and mass demonstrations.

Pope Leo XIII condemned the Plan, and Parnell dismissed it at a Liberal Eighty Club dinner. It had, however, the support of Dublin's Archbishop Walsh[397] and Archbishop Croke of Cashel. Chief Secretary Balfour denounced it as 'an unlawful and criminal conspiracy', and proposing 'perpetual' coercion, introduced the Perpetual Crimes Bill for Ireland in March 1887.

On the day fixed for its second reading in the Commons, 18 April 1887, *The Times*, organ of the establishment, published the facsimile of a letter purporting to be from Parnell. The letter, which appeared to implicitly approve the Phoenix Park murders, followed on three articles, entitled 'Parnellism and Crime', which had been published the previous week. The series was designed to discredit Irish parliamentarians, and the facsimile was intended as a mortal blow.[398] Leading members of the Irish party stood accused of criminal conspiracy. They were 'a nest of cobras' and complicit in Land War atrocities. The government, its hand strengthened by *The Times*' accusations, arrested twenty members of the Irish party. It would be an *annus horribilis* for Irish MPs.

In June, the Jubilee Plot, an assassination attempt on Victoria and her ministers, was sponsored by British intelligence in an attempt to incriminate Irish Nationalists. Covert agents, intent on troublemaking, whipped up public panic and paranoia. The arrangements were haphazard, and the Jubilee procession went off without a hitch. Later it came to light that Lord Salisbury and the proprietor of *The Times* had prior knowledge of the plot. It was establishment intrigue at its rankest; a swift sequel to the 'Parnellism and Crime' articles, and its purpose was to destroy all sympathy for the Irish cause.

Adopting a zero-tolerance approach, the new regime was intent on the obliteration of the enemy at the heart of Empire. *The Times*' damaging accusations and the disinformation surrounding the Jubilee Plot implicated the Nationalist movement in high treason. The poison was laid and the Criminal Law and Procedure (Ireland) Act, otherwise known as Perpetual Coercion, passed with a comfortable majority.

In September 1887, William O'Brien was expected for trial in Mitchelstown, County Cork, for inciting non-payment of rent. John Dillon was present and an angry crowd gathered in protest. The police arrived and moved in on the demonstrators. Three men were killed and many seriously injured in the ensuing riots. The violent reprisal is remembered as the Mitchelstown Massacre.

In mid-November there was a mass demonstration in Trafalgar Square to protest against coercion and to demand the release of William O'Brien. The rally was organised by the Social Democratic Federation, the first organised socialist party in Britain, and the Irish National League. Irish-born men and men of Irish descent made up a significant part of the workforce, and British and Irish radicals were making common cause.

Lord Salisbury's government was determined to put down the protesters and sent in 2,000 police and 400 soldiers to 'defend the classes against the masses'. A regiment of mounted police rode roughshod into the crowds. At least three people were killed and many were badly injured. Women and children were savagely beaten in what was described as 'real warfare'.

The following day, *The Times* denounced the demonstrators as looters: 'It was a simple love of disorder, hope of plunder', which attracted such large numbers to the square on a Sunday afternoon.

On his release, William O'Brien made a powerful speech in the Commons. 'Bloody Balfour', the Irish Chief Secretary's coercive policy had advanced 'the Nationalist cause by attracting to it the humane sympathy of the English masses'. Co-operation between the Irish National League of Great Britain and the Liberal party was strengthened. 'Remember Mitchelstown' had entered the Anglo-Irish lexicon.

Davitt married his American bride on 30 December 1886 and returned to Ireland the following February. A cottage in Ballybrack, close to Killiney Bay and with a panoramic view of the Sugar Loaf, was a wedding gift from friends and well-wishers.

After the heady days of the American tours and the Land War, Davitt had a falling out with John Devoy and was disillusioned with Parnell and the party. He now worked as a labour activist in Britain. Former Land League executives Patrick Egan and Thomas Brennan were living in the United States.

Davitt was anxious to see O'Connor Power back at Westminster and spoke to Parnell, 'Mr Davitt being located in London renewed his intercourse with Mr O'Connor Power and at our last meeting wished that Power could get an English seat'.[399] Davitt appreciated that work for Ireland was most effective at the heart of Empire, among the Irish in England and sympathetic English radicals, 'We have friends in this country and we must help them to help us.'[400] He urged O'Connor Power in one letter to meet with F.J. Schnadhorst, secretary of the British Liberal Federation. O'Connor Power did not accept a nomination, 'Mr O'Connor Power had declined to allow his name to go forward as a Liberal candidate at the Borough of Chelsea at the next election.'[401]

At the end of 1887, the *Manchester Guardian's* Irish correspondent wrote of the unrest in Ireland:

> The ordinary work of imprisoning public men, which is the normal business of Mr Balfour, has gone on as usual … members of Parliament are practically outlawed if they dare to lift their voices against landlordism.
>
> The Liberal Unionists have not 'modifed the grim savagery of the Tory regime … Such an administration loosens all moral bonds of society, saps the true foundation of law … The policy of repression may break up press and platform, but as surely as it 'drives discontent underground' so surely shall we have Ribbonism and its kindred societies rising again as the policy of outrage and despair when other methods have been crushed by our sapient Chief Secretary.

The correspondent pondered whether some counter-movement was in progress:

> The very remarkable letter written by Mr Davitt to Mr Philips, in which he builds a bridge of return for that dimmed luminary O'Connor Power, strengthens my conjecture, and I should not wonder if new methods were soon to be taken up on lines less likely to suit Mr Balfour's calculations than those with which he has had hitherto to deal.[402]

The Times reported on the 'remarkable' letter Davitt sent to a Mr W. Phillips 'in defence of his friend O'Connor Power', in which he wrote, 'I believe the attacks on Mr O'Connor Power are wrong.' The newspaper questioned Davitt's *volte-face*:

…we may ask on what grounds Mr Davitt accepts again the brotherhood of Mr O'Connor Power? We ask because we have not seen that Mr O'Connor Power has joined the League, or made his peace with the authors of the Plan of Campaign. Mr Davitt is here perfectly candid 'Mr O'Connor Power is now one of the Liberal party; and surely if *United Ireland* can embrace in home rule fellowship Earl Spencer and Sir George Trevelyan, it can sufficiently relax its cast iron consistency to right of free speech at public meetings to Mr O'Connor Power in England' … The Irish party is not as independent as it was. It sails in the wake of the men mentioned.[403]

A few days later, *The New York Times* noted a change in presentation, 'Michael Davitt has written a letter to explain his attitude toward O'Connor Power. He says he did not urge the readmission of Mr Power to the Parnellite ranks but he considers that since the Liberals have become allied with the Parnellites the latter ought to cease attacking Mr Power.'[404] He believed the disruptions at meetings where O'Connor Power was a speaker were wrong and vindictive. A few days later, he wrote again to the newspaper, asking that rowdies 'stop hounding him'. He was 'working as a Liberal in the interest of Home Rule' and he should be permitted to do this work where 'he renders invaluable service'. He did not urge 'his readmission to the National ranks'.

O'Connor Power was, in fact, intent on a trip to North America, and the *Toronto Daily Mail* of 23 December 1887 announced his impending arrival. It was eleven years since his last visit, and he would revisit old haunts and renew friendships. He was to promote Home Rule and investigate possibilities for Irish settlers. His election as Prior of The Johnson Club, on 13 December, had been a vote of confidence in difficult times, an appreciative *bon voyage*.

A series of bad harvests meant emigration had again become an unsought option. Thousands of farmers left never to return. Canadian agents toured Ireland and Scotland, hiring agricultural labourers to work in the Prairie Provinces. A quarter of the American population was of Irish birth or descent. During the Famine years the Irish had been effectively deported – 'enforced emigration was the "*fons et origo mali*"', the fountainhead of the evils which affect Ireland'[405] – and no thought put into their relocation. They migrated not to agricultural states, where their skills would be put to good use, but to industrial towns and cities where they found it heartbreaking to adapt to new ways. In April 1883, O'Connor Power had spoken passionately of the emigrant's plight, 'It was, above all, necessary that emigrants should not have rankling in their minds, on their arrival in Canada, or the United States, a burning sense of wrong, or injury, or banishment, or repatriation.'[406]

O'Connor Power made his exit. He arrived in New York in February and spoke on Home Rule, praising the Canadian Confederation. His long letter on the subject was published in the *New York Herald*. On 18 March 1888, the *Chicago Daily Tribune* reported that he was 'the social toast of the hour' in Louisville (home of the Kentucky Derby), where he was the guest of honour at the St Patrick's Day festivities. He told his audience that the true patriot is not the one who clamours to lead the parade but the man who walks last.

O'Connor Power had always claimed that 'intelligent patriotism in America was entirely on his side'.[407] Irish America was turning to support constitutional politics, and Clan numbers were down significantly. John Finerty, editor of the *Chicago Daily Tribune* and a leading Clan figure, moved in 1892 to champion Home Rule.

In Canada, Home Rule was of immense interest to the Irish community. Edward Blake, a distinguished lawyer of Irish descent, was leader of Canada's Liberal party, 1880–7. In 1892, he travelled to Ireland and, standing as an anti-Parnellite, won a seat in South Longford. He collected significant funds for the Irish Parliamentary Party among the Canadian friends of Home Rule and raised finance for the 1798 centenary celebrations. Blake remained at Westminster until 1907, when, in failing health, he returned to Canada.

O'Connor Power was in Quebec in mid-May and was interviewed by a representative of the *Quebec Daily Telegraph*, 'In appearance he is a man of about 55 years of age, tall and well built. He is deeply pitted by smallpox. He is a very agreeable conversationalist, has a merry twinkle in his eye, and just the slightest touch of the brogue in his speech.' His visit was 'entirely private': 'I am going up the Canadian Pacific line to Vancouver, I expect, tomorrow night. I am a lawyer, you know, and am on legal business entirely … I am out of political life and intend to remain out of it.'[408]

The transcontinental Canadian Pacific Railway was the longest railway in the world and was built to define and unify the newly created Canadian Confederation. Inspired and promoted by the Prime Minister, Sir John A. Macdonald, it was a symbol of national pride, forging a geographical identity distinct from its neighbour, the United States. The route opened up the prairies to settlement and agricultural development. Towns along its path quickly prospered. In May 1887, the first official train undertook the trip (almost 3,000 miles) from Montreal to Vancouver. O'Connor Power's transcontinental journey was made a year later. He wrote 'another interesting letter' on British Columbia for an Iowa newspaper.[409]

In June he was in Winnipeg as a guest speaker at the Manitoba Club, a bastion of high society.[410] From there he travelled to Montreal:

'O'Connor Power'

This young man, who has been lionised in Manitoba, and is anxious to find some quiet spot in Canada, to place his discontented countrymen at home, is in Montreal ... Mr O'Connor Power if he lives long enough will perhaps find many Irishmen in this part of the world emigrating to their native land as soon as Home rule is established.[411]

His detractors were still active. A *New York Times* reporter wrote in July, 'Mr O'Connor Power asks me emphatically to deny the report that he has a mission from Lord Salisbury's Government to further an emigration scheme.' He was in Toronto to give a lecture to St Michael's College, 'Our hearts thrilled when O'Connor Power addressed us on Irish Home Rule.'[412] In early October he spent time in New York. The *Manchester Guardian*'s correspondent reported, 'Mr O'Connor Power, formerly MP for Mayo, is at present staying in New York. Since January last, he has been travelling in various parts of Canada and the United States. I hear that it is his intention to write an account of his experiences across the water.'

Patrick Egan was also in New York, and in an interview in *The New York Times*, he commented on *The Times*' allegations and predicted fireworks:

Nothing new has developed yet to talk about. What has been said so far is simply a rehash of charges, without proof, that has been made for the last five years. But wait until the evidence for Parnell is produced. The whole *Times*' case will be exploded and indisputable evidence produced which will show Parnell guiltless and the true character of the allegations against him. You may expect some sensational testimony ... I have no doubt of the complete vindication of Parnell and all his associates and this will greatly injure the government.[413]

The British government's reign of terror, 'eternal repression', continued unrelenting for three years, uniting Nationalists against a common enemy. Robert Anderson, British intelligence supremo, was always several steps ahead of the Brotherhood. Leaks had come from Clan na Gael, from the very top of the organisation, and over an extended period. Now aggressive Secret Service infiltration, wire tapping and surveillance simultaneously revealed the nature and extent of its penetration.

In July 1888, Frank Hugh O'Donnell, possibly in a precursory testing of the waters, took an unsuccessful action for libel against *The Times*. In court, the Attorney General read out more incriminating letters, which, it was claimed, were written by Patrick Egan and James O'Kelly, and addressed to Parnell. During the proceedings it came to light that Richard Pigott, a former newspaperman, had given these letters to the paper, and had been 'researching' for *The Times* for some time. As a result of the damaging publicity, Parnell, whose good name was in question, was advised to demand an inquiry.

The Special Commission on Parnellism and Crime, sometimes called the 'Forgeries Commission', was set up with three judges to examine *The Times'* letters and allegations. Sessions began on 17 September 1888 and were held in Probate Court 1 in the Royal Courts of Justice on the Strand. The commission, in effect a political trial, met 128 times, ending on 22 November 1889. Sir Charles Russell, QC, a future Lord Chief Justice, with his colleague H.H. Asquith, a future Liberal Prime Minister, conducted the defence.[414] Russell, his biographer tells us, was a man, proud of his Irish brogue and 'devoted to Irish and Catholic rights'. Representing his country's interests, he relinquished his generous retainer from *The Times*.

Parnell and sixty-five named Irish parliamentarians were charged with belonging to a lawless, murderous organisation, whose aim was to overthrow British authority in Ireland. They stood accused of complicity in the Invincibles' assassination of Cavendish and Burke: 'the writers of Parnellism and Crime intended to convey to the public mind that Mr Parnell and Mr Parnell's colleagues knew of, and were parties to, the Invincible conspiracy'.[415]

Attorney General Sir Richard Webster's opening speech lasted five days. He claimed the Land League was a criminal conspiracy and under the control of the American physical force party. Its members, in and out of parliament, made speeches intended to incite disturbance. In earlier periods of unrest, landlords had been the targets, but, during the Land War, it was tenants who were the victims of violent crime.

On the third day, the AG produced the facsimile letter, dated 15 May 1882, a few days after the Phoenix Park murders. For security reasons, witnesses were not named in advance, and on the seventh day he unexpectedly called Captain O'Shea to the stand.[416] The Captain was asked if the signature on the letter was Parnell's. He said he was 'not an expert', but he believed that it was.

The defence had not been given notice that O'Shea was to testify and were taken by surprise. Russell asked him if he had met Pigott. O'Shea replied that he only knew

Pigott by reputation. When O'Shea was immediately called away to the Continent on business, cutting short the defence's cross-examination, Russell cried foul.

Subpoenaing witnesses from all over Ireland, the counsel for *The Times* led a litany of agrarian outrages, which continued for months. Landlords, agents, members of the Royal Irish Constabulary and parish priests were lined up to give evidence.

Finally, on 5 February, Thomas Billis Beach, alias Major Henri Le Caron, was called. Le Caron, an American Civil War veteran, was a founding member of Clan na Gael, and a man who could turn every opportunity to advantage. At the end of the conflict, he trained as a doctor and invested in several drug stores. To further supplement his income, he ran a grave-robbing business, supplying corpses, preserved in pickle barrels, to local hospitals.

Le Caron regarded himself as a military spy and informed the commission he had operated as a British agent for over two decades. As far back as the 1860s, he alerted the authorities to the Fenian incursions into Canada. In the early 1880s, his double life took him to the House of Commons, where he claimed Parnell gave him a message of armed revolution for Clan leaders. He posed as a close ally of John Devoy and Alexander Sullivan and was superbly placed as a conduit to his spy master, Robert Anderson. In 1885, when he stood for election to the US House of Representatives, he was denounced as a Fenian: his cover was copper-fastened. *The Times* paid him £10,000 to implicate Parnell in terrorist activity. The incriminating 15 May facsimile was addressed to 'Dear Sir', who was generally believed to be Patrick Egan. Le Caron met Egan in Paris when he took delivery of 'sealed packets' from Clan leaders. Egan, he said, told him he approved of the dynamite policy.

Le Caron was undaunted by the defence's cross-examination and retained a calm composure. His confidence remained undented. The following year, his account of his days as a Victorian super spy appeared under the title, *Twenty-five Years in the Secret Service* and sold remarkably well.

Several agents, on both sides of the Atlantic, were unmasked in the weeks that followed, and it became clear that the well-briefed British Secret Service had been forewarned of every twist and turn of Fenian activity.

Michael Davitt, working with the defence team, cross-examined witnesses. He had interviewed prominent players, and his investigations took him to Paris, where his sources were often disaffected double agents and informers, with tangled allegiances. Richard Pigott, with a compulsion to betray, was, according to Davitt, 'perfectly impartial in his scheming propensities'.[417] Davitt's black notebook, the 'black diary' and its contents, detailing accounts of conversations with this underworld, was used to great effect during the interrogations of *The Times*' witnesses. Davitt believed he could prove the involvement of the Secret Service in the Jubilee Plot, and he hoped the revelations would topple the government.

The disputed letters were examined. The facsimile appeared to approve the Invincibles' actions. The body of the letter was not in Parnell's writing, but the signature was similar. *The Times* had not troubled to authenticate the letters nor had it investigated the character of Pigott, who supplied them to their agent. The newspaper ignored the counsel of its legal advisor, who had advised against publication.

Patrick Egan, who had made a new life in America, had corresponded with Pigott in the early 1880s and he noticed similar wording and misspelling in letters, which were made public in the F.H. O'Donnell libel case. Russell had applied in October 1888 for a commission to examine Patrick Egan in the United States. The application was refused but Egan furnished Russell's team with correspondence and shared his conclusions.

Sir Charles Russell was well prepared for his cross-examination of Pigott, which began on 21 February. He asked him to sit at a desk and write the following words: 'livelihood', 'likelihood', 'proselytism', 'Patrick Egan' and 'P. Egan'. These initial requests were fed slowly to the witness so as to throw him off his guard. Finally, Russell asked him to spell 'hesitancy with a small h'. Pigott wrote it with a second 'e', 'hesitency', a misspelling, and Russell linked this to a letter written to Patrick Egan in 1882 when Pigott was negotiating the sale of his newspapers to Egan, the Land League treasurer. It was well known to friends and colleagues that Parnell had a fetish about correct spelling and was incapable of such an error. Phrases in the letters were similar to wording used by Pigott in his letters to Egan. This was more than coincidental.

Under Russell's cross-examination, Pigott denied he knew what *The Times* intended to do with the letters. However, Russell, in a dramatic confrontation, produced Pigott's letter to Archbishop Walsh, written three days before the first 'Parnellism and Crime' article, in which he claimed there were proceedings 'in preparation with the object of destroying the influence of the Parnellite party in parliament ... to be followed in all probability by the institution of criminal proceedings against these parties by the Government'. Russell proceeded to expose Pigott as an inveterate blackmailer. He portrayed him as a miserable wretch. His prey crumbled.

On the fifty-sixth day, 26 February 1889, it was announced to the court that Pigott had left the country. The Attorney General said he had run away, but Russell called it a 'foul conspiracy' and declared Pigott had already made a full confession. A warrant was issued for his arrest. He was found dead in Madrid.

On the sixty-fourth day, 2 April 1889, Russell began his opening speech for the defence, an epic presentation which lasted eight days. He identified the two sides of the case and asked, 'Who are the accusers? Who is the accused?' Attacking *The Times*, he said its longstanding and unrelenting hostility to Ireland was a major factor in the failure of British policy. The newspaper was blinded by animosity.

The speech was an extensive and comprehensive history of Ireland as a subject nation, neglected and abused over many centuries of occupation. In an indictment of English rule, Russell described at great length the draconian penal laws, which had destroyed the fabric of Irish society. Ireland's religion had been proscribed, its language scorned, and its people dispossessed, despised and disarmed. The Irish had been barred from the professions. Restrictions had been placed on their participation in manufacturing and commerce. In 1800, the Act of Union united the legislatures but not the peoples.

The Irish lived with fear and the memory of the Famine. Agrarian unrest, disaffection and ostracism were historical facts of life, and the only possible weapons of protest against a repressive regime.

There had been some attempt to address the land question, and he again instanced the Compensation for Disturbance Bill:

> That being the scheme which yesterday, in connection with the Compensation
> for Disturbance Bill, I pointed out to your Lordships was formally introduced in
> the House of Commons at the instance of the Land League by Mr O'Connor
> Power, then one of the members for Mayo, and the principle of which was afterwards adopted by the Government of the day and passed, by the second reading
> of the Compensation for Disturbance Bill through that House.[418]

Russell found that the 'rubbishy collection' of 'trumpery stories' presented against the Irish members was so flimsy that in the normal course of events 'the muddle of evidence' would not have been allowed to go before a jury.

In his summing up, on 12 April, he spoke for the land of his birth, 'Your Lordships are trying the history of a ten year revolution in Ireland.' The Irish have now moved to 'constitutional means of redress':

> This inquiry, intended as a curse, has proved a blessing. Designed, prominently
> designed to ruin one man, it has been his vindication. In opening this case I said
> that we represented the accused. My Lords, I claim leave to say that today the
> positions are reversed – we are the accusers and there [pointing to the representatives of *The Times*] are the accused.

Barry O'Brien's source was delighted:

> … I believe he has raised the Irish cause to a position which it never before held in the eyes of the people of England. I could not describe to you the scene in court this morning. Every nook and corner was packed with people and everyone listened in breathless silence.

Cardinal Manning was generous in his praise of Russell's masterful exposition, 'What I thought was the chief excellence of your defence is this: you lifted the whole subject to the level of a great national and historical cause.'[419]

The defence called Dr Walsh on 9 May. He testified that boycotting might be seen as 'exclusive dealing', not intimidation. Rebellion was provoked, 'Crime followed eviction.' Davitt confirmed on 2 July that Irish Americans now favoured a Home Rule solution.

On the 107th day, 16 July, Russell and the counsel for the defence withdrew from the case.

The publicity surrounding the articles, letters and proceedings was intended to deal a death blow to Irish Nationalism. Not only was the Land League savaged as a murder machine but the deeds of named Fenians had been ruthlessly examined in the press. The Pigott letters exposed the rifts in the ranks, and the devastating exposure of a British spy in the top echelon of Clan na Gael begged humiliating questions. Disclosures fed dissension, suspicion and paranoia and threw the American brotherhood into vengeful disarray.

Exposing the history of the IRB and airing the inner workings of the Supreme Council, did a great deal of damage, but in the eyes of the faithful, these men were heroes. Michael Davitt, Matthew Harris, James O'Kelly, Joseph Biggar and the 'long gentleman', John O'Connor had given evidence. Patrick Egan was rewarded and his diplomatic appointment as United States Minister to Chile took effect in March, shortly after the cross-examination of Pigott. Nationalists had united against a powerful enemy and triumphed.

On 13 February 1890, the commission report was published. It concluded that the defendants did not 'incite directly to the commission of crime' but they did 'incite to intimidation'. *The Times* paid £200,000 in costs for a trial which was a *de facto* State prosecution. It reportedly lost circulation and its authoritative pre-eminence, the newspaper of record, was called into serious doubt. Parnell was awarded £5,000 in libel damages.

In early March, parliament debated the conclusions of the commission and Timothy Harrington made accusations in the House, 'I'll prove a foul conspiracy by statements which will show that while we were accused of associating with dynamitards and murderers, our accusers were in constant association with dyna-mitards and were trying to obtain the testimony, true or false, of alleged murders and assassins.'[420]

John Dillon, seven years later, would question the use of Secret Service money, 'for years the established policy of the Home Office to keep in their employ and in their pay, men who did not scruple for the detection of crime … to plan, promote and assist in the organisation of crimes for the pretended purpose of preventing them'.[421]

Lord Salisbury's administration had targeted the Home Rule agenda, which threat-ened Tory and Unionist supremacy and the integrity of the Empire. The government had been foiled and their machinations exposed. The Irish around the world cel-ebrated. The Liberal party, by its long association with the Irish, had also been on trial. Gladstone led a standing ovation when Parnell returned to the House of Commons, and the National Liberal Club gave the Irish leader a lifetime membership.

In his autobiography, Dr Mark Ryan provides a provocative footnote, 'Anderson created a big political sensation on 6 April 1910, by revealing that he himself was the writer of the articles "Parnellism and Crime".'[422]

Part Five

Hearts and Minds

… we must construct a society in which selfishness is openly discredited.

In December 1888, O'Connor Power returned to London and resumed his career at the Bar. In Piam Memoriam, he moved, as befitted a Prior of The Johnson Club, to chambers at 2 Brick Court, Oliver Goldsmith's former home.

During the Special Commission proceedings, he remained behind the scenes, and in early 1890, his collaboration with Michael Davitt moved seamlessly to a joint publication and correspondence dealing with the launch of Davitt's newspaper, *Labour World*.

O'Connor Power was prolific, and several articles signalled his commitment. In March 1890, 'The Gospel of Wealth (A Reply to Andrew Carnegie)', appeared in the *Universal Review*. He presented a deceptively soft-gloved, even-handed response to Carnegie's 'The Gospel of Wealth', which first appeared in the *North American Review*. 'Mr Carnegie, who is one of the best of millionaires', republished his article in England at the request of Mr Gladstone. As 'the impartial inquirer', O'Connor tackles Carnegie's propositions in a dialogue, engaging with Adam Strong, the 'honest, upright' carpenter.

'The problem of our age is the proper administration of wealth,' writes Carnegie. Adam Strong's retort is to turn the proposition upside down and examine the question of acquisition, in 'just proportion to those engaged in its production … The millionaire naturally feels that the public ought not to ask how he has acquired his wealth, but how he administers it.' He questions the relevance of Carnegie's social philosophy, 'the law of competition', 'the law of accumulation of wealth', to Ireland:

Let the Irish landlord make his own bargain about rent, and the English or American manufacturer his own bargain about wages, and see that these bargains are enforced! According to Mr Carnegie, this is all you need do. If you interfere with what he calls the 'law' of competition you prevent the 'survival of the fittest', and enter upon a useless struggle against the law of nature. In the face of this, Mr Gladstone's policy in regard to Irish land is a huge mistake from first to last.

Adam objects strongly to the premise that 'collective property [is] the note of barbarism, while individual property is the note of civilization'. Is it possible to defend the condition of the poor, who live in degradation and filth, in England's cities? He challenges the belief that 'the chief motive for personal exertion is the desire to accumulate wealth':

> I hold, on the contrary, that the individual is capable of still greater exertion from the nobler motive of benefiting the race, and that we must construct a society in which selfishness is openly discredited if we would secure the highest development of the powers of the individual, and of the faculties of the human mind ... Mr Carnegie's distrust of the masses in the matter of money would do credit to the staunchest supporter of aristocratic government.

Philanthropy is all very well, but the recipients must be free to choose how they spend the money:

> Mr Carnegie's theory of the administration of wealth is impracticable, and if it were practicable it is undesirable. It is designed for a community of paupers, and not for a race of free men ... If Socialism be a dream, Mr Carnegie's idea of individual philanthropy producing universal prosperity is the maddest of mad delusions ... The millionaire is a product of our civilization, not according to the gospel of wealth, but according to the gospel of plunder.

Nine years earlier, O'Connor Power had recommended that the 'impartial inquirer' study socialism.[423] A Gaelic scholar, he knew that in Ireland's prehistory property was held in common.

In 'Edmund Burke and His Abiding Influence', he reminds us of that distinguished member of Samuel Johnson's Literary Club, Adam Smith:

> To be satisfied that any nation is fairly prosperous, we want to know not only that the amount of the national income is considerable, but that the great body

of the people enjoy their proper share of that income. Nor is a high rate of wages any criterion, for everything depends upon the purchasing power of money. And the surest test of material prosperity is the facility with which food, clothing, and shelter may be obtained. As Adam Smith – a contemporary of Burke's – justly says, 'accumulation makes a people rich, but distribution makes them happy'.[424]

He had championed the working man in 'The New Reform' (1885):

> The workman who has long sought direct representation can no longer be put off with the assurance that he is best represented conjointly with other classes. He feels that the best representative of working men is a working man, and the feeling is neither unnatural nor unreasonable … much of the voting power in the counties will henceforth rest with the agricultural labourers, the land legislation of the future will be conceived largely in their interest.

The Marxist *Time*[425] featured his article 'Irish Wit and Humour', a theme he had lectured on for decades. There was at least a dalliance with the Fabians. In August, he spent a pleasant Sunday with Beatrice Potter at her home, Box House in Minchinhampton. Beatrice wrote to her future husband, Sydney Webb, 'and this morning I mean to be idle and entertain my friends O'Connor Power and G. Wallas'.[426]

'The Government Plan for the Congested Districts' appeared in May 1890 in the *Nineteenth Century*. It was the second in a series of three articles, the first written by Michael Davitt, under the umbrella title 'Ireland'. O'Connor Power recalls the record of the House:

> That the chronic distress prevailing in certain congested parts of Ireland can be most safely and efficaciously relieved by a judicious and economic system of migration and optional emigration, together with a consolidation of the holdings from which tenants are removed; that in the present condition of Ireland such a scheme can be successfully carried out only by a Government Commission, with certain statutory powers, including those of purchase and sale; and that in the opinion of this House this is a subject which demands the serious attention of her Majesty's Government with a view to early legislation.[427]

And reminds his reader:

> I asked the House of Commons in 1883 to give the people the option of migration, and allow them to decide for themselves whether they would go or stay.

Many who have relatives abroad to receive them, and who have not family ties at home to bind them, will go, and will be happy and prosperous in their new homes beyond the sea. A still larger number will, I trust, elect to stay and carve out their fortunes from the developed resources of their own country.[428]

Ireland is not overpopulated, but on the western seaboard, for reasons of social and political history, the countryside is overcrowded, 'congested'. Soil is often of poor quality, providing bare subsistence, but there is plenty of semi-waste and unoccupied land where families might be accommodated.

Remedial long-term measures are the solution, not reactive responses in a crisis. Parliament, the Irish Church Surplus and charitable contributions from overseas, particularly the United States, prevented a great famine in 1880. The cost to the exchequer at that time and over many decades has been enormous. It would be more efficient to attack the causes rather than the symptoms.

A Congested Districts Board would be authorised to provide seed potatoes and seed oats to help resettlement. Roads would be built and harbours and piers improved. The Board would be granted large powers to aid Irish industry:

… in the development of the fisheries, in the instruction of persons in the curing of fish, and in teaching the knowledge of practical and scientific agriculture, and of the breeding of live stock and poultry, and in the improvement and development of weaving or spinning, or in any other industries.[429]

He is inclusive: the crofters of Scotland are also victims of the old system of eviction and ought to be helped in a similar manner. Nor does he forget urban dwellers in equally desperate straits, 'The overcrowding which festers in the large towns of the United Kingdom stands on the same footing. It is as great a scandal to our religion and our laws. It is equally dangerous to the State, and appeals with as loud a voice to all the instincts of humanity.'[430]

A report noted that the intentions of the government were excellent in theory, but the practical effect of relief measures was 'disappointing'. The 1891 Act restricted the board to the purchase of untenanted land. The following year, a major Land Purchase Act was carried, and the sum of £30 million pounds was allocated to tenant farmers to buy their holdings. Long-term mortgages became available. The Board:

… enlarged the holdings of small cottiers; taught them better methods of tillage, improved the breed of their live stock, and gave assistance to deep-sea fishing and other struggling industries. It also relieved the congestion in particular districts by acquiring untenanted land elsewhere for some of the landless inhabitants of those districts.[431]

Five years later, another Land Act would speed up the Board's workings, with compulsory powers of purchase. The Congested Districts Board was dissolved in 1923, and the staff was absorbed into the Land Commission.

A lightning rod for controversy, O'Connor Power was reported to be at a mass meeting protesting against the treatment of Russian prisoners and the persecution of Russian Jews.[432]

The Daily Chronicle

'The most influential paper in this country is the *Daily Chronicle*.'

Nothing is so fatal to corruption as publicity and discussion.

Michael Davitt's weekly newspaper, *Labour World*, was modelled on the *Boston Pilot*, the oldest Catholic newspaper in America, 'it is my opinion just the size and shape required' and will be 'a journal for the masses'.

Michael Davitt, at this time, had only the slightest association with the Irish Nationalist Movement, 'His ambition was to become a British democratic leader, with an advanced programme of social reform. He had founded in London a weekly paper, the *Labour World*, and in it he called upon Parnell to retire from public life as an atonement to public sentiment for his misconduct.'[433]

In his letters to O'Connor Power he called his project the *Weekly Earthquake* and he had high hopes for its impact. He had taken a legal action against *The Spectator*, and if it was successful, it would provide funds for the enterprise, 'My friends here are divided in opinion on the advisability of the project. The sagest of them think that Parnell and Co. will consider such an organ – although published in London – as a menace to their influence, and he believes they will try their best to ruin it.'[434]

Some months later, Healy wrote, '[Davitt] came out with an onslaught on him [Parnell] in his *Labour World*'. The 'attacks on Parnell were fiercer than anything we had said or written'. He used phrases like 'blasted reputation' and 'the imposture called Parnellism'.[435]

H. W. Massingham was universally regarded as one of the leading journalists of his generation. For a time, he was a member of the Fabian society, which purposed to move Britain firmly to the left. He 'knew everyone' and rowed in behind Davitt's venture.

In April 1891, Davitt resigned as editor of *Labour World*, and Massingham took over for the last few weeks of publication. His assistance was in vain, and the under-capitalised newspaper closed after less than a year.

Massingham, a Johnsonian, holidayed regularly in Ireland and shared O'Connor Power's radical politics and his enthusiasm for the playhouse. In 1891, he moved to the *Daily Chronicle*, 'the most literary of the dailies', and was editor from 1895 to 1899. The paper was independent, but, close to the left wing of the Radical party, it enjoyed the confidence of the trade union movement and the working man.

As a member of the National Liberal Club, Massingham trained likely candidates in practical politics and, as a parliamentary reporter, he wrote the *Chronicle*'s 'House and Lobby', a mixture of straight news and commentary. *Workman's Time* praised him, 'No man has striven more earnestly to use the Liberal Party for Labour ends.'[436]

When Massingham joined the paper, E.A. Fletcher was editor, and O'Connor Power was already one of the leading lights:

> Massingham remarks that under Fletcher, the *Daily Chronicle* reached a new standard of literary excellence through a specialisation in its editorial staff more complete than in any other paper, except *The Times*. In the Fletcher period, the political leader-writers were Robert Wilson, whom Massingham singles out as distinctly 'brilliant', O'Connor Power, MP, William Clarke (a specialist on economic problems and on American affairs, generally) and then, in 1891, Massingham himself.[437]

The *Chronicle*, founded in 1872, had the largest circulation of any daily newspaper in London. It ran to ten pages and sold for one penny. On the eve of the First World War, its editor claimed its net sales exceeded those of *The Times*, *Daily Telegraph*, *Morning Post*, *Evening Standard* and *Daily Graphic*, combined.

In the *London Daily Press*, Massingham described it as 'the most influential paper in the country' and praised its 'reasoned idealism': 'Its liveliness, variety, serious tone, and intellectual thoroughness afford a welcome relief to the slovenly and unthinking opportunism which is the curse of the modern paper.'[438] He wrote of O'Connor Power's role in the widely read paper, 'Mr O'Connor Power, one of the most polished orators that the House of Commons has ever known, has also a large and useful share in the formation of *Chronicle* opinion.'[439]

As leader-writer, O'Connor Power was positioned to promote issues close to his heart. The paper had shown 'a shyness on the Irish question'; 'How is the *Chronicle* going on Home Rule?' was a frequent enquiry. His persistence won through:

'By the end of 1892, the *Daily Chronicle*, which had previously not committed itself to Home Rule came out in its support, O'Connor Power, MP, a member of the *Daily Chronicle* staff, bringing the paper around, according to Herbert Gladstone.'[440]

O'Connor Power wrote Parnell's obituary on 8 October 1891. The *New Zealand Star* commented on the obituary in the *Chronicle*, 'he remembered only what was greatest about the uncrowned King of Ireland and obscured his manifold weaknesses'.[441]

O'Connor Power contributed to a leading Radical weekly, the *Speaker*, but the extent of his journalistic output cannot be easily gauged. Articles were not always attributed, and, in the nineteenth century, as often as not, opinion pieces, if not anonymous, were written under a pseudonym.

The Liberals returned to power in 1892, and Gladstone remained as Premier to pursue his dream of a lasting peace for Ireland. Early the following year, he introduced the second Home Rule Bill, and, despite well-organised opposition, it passed all three readings in the House of Commons. A week later it was vetoed by the House of Lords. Gladstone had a final acerbic comment, 'The question is whether the work of the House of Lords is not merely to modify, but to annihilate the whole work of the House of Commons?'[442] Home Rule took up more time in British politics than any other nineteenth-century issue, and the Empire was heartily sick of the Irish Question, the festering sore on the body politic.

Ulster remained to be conciliated, and when the legislation collapsed, Unionist Clubs, with over 80,000 members, celebrated with bonfires and attacks on Catholic communities.

William O'Brien pointed out that the principle of self-government was accepted:

> ... there remains the supreme fact that a proposal for an Irish legislature completely satisfactory to Irish patriotism has been drawn up in black and white by the greatest British statesman of the century, and passed through all its stages by a British House of Commons in a hundred deliberate votes on principle and details. That is a fact which can no more be blotted out of the constitutional history of England than the Petition of Rights.[443]

In a contemporary biographical study of Gladstone, O'Connor Power's affectionate portrait was quoted in the final chapter:

> Mr O'Connor Power furnishes us with a single incident of its influence [his spiritual energy]. He says:

The division lobby is often one of the most interesting sights in the House of Commons. There are huddled together for a brief space all the strange and varied personalities of the House. Even in the lobby, however, the great personality of Gladstone stands out. It is his usual custom to rush to one of the writing tables, and after his fashion, on which the grand symmetry and orderliness of his great life have been planned and relentlessly pursued, he will not wholly lose even the brief space of time which is there expended. Accordingly he is to be seen writing away for dear life – sometimes holding the blotting-pad on his knee when he goes back to the House, and often calmly pursuing his work amid the shouts of hatred or triumph around him.

But on Tuesday night, for a moment, he allowed the natural man to conquer. Selecting a seat in a quiet corner, he fell into a brief, hurried, but profound slumber and was lost to the world of teeming and shouting life around him. The pallid look on the face told of the fatigue of the day, but the splendid mouth, firm set was there – with that look of unalterable determination which conquers all things. It was a beautiful and impressive picture and, by a quick and electric communicativeness, all its pathos and splendour and historic significance were gathered by the crowd. The usual noise of the lobby was stilled. Silently, reverently, members paused for a moment as they went by, whispered a comment in low accents, and passed on with hearts stirred silently, but profoundly, to reverence, love, awe.[444]

The Special Commission disclosures and the seismic Parnell split had done a great deal of damage to the Irish cause, and a fresh approach was urgently required. An amnesty campaign again became the focus for Nationalists.

In 1886, the dynamitards were behind bars in Chatham. Imprisoned under the Treason Felony Act, they were known as the 'special men' and singled out for particularly harsh treatment.

Four years later, John Daly, the militant Limerick man, remembered for his intransigence to any form of gradualism or compromise, was at the centre of an enquiry. He claimed medical attendants had given him an overdose of belladonna for the treatment of a syphilitic sore. This was an attempt on his life, he alleged, and a punishment for his refusal to assist the Special Commission in its investigations – the Home Office had given permission for Richard Pigott and a representative of *The Times* to question the Irish political prisoners.

Chatham inmate Tom Clarke, who would be executed in 1916, described the appalling conditions and the effects on the mental health of the prisoners. There was petty tyranny and 'perpetual and persistent harassing'. Some died or lost their sanity. Others lived in terror of a similar fate, 'One by one I saw my fellow prisoners break down and go mad under the terrible strain – some slowly and by degrees, others suddenly and without warning.'[445]

By 1890, Daly's accusations of ill treatment had made headlines in the press, and the Visitors of Chatham, the official prison visitors, were asked to carry out an investigation. Medical officers, who were not under oath, denied the drug had been incorrectly administered. The Visitors asked for a further analysis of the belladonna compound.

At the enquiry, Fr William Alton, the Roman Catholic chaplain, told the Visitors he believed Irish prisoners were discriminated against on grounds of nationality. The prisoners had no legal representation. They had to stand for long periods and were acutely aware that when they returned to their cells they would be at the mercy of the jailers. However, in an unprecedented step, they were permitted to give written and verbal accounts of their complaints and to question witnesses.

The proceedings were reported verbatim and recorded in March 1890. The Chatham Visitors' Report was subsequently presented to both Houses in parliament.[446]

William O'Brien led an offensive at Westminster. In the press, O'Connor Power accused the Visitors of whitewashing the actions of Chatham officials and of being asked to sit in judgement on themselves. He argued that a common prisoner who had almost died from an overdose, due to medical negligence, would have been freed. Why not a political prisoner? The dynamite campaign was long over and 'the policy of dynamite had been abandoned as a futile and wicked policy': England was alone in her 'implacable severity' towards political prisoners: even the exiled Communards had been allowed to return to their homes, and many were now active in French political life.[447]

In the 1891 census, O'Connor Power was lodging with Olinthus Vignoles in 23 Dorset Street, Marylebone. Of Huguenot stock, Olinthus was the son of Irishman, Charles Vignoles, a distinguished railroad engineer. He was Minister at Marybone Chapel, close to Oxford Street, and had written variously on crime and prison. Some of his work was compiled and published as *War with Crime*. His wife, Susan, was born in Fermanagh.

The *Chronicle* ran a strong campaign for prison reform. A series of articles in 1894 analysed 'prison methods and achievements' and was dubious of the success of either the system or its initiatives. The newspaper continued to preserve the anonymity of its columnists.

Its journalists demanded domestic reforms but they also challenged the Empire's foreign policy. In 1899, Massingham opposed the Boer War. Sovereignty, he wrote, was the only reason for the conflict. The *Chronicle's* proprietor, a 'jingo paper manu-facturer', blamed a drop in circulation and revenue on the paper's anti-war stance and insisted there was to be no more criticism of government policy. Massingham resigned. 'I only resigned when I was peremptorily required to maintain absolute silence on the policy of the Government in South Africa until after the conclusion of the war. That was impossible.' Prominent members of staff, including O'Connor Power, left with him. In some quarters it was believed that Ireland's opposition to the war set the Home Rule agenda back by a decade.

In November 1891 ... Davitt, hopeful of a parliamentary seat, wrote to O'Connor Power from Ballybrack, his Dublin home, about his legal status. He was selected by the Kilkenny Convention and asked if his ticket-of-leave status disqualified him from taking a seat at Westminster, 'And would you look the matter up and let me know how the law really stands on this question.'[448]

O'Connor Power was heavily involved with the planning and direction of the election campaign, not only in preparing candidates but also advising on the Irish vote. He ran in West Mayo as an Independent Liberal, but was defeated decisively by John Deasy, the anti-Parnellite candidate. *The New York Times* reported the sur-prising result:

'British Election Strain'

In West Mayo, there was a somewhat different situation. There O'Connor Power, who is one of the most eloquent speakers alive and a man of large attainments and great personal popularity ... [failed to win a seat].[449]

The Pilgrim Soul

... a keen appreciation of homely joys.

On 28 September 1893, at the age of forty-seven, John O'Connor Power wed Avis in a ceremony at St Peter's and St Edward's Roman Catholic Church, Palace Street, Westminster. The church was also known as the Guard's Catholic Chapel, and Cardinal Manning regularly said Mass there. It closed as a parish church in 1913.

The marriage was of mixed faith, but as O'Connor Power said in his Bristol elec-tion address, 'I am a supporter of religious liberty and equality, without distinctions of any particular creed.'

Avis's sister Florence Hooke and her young nephew Harry Morrison were wit-nesses, and Frederick Percy-Perring, a mercantile clerk, was best man. O'Connor

Power gave his address as 2 Grosvenor Place, St Georges, Hanover Square, a town house of the Earl of Northumberland.[450]

Fr James Butler married the couple. For fifteen years (1889-1904), he was parish priest of Aiskew and Northallerton, in North Yorkshire, a recusant stronghold, and served as chaplain to Her Majesty's Prison Service in the county jail. Born in 1837 in Barnes, Surrey, he had lived in the Oblate Community of St Charles College, a congregation of secular priests, founded by Manning. At the time of Newman's elevation to Cardinal, he was resident at St Mary of the Angels, Bayswater. His diaries record he was not happy with the move to the Yorkshire parish.

Avis, who was six years younger than O'Connor Power, was from a close-knit middle-class family, the Hookes of Camberwell. She was born and grew up in Stoke Newington, an established nonconformist village. The Quakers, with two Meeting Houses, had a strong presence in the north London suburb, and Avis may have been educated in the Quaker model school in the grounds of nearby Abney Park. Her father, Edwin, was a Captain in the 1st Middlesex London Regiment and later Chief Accountant for the London Docks Company in Wapping. On his appointment, the family moved to a terraced Georgian home on Pier Head, purpose-built accommodation for officials of the company. Edward Hooke, her uncle, was a lawyer at Lincoln's Inn, and Avis was named for his wife, who was a Lamont and raised in Jamaica.

Following in the footsteps of Florence Nightingale, Avis worked in a caring profession. In the 1881 census, she is living with her parents, giving her occupation as a trained nurse. Quakers believe women are equal partners with men, and the school in Stoke Newington providing an outstanding education, prepared its students for a vocation outside the home. Realistically, the only profession open to women, apart from teaching, was nursing.

The honeymoon was extended. O'Connor Power was absent from The Johnson Club suppers in 1894, the year following his marriage. From 1883-99, he practised on the South Eastern Circuit, indicating he lived with Avis and young Hubert in her Ramsgate home for the first five years of the marriage. In 1899, the couple moved to Chasseral, 20 Liverpool Road, Kingston Upon Thames, close to beautiful Richmond Park, the largest urban green space in Britain, and not far from Camberwell.[451] Over fifteen years later, they moved to a new home in Luttrell Avenue, in the borough of Wandsworth, and a short walk from Putney High Street and Putney Common.[452] The two houses were approximately five miles distant by road, on opposite sides of the famous park.

Avis may have met her first husband, Hubert Foveaux Weiss, in St Bartholomew's Hospital in London. In the hospital's archive there is a record of his registration as a student on 1 October 1872. In the Register of Probation Nurses, Avis Hooke, aged twenty-four, was awarded her certificate on 30 April 1878. She left the same day to work in the West London Hospital, which was established that year to cater to the needs of the working-class population in the area. She was later joined by Hubert, who took up a post as assistant surgeon in the skin department and made 'great efforts in the direction of forming a School of Medicine but without success'.[453] Information is scant, as the hospital's records did not survive the bombings of the Second World War.

Hubert attended the Rotunda lying-in hospital in Dublin in 1878 and received a diploma in midwifery. O'Connor Power's star was in rapid ascent and their paths may have crossed at a political meeting or in Doran's of Molesworth Street. They were both young, energetic men, who loved theatre, music halls, and living life to the full.[454]

It is possible that Avis and Hubert were prison visitors, and a mutual concern for the conditions of England's prisons and the inmates brought them into contact with O'Connor Power. The formidable founder of the Stoke Newington school, Susanna Corder, wrote a biography of Elizabeth Fry, whose pioneering work led to major reforms in the penal system. Fry was a role model for altruistic middle-class women.

Hubert's grandfather, Johann Weiss, had arrived in England from Rostock, Germany, in the late eighteenth century. He was descended from a family of Master Cutlers, and, with his skill and inventive brilliance, found fame and fortune in England, designing and manufacturing surgical instruments. He invented the first gastric pump, 'Patent syringe for the extracting of poisons from the stomach' and a special saw for amputations. Prior to the Weiss saw, a relay of saws had to be used, causing delay and unnecessary danger and discomfort. For veterinary use, he developed a spring fleam which facilitated bloodletting in horses. As recognition for his distinguished services in the field of medical science, Johann was made a Freeman of his native Rostock. As a supplier of quality medical instruments to the British armed forces, he was granted the Royal Arms.

Weiss surgical knives, of proven quality, were the silent weapons of choice for the Invincibles.[455] The attack in the Phoenix Park was carried out close to the Viceregal Lodge and its security cordon, and gunfire would have immediately alerted the RIC and the nearby army barracks.

Johann's son Frederick joined him in the firm, John Weiss & Son, which operated from the Strand in London. Today, John Weiss International continues to flourish in Milton Keynes as part of the Haag-Streit group.

Frederick's second son, Hubert Foveaux, was a Fellow of the Royal College of Surgeons and of the Royal Geographical Society. Well liked and respected, he was a gregarious and hospitable man, noted for his good humour. He married Avis in

1887, and the following year they had a son, also named Hubert Foveaux. In 1891, Hubert retired, moving to a family home in Ramsgate, possibly for health reasons. A physically active man all his life, he loved sailing, and in July, the following year, he died of pneumonia in Portsmouth harbour aboard his yacht, *The Cruiser*. 'He was a thoroughly good fellow, loved by his many friends for his geniality,' reported the Royal College of Surgeons' *Lives of the Fellows*. In his late thirties when he died, he left Avis a young widow with a small child. Fourteen months later she married O'Connor Power.

It is also possible that Hubert and Avis met O'Connor Power at one of F.C. Burnand's parties in his Ramsgate home. *Punch's* editor was a friend of O'Connor Power's and in Burnand's *Catholic Who's Who*, 1908, 1919, the entry for O'Connor Power gives appropriate mention to Hubert, 'Power, John O'Connor – born 1846, son of Patrick Power of Ballinasloe; Called to the Bar at the Middle Temple 1881; represented Mayo, as a Home Ruler 1874–85; Married (1893) Avis, widow of Hubert Foveaux Weiss, FRCS.'

Young Hubert was a student at Epsom College for two years. The school, with a strong tradition of medical families, gave scholarships to boys intent on studying medicine. From 1902 to 1906, he attended King's College School, which moved from its original site on the Strand to Wimbledon in 1897. The school's famous rowing club, with its boat house on Putney embankment, is only a short walk from Luttrell Avenue, and Hubert may have inherited his father's love of water sports. Originally, the school was the junior department of King's College, University of London, where Hubert went on to read medicine. In 1912, he entered the Home Civil Service as assistant surveyor in the General Post Office. At the end of February 1918, he joined the Post Office London Regiment Territorial Force. Seven months later, a Second Lieutenant in the Medical Services, he died of his wounds in France, in the last weeks of the First World War.

A month before he died, he made his will, dated 3 August 1918, and gave Luttrell Avenue as his address. Leaving his mother the bulk of his estate, he made small bequests to his cousin Edward Green and to his friend and colleague, assistant surveyor, William Stellman Harrison. Harrison was married to Eunice Affleck Graves, a member of the Irish literary family. She was born in Ballinasloe and married William in Westport, County Mayo.[456]

Avis was a woman with a strong sense of purpose. Not only had she worked for many years as a nurse, a demanding vocation, but she married two very remarkable men. She survived them both and lived to the age of ninety-six, dying in 1948. She had lost two beloved husbands, and her only son. Many family members and friends also died in the world wars.

At the age of sixty-nine, she travelled to New Orleans, probably *en route* to Barbados and Jamaica. At eighty-one, she made the long journey to South Africa. These would not have been excursions to the sun.[457]

In her will, drawn up a couple of months before her death, she left token legacies to sons of a prominent Quaker family in Northumberland, 'to my three friends, William, John and Arthur Kitching'. All her important connections appear to be Quaker, nonconformist, and many names are traceable in academe. The Chaning Pearce family were dear to her. Dr Joseph Chaning Pearce was celebrated in several fields, and his wife was a prominent member of the National Union of Women's Suffrage, Ramsgate branch. Melville Chaning Pearce, whom Avis knew from the cradle, was a renowned theologian. To her 'old friend' Nellie Chaning Pearce, a graduate of Girton College, Cambridge (the first Oxbridge college to offer places to women), she left her three-stone diamond ring. Nellie (Elinor) took a year out when at Girton. Her younger brothers and sisters were dangerously ill with scarlet fever, and she was called home to Ramsgate to care for them. Avis may well have helped nurse the Chaning Pearces in that fateful year, 1892.

There was a small bequest to Dr Herbert Owen Taylor, the son of an old friend and of an age with young Hubert. Avis left the bulk of her estate to her nephew Edward Green, who remained close to her after the death of her son and husband.

She stipulated in her will that all her papers, letters and diaries, kept in a locked drawer in her desk, were to be burnt and her remains cremated, 'I desire my body to be cremated and I command my Executors to burn unopened my private letters and diaries and especially a presentation book to me from Barbadoes and any other mementoes in a locked drawer in my desk.'

Avis and O'Connor Power were together almost a quarter of a century. She was at his side when he died of heart failure, only a few months after the death of her son. She buried him in her family's plot in Abney Park, the first nonconformist, nondenominational cemetery in England. All classes and creeds had access to its plots, and its chapel provided space for services of all faiths. Abolitionists and radical thinkers are buried here.

Inspired by Mount Auburn in America, it is a charming Victorian 'rural' cemetery. No longer used for burials, it is maintained as a wildlife sanctuary and open to the public. One of the admired features in the thirty-two-acre park is the arboretum. The entrance – Egyptian Revival – is striking, and the ruined chapel, deep in the interior, with its rose windows and castellated turrets, draws one to prayer.

The Quaker model school, Newington College for Girls, was originally in the grounds of Abney Park. Avis would have known the landscape intimately, and it may have been a comfort to bury her husband in a place where she had many childhood memories.

An ecumenist, O'Connor Power had friends of all faiths, but he was a Catholic to the end. The headstone reads:

To the Memory of
John O'Connor Power
Born 13 February 1847 Died 21 February 1919
RIP

The stone gives 1847, and the cemetery records 1845, as the year of his birth. Both are incorrect.

Our Lady of Pity and St Simon Stock[458] is just around the corner from Luttrell Avenue and in the last decade of his life was his parish church. The death notice was read on Sunday, 23 February, and the Requiem Mass was celebrated at 10.15 a.m. on Thursday 27 February. The burial was the following day.

St Simon Stock, a jewel in the Church's building programme, was partly designed by Westminster Cathedral's architect. Long in the planning and completion, the cathedral symbolised a Church Triumphant. In earlier, less tolerant times, prominent Catholics had worshiped in the chapels of foreign ambassadors.

Disraeli allows his character in *Lothair*, Miss Arundel, to illustrate the grand design:

Had I that command of wealth of which we hear so much in the present day, and with which the possessors seem to know so little what to do, I would purchase some of these squalid streets in Westminster, which are the shame of the metropolis, and clear a great space and build a real cathedral, where the worship of heaven, should be perpetually conducted in the full spirit of the ordinances of the Church. I believe, even this country might be saved.[459]

O'Connor Power was established professionally and socially long before he married Avis. At the time of their marriage, he had been practising at the Bar for over a decade. A respected journalist, he had made his mark, with name recognition on several continents, wherever the Irish had settled.

In 1881, he was a guest at the dinner tables of senior politicians, and attended the parties of the society hostesses of the day. In 1881 and 1882 he was dining with the Earl and Countess of Jersey and Sir Arthur and Lady Hayter. A political agenda was not only advanced at Westminster, but by contacts and friendships forged in Fleet Street, club land and the social round of London and country house parties.

Leading hostesses might wield immense power. Anthony Trollope's Lady Glencora, Duchess of Omnium in the Palliser novels, made and broke many a political adventurer. The Byronic Disraeli, a rank social outsider, rose to the highest office, and it was no small thanks to the charm he used to full advantage in society's drawing rooms. Queen Victoria was smitten by Dizzie's flattery, which he laid on 'with a trowel' for royalty.

Sir Edward Hamilton, private secretary to Gladstone, recorded an encounter at Lady Hayter's when O'Connor Power bent his ear:

> On Saturday at Lady Hayter's I met O'Connor Power, and he volunteered to me some not uninteresting and useful information. The gist of it was this: Parnell had approached O'C. Power before Parliament met, and having no false pride or feeling of resentment, he (O'C. Power) expressed himself as willing to resume if possible their parliamentary relations. He accordingly again attended the meetings of the Irish party on their return to London. To his regret, however, he found Parnell perfectly uncompromising, unpractical, and closed to reason, swayed by violent counsels such as those which proceed from O'Donnell, the most unprincipled and violent of the whole lot; and O'C Power therefore found it necessary to part company again with Parnell.[460]

T.P. O'Connor linked O'Connor Power's name to Lady Jersey's.[461] Margaret, Countess of Jersey, the foremost among the political hostesses of her day, had a particular interest in the Irish Question, and toured Ireland with her parents before her marriage, 'As a girl, Margaret had arrived in the dark at Glengariff and 'awoke to glorious scenery quivering in sunshine and colour'.[462] One of her daughters married a Packenham, another a Dunsany. The third daughter married a Welshman. Lady Jersey claimed she spent her summers moving between her daughters' Celtic castles.

Sir William and Lady Gregory were guests at her parties. Sir William's career had been meteoric. A close friend of Anthony Trollope, he may have supplied some of the qualities of Phineas Finn, who rose rapidly in social circles, thanks to his charm and gallant way with the ladies.

She was a dedicated hostess, 'Emollience was, perhaps, Margaret's most useful contribution to the political life of her time.'[463] Her obituary was affectionate: 'To English society her absence will be a terrible loss, as, with the utmost simplicity, she is the one person left in England capable of holding a salon and keeping it filled to the advantage of all who enter it.'[464] She was a polished speaker and an accomplished author. Her autobiography, *Fifty-One Years of Victorian Life*, was well received. An article on the role of women in society, 'Ourselves and Our Foremothers', appeared in January 1890 in the *Nineteenth Century*. Not a feminist in the suffragette mould, she believed that any woman worth her salt might make a decisive contribution to the events of the day, for, like an experienced civil servant, she knew you can accomplish anything if you allow another to take the credit. She was susceptible to male charm and, records in her autobiography, that when sitting next to Cardinal Newman at dinner, despite her aversion to Rome, found him 'very attractive'. A lifelong Tory, she happily offered friendship and hospitality to those of all religious and political persuasions, filled her salon with society's leaders, and provided a safe and reassuring forum for informal interaction between men and women of divergent views.

On the death of the Queen Empress, the Victoria League was established in 1901 to honour her memory. The first meeting was held in Downing Street and attended by the wives of leading politicians of the major parties. Lady Jersey was appointed president and held the position for twenty-five years. The League promoted Commonwealth friendship and lobbied successfully for radical factory legislation in the colonies. Imperialist Rudyard Kipling believed it was 'the first attempt to organise sympathy' among the countries and peoples of the Empire. The League continues to offer hospitality to Commonwealth students visiting England.

Throughout the history of Britain's colonial period, women led the way in easing social contact, conciliating and building relationships. In London, on 26 May 1897, O'Connor Power addressed the annual conference of the Women's National Liberal Association:

Colonial policy formed the first subject of discussion. Mr J. O'Connor Power moved – 'That this Conference views with profound apprehension the policy of handing over in any part of the British Empire what is practically unlimited power to chartered companies, a policy which has resulted in great friction with neighbouring States and high-handed and unjustifiable treatment of native races; and it calls upon the Government to retain full control in its own hands of all Imperial responsibilities.' Mr O'Connor Power drew attention to some of the lessons which might be drawn from the recent history of our colonies. Canada, the most disaffected of all at the beginning of the Queen's reign, was now one of the most loyal. It was then governed from Downing Street; now it is a free federation of self-governing provinces. Canada had taught us that the great principle of federation was compatible with the British Constitution. There was a movement in favour of federation in the Australian colonies, and he hoped it would succeed. In South Africa we were finding out the evil of government by commercial companies, though we had had plenty of opportunities of forming an opinion upon that point previously. We ought to see, too, that alcoholic liquors were not supplied to the natives and that slavery was not established under the name of forced labour.

The resolution was seconded and carried unanimously.[465]

The day after his birthday, on 14 February 1878, O'Connor Power had registered in the Middle Temple (*alma mater* of Edmund Burke, Brinsley Sheridan, Oliver Goldsmith and Thomas Moore), and was called to the Bar, Michaelmas Term, 17 November 1881. The Honourable Society of the Middle Temple gives details:

> Admission to the Honourable Society of the Middle Temple, Register of Admissions:
> John O'Connor Power, of 10 Molesworth Street, Dublin, and M.P., Gentleman, (32), the third son of the late Patrick Power, of Ballinasloe, Co. Galway, Gentleman, deceased is specially admitted into the Honourable Society of the Middle Temple and he gives for a fine £10.

O'Connor Power's paternal uncle was a tenant farmer. What was his father's occupation? 'Gentleman' was a catch-all term and might mean unemployed, 'the appellation of gentleman, though now lost in the indiscriminate assumption of Esquire, was commonly taken by those who could not boast of gentility'.[466]

His London address was 269 Vauxhall Bridge Road, S.W. He kept eleven of the requisite twelve terms prior to his call, and bencher Charles Henry Hopwood attested that he was 'a fit and proper person'.

During his early years of practise, he was still an MP and a popular after-dinner speaker. He occupied chambers at 5 King's Bench Walk (1882-7), 2 Brick Court (1888-96) and 1 Essex Court (1897-1916). The Head of Chambers at Essex Court was (Charles) Willie Mathews – 'Spy' presents him as 'He Can Marshall Evidence'. Mathews, a Liberal, was a well-known criminal lawyer with a love of theatre and sport. In his later years, he was Director of Public Prosecutions.

In his legal life O'Connor Power was versatile – murder, burglary – and might be 'troublesome'. In 1885 he delivered the Travers' lecture on 'A Commercial Code' at the London Institution, signalling his expertise in the codification of international trade law.

From 1883, he practised on the South Eastern Circuit. From 1899 until 1918, he was involved with the North and South London sessions and the Central Criminal Court. The law firms currently at the addresses he occupied have no relevant archival material.

We'll Never Have Better

I will do my utmost, at every risk, while life lasts …

Hopes for Home Rule were in abeyance. The struggle for independence was in the doldrums. In 1894, IRB veterans met and formed the Old Guard Union. The Brotherhood reinvigorated its mission statement and, seeking to attract a new generation, emphasised the romance and idealism of the Fenian cause. The sacred principle of self-government was non-negotiable, but while it rejected extreme methods, the Union could 'accommodate diversity'. Each man played his part. There was pride in the past, no regrets and no apologies. Patriots, they had faced dangers and setbacks, and, despite strong disagreements, they were bonded by memories of former campaigns. Trading colourful insults was often a practised rhetoric, and a mutual commitment to Ireland contained difference.

The emphasis was now on co-operation and building on the movement's unquestionable strengths. Statements from the early seventies illustrate the agenda:

Common sense would also point out to us the advisability of giving the preference to our friends in all our dealings, we should thus make it the interest of many at present half hearted or indifferent to openly join the national ranks.[467]

… [the IRB] shall confine itself in time of peace to the exercise of moral influences – the cultivation of union and brotherly love amongst Irishmen, the propagation of republican principles and the spreading of the knowledge of the national rights of Ireland.[468]

The sad fact that great numbers of our brothers are constantly emigrating to America and Australia having been touched upon, the convention most strongly advised the immediate formation of branches of our organisation in every place where the Irish emigrant plants his foot, in order to preserve his services to his country. Such branches would be of great use in developing a spirit of brotherly kindness among our people in those countries, and would be of great benefit to those whom circumstances may compel to tear themselves from our beloved country.[469]

The Old Guard confirmed an apostolic link. The Bold Fenian men built a bridge between past and present, and planned the future. They shared an identity, a history and a common purpose. The Grand Old Irishman of the North, Bernard McAnulty, took his place on the platform with William O'Brien at the 1894 St Patrick Day's celebration in Tyneside's Co-operative Hall. If they laid down their arms, it was because armed insurrection was impracticable, not because it was immoral. In the main, they were Irish Catholics but remained independent of the Church, which had supported Parnell to preserve its power. Guardians of the Fenian legacy, chieftains in their communities, they were supremely confident of their role in the Gaelic world.

A month later the Irish Trade Union Congress was formed in Dublin.

An Irish-Ireland movement heralded the rebirth of Gaelic civilisation, a cultural entity which had been all but obliterated by centuries of British misrule. Now it experienced a burgeoning power and demanded respect. Tir na nÓg, an unvanquished Eden, was re-imagined. Autonomy – cultural, political and economic – was the compelling aspiration, and, with a fluid line between art and politics, literary romantics and revolutionaries flaunted a renascent heritage. Excellence in endeavour would muster pride and confidence. Orange and Green were to be reconciled.

IRB men were prominent in new societies and associations. The Gaelic Athletic Association was founded in 1884, and Archbishop Croke accepted the invitation to be its first president. Four of the original seven members were Fenians. The GAA swiftly took root in villages and towns.

Hurling was a traditional Gaelic game, with prehistoric origins, and, in 1891, an All-Ireland Championship proudly acknowledged an old love and skill. With passion and purpose, Sunday hurlers took to the fields and country roads. The Ballyduff 'boys' in North Kerry claimed victory the first year. The village was an IRB stronghold and one of the team, James McDonnell, was a founding member of the GAA in the Kingdom.[470]

The association was a nursery of the revolution, and the hurley, a symbol of a native strength and vigour, boldly challenged British authority on Irish soil. Clubs flourished across the world and an Irishman in a foreign land made the local GAA a home from home.

Racing was the sport of kings, and Irish horses and greyhounds were highly valued throughout the islands, winning prizes at major meetings. Fenians continued to gather discreetly at coursing events and at the race track.

The introduction of National Schools in 1831, when English became the medium of education, dealt a blow to the Gaelic language. After the Great Famine, the national language was no longer viable as a life skill. Parents spoke English to their offspring, preparing them for the inevitable one-way ticket to a precarious new life. If a child spoke the vernacular, he was frequently punished. Teachers strung a wooden tally around a child's neck, and if a word of Irish was uttered in the home, the parents were to mark it. Each notch earned a blow from the teacher. The rejection of the mother tongue, with its disconnection from a Gaelic past, delivered a deep psychological wound to national self-esteem.

In 1893 the Gaelic League was formed to restore Ireland's first language. It provided classes, lectures, social and musical gatherings and promoted the study of Irish literature, history and archaeology. Irish place names were reintroduced. The educated middle classes acquainted themselves with the native tongue. Irish music, dance and folklore became fashionable. Children were baptised with long-neglected Celtic names, and Fenian songs lulled babes to sleep. Native industries were fostered and traditional crafts revived. What had been a subculture moved into the mainstream. There was a deep nostalgia for the old ways, the old values, 'Rare now is it, to find the old-time hospitality, the charity to the poor, the neighbourliness, the common sympathy, the contempt for wealth, the self respect, to which travellers, native and foreign, bore abundant testimony, as the appanages of our people.'[471]

A literary revival flourished: Yeats, Moore, Wilde, Shaw, Stoker, Synge were leading lights. Aloysius O'Kelly and Jack B. Yeats painted a new image of Ireland. Arthur Perceval Graves and Charles Villiers Stanford collaborated on a collection of Irish songs. Poetry, plays, novels, music, and painting showcased Irish genius. In London, the Irish Literary Society grew out of the Southwark Irish Literary Club, taking over its library, Irish classes and members. Barry O'Brien (president), Arthur Perceval Graves (secretary), Charles Russell and W.B. Yeats, met on 13 February 1891 to inaugurate the society. In his biography of Russell, Barry O'Brien writes that Russell 'had indeed become an original member and a vice-President at my request. He occasionally presided at our meetings, and even took part in our discussions.'[472]

In 1899, the Irish Literary Theatre, later renamed the Irish National Theatre Society, was founded by W.B. Yeats, Lady Gregory and Edward Martyn. The society staged new Irish plays in the Abbey Theatre and toured Ireland with the productions.

The Abiding Influence

He annexed morality to politics …[473]

Edmund Burke represented the bustling port of Bristol, 'England's second city', at Westminster. In 1895, O'Connor Power followed in his footsteps and stood as a Radical Liberal in Bristol South. The old enemy, *The Times*, accused him of gun running and membership of an illegal organisation. He responded with a threat of legal action.[474]

On the hustings, he repeated his conviction that the power of the House of Lords must be restrained:

> The reforms to which the whole Liberal Party is pledged will find in me a staunch supporter. Among these, one of the most important is the assertion of the supremacy of the representative branch of the Legislature. It is not right that the verdict of the Country should be set aside by hereditary legislators, acting not as a revising chamber, bona fide, but as the instrument of one political party.

He believed that a system of local assemblies, and Home Rule for Ireland, would make the business of government move efficiently:

> I am convinced that the delegation to local assemblies and of all legislation of a local character is required alike in the interest of the efficiency of the Imperial Parliament and the contentment of all parts of the United Kingdom. In other words a system of Home Rule, limited by the fullest guarantee for the maintenance of the Union and of the supreme authority of the Imperial Parliament.

He was in favour of 'a conciliatory foreign policy'. The colonies should be bound to the mother country 'by interest and affection'.

All his life he had taken a great interest in workers in town and country, and in two parliaments had fought for a less expensive administration. He was in favour of social reform and help for the poor, but would not want to interfere with the Friendly Societies, who do so much good, 'Social reforms will always receive my attention and sympathy … in making provision for the aged poor, without interfering with the actions of the Friendly Societies which are now doing so much good in the same direction.'

He acquitted himself well in the poll but was defeated by the sitting Tory member: (Conservative) 5,190, (Liberal) 4,431. Three years later, in 'Edmund Burke and His Abiding Influence', published for the centenary of Burke's death, he has his say, 'On the national question Burke was opposed to separation, but in favour of legislative independence. He held that "a natural and cheerful alliance is a more secure link of connection than subordination borne with grudging and discontent."'

Burke lost his Bristol seat because of his opposition to restrictions on Irish trade and his championship of Catholic Emancipation. He claimed 'the exercise of an independent judgement as an inalienable right'.

With regard to Ireland: He had mastered all her problems, and his devotion to her interests cost him a distinction which he greatly prized – the representation of the ancient city of Bristol.

I do not suppose that Burke was troubled by the distracting claims of a dual allegiance – to England as the sphere of his duty, and to Ireland as the place of his birth. In this very Bristol speech he raises the point himself, and disposed of it effectually by declaring that he was an American in the affairs of America as much as he was an Irishman in the affairs of Ireland.

His statue in Bristol bears the inscription, 'I want to be a Member of Parliament in order to take my share in doing good and resisting evil.'

United Irish League

The Rising of the Moon.

There are centenaries to mark, and early in 1897, a dinner honoured Edmund Burke's birthday. O'Connor Power presided, and there were over seventy Nationalists present.[475] The following March, the 1798 Rebellion was remembered, and he celebrated with Irish leaders on St Patrick's Day. He was a guest of honour at John Dillon's table at the Ninety-Eight Celebration in London and, together with William O'Brien, gave the principal toast. Centenary events took place across the world.[476]

In the west of Ireland, several groups vied for control of the celebrations but William O'Brien, who was living in Westport, secured the backing of Archbishop MacEvilly of Tuam and the Mayo clergy. James Daly, who had sold the *Connaught Telegraph* ten years earlier, remained a force in local politics and was elected president of the Connacht '98 Council.

O'Brien, working closely with Daly, laid plans for a countrywide organisation. The United Irish League was inaugurated early in the centennial year of the Rising and named to honour the memory of the United Irishmen. John Dillon, MP for Mayo East, was present at the launch in Westport. The League's purpose was to re-energise Nationalists and take the initiative from a divided Irish party now, in an apparent state of inanition. Parnellites and anti-Parnellites were 'an assemblage of jarring atoms'.[477]

The League swiftly became a dynamic force, and branches were established across Ireland. Chief Secretary Gerald Balfour's strenuous efforts to suppress the new organisation helped to make it popular; the UIL soon had a presence in every parish, and its membership topped 80,000.

The 1898 Local Government (Ireland) Act gave its *raison d'être* a practical focus and UIL candidates stood successfully at elections. Seventy-five per cent of seats in county, urban and rural district councils were taken by Catholics. Power was devolved to locals and away from Westminster and the landowning gentry.

The following year, Gerard Balfour's Land Act put in place a Department of Agriculture for the development of the industry.

The League's Divisional Executive, with delegates from every branch, sent a delegate to a National Directory. Michael Davitt was President of the Directory and James O'Kelly was Vice-President. There were officers from the Parliamentary party on the Directory, but the selection of delegates was democratic, ensuring grass-root concerns were not ignored. Bureaucracy was kept to the minimum, with few meetings. Work was decentralised, and the programme encompassed agrarian and urban issues.

The UIL was preparing the ground for home government, training branch executives in organisation and decision-making. The ultimate goals were land ownership and legislative independence. The weapons of resistance remained the non-payment of rent and the boycott. Staying within the law, the UIL pursued its aims by peaceful means but every membership card had a picture of Wolfe Tone, encircled by pikes, with the words 'who fears to speak of '98'. The pikes recalled the rebellion and its marching song, 'The Rising of the Moon' – 'a thousand pikes were flashing by the rising of the moon'. Emphasising solidarity, the Directory notepaper, with an image of a stook of grain, was headed 'Union is strength'.

Many priests were involved, although, as an institution, the Church did not take a leading role. The League was determined to show its independence and demonstrate that the Irish were not a priest-ridden people.

Land and local government reforms did not impinge on Irish America. Thousands of miles across the Atlantic Ocean, the Clan, its attention diverted by the United States war with Cuba, took no part in the '98 celebrations.[478] Patrick Ford, editor of the Boston *Irish World*, wrote to Davitt offering encouragement and some money, but explained it was difficult to arouse sympathy or interest. Davitt solicited support from Irish newspaper editors across the world.

On 1 March 1899, the Irish National League of Great Britain held a mass meeting in East London in support of the UIL. Many Irish MPs did not take kindly to the incursions on their power base, and in William O'Brien's correspondence, difficulties with the invitation list for London's St Patrick's Day Banquet are discreetly aired.

A National Convention was held in Dublin on 20 June 1900, to consider the Act of Union, the hundred years of rule from Westminster. The programme and constitution of the UIL was presented and accepted, and the machinery for its future working confirmed. The League became the recognised constituency organisation of the Irish party, which reunited under the leadership of John Redmond. Irish MPs who were reluctant to participate put their seats at risk. O'Connor Power was invited to address the convention:

> He came again before the public in 1900 in the establishment of the United Irish League. He visited Mayo, and was well received.

> Mr O'Connor Power, whose rising to address the convention created some surprise and astonishment among the delegates, said he wished to express his hearty approval of the programme of the convention. The effect produced in Great Britain would be enormous.

He submitted the following clause:

> … putting an end to periodical distress and famine in the west by abolishing, on terms of just compensation to all interests affected, the unnatural system by which all the richest areas of the province are monopolised by a small ring of graziers, and restoring to the people the occupation of those lands in holdings of sufficient size and quality.[479]

It was an opportunity to visit his brother in Galway and his friends in the West.

In the general election in the autumn of 1900, the UIL, now with 100,000 members, ran candidates, and O'Connor Power, working closely with the election team, was considered for several constituencies. He was one of three candidates nominated in South Mayo, the seat vacated by Davitt in protest against the Boer War.[480] The UIL nominated him for West Cavan in October 1900.[481]

The following year, at the end of May, he was present, as a delegate from Kingston Upon Thames, at the UIL annual convention, which was held at the Royal Hotel in Bristol. He proposed and it was 'resolved to tender the proprietors of the *Irish People* and the *Sligo Champion* the heartfelt sympathy and cordial thanks for their patriotic resistance to the government of Dublin Castle'. He recommended that non-members of parliament be eligible to sit on the UIL executive.[482] He condemned the war. *The Times* reported:

> Mr O'Connor Power said that the salvation of Ireland and Great Britain, if it came at all in the present generation, would come through independent, uncorrupted and disinterested action of an independent Irish party in the House of Commons.

There was no hope of progressive forces of Great Britain returning to power until they had purged themselves of complicity in a cruel and unjust war.[483]

In October 1901, a month before the death of his brother Tom, he looked for support for his candidature in Galway and wrote to Fr P. Dooley, parish priest of Galway and chaplain for over forty years to the Catholic members of the military stationed in the city. Fr Dooley was landlord of 6 Victoria Place, home for a time to Eileen O'Shaughnessy, O'Conner Power's niece.

Chasseral,
Liverpool Rd,
Kingston Hill,
Surrey.

11 Oct. 1901

Dear Fr Dooley,

I was much pleased when his Lordship, the Bishop, informed me that you had kindly promised to support my candidature for the vacancy in Galway and I beg for you to accept my warmest thanks.

May I therefore place before you the following facts? I am a member of the United Irish League of Gt Britain, and I attended the annual Convention of that body, at Bristol, on May the 25th of this year, as the delegate of the Kingston-on-Thames branch.

At the banquet which followed the Convention I was entrusted by the President of the League with the toast, 'The United Irish League', to which the Secretary, Mr J.F.X. O'Brien, MP and Mr J.C. Flynn MP responded. I spoke also at the Convention, and at the public meeting held on the following day, in company with the President, Mr T.P. O'Connor MP, Mr Blake MP, Mr J.F.X. O'Brien MP, Mr Wm Redmond MP and the representatives of the U.I.L. assembled from all parts of Gt Britain.

I attended the National Convention in Dublin which was held prior to the General Election of last year and assisted in constituting the U.I.L. the national organisation of Ireland. I was entrusted on that occasion by the President of the Convention, Mr John Redmond, with the resolution relating to congested districts and grass farms; and congratulated, afterwards, on my return to Irish politics, which had taken place two years before, at the Ninety-Eight Celebration in London, over which Mr John Dillon presided. I was specially invited to that Celebration to speak to the principle toast in company with Mr William O'Brien MP thus the public reconciliation between old colleagues and myself has been reported and commented upon in the public press. There is therefore no room for misapprehension as to my political attitude.

And it only remains for me to add that I am prepared, if adopted as a Parliamentary Candidate, to sign and observe the party pledge to sit, act and vote with the Irish Party; and to resign my seat, if in the opinion of the party I fail to act up to the spirit or the letter of the pledge. I have not the precise terms of the pledge before me, at this moment, but I know its purport; and you may inform the Convention that I accept it unreservedly.

I have not communicated with any of the Leaders of the party regarding my candidature, out of respect for their repeated declarations that they would not interfere with the free choice of the Convention.

Mr Redmond, if I remember right, emphasised this point, on behalf of himself and Mr O'Brien in his recent speech at Westport.

I assume, as a matter of course, that it is open to anyone who has adopted the programme of the League, and especially if he is a member of it, no matter how humble his position may be, to offer himself as a candidate, and to solicit, without let or hindrance, the confidence of his fellow members.

Any requirement as to recommendation or endorsement from a leader would be in direct conflict with the declaration of the Leaders themselves, and contrary, it seems to me to the Constitution of the League.

Believe me
Yours ?,
J. O'Connor Power

Revd Fr Dooley P.P.[484]

The refusal to seek the backing of the UIL leaders was in compliance with the democratic grass-roots policy of the League's Constitution. There were to be no accusations of place-hunting and no repeat of the high-handed behaviour of the Parnellites. O'Connor Power's acceptance of the party pledge confirmed the new beginnings of a united Irish party. His statement of a 'public' reconciliation is a reminder that a private split may never have been in question.

His candidacy was pre-empted by the decision to run Arthur Alfred Lynch in Galway. A meeting was held in the Racquet Court Theatre on 17 November, and

Davitt proposed Lynch for the vacant seat. Lynch was a local man, who had spent many years in Australia. A journalist, he had served in the Second Irish Brigade in the Boer War. He had been found guilty of high treason. Davitt told his audience, 'Colonel Lynch could not come to Galway because there was a price on his head, but if he was made MP for Galway the British government would not dare lay hands on him.'[485]

Lynch was unanimously adopted as Nationalist candidate, and was subsequently elected. The UIL was triumphant, but the Tory government was not impressed, 'In Galway the so-called "Colonel" Lynch was elected by a constituency because they knew he was a traitor and they voted for him because he was a traitor.'[486]

In February 1903, in his absence, O'Connor Power's name was put forward for the Galway vacancy.[487] In 1905 he was a guest at a St Patrick's Day dinner in London to fundraise for the Irish party and seconded the vote of thanks.[488]

A coalition of Tories and Unionists governed from 1895 to 1905, and expansionist policies held sway. The Boer War (11 October 1899-31 May 1902), 'conceived in greed and brought forth in violence', dominated the political scene. An enraged and vociferous Ireland made its objections clear. Irish soldiers served with distinction in the conflict but, at home, the country was horrified by accounts of atrocities in the popular press. The death rate among children in concentration camps was not to be tolerated – Davitt writes of 'Herodian infamies'. The *Manchester Guardian* reported, 'the lawful returns from the concentration camps came to our knowledge'.[489] The UIL led anti-war demonstrations across Ireland and organised relief funds for the widows and orphans of valiant Boer soldiers. Queen Victoria made a three-week visit to Ireland.

The general election in 1900, fought on a jingoistic platform, split the Liberals. Lloyd George, the messianic Welshman, was vehemently opposed to the war. It was unjust, and the money spent on it was needed for social reform and old age pensions. C.P. Scott, editor of the *Manchester Guardian*, who had founded the Manchester Transvaal Committee in July 1899, condemned the conflict. Irish voters in England were asked to register their disapproval:

Our London Correspondent on War and Election

The immediate question is the attitude of Irish Voters, who are certainly hostile to Mr Maguire. They are to be addressed on Monday by Mr O'Connor Power whose views on the war are pronounced and whose advice may have important consequences in regard to the relations between the Irish and the Liberal parties during the election.[490]

Davitt resigned his South Mayo seat in protest. He had not been comfortable in his parliamentary role. He disliked the bad behaviour of his colleagues, 'a pack of drunken rascals', and was disillusioned with Westminster politics. His health was poor and he was advised that a warmer climate might help.[491] The Tory Government was returned with a large majority.

In November 1902, O'Connor Power wrote to C.P. Scott, editor of the *Manchester Guardian*, 'I hear from a good authority that the Government contemplate important changes in their Irish policy administrative and legislative – and I wonder whether you would consider this an opportune time for a series of letters dealing with the social and industrial condition of Ireland.'[492]

He offered to spend a few weeks in Ireland, 'a preliminary investigation'. 'The revolt of the moderate landlords, and their adoption of the idea of a conference with the tenants' representatives is, I think, a hopeful sign.' He asked that Scott 'treat this note as strictly confidential'. Scott noted his reply, commenting on 'the cheerful policy, you foreshadow', and requested articles rather than letters.

The following month, December, the Land Conference, which included a small group of progressive landlords, met and prepared the ground for the Irish Land (Wyndham) Act in 1903. William O'Brien saw it as 'Conference, Conciliation, Consent', a recognition and acceptance of mutual interests. Tory Premier, A.J. Balfour, killing Home Rule with concessions, pushed the Bill through the Commons and the Lords. It was a conciliatory move, with a transfer of land to tenants, and was considered by many as a giant step towards peasant proprietorship. £100,000,000 was made available for purchase loans and, over time, almost 200,000 tenants became owner occupiers.

The Racquet Court and Billiard Hall

Remember me to them all.

O'Connor Power had no children of his own and his relationship with his brother's family was an important one. At the end of 1880, Thomas was posted home from India and arrived in England the following spring. The family is listed in the April census form for Alverstoke Barracks on the south-east coast. O'Connor Power, a restless bachelor with a strong appreciation of family ties, now had a sister-in-law and an ever-growing number of nephews and nieces to cherish.

In 1883, Thomas returned to Ireland and settled in Galway City. On 1 April 1885 he was promoted to Barrack Sergeant-Major. In the 1901 census he is listed as Barrack Warden, Army Service Corps, and is living in William Street with his wife,

Elizabeth (Gabby), his daughters Everina, Mary and Ursula and his son, Patrick. Everina helped behind the counter of the family tea shop. Mary, with a beautiful singing voice, was known as Birdie and was a student teacher. John was in South Africa serving with the Irish Rangers.

The two oldest surviving children, Emily and John, were born in what was then British India.[493] Everina was born in Southwark in 1882 and Mary two years later in Tipperary. In Galway, there were more children, while the family was living in Eyre Square. Kathleen and Thomas Henry died of TB in March and April 1890, respectively. Still toddlers, they had been in the care of the convent on Nuns' Island. Infant mortality was a cruel fact of life.

Ursula, born in 1892, and Patrick (1896) survived to a brief and harsh adulthood. In September 1916, at twenty-three years of age, Ursula died a painful death, again TB. In the early 1900s, tuberculosis, sometimes known as the 'Irish disease', was the cause of death of more than 15 per cent of the population.

Despite the pleas of his mother, Patrick enlisted with the Connaught Rangers to fight in the First World War. His much older brother, John, an experienced soldier, had tried his utmost to dissuade him. Like many other Galway men Patrick died in France and was buried there. The family has his medal and a photograph of the grave.

Thomas maintained contact with the family in Ballygill.[494] A local historian reported that John O'Connor Power wrote regularly to his uncle for whom he was named. Uncle John had no surviving sons. His daughter Honoria married a Brady from a nearby townland, and the couple took over the Power farm. In the 1901 census, Norah and Agnes Brady are living and working with their cousin, Thomas's daughter Eileen, and her family in Galway. The eighteen-year-old Agnes Brady is listed as a nursery maid and Norah Brady, at twenty-two, is a governess.

Christened Emily, Eileen, the eldest Power daughter, was born in Agra. She changed her name to the Irish version and, as Eileen, married Peter O'Shaugnessy, a Galway publican. In 1901 they have a young family: Emily, Flossie and John. As well as the Brady sisters, the second cousins from Ballygill, there are several lodgers in the house: a stage carpenter, a billiard maker, and two porters. There was already an involvement with the Racquet Court. The Bradys were a great help with the small children, while Eileen ran the house and helped out with the business. The O'Shaughnessys had two more children. Mary Eveline was born in 1904 when they were still living in Victoria Place, and Peter arrived in 1906.

The Valuations Office records that in 1902 Peter O'Shaughnessy held the lease on the Racquet Court and Billiard Rooms in Middle Street.[495] The family continued to live in Victoria Place until 1906.

Before rail travel, the coach journey to Dublin took a full two days, usually with one overnight stop. Galway, a prosperous trading and fishing port, was, by default, the focus for provincial society, and every important family in Connacht had a townhouse in the city. It was cosmopolitan, and foreigners were part of the landscape; its architecture, with its narrow streets and courtyards, and its population still reflect a strong Spanish influence.

Theatrical events and the visits of touring companies have a long history in Galway and, in 1820, James Hardiman writes:

A new theatre, however, in an open and central situation appears necessary. The assembly-room in Middle Street frequently displays an assemblage of native beauty, elegance and fashion, which would grace the drawing rooms of a court.

These with occasional concerts and incidental public exhibitions are the only species of amusement which engage the attentions of the inhabitants of Galway.[496]

The Racquet Court was a fashionable venue in the 1850s. The *Galway Express* reported, in August 1875, that a subscription had been raised by the residents for a new roof for the theatre, at that time known as the Eglinton Racquet Court.

The Court was the city's theatre and concert hall, and, in the last decade of the century, it was managed by a Thomas O'Connor. The 1894, Salters directory lists him as the proprietor. Up for sale on 5 March 1898, the business appears to have had no takers. Thomas O'Connor died in 1906.[497]

A substantial establishment, the Court had fifteen rooms, which included two licensed bars, two billiard rooms, a proscenium and toilets. There was a large yard and stabling facilities. The auditorium, with its long, low room and four square windows, seated 500, and was available for concerts and meetings.

Historian John Cunningham gathered some interesting facts, 'It was during a variety show there in 1897 that the "renowned Cinematographie, the most wonderful discovery of photography and electricity known" was first encountered.by Galwegians.'[498]

The *Galway Observer* recorded the first showing of the 'renowned Cinematographie':

The first scene shown was of the departure of employees from a Manchester factory, followed by a picturesque view of Galway Bay, a regiment of cavalry on parade, a railway station in France, a comic scene in a barber's shop, and another amusing scene in which a gardener was seen watering flowers.[499]

In the age of the music hall, live shows of touring musicians, singers and variety artistes provided a lively programme. From October 1911, the Court showed films every night, and the feature-length adaptation of Boucicault's *Colleen Bawn*, shot on location in County Kerry, drew large audiences.[500]

Peter O'Shaughnessy died young.[501] In the 1911 census, Eileen, recently widowed, is running the Court with her mother and sisters. Agnes Brady and the teenagers, Ursula and John, are not recorded in the census returns.

'Mrs O'Shaughnessy's' (with a hard G), was the heart of the social scene. The Mechanics Institute, with a radical clientele, was close by. A university city, Galway had many students, and billiards was particularly popular. Boxing contests were held in the auditorium. One event, 'a theatrical disturbance of another kind', caused quite a stir:

> On Saturday night there was a considerable uproar at the Court Theatre, Galway, owing to the failure of one of the parties in a boxing contest for £15 a side failing to put in an appearance. The students of the Queen's College, who attended in large numbers, started by throwing chairs from the auditorium to the stage, and the 'gods' threw seats from the gallery. Later on the students and the 'gods' got into handigrips, with the result that the students were routed from the theatre and chased through the streets. A number of persons were struck with stones. The police dispersed the crowds in the street and escorted the students to their homes.[502]

Peter left a large family and a successful business when he died, and Eileen, with her mother and two older sisters, took over the management. As proprietor, she had a difficult role. With no adult male in the family, there must have been many a time when she wished for a strong arm at her side. Agnes Brady served in the mineral bar, and the other women played their parts and were constantly on their feet.

Walter Macken, a stage carpenter and actor, was one of the company. In 1911, he married Agnes Brady, and the union was blessed with three children. When, at the outset of the First World War, he joined the British army, he wrote regularly to his wife from the front line in France.[503] In his letters he asked after Ursula and for news of Mrs O'C. and the Racquet Court, 'How is Mrs O'C. and all at the Racquet Court, I hope they are all well. Did poor Ursula come out of hospital yet? How is she? Remember me to them all.' And again, 'How is Mrs O'C. and all the Racquet People getting on remember me to them, Are the pictures doing well?'[504] (Until relatively recently, films were called 'pictures', a reduction of 'animated pictures'.) 'Poor Ursula' was seriously ill and died of TB in the Galway Regional Hospital, which was built on the site of the old Union workhouse. The Mercy Order originally ran the workhouse and then established the hospital. Ursula's illness was long and painful and her death a release. Agnes and Walter's son Walter, actor, novelist and playwright, stayed in contact with his cousins throughout his life.

There are many mentions in family lore of O'Connor Power's generosity and he may have sponsored the little theatre. His friendships with Dion Boucicault, F.C. Burnand and Lady Gregory were underpinned by a common passion for the arts.

In 1903, the Irish National Theatre Society put on several plays there – Yeat's *Cathleen Ní Houlihan, The Pot of Broth* and Æ's *Deirdre*.[505] In September 1906, Lady Gregory's comedies *Spreading the News* and *Hyacinth Halvey* were staged. The programme was catholic, and Samuel Franklin Cody and his man-lifting kites entertained local audiences. In 1905, Kodak gave a photographic demonstration and a display of Dekko printing to a large attendance.[506] A youthful John McCormack sang on its stage early in his career.[507] A few years later the watchdogs of the Vigilance Associations would make life difficult for strolling players, vaudeville and popular theatre

On the first Sunday of February 1907, when many of the Powers were in Dublin for Birdie's wedding,[508] a 'sacred' concert was held in the theatre. At 3 a.m. a fire broke out. It started in the main billiard room, spreading to the second billiard room, close to the auditorium. Scenery and props were destroyed. Firemen worked tirelessly but the bar under the billiard rooms was gutted.

The Court was restored. Less than a year later, J.M. Synge's *Riders to the Sea* was performed (6-10 January 1908) on its 32ft by 30ft stage. After the riots provoked by *The Playboy of the Western World*'s première in the Abbey, it was considered unwise to stage Synge in Dublin. Lady Gregory regarded herself as a Galway woman and had a hand in arranging the engagement, 'I suppose Lady Gregory will go to Galway, the date is the 6th of January.'

The Abbey's manager, Frank Fay, did not have an easy relationship with Lady Gregory, and there was a disagreement about the programme content. She wrote to him, 'I particularly didn't wish to have "Gaol Gate" [in Galway] in the present state of agrarian excitement, it [might] be looked on as a direct incitement to crime.'[509] However, she was in the audience on the Thursday and Friday nights of the five-day run, and her Nationalist friends were encouraged to attend. Fears of a violent reaction from the public came to nought, and, disappointingly, the company played to poor houses. Fay resigned a few days later.[510]

Political meetings were held in the Court, and the Galway Workers' and General Labourers' Union (GWGLU) first came together there in 1911. Later, the GWGLU affiliated with the Liverpool-based National Union of Dock Labourers (NUDL). In 1919, The Society for Discharged Soldiers and Sailors gathered at Mrs O'Shaughnessy's.

Robert Hogan interviewed Michael Conniffe, and the Gaelic playwright Seamus O'Beirn entered the narrative. Conniffe mentions the *Seaghan na Scuab* production in 1904 in the Racquet Court:

> ... and that is the first place we met the noble gentleman and patriot, Sir Roger Casement. Sir Roger Casement was so full of enthusiasm for the players that he joined them the next day on the sidecars into the village of Tawin fourteen miles away, and travelled on the sidecars with us. And the countryside applauded.[511]

Roger Casement, diplomat, poet and revolutionary, was a well-known figure in Galway and was very popular. He was executed by the British in August 1916.

The O'Shaughnessys continued to rent 11 Augustine Street after the death of Thomas Power, and held the lease on 6 Victoria Place, later used as a cinema. Both houses had yards for storage purposes.

The Powers were a close family. O'Connor Power's cousins and nieces lived and worked together in Galway. The Macken children spent summers with their Uncle Frank in Ballygill. O'Connor Power visited Galway regularly. In 1905, he had lunch in Dublin with his godson John's fiancée, Delia, who was charmed by his old-style courtesy.

The eldest Power brother came home from his travels in the early 1900s and spent some time in Galway. He slept with pearl-handled pistols under his pillow, and his party turn was to twirl them *a la* Doc Holliday.

When Birdie fell in love with a sergeant about to be posted to India, the couple needed special permission to marry, and Lord Russell, the second baron, expedited the papers. They named their first born for him. Deeply devout, they attended daily Mass and said the rosary every night. Birdie loved to sing, and in the early years of her marriage she starred in amateur productions in Simla. Her husband, Tom Stanford, a soldier in the Connaught Rangers, was one of the 'wild, reckless and undisciplined but brave and gallant' band of men, known as 'The Devil's Own'. They were fiercely loyal to Ireland, and the British government, fearful of mutiny, disbanded the regiment in the early 1920s.

Tom was successful in the Indian Civil Service exam and became dairy manager for the province of Agra. The Indian climate felled many young men of the Empire, and he died aged thirty-five of heat stroke. Birdie was expecting their third child when she heard the news of his death. She stayed in a bungalow in the grounds of the Taj Mahal until, with the end of the First World War, safe passage to Ireland was possible. She returned to Galway with her two sons and the new baby and took up residence in Augustine Street. The following summer, the family moved to

Dublin for the boys' education, and Birdie went back to her singing, taking roles in the Rathmines and Rathgar Musical Society shows. Her younger son married the daughter of Seamus O'Beirn, a founding member of the Irish language theatre An Taibhdhearc. The mothers were friends from school days and made the match at the Galway races.

Birdie had a close friendship with her cousin Agnes Brady. They were born within a year of each other and both married British soldiers. Like so many other young women, they were widowed early, and had families to rear in hard times. Agnes named her first girl for her cousin Eileen, and the second, Noreen, was nicknamed Birdie.

Everina, Eva, loved the stage and made it her career. When the curtain was falling on the Racquet Court, when Eileen and Gabby were dying, she moved to Dublin with Birdie and her family. She married and 'ran off to the music halls in England'. When her only daughter, Terry, was five, Eva became seriously ill. Shortly before her death, she sent the little girl back to Dublin where she grew up in her aunt's care.

Eileen put the theatre up for sale in 1920. On Friday 30 July, at noon, the Court was auctioned in Eyre Square.[512]

The Making of an Orator

Oratory may be defined as the art of persuasion, and its legitimate purpose, as I view it, is twofold – it is to establish the truth, and to stimulate men to righteous action.[513]

When I entered parliament it was still the day of the great orators: of Disraeli, Gladstone, Bright, David Plunkett, O'Connor Power.[514]

O'Connor Power's book on oratory was published in June 1906. The preface explains:

The object of this book is to indicate in popular language, a course of practice in oratory, based on the writer's observation and experience in the House of Commons, at the Bar, and on the platform. It is intended for the use of students, young and old, who have had no practice in public speaking, and for speakers who are not unwilling to consider suggestions made by another. The various examples have been selected as models of the form and structure of great speeches, and will, it is hoped, appeal to all lovers of noble eloquence, as well as to those who aspire to oratorical eminence.

In 'Pages in Waiting', *The New York Times* announced the book's publication and, two weeks later, reviewed it favourably, 'full of excellent advice'. *The Irish Times* critic gave it high praise:

> Every man is interesting when he writes about an art of which he himself is a master, and hence the name of Mr O'Connor Power is a guarantee that anything he has to say on the subject of oratory will repay attention ... most lucidly written chapters ... Mr Power's style is so clear and anecdotal that his book far from being a dry treatise on the rules of speech-making, is more interesting than the average novel, and indeed it is hard to put down until the last page has been turned.

O'Connor Power is 'dogmatic' on one subject and that is the 'absolute necessity of strict truth'.[515] His approach is encouraging, assuring the reader that everyone, with guidance and practise, can learn to speak well in public. The tone is one of helpful suggestion, and, unlike many books on the subject, rules and regulations are not laid down. He believes a teacher must nurture his student and 'encourage his natural freedom of speech, and impress upon him that oratory is not dependent on rule'.

A few years after the book's publication, the Limerick Jesuit Michael Phelan recommended it and repeated the advice, 'Every man can become an orator. The teacher's duty is not to create but to draw out and develop the inborn gifts.'[516]

The voice, the chief instrument of a speaker, must be developed. Elocution is vital to achieve distinct articulation. Reading aloud is a useful way to strengthen the vocal chords. However, reading aloud, giving voice to the thoughts of others may leave one passive, unengaged. An orator must think and act.

Familiarity with a subject is a basic requirement, and management of facts, order and method, are essential when preparing a presentation. Watch, listen and learn. Study polished speakers – in church, at political meetings and in courtrooms. Analyse content and delivery critically. Audibility, lucidity, simplicity are as essential in a teacher and college lecturer.

Parliaments are 'legislative workshops' and parliamentary speeches are for public information and scrutiny. Aspiring politicians must be aware that their words will be reported and studied carefully by contemporaries and posterity.

An extempore, unrehearsed speech should be the rule and a written speech the exception. Men trained in debate and familiar with their subject, may, with a little forethought, make excellent extempore arguments, 'Oratory has its origin neither in reading, nor writing, but in conversation ... It should be taught like a living language, as if talking to friends. It is important to talk about what you know, to be comfortable with your subject.'

Describing how one fledgling statesman rose to speak but was inaudible, he recommends perseverance.[517] John Bright, the distinguished English orator, faltered at
first, but learnt to speak effectively, and 'spoke in the tone of friendly conversation'.

To recite a piece verbatim is not oratory. It should not be a test of memory but the
exercise of 'rapid thinking and ready speaking'. He quotes educationalist Alexander
Bain, 'An unnatural memory may be produced at the cost of reason, judgement and
imagination.' A logical sequence of ideas powerfully aids recall. A few notes, a single
word, are enough to jog the memory and retain the flow and order of thought.

Study the 'reported masterpieces of ancient and modern eloquence'. Translation
extends vocabulary, increasing word power. Quotations may be used skilfully.
Remember 'the essence of every style is the individuality of the speaker', 'the finished orator, whose power of expression is limited only by the resources of the
language he employs'.

Unlike books and paintings, oratory must appeal to a cross section of the public.
Approach the audience with deference; much depends on 'a happy introduction'.
Maintain the interest and attention of the listener, 'Orators should vary their topics
and their style. You cannot persuade anyone unless your matter is sufficiently interesting to engage his attention.' He warns, 'And it may be observed that there is no
form of art of which the populace is so good a judge as it is of oratory.'

The style and structure of speeches of famous orators should be studied. He
describes Daniel O'Connell's rhetoric, 'as Sheil graphically expressed it, "he flung
a brood of sturdy ideas on the world without a rag to cover them"'. Yet it was
'his clarion voice, his persuasive tones, his expressive manner, his alternate strokes
of deep pathos and broad humour, his combativeness and his commanding presence, that swayed the multitudes who hung upon his words'. Length of speech
is not important, he says, and that most powerful speech, Abraham Lincoln's at
Gettysburg, is quoted in full.

Oratory is a potent weapon in the fight against the forces of evil. In the House of
Commons, Richard Brinsley Sheridan denounced Warren Hastings, India's ruthless
British overlord, demanding his impeachment. Edmund Burke, Charles Fox and
William Pitt believed this speech to be the greatest ever delivered in ancient or in
modern times.

The Pitts, the Elder and the Younger, are praised, as is William Wilberforce,
whose words and actions dealt a mortal blow to slavery. In 'Edmund Burke and His
Abiding Influence' he writes:

> Then, remembering all the orator has to contend with and all that depends upon
> the issue, we surrender our judgment, affections, and emotions to his absolute

control, and feel that we are overwhelmed, not by speech alone, however eloquent and transcendent, but by the resistless moral force of heroic action.

Demagogues, rabble rousers, who use words to no good purpose, with no moral end in sight, are the 'commonplace of history', and are not orators.

Every man finds his own style and it is his conviction of the rightness of his purpose and the vigour and force of his argument which make him an effective orator, 'but he who bravely puts all to hazard in a just cause, and throws his own personality unreservedly into the argument for truth, and right, and honour, becomes at once the teacher and the benefactor, and it may be the saviour, of his country'. In conclusion he notes a review:

> Nor is any man a great orator who has not many of the gifts of a great actor – his command of gesture, his variety and grace of elocution, his mobility of feature, his instant sympathy with the ethical tone of this or that situation, his power of evoking that sympathy in every member of his audience; and this is surely what Demosthenes meant by making ... acting, not action – the secret of all oratory.

He comments:

> This is well said, but the writer might have gone further, and insisted that the great orator must be not only an actor, but a dramatist as well. He must, indeed, have the dramatic instinct in the first place, the power of conceiving the parts and inventing the situations of which he is the interpreter to the audience.

More than one contemporary described O'Connor Power's style with the words 'earnest' and 'pleading'.[518] With close reasoning and persuasive eloquence, he swayed his audience, appealing to logic's symmetry and the heart's sentiment:

> No musical instrument, that ever was devised, is so variously susceptible as the human heart. Its moods are innumerable, and range in expression through all the notes of passion and feeling by which we are roused to action or lulled to repose, by which we are stirred to joy or sorrow, to love or hatred, to fear or confidence, to admiration or contempt, to approval or indignation, to emulation or envy, to pride, anger, shame, pity, or remorse, to acts of mean selfishness or deeds of heroic benevolence.[519]

A Broken Treaty

We of the twentieth century must find a twentieth-century policy.

I ask is faith not to be kept with the dead?

With the death of Victoria early in 1901, the certainties of Empire seemed no more. Her colourful and popular son Edward ascended to the throne, and a new monarch and a new century ushered in a changed society. The insular Victorian became the Edwardian European, and the genial King, a roving royal ambassador, developed strong relationships with France, Russia and Germany. A modern man, he deplored discrimination whether of race, class or religion. He was no stranger to Ireland, paying frequent visits to attend major events of the racing calendar.

The gulf between rich and poor yawned more cruelly than ever before. A third of Britain's population was hungry, living in urban slums. Blinkered to the misery and suffering which surrounded them, the rich displayed their wealth with ostentation and crass insensitivity. Class hatred festered and finally suppurated. Working men took on the government, and strikes, an unpleasant phenomenon for the ruling caste, caused major upheaval. The Fabian Society, led by Sydney and Beatrice Webb, George Bernard Shaw and Bertram Russell, gave socialism an intellectual framework. Backed by the trade union movement, the Labour party was poised to become a political force and would soon replace the Liberals as the engine of reform.

Women were rejecting domestic duties, claiming a larger role in society. Articles with such titles as 'The Influence of Women's Clubs' and 'Feminine Mind Worship' appeared alongside advertisements for the standardised typewriter. Opening up career opportunities for twentieth-century women, the typewriter was perceived as an instrument of female independence.

Suffragettes demanded the vote, education and the right to manage their own fertility. In response, birth control, giving women the power to order their lives, was denounced as a threat to the future and vigour of the race. Predictions of runaway promiscuity, divorce and syphilis ratcheted up suspicion. Militant women, enraged, used violence, no holds barred, to pursue their agenda. Vandalism, arson and stormy protests at Westminster, in Downing Street and other public places, led to imprisonment and hunger strikes. Golf greens were torn up. Lloyd George's country house was fire bombed. In 1913, during the Epsom Derby, a young woman died after she threw herself under the pounding hooves of the King's horse.

Germany's naval power, challenging that of the Empire, threatened the 'Freedom of the Seas', and an arms race, with fear of conflict, raised the levels of disquiet.

Invasion literature became a fashionable genre, and Erskine Childers's *The Riddle of the Sands* exposed the German naval threat in a compelling boy's own story. Powered flight was a disturbing reality, and the disaffected Fabian H.G. Wells had a huge success with *The War of the Worlds*, in which the invading force arrives from outer space. His futuristic novella *The Time Machine* is an alarming allegory for the class war, in which slum dwellers, the terrifying underground Morlocks, are ever ready to pounce on the Eloi, the beautiful folk who live in a parasitic paradise.

Catholics were up in arms. Victoria's reign had been of such length that when the new King's coronation and the accession oath became topics of the day, traditional procedures were rigorously re-examined. In August 1902, Edward VII, King of the United Kingdom and the British Dominions, and Emperor of India would use the words 'superstitious and idolatrous' to describe the sacrament of the Mass and the veneration of the Virgin Mary. The oath was a grievous affront to the twelve million Catholics throughout the Empire, and Cardinal Vaughan and the Irish party campaigned for the wording to be modified. In the *Westminster Review* O'Connor Power writes for his co-religionists:

[Catholics] bear equally with their Protestant fellow-subjects the burden of citizenship, and they will not be content with anything less than equality of treatment. Their demand in the present case, however, does not go the length of equality: they ask only for freedom from insult ... We of the twentieth century must find a twentieth century policy ... It is the declaration of his Majesty as Sovereign to which the Cardinal objects and his co-religionists object, and not to Protestant freedom of opinion which they in no way call in question. If Mr Greenwood would know what Catholics want besides 'equal freedom of opinion' I should say – equal respect for their opinion, in all formal acts of State, and relief from the stigma under which their religious beliefs are singled out from all others, in a diversified Empire of many religions and many nations, for special reprobation on every accession to the Crown.[520]

The King, himself, was no bigot. 'Popish Ned', as he was often called, visited the Pope on several occasions and was the first monarch for over 300 years to attend Mass publicly. On a trip to Ireland he included St Patrick's College, Maynooth in his itinerary.

Over a twenty-year period, the Liberals had held power for only two and a half years. Finally, in December 1905, after eleven years in opposition, their leader, Sir Henry Campbell-Bannerman, formed a minority government. Early in the New Year, promising a New Liberalism, cheap food and a decent standard of living for the working man, he led a united and determined party into an election, winning with a sound majority. Twenty-nine Labour MPs were also elected.

Liberalism meant liberty and the freedom of the individual, and its principles – democracy, social progress, an end to poverty – replaced the drums of war. There was to be a reduction of expenditure on armaments and a curb to dangerous foreign adventures.

A new weekly paper, the *Nation*, was launched and Massingham, its editor, encouraged young talent, while preserving what was best in an older cadre. His weekly lunches were famous, and statesmen, writers and prominent thinkers were among the many invited to attend and vent the issues of the day.

The administration, beleaguered by daunting domestic problems, put Irish demands on the back burner. Campbell-Bannerman, who had briefly been Irish Chief Secretary in 1884, favoured Home Rule, but there was still strong opposition within the party. A compromise was reached: a pledge of intent, the Irish Council Bill, 'a modest shy humble effort', was proposed as the next step on the way to devolution. The Bill was rejected on all sides.

O'Connor Power did not run in the election but, within the National Liberal Federation, he continued to train political recruits.[521] MPs remained unsalaried, and lack of means deterred good candidates from seeking election. Labour members survived on sponsorship from the trade union movement until the courts made this illegal. In 1911, the Liberals, the Irish and Labour members came together, and Lloyd George, the Chancellor of the Exchequer, brought in a £400 'allowance' for all serving members in the House of Commons. Irish MPs were no longer dependent on precarious party funding. In a very few years, when John Redmond, the IIP leader, encouraged his countrymen to enlist, physical force Nationalists would claim the parliamentary allowance was a 'blood tax'.

In 1909, Prime Minister Asquith introduced old age pensions for the over seventies. Lloyd George presented his 'People's Budget', proposing a land tax and increased death duties, a redistribution of wealth from rich to poor. His budget, presenting a long-gestating Liberal programme, the beginnings of a Welfare State, was deliberately provocative. The opposition, incensed, condemned it as 'pure, unadulterated socialism'.

Rising to the bait, the House of Lords, dominated by the Tories, ignored the tradition that a Finance Bill should pass without interference and used its veto to reject it. There was a stand-off. The National Liberal Club denounced 'the revolutionary act of the Lords'. Asquith advised dissolution. The Cabinet resigned.

The abolition of the feudal Lords' veto was the major plank of the Liberal manifesto, and Asquith, associating it with Home Rule, promised 'a full self-government in regard to purely Irish affairs'. Winning two general elections in 1910 (January and December), his party's mandate was confirmed, and the Liberals returned to power with the support of Irish and Labour members. Here was the strong wind of hope Nationalists had worked for, and William O'Brien was in readiness with the All-for-Ireland-League. The AFIL had split from the Irish party, winning eight seats; non-sectarian and anti-partition, it hoped to negotiate a solution to the Irish impasse. William O'Brien again emphasised 'conference, conciliation and consent'.

Lord Morley, former Irish Chief Secretary, and Augustine Birrell, serving Chief Secretary, advised that Home Rule be brought in immediately, but the Lord's veto continued to block the way. In the National Liberal Club, O'Connor Power 'seconded a motion carried unanimously of firm support of Mr Asquith's Reform of the House of Lords'.[522] A hereditary Chamber was inconsistent with the principles of democratic and representative government. The Lords had delayed Catholic Emancipation, 'mutilated' the 1870 Land Bill, obstructed the 1884 Reform Bill and rejected the 1893 Home Rule Bill.

In 1911, with Home Rule again under consideration, the Parliament Bill was introduced to remove the Lords' veto on Bills which had passed three times through the House of Commons. Lord Morley, in the House of Lords, enabled the passage of the Parliament Act 1911. If the Lords did not agree to the new measure and it was defeated, George V, using the King's Prerogative, would flood the Upper House with a large number of compliant Liberal peers. Impaled on the horns of a dilemma, the Lords conceded with a poor grace and the Bill passed by a narrow margin.

Traditionally, Tories and Unionists depended on the Lords to stymie unpalatable legislation, and when the third Home Rule Bill was introduced in the Commons by Asquith on 11 April 1912, they obstructed its passage for months. An initial defeat in the Lords, who still had a stay of execution, delayed it for almost two years.

The reconciliation of stubborn Ulster remained a stumbling block. The northeast's economy, with an efficient industrial base, kept step with England's. Belfast's Harland and Wolffe shipyard built 'the largest vessel afloat', and Ulster's pride, the *Titanic* set sail from Southhampton on 12 April 1912. The linen and woollen industries prospered. Ulster's successful linen trade was dependent on its stable land tenure for the successful growth of flax:

> Without that security of tenure Ulster's prosperity might have been a dream, and never would have become a reality – and for this reason, that there would be not regular supply of the material to keep the looms going. Flax is the most costly – the most troublesome and the most precarious – of all crops. It can be grown in good condition, only once in nine years on the same ground. If the Ulster tenant

farmer held his land on the same uncertain tenure on which it is held in the other three Provinces of Ireland, he never would enter extensively on the cultivation of a crop involving nine years rotation.[523]

Resources in the south remained underdeveloped. Northern merchants and manufacturers feared ruin in a united Ireland. Southern Unionists believed a partitioned island was not a viable entity. Tory leader, Andrew Bonar Law, warned that armed intervention would be necessary to enforce Home Rule and that he would not be siding with the government.

In 1912, Jim Larkin and James Connolly founded the Irish Labour party, and in August 1913 they led the Irish and General Transport Workers' Union in a major strike. IGTWU members were blacklisted by employers. The union demanded that it and its members be granted recognition. In pitiless retaliation, employers, headed by the Catholic newspaper proprietor William Martin Murphy, locked out the entire workforce.

Dublin slums were the worst in Europe, and a grim, inescapable poverty drove the destitute to despair. Mobs ran amok, and police and military came out in force, attacking rioters and looters with horrendous brutality. Two months later, following on the Dublin lockout and its violent aftermath, Larkin and Connolly formed the Irish Citizen Army, the military arm of the IGTWU, to defend the working man.

On New Year's Day 1913, Edward Carson moved an amendment in the Commons. Home Rule, the Government of Ireland Bill, was to be worded to exclude all nine counties of Ulster. Towards the end of the debate, Bonar Law warned of the threat from Germany, 'These people in the North-east of Ireland, from old prejudices perhaps more than anything else, from the whole of their past history, would prefer, I believe, to accept the government of a foreign country rather than submit to be governed by honourable gentlemen below the gangway [i.e. the Nationalists].'[524]

The Ulster Volunteer Force was formed the same month. In the south, the Irish Volunteers grouped in November 'to secure and maintain the rights and liberties common to all the people of Ireland'. With the threat of an imposed partition of the island, its membership increased dramatically.

At the end of October, O'Connor Power replied (we have no record of the request) to William O'Brien:

In reply to your question: I hate needless publicity and an (X) MP is not listened to in public; but I see a good many people, and my views are pretty well known to those who have influence.

If I were in the House I should raise the plea for a quiet settlement by an amendment to the Address at the opening of the session; but two things are in my opinion essential – admission of the principle of the Bill; and keeping it within the scope of the Parliament Act.

In a postscript he commented on the labour unrest in Ireland:

The Dublin labour dispute is a significant indication of the work that lies right in front of the Home Rule Parliament. No imprisonment of the men's leaders will kill the revolt. When their men are organised as they will be later on, in Cork, Limerick, Waterford and the towns generally, there will [be] a big problem.

What is your policy for the first Election to the Irish Parliament? It is not too soon to think about it, and it requires the constructive spirit.[525]

In the new parliamentary session, the King's speech in the Lords addressed the Irish Question:

The measures in regard to which there were differences between the two Houses will again be submitted to your consideration … it is my most earnest wish that the goodwill and cooperation of men of all parties and creeds may heal dissension and lay the foundations of a lasting settlement.[526]

The British army was divided in its sympathies, and in March 1914, as the situation worsened, army officers in the Curragh camp made it clear they would resign or accept dismissal rather than attempt to contain a worsening situation in Ulster. The government backed down, and its cowardly retreat drove many more recruits into the ranks of the Irish Volunteers. The Irish Guards rode past the Houses of Parliament, waving rifles sporting green flags with the yellow harp on the muzzles.

Threatened by the spectre of parliament's dissolution, conjured by a virulent Opposition, the Irish party conceded special conditions for Ulster. On 8 July 1914, an amending Bill was brought forward in the House of Lords for the temporary exclusion of Ulster. There were still major details to be addressed on the status of the province. Were four, six or nine counties to be excluded? Was an exclusion to be on a temporary or permanent basis? Was Ulster to be coerced or reconciled? A partition of Ireland would leave southern Unionists isolated in an economically backward Catholic State. Northern Unionists wanted a permanent exclusion. Neither partition nor the coercion of Ulster could deliver an acceptable solution. Asquith feared an amended Bill would lead to civil war.

William O'Brien was not alone in attempting to accommodate Unionist concerns. In a St Patrick's Day letter in the *Daily News*, O'Connor Power made his position clear, and his words were given space in the *Irish Independent*:

'Indissoluble Unity'

Letter from Mr O'Connor Power:

'I believe in the everlasting and indissoluble unity of Ireland from Derry to Cork, and from Dublin Bay westward to the Atlantic main.' Thus is Mr O'Connor Power in the *Daily News*. 'No solution to the Irish Question can,' he insists 'be deemed satisfactory which does not secure unity.'

Conciliation Mr Power regards as 'perfectly feasible for all who are willing to be conciliated'. He regrets that the Premier felt compelled to lay aside 'his own favourite method of conciliation, viz, to give Ulster, for a limited time, I presume, the right of vetoing any Irish legislation exclusively affecting herself until it was approved by a vote of the Imperial Parliament. It is, I think, fortunate that the Opposition have rejected the offer actually made, and I hope that those who objected to the Prime Minister's own plan will see now, on further reflection, that it is the best of all. It is at once simple and effective, and has the double merit of preserving the unity of Ulster and the unity of Ireland.'

'The Bill,' says Mr Power 'has a larger mass of representative opinion behind it than any measure which has been brought forward in our time.'

Ulster in 1972
Mr Power urges that any ballot opponents should be confronted with the platform of 1792 of 'their own Protestant ancestors' – 'to forward a brotherhood of affection, an identity of interests, a communion of rights and a union of power among Irishmen of all religious persuasions'.

Concluding, Mr Power says that 'Home Rule is worthless unless it reverses the traditional policy of Dublin Castle, which always has been to keep Irishmen divided among themselves, and then to reproach them with their dissensions.'[527]

Despite overtures of persuasive reasonableness, extra-parliamentary forces, two citizen armies, took up positions. Nationalists and Unionists, north and south prepared to engage, and civil war seemed inevitable. The Ulster Volunteer Force armed, drilled and was primed for action. Guns from the Boer conflict had been easily sourced and smuggled in with fishing catches. In April 1914, a blind eye was turned to UFV gunrunning in Larne; 20,000 rifles and 2,000,000 rounds of ammunition were landed, and no one arrested.

In Howth, three months later, the Irish Volunteers brought ashore guns, purchased in Hamburg. On this occasion, the police and army did not stand idly by. Soldiers moved in, killing four and injuring many in the crowd which had gathered to watch the confrontation.

Anger at partition proposals and fear of conscription spread rapidly throughout the Nationalist community. There was a deep sense of betrayal. War taxes – Ireland was now paying out more than it received – were seen as a grave injustice. There were other grievances; the south received few war contracts, and there was no significant development of native resources. Food was exported while Irish families went hungry. As tensions mounted, money was transferred out of Ireland, and in England preparations were made to house refugees.

In defiance of law and order, Tories, shorn of hereditary ascendancy, supported Ulster and actively encouraged disobedience. Deprived of the legislative bulwark of the Lords, they turned to Orangemen, rendered resolute by a Protestant identity, undiluted by class divisions, as the means to bring down the Liberal administration. For the first time in over a century, the code of gentlemanly conduct, whatever the political disagreement, was broken. At Westminster, and on social occasions, Liberals and Tories 'cut' each other, refusing to attend parties where they might meet. Hostesses contended with 'war to the knife and fork'. The government had lost control of the Irish Question and the parliamentary system seemed on the brink of collapse.

On 18 September, despite a state of war and deepening domestic hostilities, the Government of Ireland Bill, under the provisions of the Parliament Act of 1911, passed through a deserted House of Lords. Michael MacDonagh, parliamentary reporter, gives us vivid details. There were scenes of unbounded delight in the House of Commons. An Irish flag was raised – 'a flash of green and a golden harp'. Will Crooks, an English Labour MP, led the singing of the national anthem, 'God Save the King', and at the conclusion roared 'God Save Ireland'. John Redmond responded with 'God Save England'. It was the first time singing was heard in the Chamber. The House cheered and cheered. The Bill, 'by and with the consent of the King, Lords and Commons in Parliament assembled', received the Royal assent and was placed on the Statute book.

Home Rule was on the Statute Book, but Asquith passed two emergency provisions. The Act would not come into operation until parliament made special arrangements for Ulster, and its implementation was suspended for the duration of the war. Concessions could not be negotiated when security issues took precedence. Self-deception ruled; Redmond thought it was a War Emergency Act and Carson believed it permanent.

John Redmond's National Volunteers (a large majority of the Irish Volunteers) followed his call to fight for the freedom of small nations and enlisted. It was understood that at the end of the conflict, which many believed would be brief, there would be an imperial conference with a view to bringing the dominions into closer co-operation with the British government and making a permanent settlement for Ireland.

At the end of May 1915, a wartime coalition was formed. Eight Unionists were included, and Carson, Ulster's leading crusader, was appointed Attorney General. John Redmond declined to accept a seat at Cabinet. As the Liberals coalesced with Unionists, Home Rule became an ever-receding mirage.

Asquith's proposal of a temporary respite, a six-year period of adjustment for Ulster, would not be acceptable to the Unionist Ministers in the Coalition Cabinet.

O'Connor Power wrote to William O'Brien of these 'degenerate' times:

26 May 1915

My dear O'Brien

It was very kind of you to send me your sympathetic words. I am much better thank you, though the precious word 'recovery' is not wholly justified. This coalition puts the whole Liberal programme on the shelf indefinitely. You may well call these times degenerate. The triumphs of National Freedom and of International Peace have been my day-dreams for half a century, and they are now darkened by this cruel brutal war. Unless a system of international law, based on justice, and enforceable by adequate authority, emerges, all the blood will have been shed in vain.

With all good wishes

J. O'Connor Power[528]

The war with Germany united the Empire. Appeals to patriotism and jingoistic slogans dissolved domestic discontent and galvanised its subjects to defend the freedom of small states and 'little Catholic Belgium'.

But at England's vulnerable back door, militant Irish forces, directed by the highly secretive IRB Military Council, collaborated with its European enemy and prepared to strike. America's Clan, seizing on England's danger, raised funds for an insurrection. In August 1915, O'Donovan Rossa's remains were sent home from New York for a hero's burial in Glasnevin Cemetery. Padraig Pearse's graveside oration – 'the fools, the fools, the fools! They have left us our Fenian dead, and while Ireland holds these graves, Ireland unfree shall never be at peace' – lent romantic solemnity to a resounding propaganda coup. Dublin Castle turned a blind eye to the provocation. Chief Secretary Birrell, negligent by temperament and conviction, was often absent from his post, spending time with his sick wife in London.

In Ulster, recruitment to the armed forces trickled to a near standstill; the province's able-bodied men were needed at home to defend their territory against their southern neighbours. The Larne and Howth gunrunners had both sourced weaponry in Germany. The Defence of the Realm Act (1914) had introduced emergency measures to prevent collaboration between Irish revolutionaries and Germany. A disloyal Ireland would open up the sea lanes to German battleships. Britain's fears were solidly grounded; the 1916 Proclamation of the Irish Republic declared it was supported 'by her exiled children in America and by gallant allies in Europe'.

The Easter Rising (24-6 April), which had been many months in the planning, was widely rumoured to be a preliminary to a German invasion. A shipload of German guns had been seized by the British. Others feared the rebellion was a citizen army socialist revolution. Martial law was immediately in force, and press censorship blocked the flow of information.

It was difficult to assess public reaction. Ireland, kept in the dark, at first appeared to have little sympathy for the Rising. This changed over the following weeks. Reprisals, a series of courts-martial, were conducted in secret, and, as the leading rebels were sentenced and executed, ignorance and indifference turned to admiration for the nation's gallant men. In Ulster, Unionist intransigence solidified.

In England there were few accurate news reports from Ireland, but Massingham in the *Nation* demanded immediate implementation of Home Rule: Ireland and England should be equals in an Imperial Federation. He was outraged by the brutal response of the British government to the rebels. He believed Birrell's resignation was a tragedy, writing him a personal letter of appreciation.

On 11 May, in the Commons, John Dillon condemned the executions and declared that the insurgents may have been misguided but they were not murderers. The next day, Asquith travelled to Dublin to prevent further executions. Two weeks later, on 25 May 1916, he advised the House of Commons that the Castle administration in Ireland had broken down, and the time was opportune for a new approach.

On 16 June, over 2,000 Republicans marched in protest against the suspension of Home Rule and partition proposals. Three days later O'Connor Power wrote a letter to the *Irish Independent*:

IS IT ANOTHER BROKEN TREATY?

A remarkable thing about this scheme is that nobody in Ireland is willing to be responsible for it. We are left to grope for the meaning of important parts through a maze of words studiously vague, where clearness and definiteness were essential to any sound judgment.

Let us look for a moment at the facts of the situation. The Home Rule that was passed after protracted discussion in the Imperial Parliament and the recorded approval of every Parliamentarian and Government in the Empire. In other words the highest and widest legal and constitutional sanction that any Act of the imperial Parliament ever received. It then occurred to a Cabinet too weak, or who thought they were too weak, which amounts to the same thing, to maintain the law against threats of Unionist rebellion, that the war could be utilised as a ground for not allowing the Act to be put in operation, and its operation was accordingly suspended. The psychological moment for giving to Ireland her hard-won Constitution was audaciously assigned as a reason for withholding it. A great opportunity was lost, in total disregard to the dictates of common sense and all the lessons of history.

REBELLION'S LESSON

No-one who has read the evidence given before Lord Hardinge's Commission can doubt that the suspension of the Home Rule Act was a fruitful cause of the recent rebellion. Disregarding this awful lesson, we are now invited to do what Irish public opinion universally condemned two short years ago, and which is again being condemned wherever a free and unfettered expression of the views of the people can be had. No matter how many party organisations in England or Ireland may approve this proceeding, I must affirm my solemn conviction that it will be even more disastrous than what has gone before. There is no provision in the scheme, as published, for taking the votes of electors on a matter vital to their lives and fortunes; and all the machinery of party being employed to reach a decision, while the whole of Ireland is subject to the rigours of martial law.

THE SUSPENDING ACT

The suspension of Home Rule Act was advocated in the name of peace and conciliation, and we know the result. This scheme is supported on the same ground and will be followed as surely by similar disillusion and disappointment.

I have read speeches of members of Parliament calling upon the young men of Ireland to go to the front because of the Home Rule Act. The brave young fellows rushed to the recruiting offices in tens of thousands: most of whom now sleep their last sleep in the blood-stained fields of Europe. They did not offer up their lives for a mutilated Ireland but for one united from sea to sea, and they did so with the promise of their leaders that national unity would never be given away. I ask is faith not to be kept with the dead? If so, the infamy of the broken Treaty of Limerick will be outdone by the betrayal of today.[529]

At the beginning of the war, voluntary recruitment had been proportionately as high in Ireland as in the rest of the UK. Now numbers enlisting dropped among the Irish at home and in the colonies. Irish America was appalled by the executions of the rebels. For many exiles, the destruction of the British Empire was as important as the establishment of an Irish State.

The Irish Convention, which met from July 1917–April 1918, failed in its attempt to reach agreement. Lloyd George, who succeeded Asquith as Prime Minister, attempted to secure a settlement, but he came to 'separate and contradictory' agreements with both sides. He feinted to link Home Rule to conscription, a *quid pro quo*, but in retrospect this was confirmed as a duplicitous tactic and masterly procrastination.

A Military Service Bill, proposing conscription for Ireland, was passed in April 1918. The Catholic hierarchy condemned it and, in protest, Irish Nationalists withdrew from the House of Commons. Silver coins were hoarded, as many expected a German victory, when English paper money would be worthless. Orange Ulster saw this as another instance of Rome Rule and treason.

In reality, conscription was unenforceable. The Irish in England and Irishmen already fighting for the Empire would not take kindly to a pressgang of their countrymen. The United States had entered the war with almost 100,000 soldiers, and it was thought impolitic to alienate Irish America.

Fear of a rebellion financed by Germany held the government's hand. But the Irish problem had reached boiling point and could not be contained. The Volunteers, now the Irish Republican Army, were organised to oversee land redistribution and resist conscription. Farmers were making record prices and food was again leaving Ireland while men, women and children starved. A general strike was called at the end of

April. Massingham's lunches at the *Nation* were dominated by the Anglo-Irish quarrel, and he attacked the government's unyielding policies as 'Balfourism'.

The war was officially over on 11 November 1918, Armistice Day. In December, on the eve of the election, the leaders of the main parties in British politics, Bonar Law and Lloyd George, issued a joint letter: Ireland could not leave the Empire and the six northern counties could not be coerced into Home Rule. Sinn Féin was declared an illegal organisation and its leaders arrested. The hard line, uncompromising approach drew a decisive response: Sinn Féin swept the board with seventy-three seats – the Irish Parliamentary Party, 'submerged by the floodtide of national passion', retained only six – and withdrew from Westminster. Many of those elected were held in English jails.

The first Dáil Eireann met on 21 January 1919. Leading Republicans were on the run. Éamon De Valera, who had famously declared 'we are not at war with Germany', was behind bars and, in absentia, was declared President of the new Assembly.

Britain was struggling to recover from the devastations of war and the savagery of a virulent pandemic. Spanish flu killed the young and healthy, and a terrified population gargled with Milton. Homemade masks were worn, and ozone, the microbe's enemy, was recommended. Industrial war resumed, taking the place of military conflict. Tube and rail strikes and blinding snowstorms crippled the islands. Army trucks gave free rides to stranded commuters. Lloyd George appealed to the country, asking that victory won by 'heroism not be dissipated by anarchy'.

On 3 February, De Valera escaped from the Lincolnshire prison and went into hiding. On 20 February he returned unobserved to Ireland.

John O'Connor Power died the following day. Three decades would pass before his great-nephew would welcome De Valera when he returned, a respected national leader, a celebrated world figure, to receive the Freedom of Lincoln Jail.[530]

Afterword

'Nothing would be done at all if a man waited till he could do it so well that no one could find fault with it' – Cardinal Newman's words preface *The Making of an Orator*.

My subject lived in interesting times, and I certainly felt inadequate to the task of recounting the events of a long and action-packed life, a life that might provide the impetus for a three-volume academic work or supply the material for a period blockbuster, Ireland's *Gone with the Wind*. All the ingredients – fixed purpose, adventure, romance, high politics – would deliver compelling entertainment. Refract the narrative, assume O'Connor Power as a pivotal figure, and a dramatic vista stretches from the Famine to the first Dàil.

The excavation of his life had the makings of a mystery novel, with an account of the serendipity of research and the satisfaction of a confident, 'whistleblower' refutation of meagre scholarly assessment. A.S. Byatt juggled the narrative of *Possession* between the generations. Josephine Tey's painstaking research restored Richard III's good name. The villains of my piece, who had distorted the facts, with misleading and malicious aspersions of illegitimacy and an opportunistic marriage, would be hung out to dry. Restitution of O'Connor Power's good name would be a righteous act. I would redress the injury. Moving between centuries, I would blow the dust off historical scholarship, review the reportage of his colleagues and revisit printed records. I planned to provide a fresh perspective and provoke considered debate.

Using the epic or dramatic form, early historians frequently depicted the world through individual lives. Ireland's past has been related through the memoirs and biographies of the main participants. After all, history is by its nature an art form, a storytelling mediated by a scholar's bias, his resources and his mastery of the facts.

A narrative is founded on contemporary records, secondary material can influence and corrupt the presentation; confidently asserted inaccuracies may be repeated down the years. Accounts may be distorted, either deliberately or with an unconscious prejudice in selection and interpretation. A scholar may confine himself to a particular period or location, and the writings between major events are not joined up. If he is in error, he may not be corrected.

I tried to stay faithful to early sources and allow the sequence of events to develop simply, with a little leavening rather than embellishment. I feared to bludgeon my reader with dates and facts, or tire him with discursive argument. When possible, I allowed O'Connor Power to speak with his own voice. His adventures could not be bettered in fiction; his life would read like a novel. I freely admit bias but, as his story was so long obscured, my prejudice is corrective and my mistakes, I hope, stimulating.

Up until recently there were few details of his life, and these were generally inaccurate. Insouciant historians variously referred to Thomas O'Connor Power and James O'Connor Power. Thirty years ago, Professor T.M. Moody of Trinity College did a great deal to restore the balance. Power family records open up new areas of research.

Several years ago, I sent a letter to American academic Donald Jordan, who had written an assessment of O'Connor Power's early career, published in *Irish Historical Studies* in 1986. My letter was returned unread. Jordan had died a year previously. In the letter I told him of the family connections, that O'Connor Power had brothers and many collateral descendants. Jordan had written of his 'drift' into constitutional politics but I did not challenge this interpretation. I knew O'Connor Power had never drifted in his life.

Here was a case of a genetic assurance in the luck of the Irish, that he, like Phineas Finn, 'was one of those Irish gentlemen who always seem to be under some special protection'. Certainly he never disappointed, pursuing his goals and harnessing his 'restless energy' to every opportunity, which might serve his vision: 'National Freedom and International Peace' were his 'day-dreams for half a century'.

He survived not only the Famine's Grim Reaper but also smallpox, 'the most terrible of all the ministers of death'. The savagery of the 1840s epidemic culled tens of thousands. It was common to see fortunate survivors, with the telltale pitted skin, and, in some villages, the unmarked were the exception. Milkmaids, with cowpox antibodies, escaped and were renowned for fair, unblemished complexions. One of the sequelae of the disease is male infertility. O'Connor and Avis did not have a family, and he may have been infertile.

When I left home at the age of eighteen, I took with me the family copy of *The Making of an Orator*. Over the years I kept an eye on O'Connor Power's reputation.

The National Portrait Gallery in London sent me a black and white reproduction of the 'Spy' cartoon, which I framed and hung on my sitting-room wall. I knew the man.

It was only in January 2007, with the purchase of a computer and a link to broadband, that I had the means and the leisure to pursue my search. Wikipedia's John O'Connor Power page introduced me to a long-lost cousin, who had a similar interest and a wealth of stories, which confirmed and enriched my own. Our fathers, first cousins, had remained in touch until the late 1950s. Wikipedia yielded Ballinasloe contacts. I was not alone.

The Walter Macken connection provided a major breakthrough. The Galway writer was a second cousin but there was a possibility that he was related through a different branch of the family. The first morning in the National Archives in Bishop Street I scored four strikes.

The 1901 census reveals that Agnes Brady of Ballinasloe, nursemaid, and her older sister Norah, governess, lived in the Eileen Power/O'Shaughnessy household in Galway City. Agnes Brady later married Walter Macken, actor, singer and stage carpenter, who was actively involved with the Racquet Court. Their youngest son, Walter, grew up to be the well-known actor and playwright famed for his beautiful speaking voice. His historical novels, with Irish themes, have been translated into several languages. They sell steadily in Ireland's bookstores and are ever popular in local libraries.

The genealogist on duty that day directed me to John Power of Ballygill in Griffith's Valuation. I now had the key to unlock the sequence of births, marriages and deaths of the Powers of Ballygill. There was much work to be done in the General Registry Office. The doors were flying open. It was a case of search and you will find. I was on a roll.

At the information desk I asked for Fenian records and discovered that they held the Kilmainham file. There was a wealth of information and again the defiant boy in the prison photograph was known to me. It was 'a family face', a composite of father, brother, nephew, cousin. 'The years-heired feature' of Thomas Hardy's poem 'Heredity', 'in curve and voice and eye!', made him as familiar to me as any living member of the clan. A Power descendant, a successful actor, is the most frequently heard male voice on radio advertising in Ireland. His mellow, reassuring tones transmit an echo from the distant past. Two family members were at the St Patrick's Day White House celebrations for the Bicentennial of American Independence. So does the wheel turn.

Elated, overwrought, I collected my bags from the cloakroom, trying to remain calm and objective. A time traveller, I must prepare myself for surprises. As I turned to leave, a young man who had heard me make enquiries introduced himself. An historian, he, also, had the 'Spy' cartoon on his sitting-room wall in his home town of Ballinasloe. Some weeks earlier we had exchanged greetings on the O'Connor Power Wikipedia site.

Many years ago I read that when the stakes are high, coincidences collide and so they did. It seemed not a day would go by but I would find some nugget, a precious piece for my jigsaw. My project became the quest. The roll became a rollercoaster. Coincidence, serendipity, synchronicity, a time of magical connections, accompanied my compulsive pursuit of this elusive man and his role in the making of his country.

Whenever I flagged, a gentle reminder would nudge me along. Someone would mention Walter Macken's name. I would find myself in a Pembroke room or espy a former Mechanics Institute. A new rich seam to mine would be uncovered. Every road was signposted, hastening me onward.

A strong wind was at my back. I trawled the internet, the National Archives at Kew, the General Registry Office, the Valuations Office, with increasing delight and excitement. The picture became larger and clearer. I tried to see the wood and not the trees of the broad span of a full life and contacted academics around the world.

My faith was constantly rewarded. Simultaneous to beginning the search, *The Making of an Orator* was republished in the United States more than a hundred years after its first appearance. Another sign? Another portent? The Internet Archive editions are downloaded with satisfactory frequency.

Not a week would go by but I would stumble on some revelation, a long-forgotten connection. The Westminster portraits, so familiar, bolstered the family stories that O'Connor Power was tall and handsome. His good looks and strong presence made the scars irrelevant. In the seated Westminster portrait he is wearing a poor quality suit. The dapper Tim Healy writes of 'his poverty' and the flippant judgement 'reeking of the common clay' was reinforced. O'Connor Power did not spend what money he had on fripperies and wore poverty as a badge of pride. All sides of the family spoke of his generosity. Open-handed, he would dispense what money he had, even if he threw his purse to you with a scowl. He left no will. In his writings he emphasises the importance of generosity in Gaelic culture. Sharing brings blessings, to deny a helping hand is a grievous sin against God and man.

Every day during the memorably disastrous summers of 2007-9, the adventures of this maddening man held me enthralled. Coincidentally, the rainfall of the years leading up to the Land War was just as relentless.

I called on the Chief Herald and told him I was researching O'Connor Power and asked why there was no biography. 'Why don't you do it yourself?' I had no answer. An Irish diplomat advised me, 'First you must find out why he was so visible and then became invisible.' It might be speculated that O'Connor Power, who had such high visibility, dipped beneath the historical radar because of his IRB god-father status. He had taken an oath not to reveal the business of the Brotherhood. Secrecy was vital, particularly after British intelligence's infiltration of Clan na Gael and the disclosures of the Special Commission. The discretion of high politics was another factor. Moving with policy makers, he had the most formidable connec-tions of any living Irishman. He hated 'needless publicity'. Doubtless, he wished to preserve the privacy of family and to protect his brother in the British army and the extended family in Galway and Ballygill. His late marriage was a cherished gift, a domestic haven.

He left no journal, no appointment diary. He did not compose his memoirs nor chronicle his times. It was a considered, deliberate choice. An experienced newspa-perman, he knew his story would make good copy. An autobiography, with name recognition, would have been an instant bestseller on several continents.

I wonder did he share my distaste for the self-serving memoirist who writes for posterity, attempting to ensure himself a prominent place in the history books? Many self-aggrandising, self-justifying narratives stand unchallenged. O'Connor Power's exploits and achievements have been forgotten, partly due to the clear field left to other men who wrote their memoirs, preserved and published correspond-ence, staked their claims.

Victorians often used overblown language, but when O'Connor Power spoke or wrote, he was to the point, 'I always prefer plain language.' There were no colourful pen portraits of his colleagues. He did not make personal attacks in print (his attack on Butt was ritualistic, not personal), 'Mere personal attacks are objectionable not only because they lower the tone of public life, but because they are irrelevant and solve nothing.'[531]

His journalistic output was, like the newspapers he wrote for, transitory, but his leading articles on Home Rule, land legislation, the House of Lords, prison reform and adult suffrage were the constant drip, drip of pressure and persuasion. The pur-pose was long term and, in the long term, effective. A teacher, he understood that a lesson, until it is learnt, cannot be repeated too often. Steadily a series of land and local government reforms were put in place. Home Rule would be the crowning achievement and never ceased to top the agenda. It was nation-building and a slow, inexorable erosion of the Union.

Shortly before his death, he gave the Irish author and journalist Michael MacDonagh his personal papers. *The Home Rule Movement*, partly based on these letters and newspaper cuttings, was published by the founding member of The Johnson Club, Fisher Unwin.

The papers – where did O'Connor Power store his memorabilia in the early days? – have long since disappeared. It is possible that among them there was evidence of foul play on the part of other men. Were they lost or destroyed? The few surviving letters among the MacDonagh papers in the National Library of Ireland are helpful. O'Connor Power did keep a copy of his reply to the Lord of the Treasury.

The National Library has his copy of the letter he wrote to Gladstone in the summer of 1877 asking for his intervention for the speedy release of Irish political prisoners. A few weeks later Gladstone visited Ireland and, within a short time, Davitt and his fellow prisoners were free. O'Connor Power was justly proud. His campaign for his comrades-in-arms had a successful outcome.

MacDonagh, a close friend of Davitt, also draws from the published work of Frank Hugh O'Donnell, John Denvir and Barry O'Brien. His chapter 'What the Irish Party Accomplished' is a lucid account of the legislative measures which prepared the way for independence.

O'Connor Power, as himself and as 'X', gives valuable information to his Middle Temple colleague Barry O'Brien, for a biography of Parnell. The description of the formation of the Home Rule Confederation of Great Britain is vivid. The influence of the Clan, the rapprochement of John Devoy with Parnell is revisited. He talks to O'Brien in interview mode, informal, unbuttoned. We hear the rhythms of his voice in intimate conversation with a fellow Irishman. He speaks of his great fondness for Butt and with genial bemusement of Parnell. He is generous in his assessment of the controversial leader – a good listener, quick learner, sound instinct, with a hatred of England. Anonymity is maintained, as X's name has not 'transpired, and accordingly cannot be published': 'transpire' is used in an earlier sense of 'leaked out, made public'.

A year into my research, I was helping a charity prepare for its conference. Moving boxes and sorting leaflets, I noticed some early twentieth-century books on the office shelves. Where did they come from? – My great uncle. Who was he? – Michael MacDonagh. Against all the odds I had hit the jackpot. Long ago I had given up all hope of finding the MacDonagh family. My many queries had been met by negatives. I now had access to MacDonagh's books and his descendants. Sadly, the O'Connor Power papers are not in their possession.

The conference was the next day. I was explosive, a rumbling volcano of excitement. Next week I would search through MacDonagh's library. That same evening I located a copy of *The Johnson Club Papers* online. The following morning my Ballinasloe contact walked into the conference hotel. What were the odds against such a series? The hounds of destiny were in hot pursuit!

Edmund Burke had indicated that he was to be buried in an unmarked grave and not in Westminster Abbey among the great and powerful. I had contacted just about every cemetery in London looking for O'Connor Power's grave and was resigned to the fact that he, also, chose to be buried in an unmarked plot, in company with the millions of Irish who died in the Famine years.

A few days before my annual trip to London, I typed the name of the doctor on his death certificate into an Internet search engine. Absentmindedly, I searched variations of the name. I hit a cemetery database and took a very deep breath. I just *knew* I was going to gold. And, sure enough, there was O'Connor Power's name and the details of the plot in a cemetery in North London. Avis had buried her husband with members of her family.

Abney Park is a renowned Victorian cemetery. I looked forward eagerly to my visit. I rang the office and the secretary arranged for a photograph of the headstone. The grave was overgrown, and the photographer would clear the ground. A few days later I made my pilgrimage to Stoke Newington. The morning was cold and wet, and the grounds of Abney Park are extensive. I was given a map and, after much searching, found my way to the grave. My new-found cousin had arranged to meet me there. O'Connor Power's last resting place is close to the derelict chapel. A local historian, an Irishman who emigrated to London in the 1950s, and guardian of the memory of Irish Chartist, James Bronterre O'Brien, came to greet us.

The headstone is simple. O'Connor Power's name is on one side and the names of Avis's nieces and brother who predeceased him by some decades are on the other. He died on 21 February 1919, having achieved his three score and ten, with a few years and days thrown in. He drew his last breath at home with the woman he loved at his side. A charmed life, indeed. But young Hubert was barely dead six months. Friends and relatives did not survive the First World War. Many of those who came home to their loved ones died in the pandemic which swept the world, the Spanish flu. Europe was in deep mourning.

When Avis died, aged ninety-six, almost thirty years later, she left instructions that she was to be cremated. She, like the Quakers, did not believe in the importance of the body after death. Were her ashes scattered on the graves of those she loved in life?

To his acquaintances, his friends and his family, O'Connor Power was a man with multiple identities. Multifaceted, he kept his personal and public lives separate. By nature he was a man of the theatre. When he took a leading role, he played his part, and, when the show was over, he retired behind the scenes to prepare for the next production. Actor, writer, producer, director, he wrote the scripts, selected the cast and determined the presentation, delighting in variety and challenge. Wilkie Collins, 'actor' and 'Roman Catholic priest' provide insight. He loved to play many parts, travel many roads. Not a follower of any man, he placed himself firmly in a pastoral role.

MacDonagh writes of his departure from the Irish party ranks in 1884 and comments that 'a little complaisance to Parnell' might have saved his parliamentary career. He does not report that the member for Mayo's constituents supported him. He was, indeed the Member for Mayo. There could be no complaisance, especially when the stakes were so high. Unleashed, O'Connor Power was one jump ahead. The move to the Liberals gave him 'a free hand' to pursue Home Rule in his own way. He was never better than as a one-man show.

He had an impeccable sense of direction. An historian, he retained objectivity, understanding the broad span of time and personalities essential for change. Scholars sometimes refer, in an almost disparaging manner, to Fenians as 'self-educated'. A police file submitted while O'Connor Power was at St Jarlath's condescended, 'he was clever in composition and recitation' and his appearance was 'smart'. Many acquired the basics in overcrowded classes; the Mechanics, reading rooms and lending libraries provided further opportunities. Men of action, with a hunger and respect for knowledge, they read voraciously. The school of life, a practical, analytical curriculum, delivered formidable, original minds. They were proud of Ireland's glorious past and were heirs to her saints and scholars, 'I believe that all historians unite in testifying that the ancient Church of Ireland was the university of the world.'[532]

I was enchanted by my visit to Moore Hall with my Mayo in-laws. During the Civil War the house was torched and only the shell remains, but it is not hard to imagine the Moore home as the patriotic hearth and heart of the West. Spectral heroes, vibrations of historic moments, inhabit the demesne.

A private viewing of the 'Spy' portrait in the archive of the National Portrait Gallery in London was a treasured privilege. The striking blue backdrop thrusts the lively figure to the fore. 'A friendly spirit', O'Connor Power is himself; no photograph could represent him with more clarity and insight.

When I wasn't reading around my subject, I was writing to maintain focus. The case, passed to the fourth generation, was almost cold, but faith, a secret dictate, overruled my hesitations. Instinctively I knew that O'Connor Power did not retire to private life when he left Westminster. He was going to keep pushing the boulder of Home Rule up that very steep hill. He had carved his niche, and the campaign continued in the press, the prisons and the law courts. The National Liberal Club, the newspaper world and The Johnson Club provided fora and platforms to press his case. An outsider, 'a square peg', he uses the word 'troublesome' frequently – 'trouble(s)' is a catch-all in Ireland and can denote anything from an insurrection to a difficult birth. Troublesome, he persisted and kept Irish issues before the British public and its governments.

If I lost heart, I was given a helping hand. I was daunted at the prospect of retelling the story of his role in the amnesty campaign. Where to begin? The 1878 publication of his speeches and the report on the enquiry on prison treatment gave me substantial assistance. My work was done for me.

I visited O'Connor Power's former home in Luttrell Avenue, Putney. There were several routes back to the village High Street. Happily the one I chose brought me past the nearby Catholic church, Our Lady of Pity, St Simon Stock, which opened in the autumn of 1906. When – moved to Luttrell Avenue it was his parish church. I knocked on the presbytery door. The parish priest, Canon Quinlan from Tipperary, was welcoming. I told him my search was full of extraordinary surprises. He understood, 'You are being led'. 'Yes,' I thought, 'Yes, I am.'

Six months later, when I was mired in 'congested districts' – how to make that part of my narrative engaging! – I had a wake-up call. Canon Quinlan contacted me with details of the Requiem Mass and the funeral arrangements.

Ecumenical in love and friendship, O'Connor Power was a strong and 'vigorous' Catholic and was on the building committee of his former parish church, St Agatha's, Wyndham Road, Camberwell, which was consecrated in 1899. He and his associates were driven by a desire to make the world a better place; they spoke and wrote robustly of moral conviction, moral energy, the moral force of right. 'Vigorous' and 'energetic' were adjectives they favoured. In recent times there has been a degradation of liberal vocabulary. Morality was not a 'Thou shalt not' but a compelling command for good works. Words, actions, were Jedi lightsabers cutting swathes through an unjust world. Moral memory and moral obligation are a national heritage: 'I start with the simple proposition that there is a moral law governing the lives of nations as of individuals. The operation of this moral law in the history of the Irish nation is what I mean by the philosophy of Irish history'.[533]

Born under a lucky star, an Aquarian, his birthday was a date on which he placed significance and presumably celebrated in appropriate fashion. In 1875, his first birthday at Westminster, he 'asked the First Lord of the Treasury the advisability of adoption of a rule fixing beyond which no sitting should be continued'. Had he plans for a night out at the theatre, followed by a late supper with friends at the Cheese? He was in no doubt that 'politics would be intolerable but for its amusements'.[534]

On his thirty-second birthday, he supported the first reading of the Contention (Ireland) Act, Repeal Bill.[535] That evening he sent his regrets on House of Commons notepaper to the Knights of St Patrick in St Louis. He cannot be with them for the celebration of the National Day. He wrote of the 'Saxon oppressors' from the

Library at Westminster. The next day he registered for legal studies in the Middle Temple. New beginnings – where next?

The raid on Chester Castle was two days before his birthday, and his arrest in Dublin, the following year, following on the Supreme Council's first meeting, was a few days after his twenty-second. Had he celebrated too well? Was his guard down? He died a few days after reaching his seventy-fourth birthday.

It was in February 1884 that he made the difficult decision to burn his bridges with the Irish party. He was encouraged by colleagues, horrified by the implications of the Parnell Tribute, and who feared the collapse of the Reform legislation and an end to all hope of home government.

Early in 1888, at the age of forty-two, he took a gap year in North America. Was it a consolidation of Ireland's diaspora base, 'the greater Ireland beyond the Atlantic', which took him away from familiar haunts? Or was it, perhaps, a pause in middle age, an opportunity to distance himself from the quagmire of current events and a hostile Tory government, and re-evaluate. If he knew Avis and Hubert prior to their marriage in October 1887, he may have been nursing a slighted heart or, at least, reassessing his single life. Or was his true purpose counter intelligence? Irish Nationalists were tapping and deciphering *The Times* transatlantic communications. Was he accumulating evidence of the Big Game, British machinations within the Fenian community? A map of his itinerary might reveal a fascinating network.

There are no sightings of O'Connor Power in 1889. Alongside Michael Davitt, he was part of Charles Russell's backroom team. The brilliant advocate's *modus operandi* was to assemble first-class researchers to devil on every case, and, in a time of national emergency, it was a question of all hands on deck. Russell's biographer, Barry O'Brien judges he was deeply interested in Irish history but was not well up on political history. Russell, he writes, asked his advice, and I have no doubt he consulted with O'Connor Power. When I first read the Speech for the Defence, a powerful account of Ireland's troubled history, I sometimes heard his voice. Both Davitt (Irishtown) and Russell (1881 Land Act) acknowledge him. Public rapprochement and collaboration between Davitt and O'Connor Power bookend the Special Commission. The report was published on 13 February 1890.

With apparent serendipity, in 1893, the Second Home Rule Bill was introduced on O'Connor Power's forty-seventh birthday. The following September, the month of his marriage, the Bill passed its third reading in the House of Commons. It was subsequently vetoed by the House of Lords.

Perhaps he sent *The Making of an Orator* to the printers in February 1906 to mark that milestone sixtieth birthday!

Professor Moody began the process of restoring the 'long-neglected' O'Connor Power to his rightful place in the national historiography. In 1977, on his retirement, his paper on the forgotten Irish leader was timed for The Johnson Club's significant date, 13 December. Was Moody a Johnsonian?

Around 1869, John Power became O'Connor Power. A new departure strategy was taking shape, he was preparing to emerge from the shadows and play a leading role. A double-barrelled name was a common practice, a fashion of the day. O'Connor Power had a mantra-style ring and would be repeated to great effect by the crowds at the monster rallies he addressed. The adoption of his mother's name honoured her and the O'Connor clan.

A few days before Christmas 2008, I was invited to a preview of the 1911 UK census. I did not look for surprises and approached the site with nonchalance. Again, the unexpected gift. O'Connor Power, age sixty-five, pinpointed for the first time his birthplace as the parish of Clashaganny, County Roscommon. Clashaganny, 'Clais Gainimhe', which translates literally to 'Sandy Hollow', is a townland close to Tulsk. The terrain is well known for fishing and hunting. Meets were held there. Stag hunting was a popular local sport. O'Connor Power Hill, a favourite haunt of the Roscommon Harriers, is close by:

> The meet of the above took place on Monday at Carns. The day was beautifully fine, and a good crowd had assembled when Matthews arrived with the hounds. Shortly after one o'clock a red deer was enlarged at O'Connor Power's Hill and after traversing a couple of miles around this famous trysting place …[536]

Carns is less than two kilometres from Clashaganny. Is it possible Patrick Power worked with horses and met his bride while delivering mounts to the local hunt?

A charming Protestant church, St George's, graced the parish, which was important enough in the mid-1880s to apply for a post office.[537] The seat of the O'Connors, the High Kings of Connacht, is nearby and there are significant prehistoric sites in the area. Tulsk, eight miles from Roscommon town, is on the pilgrim route to Croagh Patrick, which, before the arrival of St Patrick and Christianity, was a pagan place of sun worship.

There is no record of O'Connor Power singing but I like to think that at the end of an evening he led his friends with renderings of Fenian songs – 'The West's Awake', 'The Rising of the Moon' and 'God Save Ireland'. Did he sing Thomas Moore's 'The Minstrel Boy' to captive audiences, rounding off the night with 'A Nation Once Again'? Perhaps he 'stepped lightly' to the dais in his bid for selection in Cavan? Did he dance? I imagine he was a skilled boxer. A great-nephew was featherweight champion of Ireland and selected for the 1936 Olympic team. Did he wear the Claddagh ring, a sign of fealty? A great-nephew, who was very like him, an Irishman in England, wore one with pride all his life – as did his son and grandson.

Was he a racing man? The track was always a good place to meet comrades and to disappear in the crowd. 'Spy' observed his subjects at a discreet distance and often at the racecourse. The cartoon was not in O'Connor Power's possession. Did he dislike it or did he just not get around to buying it? I intuit he was vain.

His enemies made much of his oath to the Queen on taking his seat at Westminster, which appeared to contradict his oath to the Brotherhood, 'gross perjury'. An oath, sworn with a sharp awareness of the four last things – death, judgement, hell and heaven – was a grave matter, and the Church's condemnation of the oath-bound society emphasised sacrilege. After his death, this apparent conflict is thrown up in the Treaty Debate. Many before and after him, making a 'mental reservation', arrived at the same pragmatic decision. In his letter to the Knights in St Louis, he wrote of a dual allegiance Irish Americans cherish – a loyalty to their new-found land and to the home country. Edmund Burke 'was an American in the affairs of America as much as he was an Irishman in the affairs of Ireland'.

The Thames Valley Legitimist Club took an oath to the Queen and to the King of Spain, and held their meetings in the Cheese. Gladstone, in a pamphlet 'Vaticanism', attacked papal infallibility which, he believed, undermined the civil allegiance of Catholics.[538] English Catholics continue to balance conflicting loyalties. Quakers resile.

The Irish in England and the Empire never made as much clamour as the Irish in the United States, but worked for justice and reconciliation, protecting the interests of the Irish at home and overseas, creating an archipelago of sympathy. If the ballot box and the gun do not succeed, change the minds and hearts.

In O'Connor Power's last years, his health was poor. The Johnsonian long clay pipe and the unventilated, smoke-filled rooms of the Cheshire Cheese and the National Liberal Club may have inflicted long-term damage on his heart and lungs. London's dense yellow fog killed thousands annually. Throughout his life O'Connor Power suffered from recurrent bouts of high fever.[539]

There were no entries for the law lists in 1917 and 1918. O'Connor Power had retired. The *Anglo-Celt* reported, 'The Veteran Nationalist, Mr John O'Connor Power, is seriously ill in London.' He died at home. There had been great sadness at the beginning and end of his life. The death of Hubert in the First World War, the collapse of Home Rule and the turmoil in Ireland caused unbearable anguish.

The eldest brother, his name escapes us, has been hard to track, but the family passed down many stories. He was a seaman who sailed from Liverpool to New Orleans. During the American Civil War, the cotton trade declined, and the number of ships sailing to New Orleans was fewer. Did he leave his life at sea because the job opportunities were drying up? It is more likely the call of adventure incited him to a career change.

In the Galway years, like Alexander Sullivan, chief of the Clan's 'Triangle', he carried pearl-handled pistols and slept with them under his pillow. A Civil War veteran, he had earned his right of citizenship. What part did he play in the fight for Ireland's freedom?

Sergeant-Major Thomas Power, the second brother, enjoyed high status. A Sergeant-Major was the most senior of the non-commissioned ranks, the backbone of the army. The British caste system was at its most rigid in the military, and to be a Sergeant-Major in the Army Service Corps was as high as a non-commissioned soldier might rise. Thomas's wife and family were proud of his success and mention his rank on every birth and death certificate.

In 1879, O'Connor Power commended our brave soldiers in Afghanistan. There is a hiatus in Tom's service record which fits neatly with the enquiry O'Connor Power made in the House of Commons on 5 April 1881. Thomas asked the Secretary of State for War, if non-commissioned officers of 'good conduct' and 'exemplary character' and with the requisite twenty-one years' service, might remain in the army 'as long as they are able and willing to serve'.[540] In May 1881, Thomas was discharged with pension. His discharge was cancelled in August 1883.

The three boys were so competent, confident and well socialised that I like to imagine that their mother managed one of the local hostelries. Men succumbed to the deadly fevers more frequently than women, and many households were headed by widows. If Patrick Power died young and there were three sons to care for, it is likely Mary turned her hand to a career behind a shop counter or managing one of Ballinasloe's many businesses. Her Racquet Court granddaughters were as ducks to water in the customer service industry. I speculate that the O'Connors of Roscommon, the maternal side, may have been the O'Connors who ran the theatre before the O'Shaughnessys took over the management. There is certainly a significant overlap of involvement in the business.

The boys' leadership and organisational gifts may have been the legacy of an institutional experience. I wonder were they better fed and educated in a well-run workhouse than would have been possible in a small homestead with many mouths to feed. With caring relatives close by they were secure. Ties of kinship were sacred, 'to speak of the holy love of kindred for which the Irish are remarkable, no matter how far apart the cruel vicissitudes of fortune may have scattered the members of the family'.[541] It is possible that O'Connor Power spent only a few months in the workhouse while recovering from his illness. He and his brothers do not show any signs of serious neglect.

We have a construct – the gifts of an actor, enormous strength and stamina, and the ability to mix at all levels of society. He joined his battles with imagination, innovation and gusto. The words chutzpah, brio and elan fly to the page. In the aftermath of every setback, undaunted, he bounded onward. A pragmatist, an opportunist, in the original sense of the word, he seized the occasion. Gifted with a phenomenal memory, he was a formidable strategist. His article contrasting two great statesmen, Gladstone and Disraeli, displays his consummate gift for reading character. He would spot an informer or an opponent's weakness at a hundred paces. He knew the board and he knew the pieces.

He had a deep affection for his family. He loved his wife and does not appear to have alienated his stepson. In the 1911 census, he writes 'son' and then amends it to 'stepson'. 'The Gospel of Wealth' explores his social creed. 'Edmund Burke and His Abiding Influence' is revelatory, a veiled apologia. 'The Irish in England' is a mission statement and a blueprint for the Irish race. In 'The Philosophy of Irish History', O'Connor Power, as historian, opens the wider question of national identity. *The Making of an Orator* presents a masterclass series. A life's mosaic acquires shape and colour; you find him in his words as in his actions.

Like Edmund Burke, he 'never attained high office' but 'his abilities were so versatile as to qualify him for any post which a cabinet minister could fill'.[542] He persisted in his refusals to accept preferment from a British government. He would not accept office, rewards or honours, 'Mr O'Connor Power has not held office under Government.'[543] Nor was he tempted by the green pastures of North America, 'The recent declaration of Sir John McDonald, the Canadian Prime Minister need not be recalled. Sir John has always been kindly disposed to the Irish people, and many years ago he offered Mr O'Connor Power a seat in Cabinet.'[544]

We find him in the men he admired. In the early days of The Johnson Club he was Ireland's voice, in much the same way as Burke, Sheridan and Goldsmith a hundred years earlier. In Burke's political writings – 'and they can be mentioned in the same breath with Machiavelli's *Prince* only for the purpose of contrasting their perfect morality with the sinister statecraft of the Italian author' – he found a Bible. And, like Burke, he did not 'fail to meet with an intrepid spirit the events of his own time'.[545]

If a story is not told, it will be lost forever. I leave it with you …

Some Biographical Jottings

Herbert Henry Asquith, first Earl of Oxford and Asquith (1852-1928): Liberal Prime Minister (1908-16). In his memoirs he recalls, 'One of its most notable figures for a time, was John O'Connor Power. He was a man of humble extraction and is said to have been born in the workhouse.' From Dublin he writes to his wife on 16 May 1916, 'You will never get to the bottom of this most perplexing and damnable country.'

John Barry (1845-1921): The son of Wexford parents, he was born in England. His early years were spent in Northumberland and later he moved to Manchester. In the late 1860s he was involved in arms trafficking with Michael Davitt and Mark Ryan. A member of the Supreme Council and founding member of the HRCGB, he was MP for Wexford (1880-95). A distant relative and close friend of Timothy Healy, with whom he toured Portugal and Spain. In the last twenty years of his life he pursued a successful business career.

Joseph Biggar (1828-1890): Born in Belfast. Home Rule MP. A prominent obstructionist, his 'rasping voice and odd and jerky mode of speaking' made him a brilliant choice, adding irritation to aggravation. He was IIP treasurer, and reputed to be 'close' with the funds, 'he had a frugal mind'. He was a member of the Supreme Council and claimed at the Special Commission hearings that he had joined the IRB to gain support for Home Rule. Timothy Healy holidayed with his family at Biggar's castle in Butlerstown, Waterford. Biggar, Healy and John Barry often celebrated New Year together in Fifeshire. Parnell did not attend Biggar's funeral.

Augustine Birrell (1850-1933): Born in Liverpool. Liberal MP, barrister, orator, author. Prior of The Johnson Club (1895). As President of the National Liberal Federation, he played a major part in the Liberal landslide of 1906. He was Irish Chief Secretary (1907-16). He was opposed to partition. The Royal Commission into the Easter Rising held him 'primarily responsible for the situation that was allowed to arise and the outbreak that occurred'. Of Disraeli and John Bright: '[They had] the great advantages of an irregular education and most leisurely occupations.'

Canon Ulick Bourke (1829-1887): Born in Castlebar. A Gaelic scholar, he was President of St Jarlath's College, Tuam (1865-77). As parish priest, he chaired a land meeting in Claremorris on 13 July 1879.

Thomas Brennan (1842-1915). Born in Mayo. He worked for several years in Castlebar and Dublin for Patrick Egan in the North Dublin City Milling Company. Land warrior. '... there are few in Ireland who know more of O'Connor Power's thoughts than I do ...' He was Secretary to the Land League and was imprisoned in 1881. After the Kilmainham Treaty, he emigrated to the United States and was active in Irish American politics.

John Bright (1811-1889): Born in Rochdale to a Quaker manufacturing family. Chartist. Orator. He entered parliament as MP for Durham. A long-time supporter of Irish land reform, he finally became disillusioned with the Irish party. 'His charm is doubtless his clearness of mind and expression; and what detracts from that is his intolerance of those who think differently from him.' (Sir Edward Hamilton)

Sir Francis Cowley Burnand (1836-1917): Of Huguenot descent. A Catholic convert, he tried a vocation with the Oblates of St Charles at Bayswater under Dr Manning. A Liberal, a lawyer and writer of burlesques, he was editor of *Punch* (1880-1906). 'Is not Punch an Irish name? And is there not Punch's Town?'

Isaac Butt (1813-1879): Irish MP, barrister, academic. Advocate for Fenian prisoners. He was leader of the IIP (1874-7). He was gregarious, generous to a fault and unable to manage his finances. He spent part of 1868-9 in the debtors' jail in Kilmainham. 'He was the most disinterested of men.' (Michael MacDonagh)

Joseph Cowen (1829-1900): Radical MP for Newcastle and editor of the *Newcastle Chronicle*. 'We had influence in Cowen's constituency, but it was not our influence that weighed with Cowen. He would have voted for Home Rule anyway. He was thoroughly Irish in feeling.' (X, Barry O'Brien, *Parnell*)

Archbishop Croke of Cashel (1824-1902): Ordained in 1846. While at the Irish College in Paris, he manned the barricades during the 1848 revolution. A Nationalist, a proponent of Gallicanism. He served in Auckland, New Zealand (1870-5). He was first President of the Gaelic Athletic Association and Croke Park, the GAA headquarters, is named for him.

Michael Davitt (1846-1906): Fenian, land warrior, MP, journalist. He was born in Mayo and his family moved to Lancashire when he was four years old. He spent seven and a half years in prison for gun trafficking. He was President of the United Irish League. In 1899, he resigned his seat at Westminster in protest at the Anglo-Boer war. He defended the rights of the Irish and British working class. He had a strong fear of the demon drink. 'Davitt is a man who must always have somebody on the spit.' (Matt Harris) 'Mr Davitt, however, was a born frondeur.' (William O'Brien, *Recollections*)

James Daly (1836-1916): Owner and editor of the *Connaught Telegraph*. Influential in the election of O'C.P. in 1874. A Home Ruler, he advocated 'unqualified control of Irish affairs by the Irish people'. He believed that land agitation, within the law, was as important as parliamentary action. He organised and chaired the Irishtown meeting which launched the Land War. His work for the Bessborough Commission provided a structure for land reform. He was a strong supporter of the United Irish League. 'A rough-spoken giant, with an inexhaustible fund of knowledge of the people.' (William O'Brien).

John Daly (1845-1916): Limerick Fenian. Member of the IRB Supreme Council during the Land War.

John Denvir (1834-1916): Born in Antrim. He joined the IRB and was involved in gunrunning. He was first secretary of the HRCGB. Journalist, author and printer, he published the Penny booklets – biography, history, songs – which were known as *Denvir's Irish Library*.

John Devoy (1842-1928): Fenian organiser. On his release from prison in 1871 he moved to the United States and joined Clan na Gael. 'He never married. The cause was for him wife, family and home.' He was the implacable enemy of O'C.P. and 'Powerism'.

John Dillon (1851-1927): Born in Dublin. IIP MP. Signatory of the No-Rent Manifesto. He supported the Plan of Campaign and the United Irish League. He opposed the Boer War. He was involved in the campaign against conscription and, in 1918, succeeded John Redmond as leader of the Irish party.

Benjamin Disraeli, Earl of Beaconsfield (1804-1881): Of Jewish parentage. Conservative politician. Leader of the House of Commons, 1852. Tory PM (Feb.1868-Dec.1868, Feb.1874-April 1880). A Byronic social and literary figure. His insight into the Irish Question, 'an alien Church and an absentee aristocracy' is often quoted. 'He was shrewd enough to see that the party of leisure and affluence was too much given up to pleasures and the refinements of life to furnish many formidable competitors for the prizes of politics.' (O'C.P.)

Sir Charles Gavan Duffy (1816-1903): Young Irelander, barrister and author. He was Prime Minister of Victoria, Australia and returned to England to promote Home Rule. He was a President of the Irish Literary Society.

Patrick Egan (1841-1919): Member of the IRB Supreme Council, treasurer of the Land League. A successful businessman and *bon viveur*, he stayed at the Hotel Brighton during his time in Paris. He was suspected of funding the Invincibles, who were responsible for the Phoenix Park assassinations. In 1883, he moved to the United States. His co-operation was vital to the Special Commission defence team. In March 1889, he was appointed United States Minister to Chile. He moved to support Home Rule, and, after the Easter Rising, in an interview in *The New York Times*, he denounced John Devoy, 'if anyone were shot it should be John Devoy who hatched the whole nefarious scheme here in New York and was personally responsible for it'.

Herbert Gladstone (1854-1930): Liberal politician. Youngest son of William Ewart Gladstone. In October 1881, he was sent to Dublin to assist the Irish Chief Secretary. In December 1885, he leaked to the press that his father was in favour of Home Rule. His purposeful indiscretion is remembered as the 'Hawarden Kite'. He was Under Secretary of State for the Home Department in 1892.

William Ewart Gladstone (1809-1898): Liberal PM (1868-74, 1880-5, Feb.-July 1886, 1892-4). He told Queen Victoria, 'My mission is to pacify Ireland.' She considered him to be a dangerous radical, and he declined her offer of an Earldom. 'All the world over, I will back the masses against the classes' (Hansard, 28 June

1886). 'He brought out what was most generous in the two peoples, and repressed what was most savage in their racial propensities' (William O'Brien).

Matt Harris (1826-1890): Born in Athlone. MP for Galway East (1885-1890). He was a stonemason and building contractor. He succeeded O'C.P. as Connacht representative on the Supreme Council and was chief supplier of arms in the west of Ireland. He was the leading Ballinasloe tenant right activist.

Timothy Healy (1855-1931): Born in Bantry, County Cork. He was secretary to Parnell and a member of the IIP. He writes to his brother Maurice on 5 June 1880, 'I received from the Land League £140 for "work at home and abroad" and have entered as a student at Grey's Inn.' Later that year he would receive a further £150 for election expenses (*Letters*, chap. vii). The UIL made great efforts to drive him out of public life, and he was expelled from the Irish party. He was first Governor General of the Free State, 1922. 'Provokes admiration and distrust' (F. Hugh O'Donnell). 'He was characteristically Irish in his qualities, winning and repellent.' (Michael MacDonagh)

Mitchell Henry (1826-1910): A wealthy businessman and a consultant physician, who promoted healthcare for the poor. He built Kylemore Castle in Connemara as the family residence. He was Home Rule MP for Galway County (1871-85) and was considered at one time for leadership of the IIP. He supported O'C.P.'s 1874 campaign and resigned from the party in 1884. In 1885 he was elected as a Liberal for Glasgow. He lost his seat when he joined the Liberal Unionists.

Charles Henry Hopwood (1829-1904): Liberal MP and lawyer. He supported Home Rule, and recommended that Britain pardon Fenian prisoners in the same spirit as the US government dealt with Confederates after the Civil War.

Fr Patrick Lavelle (1825-1886): Born in Mayo. Nationalist Catholic priest. An outstanding scholar, he taught in the Irish College in Paris. In 1862 he lectured on 'The Catholic Doctrine of the Right to Revolution'. He was a controversial figure, with a penchant for litigation. Fr John O'Malley gave his graveside oration, 'We all know he was impulsive, but we also know that he was at the same time the most generous, the most unselfish of men.'

David Lloyd George, first Earl (1863-1945): Born in Manchester of Welsh parentage. Orator, lawyer, journalist. Liberal PM (1916-22). Known as the 'Welsh Wizard', his first language was Welsh. He opposed the Second Boer War and war profiteering. In 1911 he introduced the National Insurance Act and the Unemployment Act.

Michael MacDonagh (1862-1946): Journalist and prolific author. He was on the parliamentary staff of the *Freeman's Journal* and later *The Times*. '[It was Labour] which supplied the driving force of the country socially and politically, which had given the backbone, the muscle and the grit to every Nationalist movement, revolutionary and constitutional' (MacDonagh, *Home Rule*).

Archbishop McHale (1791-1881): Born in Mayo, a native Irish speaker. He was an outspoken leader of his people and was the author of an Irish catechism and a translation of Moore's *Melodies*. Known as 'The Lion of St Jarlath's' or 'the Lion of the West', he was fearless and opposed and voted against the dogma of Papal infallibility at the First Vatican Council in 1870. 'He kept a good table and meat was always available on Fridays for guests who had a dispensation' (George Moore, *Hail and Farewell, Ave*).

Henry Edward Manning (1808-1892): Brilliant academic. A close friend of Gladstone at Oxford. Lord Goderich, father of Lord Ripon, found him a job in the Colonial Office. He entered Holy Orders and converted to Catholicism in 1851. In 1865 he was appointed Archbishop of Westminster. He was made a Cardinal in 1875. He was an advocate of social justice. Westminster Cathedral was his project. Lytton Strachey's *Eminent Victorians* includes an unflattering biographical essay.

W.H. Massingham (1860-1924): Journalist and Johnsonian. 'A thorough going radical', he was editor of the *Daily Chronicle* and later the *Nation*, which was founded in 1906, marking the return of the Liberals to government. He visited Ireland often and supported Home Rule wholeheartedly. He had a strong interest in theatre. An early member of the Fabian Society, he moved, as did many Liberals, to the Labour party. His son H.J. Massingham was a prominent environmentalist.

George Henry Moore (1811-1870): Catholic landlord and politician. MP for Mayo (1847-57, 1868-70). He was a founding member of the Catholic Defence Association (the Irish Brigade) and the Independent Irish party. He supported tenant right and amnesty and worked closely with the Fenians. 'Nobody but Archbishop McHale was allowed punch in my father's house.' 'My family never yielded to peasant mistresses' (George Moore, *Hail and Farewell, Ave*).

John Morley (1838-1923): Liberal politician and journalist. Home Rule MP for Newcastle Upon Tyne and Chief Secretary for Ireland (February-July 1886, 1892-5). In 1908, created viscount, he moved the Home Rule agenda to the House of Lords. Editor of the *Fortnightly Review*, 1867-82. 'One should take care lest in quenching the spirit of Midlothian [Gladstone's election speeches, 1880] we leave the sovereign mastery of the world to Machiavelli.' (Cited in *The Making of an Orator.*) He opposed the Boer War: 'You may make thousands of women widows and thousands of children fatherless. It will be wrong. You may add province to your Empire. It will still be wrong. You may increase the shares of Mr Rhodes and his Chartereds beyond the dreams of avarice. Yea, it will still be wrong.' And in 1921, 'If I were an Irishman, I would be a Sinn Féiner.'

P.W. Nally (1856-1891): Born in Balla, County Mayo. He was an outstanding athlete and the leading Fenian in the county. In 1882, he was elected a Poor Law Guardian. He publicly condemned agrarian violence while secretly importing arms. He died in Mountjoy shortly before he was to be released.

John Henry Newman (1801-1890): A High Church Anglican who converted to Roman Catholicism in 1845. He was ordained two years later. He was Rector of the Catholic University of Ireland (1854-8) and was made a cardinal in 1879.

J.F.X. O'Brien (1828-1905): Assistant surgeon in the American Civil War, journalist, member of the Supreme Council (1869). MP for South Mayo (1885-95) and for Cork City (1895-1905).

R. Barry O'Brien (1864-1918): Born in County Clare. Barrister, historian and journalist. He was a member of the HRCGB and secretary to Parnell. There was a bust of John Bright in his father's home. T.P. O'Connor attempted to prevent the circulation of his biography of Parnell (Healy, *Letters,* chap. xix). His works include *The parliamentary history of the Irish Land Question 1829 to 1869* (1880), a biography of Charles Russell and a monograph on John Bright. He was careful to protect his sources.

William O'Brien (1852-1928): Fenian, MP, land reformer, journalist, author. He resigned from the IRB in the mid-1870s. He was editor of *United Ireland* and launched the No Rent Manifesto while in Kilmainham. He was the main mover behind the Plan of Campaign, 'He inspired and directed the Irish Nationalist Movement, agrarian and political, for the four stirring years 1886-1890.'

He organised the United Irish League and later the All-for-Ireland-League. 'He was acknowledged leader because of his ability, his passionate earnestness, his soaring faith in his cause.' (Michael MacDonagh)

John O'Connor (1850-1928): Born in Mallow, County Cork. MP for Tipperary South (1885-92) and later North Kildare (1902-18). He was a distinguished lawyer. A Secretary of the Supreme Council, he was present at the New Departure talks in 1878. In 1888, Devoy branded him a 'renegade' and accused him of being implicated in attempts 'to depose Parnell in favour of Davitt' (McConnel, *Fenians at Westminster*, p.55). For an affectionate portrait see Stephen Gwynn's 'Long John – A Parliamentary Memoir' in *Memories of Enjoyment* (Tralee, 1946). 'Once he took me to dine at the Johnson Club.' Gwynn was a grandson of Young Irelander William Smith O'Brien.

Thomas Power O'Connor (1848-1929): Born in Athlone. Home Rule MP, journalist and popular author. In December 1918, he retained his Liverpool seat, when Sinn Féin swept to victory.

F. Hugh O'Donnell (1846-1916): MP, prominent obstructionist, journalist, historian, playwright and educationalist. In 1875, together with O'C.P. and two Indians living in London, he inaugurated the Constitutional Society of India, a 'Home Rule for India'. 'Mr O'Donnell's grand passion in politics was a confederation of all the discontented races of the Empire under the lead of the Irish party. He once brought down some scores of dusky students of all the races and creeds of Hindustan to the House of Commons' (William O'Brien, *Recollections*, 247 fn). After obstruction, 'Twenty years later he was an Irish secret agent for the Boer government then at war with Britain' (McCracken, 106). He called the British 'Imperial pirates' and was anti-clerical, 'In Ireland material ruin has accompanied clerical despotism.' His 'matter is often better than his manner'. (Belfort Bax)

James J. O'Kelly (1845-1916): Fenian, soldier of fortune, war correspondent, art dealer and MP for Roscommon (1880-92, 1892-1916). A Secretary of the Supreme Council, he was present at the New Departure negotiations with George Moore and in 1878 Dr Carroll and Parnell. Named by colleagues 'the Fenian Whig'. In May 1881, he introduced Parnell to Henri Le Caron. He was Vice-President of the UIL Directory. '[O'Kelly] shares our ideas in everything – excepting a more 'charitable' opinion of O'Donnell and Power' (Davitt to Devoy, 31 October 1878). His brother was the painter Aloyisius O'Kelly.

William O'Shea (1840-1905): Irish Catholic MP. He was married to Katherine Wood, who, after the divorce, married Charles Parnell. He negotiated the release of Irish MPs from Kilmainham Jail, later referring to it as Parnell's 'surrender'. For him, the Fenians were the 'real boys'. Parnell believed O'Shea was behind the Pigott forgeries.

Charles Stewart Parnell (1846-1891): Born in Avondale, County Wicklow. MP for Meath (1875-80) and Cork City (1880-91). He was leader of the IPP (May 1880-91). He had many health problems and was an 'inveterate sipper of water'. 'Talking yesterday of the Opposition, or rather Oppositions, Mr G. [Gladstone] said he felt towards Sir S. Northcote much the same as he did towards Parnell. Neither of them were really big men or pleasant antagonists; but their places might be taken by worse men, and therefore he preferred keeping them.' (Hamilton, *Diary*, 558) Of obstruction tactics, 'How far Mr Parnell saw ahead of him at this time, what his motives were, and what secret influences were acting upon him may, perhaps, never be revealed' (*The Times* obituary, 8 October 1891).

Lord Ripon (1827-1909): Radical Liberal. He was born in 10 Downing Street, the son of a Prime Minister. His mother was born in Ireland and he had strong connections to the country. He converted to Catholicism in September 1874. He was Viceroy of India (1880-4) and Secretary of State for the Colonies (1892-5). He was president of the St Vincent de Paul Society.

Jeremiah O'Donovan Rossa (1831-1915): Born in Ross Carbery, County Cork. Journalist and leading organiser of the IRB in the late 1860s. He was imprisoned in 1865, and, while still in Chatham Jail, won a parliamentary seat in County Tipperary. Sometimes called 'O'Dynamite Rossa', his Skirmishing Fund came under the control of John Devoy and financed the dynamite campaign. His two sons were educated at St Jarlath's College, and the fees were paid by Richard Pigott. Padraig Pearse gave the graveside oration at his re-interment in Glasnevin.

Charles Russell, first Baron Russell of Killowen (1832-1900): An Ulster Catholic, his uncle was President of Maynooth. He was a lawyer and member of parliament for Dundalk (1880) and Hackney South (1885-94). He was consulted on the 1881 Land Act. His eight-day epic speech for the defence at the Special Commission was a comprehensive account of Irish history. When the Liberals returned to power in 1892, he was appointed Attorney General and then Lord Chief Justice – the first Catholic to hold the office since the reign of Henry VIII. Gladstone would have made him Lord Chancellor but the position was out of bounds to Catholics. He was a man of action, a boxer and lover of theatre first nights. He was noted for his hospitality and his party pieces were drawn from Moore's *Melodies*. He was a talented card player. A racing man, he lived at Tadworth Court, close to Epsom.

Mark Ryan (1844-1940): Born in Tuam, County Galway. His family was evicted and moved to Lancashire, where he joined the IRB. He returned to Ireland to study at St Jarlath's and then medicine at University College, Galway. He continued to be active in the IRB. When he qualified he moved to England. His autobiography, *Fenian Memories*, was published after his death.

P.J. Smyth (1823-1885): Born in Dublin and educated at Clongowes Wood College. Young Irelander, Home Rule MP and outstanding orator. He organised the escape of John Mitchel and other Young Ireland leaders from Tasmania in 1853. He was opposed to the violent methods of the Land League, 'a League of hell', and resigned his seat in 1882.

Time Line

(13 Feb.) John O'Connor Power is born in Clashaganny, Tulsk, County Roscommon. Third son of Patrick and Mary Power (*née* O'Connor). Patrick was from townland of Ballygill, Creagh. Ballinasloe. Family reportedly of Mayo extraction. Shortly after birth he was taken home to Ballinasloe. Contracts smallpox. Spends time in workhouse.

1860
(23 Jan.) Thomas Power, O'Connor Power's older brother, enlists in 59th Regiment of Foot, 2nd Nottinghamshire Brigade. O'C.P. emigrates, following his brothers to England. He works with relatives in the house-painting business and in flannel mills during winter months. He joins the Irish Republican Brotherhood, travelling extensively in the north of England and in Scotland, recruiting members, building the network and growing reputation as organiser, platform speaker and journalist.

1867
(11 Feb.) Evades arrest after aborted raid on Chester Castle. (5-6 Mar.) Fenian Rising. (18 Sept.) Takes part in rescue of Fenian officers from prison van. Three

men were executed and remembered as the 'Manchester Martyrs'. Travels to America to discuss reorganisation. (13 Dec.) Clerkenwell Prison explosion.

1868
(Jan.) Returns to Ireland. (13, 14 Feb.) IRB Supreme Council meet for first time. (17 Feb.) Arrested in Dublin, spending five and a half months in Kilmainham. Known to Dublin Castle by several aliases – John Webster, John Fleming, Charles Ferguson, and later, John Delaney. (29 July) He was the last of the Fenians arrested on suspicion to be released. Sets up structures of IRB. Connacht representative on Supreme Council. Travels to Mayo to establish units in the county. Irish Liberal Alliance. (Nov.) Campaigns for George Henry Moore.

1869
Meets with Moore to discuss amnesty for Fenian prisoners. (29 Jun.) Amnesty Association founded. Tours England and Scotland with Edmond O'Donovan. Explores ways to forge alliance between physical force Nationalists and constitutionalists.

1870

Disestablishment of Church of Ireland. Land Act. (12 Jan.) Fenians condemned by Pope Pius IX and IRB members automatically excommunicated. O'C.P. convenes All-Ireland revolutionary parliament in Cork. (19 Apr.) Moore dies before the full implementation of the home government initiative. (19 May) Founding of the Home Rule movement.

1871

(Jan.) Enrolls in St Jarlath's College in Tuam, County Galway. Studies Greek and Latin, Irish language and history. Excels in debate and college dramatics. Continues arms trafficking and Fenian activities. Pays fees by lecturing for Amnesty Association in Britain and America and teaching Irish history in college.

1872

(18 Jul.) The Ballot Act introduces secret voting. (19 Aug.) Local Government Board Act.

1873

(8 Jan.) Home Rule Confederation of Great Britain in Manchester. (17 Mar.) IRB Solemn Convention of the Irish Republic. (Sept.) Archbishop McHale supports Home Rule. (18-21 Nov.) O'C.P. gives qualified support for Home Rule League at a conference in Rotundo, Dublin.

1874

(5 Jan.) Home Rule meeting, Free Trade Hall, Manchester. (Feb.) Leaves St Jarlath's to campaign. (May) Elected MP for Mayo. (2 July) Promotes federal solution at Westminster. (13 July) Launches amnesty campaign in House of Commons. Works for improvement in prison conditions and support for prisoners' families.

1875

(Mar.-Apr.) Spends time in Italy and has an audience with Pius IX. (15 Mar.) Manning made Cardinal. (10 Jun.) O'C.P. present in Tuam for Archbishop McHale's Jubilee celebration. (13 Jun.) Present at meeting of Supreme Council in Dublin. (8 Jul.) Questions the benefit of the Prince of Wales's visit to India, 'either for the people of England or the people of India'. Founding member of the Constitutional Society of India. (15 July) In Castlebar to address his constituents. (2 Aug.) Addresses gathering of over 100,000 in Hyde Park on amnesty. (6 Aug.) O'Connell centennial celebrations in Dublin. (8 Aug.) The Supreme Council meet in Imperial Hotel, Dublin. (20 Sept.) Cardinal Cullen's pastoral letter condemns 'secret societies and illegal combinations'. (Sept.-Mar. 1876) Tours North America as accredited agent of the Supreme Council and fundraiser for the Home Rule League. Parallel action.

1876

(13 Mar.) Arrives Liverpool on White Star steamer *Republic*. (May) Ballinasloe Tenants Defence Association founded. (28 May) Attends meeting of Supreme Council in Dublin. (4 Jul.) Guest speaker, Durham Miner's Gala. (1 Aug.) Amnesty question reopened at Westminster. Presides over mass amnesty rally in Hyde Park. (17 Sept.) Addresses constituents in Mayo. (19 Sept.) Lectures on 'Irish Wit and Humour' in Manchester. (20 Sept.) Resigns from HRCGB executive. (30 Sept.) Arrives New York on SS *Britannic* bearing congratulatory address from the people of Ireland on the Centennial of American Independence. Meets informally with President Ulysses S. Grant in New York. (20 Dec.) Presents House of Representatives with an illuminated address.

1877

(3 Mar.) In Quebec to lecture on 'English Rule in Ireland'. (17 Mar.) Guest of the Knights of St Patrick, St Louis. (13 Apr.) Arrives in Cork on SS *Adriatic*. (Apr.) Obstruction of Mutiny Bill. (5 Jun.) Proposal to Amend the Prison Bill. (Aug.) Obstruction of South Africa Bill. (9 Sept.) In Manchester to speak on 'The Present Position of the Irish National Cause'. (Oct.) Gladstone visits Ireland. (Dec.) O'C.P. in Mayo for unveiling of a monument commemorating the French soldiers who died near Castlebar during the 1798 Rising. (19 Dec.) Davitt released.

1878

(14 Jan.) Davitt, Chambers, McCarthy and O'Brien visit O'C.P.'s lodgings in Dublin to thank him for his 'unceasing exertions' on behalf of prisoners. (14 Feb.) Registers as law student in Middle Temple. (28 Apr.) Speaks on 'Irish Independence' in Liverpool. In House of Commons moves amendment with object of bringing native soldiers in India under the operation of the Army Bill. (26 Oct.) Addresses founding meeting of the Mayo Tenants Defence Association, Castlebar. Delivers battle cry, 'The land of Ireland for the people of Ireland', as reported in the *Connaught Telegraph* (2 Nov.). 'Irish Political Prisoners: Speeches of John O'Connor Power in the House of Commons on the subject of amnesty, etc., and a statement by Mr Michael Davitt on prison treatment.' 'Irish Political Prisoners: Enquiry into the prison treatment and cause of death of the late Color-Sergeant McCarthy, and the letter to James Ingham'.

1879

(20 Apr.) Addresses tenant right meeting in Irishtown, County Mayo. (10 Aug.) Speaks at Home Rule demonstration at Crystal Palace. (16 Aug.) Land League of Mayo. (7 Sept.) Constituency meeting in Castlebar. (21 Oct.) Founding of Irish National Land League. (1 Dec.) Addresses monster rally in Hyde Park to protest at imprisonment of Land League leaders Matt Harris and Michael Davitt. 'Fallacies about Home Rule', *Fortnightly Review*. 'The Irish Land Agitation', *Nineteenth Century*.

1880

(Apr.) Tops poll in Mayo in general election. (20 Apr.) Attends first anniversary of Irishtown meeting. (26 Apr.) Lectures on 'The Philosophy of Irish History' in the Round Room at Rotundo. (28 May) Introduces Compensation for Disturbance Bill in the House of Commons. Strong contender for leadership of the Irish party. (Sept.) Boycott campaign. (Nov.) Speaks in Galway on objects of the Land League and freedom from British rule. 'The Irish in England', *Fortnightly Review*.

1881

Thomas Power and family return from India. (17 Mar.) Guest of the Manchester Irish Literary Association in the Clarence Hotel. (Apr.) Tours North of England to protest against coercion. (20 Jun.) Lectures in Liverpool on 'Nationality'. (17 Nov.) Called to the Bar. Works with Gladstone and Charles Russell on land legislation. Land Law Ireland Act.

1882

(Aug.) Arrears Act.

1883

(10 Apr.) Moves resolution in House of Commons for relief of chronic distress in Ireland by migration and optional emigration.

1884

(24 Apr.) Formally leaves Irish party. (8 Jun.) Warm reception in Cork. (Jun.) Unanimous vote of confidence at Castlebar constituency meeting. Attends British Liberal Conference in Belfast with Charles Russell. (12 Oct.) Attends Liberal meeting in Rochdale. (5 Nov.) Attends stone-laying of National Liberal Club's new premises. (13 Dec.) The Johnson Club's inaugural meeting.

1885

Third Reform Act. Redistribution of Seats Act. (1 Feb.) Lectures on Thomas Moore at Vauxhall. Land Purchase Act. (1 Apr.) Thomas Power promoted Barrack Sergeant-Major. (6 Jun.) O'C.P. a guest at the annual dinner of the Oxford Palmerston Club. (Jul.) John Bright endorses his candidacy for Kennington. (Nov.) Stands unsuccessfully as Liberal candidate in Kennington. Member of administrative council of Indian National Congress. Active member of the National Liberal Club. 'The New Reform', *Nineteenth Century*.

1886

(6 Apr.) First Home Rule Bill introduced in House of Commons. (24 Oct.) Launch of Plan of Campaign. (25 Dec.) 'Spy' cartoon 'The brains of Obstruction' appears in *Vanity Fair's* 'Men of the Day'. 'The Anglo-Irish Quarrel, A Plea for Peace.'

1887

(9 Sept.) Mitchelstown Massacre. (19 Oct.) Hubert Foveaux Weiss marries Avis Hooke. (13 Nov.) Bloody Sunday, Trafalgar Square. (13 Dec.) O'C.P. takes office as Prior of The Johnson Club. (End Dec.) Davitt public letter asking party to make peace with O'Connor Power. (23 Dec.) *Toronto Daily Mail* announces O'C.P.'s trip to North America.

1888

(Jan.-Nov.) O'C.P. tours the United States and Canada to promote Home Rule. Explores settlement options in Canada for new wave of emigrants. (Oct.) Spends time in New York. Lecture series arranged by impresario Major Pond. On return to London moves to chambers in Oliver Goldsmith's former lodgings.

1889

(17 Sept. 1888-22 Nov. 1889) Special Commission.

1890

(13 Feb.) Special Commission Report published. (Aug.) Chatham Visitors' Inquiry and Report. O'C.P. accuses prison Visitors of whitewashing actions of prison officials.
'The Gospel of Wealth, A Reply to Andrew Carnegie', *Universal Review*.
'The Government Plan for the Congested Districts', *Nineteenth Century*. 'Irish Wit and Humour', *Time*.

1891

Land Purchase Act.

1892

Leader-writer for *Daily Chronicle*, which commits to Home Rule. Takes strong stands on prison reform, adult suffrage and House of Lords veto. (4 Jul.) Hubert Foveaux Weiss dies in Alverstoke. (Jul.) Fails to take seat as Independent Nationalist in Mayo West.

1893

(13 Feb.) Second Home Rule Bill introduced. (1 Sept.) H.R. passes third reading in House of Commons, subsequently vetoed by House of Lords. (28 Sept.) Marries Avis Weiss (*née* Hooke), widow of surgeon Hubert Foveaux Weiss, in St Edward's Roman Catholic Church, Westminster.

1894

Continues to practice on the south-eastern circuit.

1895

(Jul.) Stands as Radical candidate in Bristol South, defeated by sitting Tory MP. Denies taking oath of illegal organisation, threatens legal action.

1897

(27 Jan.) Opposes Anglo-Turkish Convention. (26 May) Addresses Women's National Liberal Association's Annual Conference in London on 'Colonial Policy'. (11 Jun.) Proposes vote of thanks at 'A Sheridan Night' hosted by the Irish Literary Society of London in St Martin's Town Hall. 'Edmund Burke and his Abiding Influence', *North America Review*.

1898

(13 Jan.) Presides at centennial dinner celebrating anniversary of Edmund Burke's birthday. Seventy Nationalists present. (16 Jan.) United Irish League launched in Westport. (21 Feb.) Local Government (Ireland) Bill introduced in House of Commons. (12 Mar.) Guest at lecture on India and Sir Henry Maine. (17 Mar.) A guest of John Dillon, he was a principle speaker at St Patrick's banquet to commemorate 1798 Rising. (July) Guest at Burke centennial memorial in Beaconsfield. (11 Nov.) Represents National Liberal Club at funeral of T.B. Potter, a Radical MP for Rochdale and founder of the Cobden Club.

1899

(2 Jan.) Speaks in Mansion House Round Room to protest against over taxation of Ireland. (13 Jul.) Vice-Chairman, National Liberal Club Political Committee.

1900

(30 Jan.) Irish party reunites under leadership of John Redmond. (2 Mar.) O'C.P. presides at National Liberal Club discussion on Licensing Reform. (2 Mar.) (20 Jun.) Addresses National Convention in Dublin. Welcome reception on visit to Mayo. (5 Oct.) At UIL convention, nominated but not selected for West Cavan. (10 Oct.) Sails from Kingstown (Dún Laoghaire) on Royal Mail Steamer.

1901

Writes a letter to the *Westminster Review*, objecting to the anti-Catholic wording of the Accession Oath. (24 Apr.) League of Liberals against Aggression and Militarism. The War in South Africa. (27 May) As delegate of Kingston Upon Thames, addresses United Irish League of Great Britain annual convention in Bristol. Speaks against the 'cruel and unjust war'. (12 Nov.) Sergeant-Major Thomas Power, his brother, dies in Galway City.

1902

(Nov.) Letter to C.P. Scott, editor of the *Manchester Guardian*, offering to write a series of letters on the state of Ireland. (Dec.) Land Conference.

1903

(14 Aug.) Wyndham Land Purchase Act.

1905

Visits Dublin for engagement of his godson, John Power.

1906

(Jun.) *The Making of an Orator: With Examples from Great Masterpieces of Ancient And Modern Eloquence*

1907

(4 Feb.) Racquet Court Theatre, Galway, damaged by fire. (6 Feb.) Marriage of

his niece Mary Power in Rathmines, Dublin. Irish Council Bill proposed and rejected.

1909

(3 Mar.) National Liberal Club guest speaker, 'The House of Lords'. (11 May) Speaks on 'Adult Suffrage'.

1910

All-for-Ireland-League.

1911

(Aug.) Parliament Bill.

1912

(12 Jan.) Chairs talk given by T.M. Kettle to Political and Economic Circle of National Liberal Club. (26 Jan.) Attends opening campaign for disestablishment of Anglican Church in Wales.

1913

Dublin Lockout. (24 Oct.) O'C.P. letter to William O'Brien.

1914

(25 May) Third Home Rule Bill passes third reading in House of Commons. (18 Sept.) Government of Ireland Act.

1915

(26 May) O'C.P. seriously ill. Replies to a letter from William O'Brien. (1 June) Private Patrick Power, Connaught Rangers, First Battalion, his nephew, is killed in action in France.

1916

(Apr.) Easter Rising.

1918

(3 Sept.) Second Lieutenant Hubert Foveaux Weiss, Post Office Rifles, City of London Battalion, his stepson, dies of wounds in France.

1919

(21 Jan) First Dáil meets in the Round Room of the Mansion House. (3 Feb.) Éamon de Valera escapes from Lincoln Jail. (21 Feb.) O'C.P. dies at home in Putney of heart failure, with Avis at his side. (27 Feb.) Requiem Mass in Our Lady of Pity and St Simon Stock, his parish church. (28 Feb.) Buried in Abney Park, north London.

1920

Government of Ireland Act. (20 Jul.) Racquet Court up for auction.

1922

(4 Jan.) Named in Treaty Debate (oath of allegiance).

1924

(22 May) Elizabeth (Gabby) Power, dies in Galway. (7 Nov.) Eileen O'Shaughnessy dies in son-in-law's home in Fair Hill, Galway. Residence on both death certificates is Middle Street.

1948

(2 Sept.) Avis dies in Richmond. Her remains are cremated.

Obituaries

Mr John O'Connor Power whose death is announced, will be remembered very well by an older generation of members of the House of Commons, in which he sat for Mayo from 1874 to 1885.

He was a man of education and a speaker with something of the grand style. In fact, Irishmen reckoned him as one of the best orators they had ever sent to Parliament.

In his youth he was connected with the revolutionary movement, and is credited with organisng the daring Fenian plot to seize Chester Castle. Its main idea was to move suddenly some hundreds of Fenians from the North of England to Chester, to take the arms in the arsenal there, to move rapidly to Holyhead, seize a steamer, and cross with weapons to Ireland for the purpose of starting the contemplated insurrection. Many Irishmen from Manchester, Liverpool and other Lancashire towns took part, including Michael Davitt. Information reached the police and preparations were made to resist the raid, the Fenians only discovering this after the parties of their members had started from various points. By extraordinary efforts, however, they managed to intercept them and get them back without losing a man.

Mr Power's career in Parliament began before the Biggar-Parnell era of obstruction. He allied himself with them for a time, then broke away and dropped out of Parliament.

He made one or two efforts afterwards to return to Parliament for an English constituency as a Liberal but failed.

Manchester Guardian, 24 February 1919

The death in London, of Mr John O'Connor Power recalls the earlier days of the land agitation, when he figured, as MP for Mayo, with Parnell and Biggar in their famous obstruction tactics in Parliament, and was one of those suspended after the great scenes in 1881 arising out of Davitt's arrest.

Belonging to a Mayo family, he was born in Roscommon in 1846, and is believed to have been one of the chief organisers of the abortive Fenian raid on the Chester Castle in '67. As a public orator he aroused the keenest enthusiasm, while in Parliament, he was forceful and eloquent. He was one of the speakers at the Irishtown meeting when the Land League was launched. In Parliament since 1874, as a supporter of Butt, he was again returned in '80 with Parnell, but the latter convinced that their policies were growing divergent, elected to sit for Cork city, for which he was also returned. Though there was no open rupture, Power and Parnell drifted further apart, and in 1885 the former dropped out, having previously had notable differences with Messrs Parnell, Sexton and Healy. Since then Power twice unsuccessfully stood for English constituencies as a Radical. Davitt and he maintained their friendship. In 1893 Power married the widow of Mr K.F. Weiss, FRCS. One of his books dealt with the art of oratory. He was called to the English Bar in 1881. The *London Evening Standard* classes him as an orator with Gladstone and Bright.

Irish Independent, 24 February 1919

Mr John O'Connor Power, the brilliant politician and orator, who represented Mayo in the House of Commons from 1874 to 1885, died on Thursday at his residence in Putney, near London, at the age of 73.

Connaught Telegraph, 1 March 1919

Notes

Part One

The Home Place

1. *The Exodus* (1864), Speranza, *nom de plume* of Lady Wilde.
2. Walter Macken, *The Silent People* (1962), chap. ii.
3. Primary Valuation of Ireland and Sir Richard Griffith's Valuation, a property valuation record, was carried out between 1848 and 1864. It names occupiers and holdings and gives the valuation of House, Offices and Land and Total Annual Valuation. Poor Law rates were assessed under the valuation, and disputes arose later over its use in setting rents. The entry reads, 'John Power, Bellagill, Parish of Creagh. Lessor, Dudley Persse. Total assessed valuation of rateable property £13.'
4. Thomas Power, farmer, Ballygill, was present at the marriage of his daughter, Bridget, on 21 November 1867, and at the death of his wife, Sabina, on 9 February 1880. He died on 16 June 1889, and the death was registered in his daughter's home in Ahascragh, a few miles from Ballygill.
5. James Fraser, *Travellers*, p.362.
6. The National Education System was established in 1831. Education was to be non-denominational to remove 'suspicion of proselytism'. Initially religious groups were not happy with the arrangements.
7. William Thackerey, *Irish Sketchbook*, p.231.
8. O'C.P., 'Condition of Ireland' (1875).
9. The workhouses were established under the Poor Law (Ireland) Act of 1838. There were 130 Poor Law Unions in the country and they served as administrative districts. Each union was governed by an elected board of guardians, which was responsible for the levying of rates to pay for the relief of the destitute and for maintaining a union workhouse. The Ballinasloe workhouse was built in 1841. William O'Brien, *Recollections*, p.445, writes that Michael Davitt's family 'was denied the shelter of an Irish workhouse'.
10. O'C.P., Hansard, 8 February 1882.

11. O'C.P., *Congested Districts*, p.796.

12. The register of St Michael's Church, Ballinasloe, records the baptism of two infants: Born 21 March 1846, baptised 13 April, Ellenora Power, daughter of John and Catherine Kelly, sponsors Michael Glynn and Catherine Coffey. Born 9 March 1846, baptised 13 April, Patrick Hogarty, son of Daniel and Bridget Glynn, sponsors Patrick and Mary Power In the register there is a record of a marriage between a Patrick Power and a Bridget Mitchell on 4 June 1841. The witnesses were John Power and Bridget O'Neal. *The Times* records in its biography of candidates, 25 November 1885, that 'Mr. John O'Connor Power is the son of Mr. Patrick Power, by his marriage with Miss Mary O'Connor of Roscommon' possibly implying that there was an earlier marriage.

13. O'C.P., 'New Reform', p.20.

14. *The Times*, 9 August 1849.

15. Record of Service, 59ᵗʰ Regiment of Foot, Nottinghamshire: Date of Enlistment 23 January 1860. Discharged to pension 28 July 1881. Discharge cancelled under Part II of the Army Act 1881. Transferred to the Bk Sec: C. & T. Corps from 8 August 1883. UK 1881 census: Thomas, a Quarter Master Sergeant is in New Barracks, Alverstoke, with his family. His birth year is given as 1842, his age thirty-nine. Birthplace, Galway, Ballinasloe.

Liberty, Equality, Fraternity

16. T.W. Moody, professor of history, Trinity College Dublin (1939-1977), read the paper to the Irish Historical Society, 13 December 1977. Cited in Donald E. Jordan, *Power*, p.48. Moody describes O'C.P. as 'this enigmatic man', *Davitt*, p.47, fn 5.

17. In the 1861 UK census, the only possible fit appears to be a John Power, sixteen, lodger, cotton-factory worker, born in Ireland. The address is 10 William Street, Gorton, Chorlton. Matthew Power (forty-six) and son Michael (nine) are also lodgers. Gorton is fifteen miles from Rochdale and was the scene of the Manchester Rescue, 18 September 1867.

18. O'C.P., 'Condition of Ireland' (1875).

19. In 1867, Disraeli's Second Reform Bill enlarged the franchise. Karl Marx's *Das Kapital* was published in the same year.

20. O'C.P., 'Gospel of Wealth', p.352.

21. O'C.P., 'Irish in England', p.411.

22. Mrs Gaskell, *Mary Barton* (1848), chap. i.

23. O'C.P., *Land Agitation*, p.958.

24. George Moore, *A Drama in Muslin*, chap. iii.

25. See Terence Eagleton, *Heathcliffe and the Great Hunger, Studies in Irish Culture*, chap. i, Verso (1995).

26. This version of the oath is in the 17 March 1873 Constitution of the Irish Republican Brotherhood, T.W. Moody, *IRB*, p.314. Before the establishment of the Supreme Council a V was the designation for the Head Centre of one of the four provinces of Ireland. The flag of the Irish Republic had four stripes, representing the four provinces, and thirty-two stars marking the thirty-two counties. Ellis Dillon, *Bitter Sea*, p.165, 261. VB was the abbreviated code for the United Brotherhood.

27. Fintan O'Toole, *A Mass for Jesse James, a Journey Through 1980s Ireland* (1990), pp20-1. Patrick Maume, *Gestation*, p.208, 'Father William Ferris of County Kerry … fantasised about a "Gaelic State", seen as a decentralised, egalitarian, frugally moral federation of artisans and smallholders.'

28. Benjamin Disraeli, The State of Ireland Hansard, 16 February 1844.

29. Disraeli, *Lothair*, chap. xi.

30. Strachey, *Eminent Victorians*, p.83.

31. T.P. O'Connor, *Memoirs*, pp83-4, '[O'C.P.] told me how he used to have to distribute over all the twenty-four hours the small amount of food he was allowed; if I remember rightly, he used to keep over from his supper a couple of potatoes for his breakfast.'

32. John Denvir, *Irish in Britain*, p.274.

33. O'C.P., *Orator*, p.201.

34. B. O'Brien, *Parnell*, p.159.

35. Philip H. Bagenal, *Agitator*, p.39.

36. O'C.P., 'Irish in England', p.421.

And Never Feared Danger

37. Padraig Pearse writing of the Fenians.

38. *Special Commission Proceedings*, ix, p.357. Cited Moody, *Davitt*, p.47.

39. Moody, *Davitt*, p.93. *Freeman's Weekly*, 1 March 1919.

40. *FJ*, 20 October 1877. The leaders of the raid met 12, 13 February, Moody, *Davitt*, p.93.

41. Arthur Conan Doyle borrowed the bishop's name for his arch-villain, Professor Moriarty. See Catherine Wynne, *The Colonial Conan Doyle, British Imperialism, Irish Nationalism and the Gothic* (2002), chap. I; *Imperial War and Colonial Sedition, Soldiers, Mollies and Fenians*, p.52.

42. O'C.P., *Speeches*, p.15.

43. *Ibid.*, p.4.

44. Moody, *IRB*, p.288.

45. Message from the IRB council to the Irish people, 24 April 1868. See Moody, *IRB*, p.302.

46. R.V. Comerford, *Fenians in Context*, p.158.

47. Abstract of cases of persons arrested under Habeas Corpus Suspension Act, iii, p.29 (S.P.O., C.S.O/1CR/16/6).

48. Michael MacDonagh, *Home Rule*, p.31.

49. O'C.P., *Speeches*, pp23-4.

50. Address of the IRB Supreme Council to the officers and men of the IRA (17 March 1873). See Moody, *IRB*, p.312.

51. Sir Charles Russell, *Commission*, p.68. Lord Leitrim was said to have had his way with the wives and daughters of his tenants. In 1877 he was murdered in Donegal.

A New Departure

52. O'C.P., *Anglo-Irish Quarrel*, p.10.

53. Moore Hall was built in 1780. George Moore, in *Hale and Farewell, Vale*, has an

enchanting description of the house and grounds. In 1923, during the Civil War, the hall, with its impressive library, was gutted by fire.

54. O'C.P., *Anglo-Irish Quarrel*, p.4.
55. Mayo County Library, *The Story of Mayo*.
56. The Ecclesiastical Titles Act, 1851, made it illegal for Catholic prelates to use territorial designations. The Act was repealed in 1871.
57. Ryan, *Memories*, p.41.
58. MacDonagh, *Home Rule*, pp115-16. Moore's widow told her son Maurice that his father was in the IRB by 1870. Maurice writes, 'Mr O'Donovan Rossa published an account of a meeting with Moore, and wrote that the latter had taken the Fenian oath. A few years ago I wrote to Mr John O'Leary to verify the fact, and after inquiry he replied that he found it to be correct, and promised to give me further information when we met', Moore, *An Irish Gentleman*, p.350, fn.
59. William O'Brien, *Recollections*, p.89, fn chapel bell.
60. MacDonagh, *Home Rule*, pp115-16.
61. Moody, *Davitt*, p.56.
62. MacDonagh, *Home Rule*, p.114.
63. *Ibid.*, p.174. William O'Brien was secretary to the Province of Munster.
64. Address of the IRB supreme council to the people of Ireland, January 1870. See Moody, *IRB*, p.310.
65. Hansard, 29 June 1869.
66. Dr Mark Francis Ryan, *Memories*, p.177.
67. George Moore's preface to his brother Maurice's biography of their father, *George Henry Moore, An Irish Gentleman*, M.G. Moore (1913). Fr Lavelle also claimed Moore died of a broken heart. *Ibid.*, p.376.
68. T. White, *Excess*, p.239.
69. 'A man who was to be for some years closely allied with Butt, a certain Captain John Dunne, relates in his memoirs that Moore in 1869 disclosed to him a plan for Irish Home rule, the success of which depended on Butt's co-operation … there can be no doubt that Butt and Moore were in agreement and what came to known as the Home Rule agitation was fully worked out when Moore died on the 19th April, 1870.' White, *Excess*, p.236.
70. Some years later, 'a Fenian leader' confided to O'Brien that he had attended the proceedings under the assumed name of James Martin. B. O'Brien, *Parnell*, pp57, 128.
71. In 1868, over 1,600 priests signed the Limerick Declaration, which stated that self-government was the solution to the Irish Question.
72. MacDonagh, *Home Rule*, p.10.
73. Disraeli, *Lothair*, chap. ix. The Monsignore claims that 'the Anglicans have only a lease on our property'.

The Long Game

74. B. O'Brien, *Parnell*, p.63, Butt to an acquaintance.
75. St Jarlath's was not 'a poor provincial college' (T.P. O'Connor, *Memoirs*, p.84.) but an intellectual powerhouse, taking third-level students. A bastion of Gallicanism, the college asserted the Catholic Church's role in national politics.
76. SJC, 1865 prospectus. Cited in John Cunningham, *Jarlath's*, p.98.
77. *MG*, 17 August 1871.

78. *MG*, 26 July 1873.
79. *Tuam News*, 28 June 1872. Cited Cunningham, *Jarlath's*, pp102–3.

A Rebel's Progress

80. B. O'Brien, *Parnell*, p.76.
81. *Ibid.*, p.99.
82. *Ibid.*, pp99–101.
83. Comerford, *Fenians*, p.203.
84. 'Proceedings of the Home Rule Conference, 1873'. Cited in, MacDonagh, *Home Rule*, pp23–4.
85. W. O'Brien, *Recollections*, p.141.
86. *Ibid.*, p.165.
87. *FJ*, 21 November 1873.
88. O'C.P., 'Abiding Influence', p.669.

Utterly Changed

89, Jordan, *Power*, p.52.
90. MacDonagh, *Home Rule*, p.31.
91. Moran, *Radical Priest*, p.146.
92, Cited Jordan, *Power*, p.51.
93. Larkin, *Home Rule*, pp253–4. Cited Jordan, *Power*, p.51.
94. *Irishman*, 28 February 1874, Cited Moran, *Radical priest*, p.149.
95. *Irishman*, 28 February 1874. Cited Moran, *Various country*, p.150. Fr Lavelle's letter to Isaac Butt has been quoted extensively and, surprisingly, up to the present time. 'You may have often heard the question put – 'who is this O'Connor Power?' – I often did but never could I get an answer. I am, however, now in a position to tell you he is the bastard son of a policeman named Fleming from County Cavan, and a housepainter by trade, who has managed to live on his wits', Lavelle to Butt, 12, 13 March 1874 (N.L.I., Butt papers MS 9686 6). 'The only truth in these allegations would appear to be that O'Connor Power was a painter who lived near Rochdale; Ryan, *Fenian memories*, p.13.' Moran, *Radical Priest*, p.199, fn 53.
96. Cited Moran, *Radical Priest*, p.149.
97. *FJ*, 7 May 1874.
98. Ryan, *Memories*, p.46.
99. Jordan, *Power*, p.50.
100. *Ballinrobe Chronicle* and *Mayo Advertiser*, 16 May 1874, Cited Jordan, *Power*, pp51–2.
101. Cited Jordan, *Power*, p.52.
102. Pat Ryan, PP, to Mitchell Henry, 18 May 1874 (N.L.I., Butt papers, MS 8706). Cited Jordan, *Power*, p.53.
103. *The Times*, 1 June 1874. Cited Jordan, *Power*, p.52. There was a precedent in the Galway by-election of 1872, when the result was overturned on grounds of intimidation. See Ryan, *Memories*, 41–4 and Comerford, *Fenians in Context*, 192–4.
104. O'C.P., 'New Reform', p.20.
105. *Weekly Freeman*, 1 March 1919. Ryan, *Memories*, p.46: Browne (1,330), O'Connor Power (1,319), Tighe (1,272).

Part Two

Confessors of Irish Nationality

106. In 1877 there were eight English Home Rulers in the House of Commons. These included John Bright (Manchester) and Joseph Cowen (Newcastle). Sir Charles Bowyer, an English Catholic convert, was Home Rule MP for Wexford, 1874-80.
107. MacDonagh, *Home Rule*, p.63. *The Times'* correspondent described it as a 'Thucydidean speech'.
108. T.M. Healy, *Letters*, chap. iii. Healy, in turn, would use similar tactics to attack O'Connor Power in February 1884.
109. Moody, *Davitt*, p.196. Hansard, 13 July 1874.
110. *Punch, Essence of Parliament* (1875), p.77.
111. *Flag of Ireland*, 17 January 1874.
112. Following extracts from *Irish Political Prisoners, Speeches of John O'Connor Power in the House of Commons on the Subject of Amnesty ... 1878*. Speeches dated 12 March 1875, 1 August 1876, 5 June 1877, 20 July 1877.
113. Winston Churchill, *Lord Randolph Churchill* (London, 1906), p.70. O'C.P. had little regard for Randolph Churchill, 'If Disraeli had lived Lord Randolph Churchill's role would have been impossible; he might never have been heard of as a serious politician at all, and it is not unlikely he would have had to wait many years more before reaching the notoriety which he now enjoys.' O'C.P., 'Two great statesmen' (1889).
114. Sean McConville, *Political Prisoners*, p.293. Du Cane to Adolphus Liddell, 3 January 1872: PRO HO 144/5/17869/4. See Moody, *Davitt*, pp156-7.
115. *Sybil, the two nations*, deals with the problems of society's two tiers, the rich and the poor. In Castlebar, on 14 August 1875, O'Connor Power told his constituents, 'Mr Disraeli, in one of his novels, entitled *Sybil*, written avowedly for a political objective, to expose the abject condition of the people, lays down the principle that political offenders should not be treated like convicted criminals, and I am not aware that he has ever retracted the opinions he there put forward.' As reported in *The New Zealand Tablet*, 22 October 1875.
116. *MG*, 3 August 1876.
117. T. Baty, *International Law* (1909), p.169.
118. *The Times*, 14 August 1877. Sir Stafford Northcote, Tory leader in the House of Commons, promised an early release.

Charles McCarthy's Death

119. *Cork Examiner*, 15 January 1878. O'C.P. also stayed at 83 Amiens Street. Thom's Directory (1878) lists John White as the occupier.
120. Hansard, 29 January 1878.
121. This forty-page Davitt account of prison life was 'missing' until quite recently. 'No copy of the original has been found.' Moody, *Davitt*, p.586.
122. *Devoy's Post Bag*, Chambers to O'Reilly, 18 February 1878. '... absolutely faithful', p.303.

123. John Denvir, *Irish in Britain*, p.275.
124. Denvir, *Old Rebel*, p.199.
125. 'Had he not at his back another ex-political prisoner, a Fenian gentleman of distinction, who boasted that he had not only the honour of a seat in parliament but also the far greater honour of a seat on a wooden stool in an English prison – Mr O'Connor Power, the member for Mayo.' Bagenal, *Agitator*, pp105-6.
126. *MG*, 13 July 1878.
127. *MG*, 13 December 1878.

A New Career

128. Healy, *Letters*, chap. v. Letter to his brother, 5 April 1879.
129. *NYT*, 27 March 1878.
130. Samuel Romilly (1757-1818), a Huguenot who attempted to reform the criminal legal system. Charles Hopwood reviewed the law on rape.

'A Towering Figure'

131. Jordan, *Popular Politics*, p.257.
132. Moran, *Radical Priest*, p.152.
133. 'Butt could not be found, whereupon [X] went off and discovered Butt at the Imperial Hotel, brought him along at once, and then he addressed us from the platform.' B. O'Brien, *Parnell*, pp118-19; O'Donnell, *History IIP*, pp136-7.
134. There was an exchange of letters between John and the SC secretary, Charles Doran, 11, 12 August 1875. Doran criticised O'Connor Power's intervention. He replied, 'even Whigs are men and entitled to freedom of speech'. Doran papers, cited Moody, *IRB*, p.327.
135. Moody, *IRB*, p.319. *NYT*, 10 September 1875, reported he had a speaking engagement at Westchester County Agricultural fair.
136. *NYT*, 4 October 1875. 'Arrivals at the hotels'.
137. *Ibid.*, 8 October 1875. *The Irish Canadian*, 20 October 1875. General Jones introduced him, 'His record is as well known to you as that of any man in the universe.'
138. *Devoy's Post Bag*, John O'Leary to John Devoy, 5 February 1875. Cited Dudley Edwards, *Parnell*, p.54. '... and there is no doubt that he is now speaking of O'Connor Power'.
139. *Chicago Daily Tribune*, 6 December 1875.
140. *The Times*, 20 June 1877.
141. McGee, *IRB*, pp53-4.
142. B. O'Brien, *Parnell*, p.63.
143. MacDonagh, *Home Rule*, p.73.
144. B. O'Brien, *Parnell*, p.64.
145. *MG*, 24 February 1876.
146. Durham Miners' Gala, 3 July 1876. O'C.P. was a regular guest speaker at the annual gala. The Durham Miners supported Irish causes and gave £100 to the Land League Relief Fund.

147. *MG*, 4 August 1876.
148. Cited in Moody, *IRB*, p.321. The Imperial Hotel was in what is now O'Connell Street. Clery's department store occupies the site.
149. The Constitution of the IRB Supreme Council, 18 August 1869, VI: 'That each member of the supreme council is, and shall be finally elected, but may be removed by a two-thirds vote of the electoral body.' Moody, *IRB*, p.304.
150. *IT*, 18 September 1876.
151. 'Mr John O'Connor Power, the member of Parliament for Mayo County, has resigned his position as a member of the executive committee of the Home Rule Confederation and started for the United States, bearing an Irish congratulatory address on the Centennial of American Independence', *Daily News*, London, 25 September 1876. 'Mr John O'Connor Power, MP for Mayo arrived yesterday on the *Britannic* bearing a congratulatory address from the people of Ireland to President Grant on the Centennial of American Independence.' *New York Times*, 1 October 1876. 'Mr O'Connor Power MP from Mayo, has arrived in this country, and will this week present to the President the congratulatory address, of which he is to be the bearer from Dublin', *The Times*, 17 October 1876. *The Times* referred disdainfully to 'Mr O'Connor Power and his friend [Parnell].'
152. Letter from the Arlington Hotel, 17 October 1876.
153. The Cuba Five were Fenians released from British jails who arrived in New York in January 1871. Together with nine others they were presented to President Grant on the steps of the White House and were granted a resolution of welcome from the House of Representatives.
154. Loomis T. Palmer, *The Life of General U.S. Grant, His Early Life, Military Achievements, and History of his Civil Administration, his Sickness and Death* (1885), p.356.
155. *Devoy's Post Bag*, Carroll to Devoy, 6 November 1876.
156. *The Times* was dismissive and F.H. O'Donnell's letter to the editor, 7 February 1877, stated '[the Address] will be duly framed and deposited in the Capitol instead of the White House'.
157. G. de Molinari, *Lettres sur les états-unis et le Canada: addressées au journal des débats à l'occasion de l'exposition universelle de Philadelphie* (1876), p.339.
158. After-dinner toast to guests at the National Liberal Club, 16 July 1886, p.xxvii.
159. Moody, *Davitt*, p.137.
160. A police report, 13 March 1877, recorded that all four members (O'C.P., Egan, Biggar, Barry) 'were compelled to resign'. Moody, *IRB*, p.295.
161. B. O'Brien, *Parnell*, p.125. *Devoy's Post Bag*, Carroll to Devoy, 16 November 1879, 'The correspondent tells how Power withdrew to avoid expulsion.'
162. *Ibid.*, p.126.
163. *Ibid.*, pp125-6
164. *Ibid.*, p.168, 'We have seen that in 1879 the supreme council of the IRB passed a resolution to the effect that the members of the rank and file might take part in the parliamentary movement at their own risk. In 1880 this resolution was rescinded, and it was declared that no Fenian under any circumstances should co-operate with the constitutional party.'
165. White, *Excess*, p.309. See also B. O'Brien, *Parnell*, pp113-14. The assault took place in Limerick on Easter Monday, 1876. A feature of Irish life up to the end of the nineteenth century was 'faction fighting' at fairs and sporting events. Fights were organised in towns and villages. Men and women took part, using fists, stones and

seasoned blackthorn sticks. Sometimes the fight was between two villages or two families; sometimes there was no apparent reason for this customary finish to a festive outing.

166. *FJ*, 20 October 1877.
167. *FJ*, 12, 16, 18, 20 October 1877. Daly supporter's letter, 18 October, referred throughout to 'Fleming'. Up to the mid-twentieth century, illegitimacy was perceived as a lifelong stigma. Eamon De Valera would also be the target of a similar accusation.
168. Thomas Brennan to Matthew Harris, 20, 24 October 1877 (N.L.I., W.G. Fallon papers, MS 22740).
169. *Devoy's Post Bag*, letters from Carroll to Devoy, 12 July 1877, 12 August 1877, 30 October 1877, 16 November 1877.
170. O'C.P., 'Irish in England', p.421
171. Lord Russell in an after dinner speech in 1898. B. O'Brien, *Russell*, p.336.

Parliamentary Manoeuvres

172. Edmund Dwyer Gray (1845-1888). Cited MacDonagh, *Home Rule*, p.93.
173. 'It seemed to be generally thought that Biggar did that of his own motion, but he did not – it was arranged by the party.' Andrew S. Kettle, *Material for Victory*, p.85. George Moore proposed obstruction of the Ecclesiastical Titles Bill in 1851 but was overruled by party colleagues.
174. W. O'Brien, *Recollections*, p.215.
175. *FJ*, 16 April 1877. Letter dated 14 April 1877 on his return from America. On 31 May he wrote a letter in support of the obstructionists, which was published in the *Freeman's Journal* and in the *Nation*, 9 June 1877.
176. MacDonagh, *Home Rule*, p.89. The correspondence was printed in the *FJ*, 24, 25, 28 May 1877.
177. Healy, *Letters*, chap. v. Letter dated October 1878.
178. B. O'Brien, *Parnell*, pp104-5. The five were O'C.P., F.H. O'Donnell, Parnell, Whalley, Biggar. Randolph Churchill named them 'the interesting quartette': O'C.P., O'Donnell, Parnell, Biggar.
179. *MG*, 26 March 1878.
180. Hansard, 28 March 1878.
181. *MG*, 23 June 1879. At the Chatham enquiry in 1890, prisoners were allowed for the first time to question the witnesses.
182. Hansard, 3 July 1879.
183. O'Donnell, *IIP*, p.417. Flogging was abolished in 1881.
184. *Wilfred Owen's Photographs*, Ted Hughes, *Lupercal*, 1960. See Stephen Fry, *The Ode Less Travelled* (London, 2005), pp309-11. 'That Irishman did in life what poems try to do in words: to make the idea fact, the abstract concrete and the general particular.'
185. Henry Lucy, *Two Parliaments*, chap. xxxv, pp486-7. Speaker Lenthall was brought to heel when Charles I stormed into parliament. The event precipitated the English Civil War. See also Bagenal, *Agitator*, p.63, where he cites the account in *The Irish Times*.
186. *NYT*, 10 July 1879.
187. MacDonagh, *Home Rule*, p.91. The seven obstructionists were Biggar, E.D. Grey, G.H. Kirk, J.P. Nolan, O'Connor Power, O'Donnell and Parnell.

188. *MG*, 16 July 1877.
189. *Ibid.*, 4 September 1877.
190. F.S. Lyons, *John Dillon, A Biography* (University Chicago Press, 1968), p.21.
191. The letter was written in the Library of the House of Commons, 13 February 1878, his thirty-second birthday. It was printed in *The New York Times*, 27 March 1878. Clan members approached Russian agents.
192. B. O'Brien, *Parnell*, p.98. Originally thirteen venues were planned but Parnell, who was superstitious, asked for fourteen. Parnell believed the colour green to be unlucky.
193. Healy, *Letters*, chap. v, 24 November 1878.
194. Hansard, 5 December 1878.
195. MacDonagh, *Home rule*, p.165.
196. B O'Brien, *Parnell*, p.116.
197. Healy, *Letters*, chap. v, 8 March 1879.
198. Hansard, 26 March 1879. *MG*, 30 March 1879.
199. *MG*, 3 July 1878.
200. Lawrence McBride, *Reading Irish Histories* (Dublin: Four Courts Press, 2003), p.33.
201. O'C.P., 'Two Great Statesmen' (1889).

Worth Working For, Worth Fighting For, Worth Dying For

202. 'Why land's the only thing in the world worth working for, worth fighting for, worth dying for, because it is the only thing that lasts.' Gerald O'Hara, Scarlett's father in Margaret Mitchell's *Gone with the Wind*.
203. Jordan, *Merchants*, p.340.
204. *Nation*, 2 November 1878. Cited McBride, *Irish Histories*, p.33.
205. O'C.P., *Land Agitation*, pp957-8.
206. Davitt, *Fall*, p.146.
207. *Ibid.*, pp149-50.
208. Cited Bagenal, *Agitator*, p.45.
209. Healy, *Letters*, chap. vi. *CT*, 21 April 1879.
210. W O'Brien, *Recollections*, pp215-16.
211. Hansard, 27 May 1879.
212. Hansard, 26 June 1879.
213. Moody, *Davitt*, p.394. On Davitt's attack from New York, 16 June, 'his name [O'C.P.] was on the original appeal to the Irish race'. Davitt's 'Appeal to the Irish Race was specially intended for Irish-Americans.' Moody, *Davitt*, p.339.
214. B. O'Brien, *Parnell*, pp125-6.
215. *Devoy's Post Bag*, pp328-9.
216. Jordan, *Power*, p.55.
217. Davitt wrote, on 6 December 1893, to Barry O'Brien, who was working on a biography of Parnell, that he had agreed to a course of 'parallel action' in 1878. Moody, *Davitt*, p.225, fn i. Moody questioned the accuracy of his recollection and believed Davitt was referring to a meeting with Brennan in January 1879.
218. Doherty Hickey, *Dictionary*, James O'Kelly entry.
219. *CT*, 11 January 1879. Cited in Jordan, *Land War*, p.215.

Land Hunger

220. Russell, *Commission*, p.163.
221. O'Donnell, *IPP*, p.148.
222. *NYT*, 14 August 1879.
223. *FJ*, 25 November 1879. Cited Moran, *James Daly*, p.197, fn 34.
224. John O'Connor Power to Fr John O'Malley, 26 September 1879 (NLI, J.F.X. O'Brien, MS 13457). The meeting was three days later, 29 September 1879.
225. Cited Doherty, *Dictionary*, Thomas Brennan entry, p.41.
226. *The Times*, 18 October 1880.
227. Trollope, *The Landleaguers*, p.162. Moore, *Parnell and his Island*.
228. O'C.P., *Land Agitation*, pp953-4.
229. *The Times*, 1 December 1879.
230. O'C.P., *Land Agitation*, pp955-6.
231. *Ibid.*, p.956.
232. O'Day, *Irish Home Eule*, pp61-2. 'The Land League was now appealing for American help not for famine relief but to fight landlords.' Moody, *Davitt*, p.400.

A Change of Government

233. W. O'Brien, *Recollections*, p.241.
234. O'C.P., *Fallacies*, p.235.
235. *NYT*, 28 March 1880.
236. Hansard, 20 May 1880.
237. B. O'Brien, *Parnell*, p.167.
238. John O'Connor Power to Fr John O'Malley, 26 April 1879. (NLI, J.F.X. O'Brien, MS 13457). Barry O'Brien, *Parnell*, refers to Parnell's dislike of the Catholic Church, p.137. Louden was a substantial grazier, 'Although Louden secured a large rent abatement from [Lord] Lucan during 1879-81, this was not passed on to tenants. He frequently imposed heavy fines on tenants for trespassing on to his grazing farm.' In 1880, he failed to win a nomination for the Mayo election. He was the only member of the League executive who was not imprisoned. Moran, *James Daly*, pp205-6. Although the Land League was a secular movement, individual priests were involved.
239. Healy, *Letters*, chap. vii.
240. Michael Davitt to Matthew Harris, n.d. (NLI, W.G. Fallon papers, MS 22740).
241. Healy, *Letters*, chap. vii.
242. *The Times*, 19 December 1910.
243. A 'plumper' voted for only one candidate, when he could vote for two.
244. Denvir, *Old rebel*, p.56.
245. B. O'Brien, *Parnell*, p.125.
246. J.J. Lee, *Modernisation*, p.72.
247. He paraphrases lines from Oliver Goldsmith's *The Deserted Village*, 'Ill fares the land, to hastening ills a prey/Where wealth accumulates, and men decay.'
248. Hansard, 20 May 1880.
249. Russell, *Commission*, p.154.
250. *MG, Our London Correspondent*, 10 June 1880.
251. Gladstone to the Duke of Argyll, 14 June 1880, cited Godfrey Locker Lampson, *A Consideration of the State of Ireland in the Nineteenth Century* (London, 1907), p.632.

252. *MG*, 'Our London correspondent', 10 June 1880.
253. Moran, *James Daly*, p.201.
254. B. O'Brien, *Russell*, pp356-7
255. Hamilton, *Diary*, p.102.
256. *MG*, 8 January 1881.
257. *Ibid.*, 18 January 1881.
258. MacDonagh, *Home Rule*, p.155.
259. *MG*, 3 February 1881. Moody, *Davitt*, p.461, 'At the instance of O'Connor Power (Parnell being absent) the party had marched out of the commons' chamber in passionate protest against this "suspension of constitutional liberty"'.
260. W. O'Brien, *Recollections*, p.271. 'The effect upon myself was that I instantly offered myself to Mr. Egan for any post of danger in which I might be useful.' fn. i
261. Hansard, 3 February 1881.
262. *MG*, 6 May 1881.
263. Hansard, 5 May 1881.
264. Hamilton, *Diary*, p.155. Davitt describes 1881 Land Act as a 'remedial set-off to coercion' and emphasises the 'magnitude and importance of the measure'. Davitt, *Fall*, 317
265. *NYT*, 30 May 1881.
266. Hansard, 30 May 1881. 'When O'Connor Power takes to calling Egan, the Secretary of the League, a swindler and a coward, there must be something hideously wicked in the constitution of the most advanced Land Leaguers.' Hamilton, *Diary*, p.143.
267. Hansard, 31 May 1881.
268. *CT*, 13 August 1881. Cited Moran, *Daly*, p.203.
269. Cited Jordan, *Land War*, p.280.
270. *MG*, 11 February 1882.
271. *Ibid.*, 29 March 1882.
272. *Ibid.*, 24 April 1882.
273. *CT*, 1 July 1882. Cited Carla King, *Lives of Victorian Political Figures*, Part III, pp176-7.
274. Hamilton, *Diary*, 8 July 1882, 302. Hamilton writes: 'There is nothing to shew that the new Coercion Bill will put an end to the worst agrarian or political outrages. But it is absurd to condemn the Land Act as a failure yet.'
275. MacDonagh, *Home Rule*, p.270.
276. B. O'Brien, *Parnell*, p.256. Gladstone would later admit that without the Land League the Land Act of 1881 would not be on the Statute book. Hansard, 21 April 1893.

Part Three

At Large

277. W.B. Yeats, *The Grey Rock* (1914).
278. The Club, or The Literary Club was founded by Reynolds in 1764. Of Edmund Burke, 'From no other speeches and writings can we so easily reconstruct the social and political life of the second half of the eighteenth century', O'C.P., 'Abiding influence', p.631.

279. Sir Boyle Roche, whose 'mental obliquity' was thought to have been caused by reading Gibbon's *Decline and Fall of the Roman Empire*, 'was so cruelly puzzled, without being in the least amused, that he often stigmatised the great historian as a low fellow who ought to have been kicked out of company, wherever he was …', O'C.P., 'Irish Wit and Humour', p.475. '[Gibbon might have been] stolen out of a corner of Burke's mind without being missed.' Mackintosh, cited O'C.P., 'Abiding Influence'.
280. Sam Weller was a popular character in Charles Dickens' *The Pickwick Papers* (1837).
281. Charles Dickens, *A Tale of Two Cities*, chap. iv.
282. Reid, *Traits*, p.62.
283. '… gloom made apparent by the antiquated lights scarcely served to show the portrait of Dr Johnson', *The Antiquary*, (London, 1888), p.74.
284. Reid, *Traits*, p.62.
285. *Johnson Club Papers* (1899), p.viii.
286. Francis Bacon, *Essays, of Studies*.
287. The Irish Council Bill, 1907. The Bill was an attempt at a limited form of devolution. Birrell introduced the Evicted Tenants Act (1907) the Irish Universities Act (1908) and Irish Land Act (1909).
288. *Johnson Club Papers* (1899), pp87-99.
289. *Ibid.*, pp139-56.
290. George Whale, *Forty Years*, p.18.
291. *City Press*, 17 December 1887.
292. Whale, *Forty Years*, p.12.
293. *Ibid.*, p.12.
294. Augustine Birrell, 'The Transmission of Dr Johnson's Personality', *Johnson Club Papers* (1899), p.4.
295. Whale, *Forty Years*, p.12.
296. J.R.R. Tolkien, *The Notion Club Papers, Sauron Defeated*, p.154.
297. MacDonagh, *The Reporter's Gallery* (London, 1913), chap. xvi.
298. Whale, *Forty Years*, p.23. Arthur Perceval Graves (1846-1931) was an Irish poet, songwriter and educationalist and was for several years President of the Irish Literary Society. He was the father of Robert Graves.
299. Cited in Ó Brion, *Birrell*, p.160.
300. To Oliver Goldsmith. A Poet, Naturalist, and Historian, who left scarcely any style of writing untouched, and touched nothing that he did not adorn. James Boswell's *Life of Johnson*, vol. iii, p.82.
301. Whale, *Forty Years*, Appendix B, p.28.
302. *Ibid.*, p.23.
303. F.W. Chesson dinner, NLC, 16 July 1886, p.xxiii.
304. Marcus Tullius Cicero, a Roman philosopher, statesman and orator. 'The righteous pagan' is remembered for his treatise on oratory, *De Oratore*.

The Artist in Irish Politics

305. Liam O'Flaherty, *The Life of Tim Healy* (1927), p.40.
306. O'C.P., *Orator*, p.109.

307. O'C.P., 'Condition of Ireland' (1875).

308. Hartley, *Christy Carew*, p.50. See Madeleine Helena Khan, *Late Nineteenth Century Ireland's Political and Religious Controversies in the Fiction of May Laffan Hartley* (Elt Press, 2005)

309. See Elizabeth Grubgeld, *George Moore and the Autogenous Self, the Autobiography and Fiction*, (Syracuse University Press, 1994), pp29-30. See also George Moore, *Parnell and his Island*, ppxix-xx.

310. MacDonagh, *Home rule*, 'strong and unmistakably Irish face', p.115. MacDonagh writes that *Parnell and His Island* was 'perhaps the most ironic criticism of the Nationalist Movement ever written'.

311. Collins, *Blind Love*, chap. xi, p.152.

312. *Ibid.*, chap. lxii, p.375.

313. Charles Dickens, *Our Mutual Friend*, chap. xii, 'The passing shadow'.

314. Victoria Glendenning, *Trollope* (1992), p.370.

315. Trollope, *Phineas Finn, the Irish Member* (1869), *Phineas Redux* (1874), *The Landleaguers* (1883).

316. Sir William Gregory, a Galway man, was at school with Anthony Trollope and was a lifelong friend. He had a meteoric political career and may have inspired *Phineas Finn*.

317. *Phineas redux*, chap. I; *Hamlet*, III, i, p.76. 'When he himself might his quietus make/ With a bare bodkin.'

318. Conan Doyle, *The Final Problem*, chap. i.

319. Conan Doyle, *The Valley of Fear, the Scourers, the Man*.

320. O'C.P., 'Two Great Statesmen' (1889).

321. *Punch*, 1 March 1884.

322. Sir Robert Anderson to Sir William Harcourt, 5 November 1883, Sir Robert Anderson's papers. Cited Sean McConville, p.285, fn 34. Mark Ryan mentions a scheme to kidnap the Prince of Wales and hold him hostage until Fenian prisoners were released, *Memories*, p.16.

323. F.C. Burnand to John O'Connor Power (NLI, MacDonagh papers, MS 11445). The letter is headed 3 May but there is no year.

324. A copy of a letter from John O'Connor Power to Lady Wilde, 21 February 1885 (NLI, Lady Wilde papers, MS 27609). It is in reply to her letter of 17 February.

325. Lady Gregory, *Irish Theatre*, p.9.

326. In 1934, the National Gallery bought the cartoon (NPG 3293) as one of a collection of *Vanity Fair* cartoons. It is now in the archive of the National Portrait Gallery in St Martin's Place in London.

327. MacDonagh, *Home Rule*, p.160.

Part Four

The Irish in England

328. Unless otherwise noted the extracts in this section are from O'C.P., 'The Irish in England' (1880).

329. Hansard, 27 June 1877. Debate on the Sale of Intoxicating Liquors on Sunday (Ireland), Committee on Re-Commitment
330. O'C.P., *Fallacies*, p.230.
331. *FJ*, 3 April 1875.
332. *MG*, 10 July 1875.
333. Disraeli, *Lothair*, chap. ix.
334. Russell, *Commission*, p.36, '[Henry Mathews, Home Secretary], with great courage as I then thought and think now, at a time when there was a great tide of popular prejudice against, and as he thought misrepresentation of, the Fenians, said some words, at least in palliation, if not in justification of their conduct and position.'
335. O'C.P., 'Philosophy of Irish History' (May 1880).

A Party Divided

336. Healy, *Letters*, chap. viii. In 1880s there was no 'pairing' in the House and attendance was important for a vote. B. O'Brien, *Parnell*, p.315. O'Brien uses the words 'submerged' and 'inactivity'. Biggar describes Parnell as 'used up'. Healy, *Letters*, chap. xix. Parnell's 'fits of nervous depression', Healy, *Letters*, chap. iv.
337. Lord Harcourt's letter to Gladstone, cited Callanan, *Parnell Split*, p.97. The 'English alliance' was the Irish Liberal pact.
338. Harcourt complained to Gladstone in April 1883, Hamilton, *Diary*, p.422. He would later favour Home Rule.
339. Lord Richard Grosvenor to W.E. Gladstone, 3 September 1882. Cited in James McConnel, *Jobbing*, p.110.
340. In 1884, Grosvenor was 'subjected to a barrage of requests for postmasterships for nominees of [Captain] O'Shea'. Miles Dungan, *O'Shea*, p.144. In 1886, Grosvenor broke with Gladstone over Home Rule and joined the Liberal Unionists.
341. *Aroha News*, 19 January 1884.
342. *United Ireland*, 9 February 1884. Cited McConnel, *Jobbing*, p.109.
343. 'A FEMALE is at the bottom of every conspiracy. Look for the woman in the Kilmainham Treaty Mystery, and you will find her in O'SHEA!', *Punch*, 27 May 1882. Cited, Dungan, *O'Shea*, p.116.
344. Agreement was reached during Parnell's ten-day parole – compassionate leave – when he visited the O'Sheas at Eltham. Healy, *Letters*, chap. xii. Parnell had attended the funeral of his nephew in Paris.
345. Hansard, 16 February 1882.
346. Letter of 10 May 1882. Cited Russell, *Commission*, p.290.
347. Paul Bew, *Emnity*, p.341.
348. MacDonagh, *Home rule*, p.198. B. O'Brien, *Parnell*, pp379–84. Healy, *Letters*, chap. xix, 'Both of us [Healy and Biggar] failed to realise the depths to which the "Chief" had sunk.'
349. Davitt, *Fall*, p.468, cited Bew, *Emnity*, p.347.
350. MacDonagh, *Home Rule*, pp171–2.
351. NLI, T.D. Sullivan papers, Folder 1.
352. *Ibid.*, Folder 2.
353. NLI, O'Leary papers, Cited McGee, *IRB*, p.158.
354. Healy, *Letters*, chap. xxxvii. Letter to John Redmond, 8 February 1910.
355. Fanny Van de Grift Stevenson and Robert Louis Stevenson co-wrote *More Arabian Nights, The Dynamiter* (1885). Robert was highly critical of the term 'dynamitard',

'Any writard who writes dynamitard shall find in me a never-resting fightard.'
Dynamite comes from the Greek *Dynamis*, meaning power.

356. Hamilton, *Diary*, 26, 28 February 1884, pp566-7.

357. *Ibid.*, 3 February 1884, pp553.

358. Michael Davitt to John Ferguson, cited Russell, *Commission*, p.497.

359. O'C.P., 'New Reform', p.24.

A Democratic Position

360. Hansard, 11 February 1884.

361. *MG*, 6 February 1884.

362. Hansard, 20 February 1884.

363. 'On the Home Rule side Edmund Burke was the icon of icons and quoted by Gladstone, Harcourt and Granville ... the Home Rulers remained loyal to "their Burke".' Bew, *Emnity*, p.349.

364. 'Healy Clause'. See account in B. O'Brien, *Parnell*, p.279. Russell, *Commission*, p.263. Healy took his seat in January 1881. He would later be sidelined by the Irish party.

365. Hansard, 20 February 1884. Cited MacDonagh, *Home Rule*, pp167-8. 'I have maintained, on fifty platforms in Great Britain and America, since my release from Portland, that to outrage and outrage alone was due the defeat and partial collapse of the Land League, and the consequent escape of landlordism – for a time ... ' Davitt, physical force letter, cited Russell, *Commission*, p.496.

366. McDonagh, *Home Rule*, p.166.

367. *The Times*, 2 June 1884.

368. *MG*, 8 June 1884.

369. O'C.P., 'Abiding Influence', p.669.

370. *MG*, 25 April 1884. Barry O'Brien relates that an MP was driven out of the party because of Whig leanings and for insulting Parnell. '"Parnell was quite willing" this ex MP said to me "to take me back but Healy and Dillon objected, and the matter was let drop"'. B. O'Brien, *Parnell*, p.538.

371. *NYT*, 29 September 1885.

372. Hamilton, *Diary*, 16 January 1884, p.545. 'It appears that Parnell is not much pleased with the idea of a Reform Bill.' *Ibid.*, p.547. On the second reading of the Bill it was only at the last moment that Parnell voted for it.

373. *Ibid.*, 28 January 1884, p.550.

374. *Ibid.*, 14 February 1884, p.565.

375. *Ibid.*, 29 February 1884, p.567.

376. *Ibid.*, 25 May 1885, p.870.

377. Hansard, 26 July 1888.

378. Kettle, *Material for Victory*, cited Bew, *Emnity*, p.344. In Winston Churchill's biography of his father he quotes Randolph in 1886, 'I decided some time ago that if the GOM [Gladstone was the Grand Old Man] went for Home Rule, the Orange Card would be the one to play.' Cited, Dangerfield, *Strange Death*, p.82.

379. The rapprochement with the Tories dated at least as far back as 27 February 1885, 'Some sort of compact is evidently being made between the Tories and the Irish Nationalists. Constant communications are going on between the two parties.' Hamilton, *Diary*, p.802. And 5 May, 'We are face to face with an Irish *impasse*. I am

afraid I may turn out a true prophet in foretelling that the Irish rock was the one which would finally shipwreck the Government.', p.856.

380. B. O'Brien, *Parnell*, pp337-8. Charles Gavan Duffy, *The Carnarvon Controversy*, chap. xviii, pp333-60. Lord Carnarvon, briefly Lord Lieutenant, was believed to be in favour of a large measure of local government for Ireland.

381. Healy, *Letters*, chap. xvi.

382. 'Hawarden Kite', *Leeds Mercury*, 17 December 1885. *The Times*, 12 January 1886.

383. *MG*, 11 December 1928.

384. Healy, *Letters*, chap. xix.

Man of the Day

385. *MG*, 24 April 1885. John Bright, letter to Kennington, July 1885.

386. John Proctor and A. Bryan, *Moonshine*, p.230, 'The Radicals called him a Fenian, and the Fenians called him a renegade.'

387. *The Times*, 3 December 1885. 'In South London a special committee was formed to prevent the return of Mr John O'Connor Power for the Kennington Division.' *MG*, 18 November 1885, 'Irish Roughs in Lambeth'.

388. *MG*, 7 April 1886.

389. Richard Cobden, 10 March 1865.

390. *MG*, 18 December 1885.

391. F.W. Chesson dinner, 16 July 1886, ppxxv–xxvi.

392. Ayerst, *Guardian*, pp217-18.

Taking a Stand

393. Of Liberal Unionists. O'Connor Power entry, *Oxford Book of Quotations* (1966), p.387:15. Attributed by H.H. Asquith, *Memories and Reflections*, vol. i (London, 1892), p.123. 'He was, I believe, the real author of a phrase which was sometimes attributed to me, that the Liberal Unionists were "the mules of politics: without pride of ancestry, or hope of posterity".' Attribution disputed by Healy.

394. London, 20 June. Reported *NYT*, 2 July 1883. On 13 October 1883, James Daly attacked the League in the *Connaught Telegraph*, 'The Land League is the most anti-national and demoralising organisation that ever cursed Ireland.' Cited Moran, *James Daly*, p.204.

395. *Universal Review*, vol. iii, January-April 1889. J.E. Thorold Rogers, MP, published John Bright's speeches.

396. Earl Spencer to John O'Connor Power, 22 January 1886 (NLI, Michael MacDonagh papers, MS 11445).

397. Archbishop Walsh (1841-1921). His appointment in 1885 was opposed by the British government. At the Special Commission proceedings his evidence helped unmask Richard Pigott. He supported Sinn Féin and opposed partition.

398. 'Parnellism and Crime' articles, 7, 10 and 14 March 1887. The facsimile letter appeared 18 April 1887.

399. Kettle, *Material for Victory*, p.85.

400. B. O'Brien, *Parnell*, p.404.

401. *MG*, 22 May 1887.

402. *MG,* 28 December 1887.
403. *The Times,* 2 January 1888.
404. *NYT,* 6 January 1888.
405. O'C.P., 'Condition of Ireland' (1875).
406. Hansard, 10 April 1883.
407. *Devoy's Post Bag,* Carroll to Devoy, 10 April 1876.
408. *Quebec Daily Telegraph,* 14 May 1888.
409. *Clinton Evening News,* 3 November 1888.
410. *The Canadian Magazine,* ed. J. Gordon Mowat (1899), p.287.
411. *Saturday Budget,* 30 June 1888.
412. *Blue Banner,* 11 November 1951, *Toronto: 75 Years Ago,* Alumni magazine of St Michael's College, now the largest Catholic university in Canada.
413. *NYT,* 25 October 1888.
414. Timothy Healy wrote that O'Connor Power 'rejected overtures from *The Times* to "form" against former colleagues at the Forgery Commission'. Healy, excluded from the inner circle of Russell's defence team, was not in the loop. Healy, *Letters,* chap. ix. Parnell offered him the brief and then, four weeks later, without explanation, abruptly changed his mind. Callanan, *Healy,* pp195-6. Davitt objected strongly to Healy holding a brief. B. O'Brien, *Parnell,* p.539
415. Russell, *Commission,* p.281.
416. Captain O'Shea wrote an unflattering article about Parnell in *The Times,* 2 August 1888.
417. Davitt, *Fall,* p.565.
418. Russell, *Commission,* p.208. Davitt dined with Russell on 8 April. Michael Davitt to John O'Connor Power, 8 April 1889 (NLI, MacDonagh papers, MS 11445).
419. B. O'Brien, *Russell,* p.257.
420. Timothy Harrington, Parliamentary Debate of Special Commission Report, Hansard, 4 March 1890.
421. John Dillon, Parliamentary Debate on Special Service Money, Hansard, 26 March 1897.
422. Ryan, *Memories,* p.143.

Part Five

Hearts and Minds

423. Hansard, 5 May 1881. O'C.P. is opposed to communism because it destroys individuality and represses energy, leading men to look to the State for support. In 1883, he promotes 'the value of self-help'. Hansard, 10 April 1883. Fenians were frequently called socialists and communists.
424. O'C.P., 'Abiding Influence', pp677-8.
425. Belfort Bax's *Time* was short-lived (January 1890-December 1891). O'C.P., 'Irish Wit and Humour' (May 1890). Other notable contributers to *Time* were Massingham, George Bernard Shaw and Michael MacDongah.
426. Letter dated Sunday Morning, 17 August 1890. Norman MacKenzie, *Letters of Sidney and Beatrice Webb* (2008), p.175, 177. G. Wallas is Graham Wallas.
427. MacDonagh, *Home Rule,* p.164. Hansard, 15 March 1892. Mr J.G. Swift McNeill,

'very clauses later dealing with the Land Purchase Act taken from plans suggested in 1883-4 by John O'Connor Power'. '[O'C.P.] formulated a scheme of migration from the congested districts to the pasture plains by which the most crowded and poorest places would be relieved, and the plains that supported only cattle be made to provide a freer and fuller life for men'. Hansard, 10 April 1883. At the end of 1884 he was on a committee with James Tuke to raise funds for the Achill Bridge and Viaduct. James Tuke letter to *The Times*, 23 December 1884.

428. O'C.P., *Congested Districts*, pp796-7.
429. *Ibid.*, p.798. Female-dominated cottage industries were fostered. Co-operative labour, 'meitheal', was encouraged. Bee-keeping was popular.
430. *Ibid.*, p.798.
431. MacDonagh, *Home Rule*, pp273-4.
432. *The Times*, 10 March 1890.

The Daily Chronicle

433. MacDonagh, *Home Rule*, p.199.
434. Michael Davitt wrote to arrange a meeting at the National Liberal Club to discuss *Labour World*. Michael Davitt to John O'Connor Power, 28 February 1890 (NLI, Michael MacDonagh papers, MS 11445).
435. Healy, *Letters*, chaps xxiv, xxvi. On 20 November, *Labour World* asks for Parnell's resignation. Davitt does not hold back, 'His honour is a by-word, his mendacity boundless, his vindictiveness and tyranny infamous, his hypocrisy colossal.'
436. *Workman's Time*, 11, 16, 23 November 1893. Cited Havinghurst, *Radical Journalist*, p.51, fn i.
437. Alfred F. Havinghurst, *Radical Journalist*, p.56.
438. Massingham, *London Daily Press*, p.144.
439. *Ibid.*, p.134.
440. Havighurst, *Radical Journalist*, p.47. O'C.P. was no longer an MP. Under Secretary of State for the Home Department, Herbert Gladstone to Lord Ripon, Secretary of State for the Colonies, 5 December 1892. Ripon may have asked for recognition of O'C.P.'s role in the Liberals' return to power. Herbert Gladstone's reply was enigmatic, 'you know all about O'Connor Power' (BL MS 43543/157). Asquith was Home Secretary.
441. *New Zealand Star*, 3 December 1891.
442. Hansard, 1 March 1894. The *Chronicle*'s correspondent compared his visit to the House of Lords to 'a visit to the funeral barrow of one's prehistoric ancestors'. Lord Roseberry succeeded Gladstone as Premier.
443. W. O'Brien, *Irish MPs*, pp746-7.
444. Frank Wakeley Gunsaulis, William Ewart Gladston, a biographical study, 'At Eventide' (1898), pp370-1.
445. Cited in McConville, *Political Prisoners*, p.365.
446. Commons Paper Index (1890), p.403. Reports of Commissioners. Chatham Convict Prison (Treatment of Treason Felony Prisoners). Report of the Visitors of the Convict Prison at Chatham, as to the treatment of certain prisoners convicted of treason felony (1890), [c6061] p.xxx vii, 629. On his release John Daly gave an interview to the *Daily Chronicle* which appeared 12 September 1896.
447. *The Times*, 14 August 1890. Cited in McConville, *Political Prisoners*, p.377.

448. Michael Davitt to John O'Connor Power, 11 November 1891 (NLI, MacDonagh papers, MS 11445).
449. *NYT*, 10 July 1892.

The Pilgrim Soul

450. Percy was the family name of the Northumberlands, and Shakespeare's Hotspur was a member of the historically prominent dynasty. The third Earl, Lord Lieutenant of Ireland (1829-30), was a patron of Oliver Goldsmith.
451. Their cook, Jessie Byerley, was the daughter of a police constable (1901 UK census).
452. The final drainage application for 7 Luttrell Avenue was submitted in April 1906. Another occupier was in residence in 1908. The 1911 census places the O'Connor Powers and young Hubert at the address.
453. *Plarr's Lives of the Fellows of the Royal College of Surgeons – England*, vol. 2, p.500.
454. *British Medical Journal*, 16 July 1892.
455. Healy, *Letters*, p.xiii.
456. Eunice Lois Affleck Graves was born 24 May 1875, married 29 April 1899 and died 29 April 1944. William died in 1939. They had a daughter, Shelagh. Eunice was related to Arthur Perceval Graves, his son Robert and Ida Affleck Graves. Robert Graves was briefly at King's College School.
457. 3 November 1921, Southhampton-New Orleans, USA, *Frisia*; 13 January 1934, Southhampton-Capetown, South Africa, *Balmoral Castle*.
458. The church was built at much the same time as the Luttrell Avenue houses. The land was donated by the Catholic Lady Westbury (1857-1941), whose maiden name was Agatha Luttrell. Her parents were born in Ireland, and her mother's family was from Glinsk, County Galway. Lady Westbury attended the International Congress of Women in 1899. Fr Joseph Livesey was parish priest, 1908-28.
459. Disraeli, *Lothair*, chap. xv.
460. Hamilton, *Diary*, February 1883, pp403-4. Aside from Gladstone, Hamilton would have 'awarded the highest oratorical prize … to an Irishman, such a man as O'Connor Power'.
461. O'Connor, T.P., *Memoirs*, pp85-6. '[O'C.P.'s] name used to appear in the list of the guests at the house of Lady Jersey and others of the then ruling *salonnières* of London'. T.P. describes Lady Jersey as a 'philanthropist', a lover of mankind, regardless of race or creed.
462. Powell, *Margaret, Countess of Jersey*, p.85. Violet Powell, Lady Jersey's granddaughter, was married to the novelist Anthony Powell.
463. *Ibid.*, p.76.
464. *Ibid.*, p.106.
465. *MG*, 27 May 1897.
466. James Boswell, *Life of Johnson*, chap. i.

We'll Never Have Better

467. Address of the IRB Supreme Council to the people of Ireland, January 1870. See Moody, *IRB*, p.310.

468. Amended constitution of the IRB and of the Supreme Council, 17 March 1873 (2). See Moody, *IRB*, p.314.

469. Address of the IRB Supreme Council to the officers and men of the IRA, 17 March 1873. Printed broadsheet in Doran papers. See Moody, *IRB*, p.312.

470. The North Kerry villages of Ballyduff, Ardfert and Causeway have a place in Charles Doran's notes. Mem. 28 Jan. 1877, Mallow. See Moody, *IRB*, p.322. According to a contemporary account, 'the brilliant play of McDonnell' made the winning goal in extra time. Cited *Ballyduff Magazine*, vol. i (1988). The ballad 'The Boys of Ballyduff' is still sung in the village after All-Ireland finals.

471. Francis A. Fahy, 'The Irish language movement', *Westminster Review*, March 1902. In 1883, Fahy founded the Southwark Literary Club.

472. B. O'Brien, *Russell*, p.14.

The Abiding Influence

473. O'C.P., 'Abiding Influence', p.678.

474. *The Times*, 5, 13 July 1895.

United Irish League

475. *MG*, 13 January 1897. Edmund Burke was born 12 January 1729 in Dublin. He died 9 July 1797.

476. *MG*, 18 March 1898, 'Banquet in London'.

477. Timon, 'Ireland militant', *Westminster Review*, July 1901.

478. 'Between 1880 and 1922 few Irish Americans visited Ireland and the effects of the expansion of local government and land reforms were not witnessed by them.' Hennessy, *Dividing Ireland*, pp30-1.

479. *The Times*, 21 June 1900; *Anglo-Celt*, 23 June 1900.

480. *New Zealand Tablet*, Home News, 1 February 1900.

481. *Anglo-Celt*, Saturday, 6 October 1900. UIL convention, West Cavan, 'Mr J. O'Connor Power had been in the constituency from the previous Saturday, urging his claims upon the electors … Mr O'Connor Power appeared in rare form, and as he stepped lightly on to the bench in the Court House next the chairman, seemed to say to himself "If I can get a hearing I can convince them that I am the man" but he didn't.'

482. *MG*, 27 May 1901.

483. *The Times*, 27 May 1901.

484. Revd P. Dooley PP to John Redmond, 13 October 1901, enclosing O'C.P.'s letter (NLI, John Redmond papers, MS 15240/11).

485. *FJ*, 18 November 1901.

486. Hansard, 2 March 1903. The Galway Vacancy. The Attorney General moved a writ for a new election. It was argued that the constituency should be disenfranchised for five years and 'the writ not be entered in the present session'.

487. *IT*, 21 February 1903.

488. *II*, 21 March 1905, *The Irish in London*.

489. *MG*, 28 November 1901.

490. *MG*, 22 September 1900. Maguire was a close associate of Cecil Rhodes. He supported the war and denounced Home Rule. He lost his seat. The London

correspondent was probably Massingham who had moved to the *Manchester Guardian*. In January 1901 he took up a position with the *Daily News*.

491. McCracken, *Forgotten Protest*, p.89.
492. C.P. Scott correspondence, November 1902.

The Racquet Court and Billiard Hall

493. Emily was born in Peshawar in 1876 and John in Daigshai in 1879.
494. Catherine Power, Ballygill, died at the age of seventy in 1872. She was married and John Power was present at her death.
495. 1902 Valuations. Peter O'Shaugnessy, 22 Middle Street, Billiard Rooms, 22a Middle Street, Court Theatre.
496. James Hardiman, *Galway*, p.315.
497. He was married and was forty-one years of age when he died on 26 May 1906.
498. Cited Cunningham, *A Town Tormented*, p.301.
499. *Ibid.*
500. *Ibid.*
501. Peter died in the Galway County Hospital on 4 August 1910 at the age of thirty-eight.
502. 'Scene in Galway Theatre', *FJ*, 17 November 1908. Cited Hogan and Kilroy, *The Abbey Theatre*, p.364. The court has been rebuilt and re-furbished.
364. The Court had been rebuilt and refurbished.
503. Private Walter Macken was killed in action at St Eloi, 27 March 1916.
504. Macken Family Archives, cited by Willie Henry, *Galway and the Great War*, pp146-7. See also Ultan Macken, *Walter Macken, Dreams on Paper*, 19-20 (Dublin, 2009)
505. John Kelly & Ronald Schumach (eds), *The Collected Letters of W.B.Yeats, 1901-1903* (1994).
506. *IT*, 8 May 1905.
507. Hayward, *Corrib County*, p.143. Hayward also mentioned 'Terry, Benson and Martin Harvey … giants of provincial touring days'.
508. *IT*, 5 February 1907. Mary (Birdie) and Everina were not in Galway. Mary married in Rathmines, Dublin, on 6 February 1907. Everina was her bridesmaid.
509. Cited Toibin, *Toothbrush*, pp50-1.
510. Ann Saddlemyer (ed.), *The Collected Letters of John Millington Synge, 1871-1909* (Clarendon Press: New York; Oxford University Press, 1983/84), pp114–116. Fay resigned on 13 January. Anthony Roche, *Lady Gregory, the Politics of Touring Ireland, Irish Theatrical Diaspora Series, 1*, Nicholas Grene & Chris Morash (eds) (Carysfort Press, 2005), pp58-64.
511. Robert Hogan, *The Rise of Realism* (1910), Appendix II, p.436.
512. *Connaught Tribune*, 17 July 1920.

The Making of an Orator

513. O'C.P., *Orator*, p.33.
514. Leslie Cope Cornford, *The Memoirs of Lord Charles Beresford* (London, 1917), p.140.
515. *NYT*, 23 June 1906. *IT*, 26 June 1906.
516. Fr Michael Phelan, *The Young Priest's Keepsake* (Dublin, 1909), pp40-3.
517. This may be a reference to Parnell's first attempt at public speaking. Parnell accepted

advice and carefully observed orators in the House before appearing on platforms in the North of England and Scotland, on an introductory whirlwind tour.

518. Sir Herbert Maxwell, *A Century of Empire* (London, 1911), p.153.
519. O'C.P., *Orator*, p.39.

A Broken Treaty

520. O'C.P., *Westminster Review*, Spring 1901. Cited in *The Advertiser*, Australia SA, 10 April 1901. Edward's coronation took place on 9 August 1902. A moderated form of the oath was used for the coronation of George V in 1910. Frederick Greenwood was founder of the *Pall Mall* gazette.
521. William A. Sandys, writing from the National Liberal Club, told Redmond that O'Connor Power asked him to approach Redmond about re-entering parliament. William Sandys to John Redmond, 2 January 1906 (NLI, John Redmond papers, MS 15246/2). 'Political Recruits', *MG*, 30 November 1908.
522. *The Times*, 3 March 1910.
523. O'C.P., 'Condition of Ireland' (1875).
524. Hansard, 1 January 1913. Cited Dangerfield, *Strange Death*, p.105. Carson calls on the Irish party, 'below the gangway', to recognise the 'seriousness of events' and lay aside its 'holiday hilarity'.
525. John O'Connor Power to William O'Brien, 24 October 1913. William O'Brien Papers, University College Cork Archives.
526. Hansard, 10 February 1914.
527. *II*, 17 March 1914.
528. William O'Brien Papers, J. O'Connor Power to Williamm O'Brien, 26 May 1915, University College Cork Archives. The *Irish Independent* 'London Letter' reported on 23 May, 'Mr O'Connor Power, ex-MP, who has been ill lately, is now much better. He is well enough to be out of doors.'
529. *II*, 19 June 1916.
530. The Anti-Partition of Ireland League (Great Britain) hosted a dinner for Eamon De Valera at the Saracen's Head in Lincoln, 7 October 1950. The toast was to Anglo-Irish friendship.

Afterword

531. O'C.P., *Orator*, p.44.
532. O'C.P., 'Philosophy of Irish History' (1880).
533. *Ibid.*
534. *MG*, 14 February 1875. O'C.P., 'Politics Would Be Intolerable', 'New Reform', p.19.
535. On the motion of P.J. Smyth, a first reading of the Bill for the Repeal of the Act of Irish Parliament to prevent 'the Election or Appointment of Unlawful Assemblies'. The statute was repealed in 1879.
536. *IT*, 23 February 1906. 'Enlarge' here means set free. A trysting place is a hunting station. In the 1911 census there is a Michael O'Connor (forty-eight) farming in Carns in the parish of Ogulla.
537. Hansard, 20 August 1883. O'C.P.'s colleague James O'Kelly, MP for Roscommon, asked the Postmaster General for a post office for Clashaganny. A request for a post office was a way of obstructing the business of the Commons.

538. When a Monsignore renounced his faith Gladstone was delighted, '[Mr G.] has the most holy terror of Ultramon(tan)ism and its demoralising effect on individual characters, and regards any secession from it as a triumph of religion and morality.' Hamilton, *Diary*, p.531.

539. *II*, 23 May 1915, 'London Letter'. *Anglo-Celt*, 13 January 1917.

540. Thomas was discharged on 3 May 1881, with twenty-one years' service, plus a hundred days. O'C.P. asked for a vote of thanks to the army in Afghanistan. *MG*, 6 August 1879.

541. O'C.P., 'Condition of Ireland' (1875).

542. O'C.P., 'Abiding influence', p.673.

543. *MG*, 20 December 1905.

544. *Ibid.*, 13 March 1889. 'London correspondent on commission'.

545. O'C.P., 'Abiding influence', pp680-1.

Bibliography

Primary Texts

'The Condition of Ireland, Social, Political and Industrial,' John O'Connor Power, text of lecture, *The Irish Canadian*, 20 October 1875.

Irish Political Prisoners, Speeches of John O'Connor Power M. P., in the House of Commons on the Subject of Amnesty, etc., and a Statement by Mr. Michael Davitt, (ex-political prisoner) on Prison Treatment (March, 1878).

Irish Political Prisoners, Enquiry into the Prison Treatment and Cause of Death of the Late Color-Sergeant McCarthy (ex-political prisoner) and Letter to Sir James T. Ingham, John O'Connor Power, M.P. (London, 1878).

'Fallacies About Home Rule,' J. O'Connor Power, *Fortnightly Review*, Aug. 1879, pp. 224-35.

'The Irish Land Agitation,' J. O'Connor Power, *Nineteenth* Century, no. 34, Dec. 1879, pp. 953-67.

'The Irish in England,' J. O'Connor Power, *Fortnightly Review*, no. 159, 1880, pp. 410-21.

'The Philosophy of Irish History,' J. O'Connor Power, text of lecture, *Weekly Irish Times*, 1 May 1880.

'The New Reform,' J. O'Connor Power, *Nineteenth Century*, Jan. 1885, 15-24.

Toast to distinguished visitors at F. W. Chesson dinner, National Liberal Club, 16 July 1886, xxii-xxviii. Raymond English Anti-Slavery Collection, REAS/12, John Rylands Library, Manchester University.

The Anglo-Irish Quarrel, A Plea for Peace, John O'Connor Power, M.P. for the County of Mayo from 1874 to 1885, a reprint of recent articles in the *Manchester Guardian*, revised by the author (2nd Ed. London, 1886).

Ireland, A Book of Light on the Irish Problem, Contributed in Union by a Number of Leading Irishmen and Englishmen. Ed. Andrew Reid, essay by J. O'Connor Power (London, 1886), 77-87.

The Government of Ireland, the Irish Magistracy, the Root of Irish Discontent, John O'Connor Power, National Press Leaflets, no. 45 (1886).

'Two Great Statesmen, O'Connor Power Contrasts Gladstone and Disraeli,' O'Connor
   Power, *Special correspondence, Ottawa Free Trader,* 26 Jan. 1889.
'The Gospel of Wealth (A reply to Andrew Carnegie)', J. O'Connor Power, *The Universal
   Review,* vol. vi, no. 23, 347-55, 15 March 1890.
'Irish Wit and Humour,' John O'Connor Power, *Time,* May, 1890, 474-81.
'The Government Plan for the Congested Districts,' J. O'Connor Power, *Nineteenth
   Century,* xxvii, no. 159 (May 1890), 795-8.
Address to the Electors of Bristol South, 1895.
Edmund Burke and his Abiding Influence, J. O'Connor Power *The North American Review,*
   vol.165 issue 493, December, 1897, 666-81.
Letter from John O'Connor Power to C. P. Scott, November 1902. *The papers of C P Scott.
   Correspondence 1901-1904.* Journalism and Politics Series 1, Ptl. Reel 7.
*The Making of an Orator with Examples from Great Masterpieces of Ancient and Modern
   Eloquence,* John O'Connor Power (New York and London, 1906) (G.P. Putnam's Sons,
   The Knickerbocker Press, Methuen, 1906).

Manuscript Sources

National Library of Ireland

NLI, Michael MacDonagh papers, MS. 11,445.
NLI, F X O'Brien papers, MS. 13,457.
NLI, W G Fallon papers, MS, 22,740.
NLI, John Redmond papers, MS, 15240/11.
NLI, T D Sullivan papers, MS, 8237.
NLI, Lady Wilde papers, MS 27,609.

University College Cork Archives, William O'Brien papers

British Library, H. Gladstone to Lord Ripon, MS 43543/157.

Various newspaper and journal articles. Irish Census returns. National Archives of Ireland.
   National Archives at Kew, findmypast.co.uk, General Registry Office, Valuations Office.
   Power family records.

Contemporary Texts

Bagenal, Philip H., *The Irish Agitator in Parliament and on the Platform, A Cmplete History of
   Irish Politics for the Year 1879* (Dublin, 1880).
Baty, T., *International Law* (London, 1909).
Collins, Wilkie, *Blind Love* (Broadview Press, Canada, 2003, first published 1889).
Davitt, Michael, *The Times'-Parnell Commission, Speech delivered by Michael Davitt in Defence
   of the Land League* (London, 1890).
— *The Fall of Feudalism in Ireland, or the Story of the Land League Revolution* (London and
   New York, 1904).
Denvir, John, *The Irish in Britain, From the Earliest Times to the Fall and Death of Parnell*
   (London 1892).
— *The Life Story of an Old Rebel* (Dublin, 1910).

Devoy, John, *Devoy's Post Bag*, 1871-1928, William O'Brien and Desmond Ryan (eds) 2
  vols. (Dublin, 1948, 1953).
Fraser, James, *A Handbook for Travellers in Ireland* (Dublin 1844).
Gormley, Mary, Compiled by, *Tulsk Parish, Aspects of its History and Folklore* (March, 1989).
Gregory, Lady, *The Irish Theatre. A Chapter of Autobiography* (G.P. Putnam's Sons, The
  Knickerbocker Press, 1913)
Hartley, May Laffan, *Hogan MP* (1876, 1882).
— *Christy Carew* (1878, 1882).
Hamilton, Sir E. W., *The Diary of Sir Edward Walter Hamilton, 1880-1885*, ed. Dudley W. R.
  Bahlman, 2 vols (Oxford, 1972).
Hardiman, James, *The History of the Town and County of Galway* (1820).
Healy, T. M., *Letters and Leaders of My Day*, 2 vols (London, 1928).
The I.R.B Supreme Council, 1868-78, eds. T.W. Moody and Leon Ó Broin, *Irish Historical
  Studies*, xix, no. 75 (March, 1975), pp286-332.
Jeans, William, *Parliamentary Reminiscences* (London, 1912).
Jersey, Margaret Child-Villiers, *Fifty-one Years of Victorian Life* (New York, 1922).
Kettle, Andrew J., *The Material for Victory, Being the Memoirs of Andrew J. Kettle* (Dublin,
  1958).
Lucy, Henry William, *A Diary of Two Parliaments* (London, 1885).
MacDonagh, Michael, *The Home Rule Movement* (Dublin and London, 1920).
Massingham, William Henry, *The London Daily Press* (London, 1892).
Moore, George, *A Drama in Muslin, a Realistic Novel* (1886), (Colin Smyth, 1981).
— *Parnell and his Island* (1887), (U.C.D. Press, ed. Carla King, 2004)
— *Hail and Farewell, Ave, Salve, Vale*, 1911, 1914, 1925. (Colin Smyth edition, 1985).
Moore, M. G., *An Irish Gentleman, George Henry Moore* (London, 1913).
O'Brien, R. Barry, *The Life of Lord Russell of Killowen* (London, 1902).
— *The Life of Charles Stewart Parnell, 1846-1891* (London and New York, 1910).
— *John Bright a Monograph, with a Preface by Augustine Birrell* (London, 1910).
O'Brien, William, *If Ireland Sent Her M.P.s to Washington, Nineteenth Century*, May 1896,
  pp746-55.
— O'Brien, William M.P., *Recollections* (New York and London, 1905).
O'Connor T.P., M.P., The Right Honourable, *Memoirs of an Old Parliamentarian*, vol. i,
  (Ernest Benn Ltd., 1929).
O'Donnell, F. Hugh, *A History of the Irish Parliamentary Party*, 2 vols (London, 1910).
Parnell, Anna, *The Tale of a Great Sham*, 1907, ed. Dana Hearne (Arlen House, 1986).
Reid, Thomas Wilson, compiled by, *The Book of the Cheese: Being Traits and Stories of "Ye old
  Cheshire Cheese"*, Wine Office Court, Fleet Street, T Fisher Unwin (London, 1901)
Russell, Sir Charles, Q.C, M.P, *The Parnell Commission, the Opening Speech for the Defence*
  (New York and London, 1889).
Ryan, Dr. Mark Francis, *Fenian Memories* (Dublin, 1945).
Strachey, Lytton, *Eminent Victorians* (London, 1918).
Thackeray, William M., *The Irish Sketchbook* (Dublin, 1990, first published 1843).
Trollope, Anthony, *Phineas Finn* (1869).
— *Phineas Redux, The Palliser Novels* (1874, Oxford University Press, 1983).
— *The Landleaguers* (1883).
Various Hands, *The Johnson Club Papers by Various Hands*, T. Fisher Unwin (London, 1899).
Various Hands, *The Johnson Club Papers by Various Hands*, T. Fisher Unwin (London, 1920).
Whale, George, *The Forty Years of the Johnson Club, 1884-1924*, privately printed (London, 1925).

Secondary Texts

Ayerst, David, *Guardian, Biography of a Newspaper* (1971).

Bew, Paul, *Ireland, The Politics of Enmity 1789-2006* (Oxford, 2007).

Boyce, D. G., *Nationalism in Ireland* (Routledge, third edition 1995).

Breathnach, Ciara, *The Congested Districts Board of Ireland, 1891-1923, Poverty and Development in the West of Ireland* (Dublin, 2005).

Callanan, F., *The Parnell Split* (Cork, 1993).

— *T.M. Healy* (Cork, 1996).

Comerford, R.V., *The Fenians in Context, Irish Politics & Society, 1848-82* (Dublin, 1985).

Cunningham John, *St Jarlaths's College Tuam 1800-2000* (SJC Publication, Tuam, 1999).

— *'A Town Tormented by the Sea', Galway, 1790-1914* (Geography Publications, 2004).

Dangerfield, George, *The Strange Death of Liberal England* (London, 1997, first published 1935).

— *The Damnable Question, One Hundred and Twenty Years of Anglo-Irish Conflict* (Atlantic–Little, Brown Books, 1976).

Dillon, Eilis, *Across the Bitter Sea* (Coronet Edition, 1984, first published 1973).

Dudley Edwards R., *Parnell and the American Challenge to Irish Nationalism, Irish University Review*, vol. 2, no. 2 (Summer 1960), pp47–64.

Dungan, Myles, *The Captain and the King*, William O'Shea, Parnell and late Victorian Ireland (Dublin, 2009).

— *Conspiracy, Irish Political Trials* (Dublin, 2009).

Edwards, Peter, *The Infiltrator* (Maverick House, 2010).

Egan, Rev. Patrick, K, C.C., *Ballinasloe, A Historical Sketch* (Ballinasloe Tostal Council, 1953).

Grey, Peter, ed., *Victoria's Ireland? Irishness and Britishness, 1837-1901* (Dublin, 2004).

Havinghurst, Alfred F., *Radical Journalist: H.W. Massingham (1860-1924)* (London and New York, 1974).

Hayward, Richard, *The Corrib County* (Dundalgan Press, 1943).

Hennessey, Thomas, *Dividing Ireland, World War One and Partition* (Routledge, 1998).

Henry, William, *Galway and the Great War*, Mercier Press (Cork, 2006).

Hickey, D.J., and J.E. Doherty, eds., *A New Dictionary of Irish History from 1800* (Dublin, 2003).

Hogan, Robert and James Kilroy, *The Abbey Theatre, The Years of Synge 1905-1909* (Dublin, 1978).

Johnson Club, *The Johnson Club 1884 – 1934*, being *Some Account of the Club with its List of Members and its Rules*. London, Chapman, Robert William (Printed by Clarendon Press for the Club, London, 1938).

Jordan, Donald E., 'John O'Connor Power, Charles Stewart Parnell and the Centralisation of popular politics in Ireland', *Irish Historical Studies*, 25, 97, (1986), pp46–66.

— *Merchants, 'Strong Farmers' and Fenians, the Post Famine Political Elite and the Irish Land War, Nationalism and Popular Protest in Ireland*. Ed. Philpin C.H.E. (Cambridge, 1987).

— *Land and Popular Politics in Ireland. County Mayo from the Plantation to the Land War* (Cambridge, 1994).

Larkin, Emmet, *The Roman Catholic Church and the Home Rule Movement in Ireland, 1870-1874*, (Dublin, 1990)

Lee, J.J., *The Modernisation of Irish Society 1848-1918* (Dublin, 1973).

— *Ireland 1912-1985, Politics and Society* (Cambridge University Press, 1989).

McConnel, James, 'Fenians at Westminster, the Irish Parliamentary Party and the Legacy of the New Departure,' *Irish Historical Studies* xxxiv, 133 (May 2004), pp41-64

— 'Jobbing with Tory and Liberal: Irish Nationalists and the Politics of Patronage,' *Past and Present*, 2005, 188: pp105-31

McConville, Sean, *Irish Political Prisoners 1848-1922, Theatres of War* (Routledge, 2003)

McCracken, Donal, *Forgotten Protest, Ireland and the Anglo-Boer War* (Ulster Historical Foundation, 2003).

McGee, Owen, *The Irish Republican Brotherhood, from the Land League to Sinn Féin* (Dublin, 2005, Second edition containing minor corrections, 2007).

Marlow, Joyce, *Captain Boycott and the Irish* (London, 1973).

Maume Patrick, *The Long Gestation, Irish National Life, 1891-1918* (Dublin, 1999).

Mayo County Library written and compiled by Rosa Meehan, *The Story of Mayo* (2003).

Moody, T.W., *Davitt and Irish Revolution 1846-82* (Oxford, 1982).

— Moody T.W., Hawkins, Richard, and Moody, Margaret, *Florence Arnold-Forster's Irish Journal* (Oxford, 1988).

Moran, Gerard P., *The Changing Course of Mayo Politics, 1867-1874*. chap. 7, '*A Various Country*', *Essays in Mayo History 1500-1900*, eds. Raymond Gillespie and Gerard Moran (FNT-Mayo News Westport, 1987).

—*A Radical Priest in Mayo Fr Patrick Lavelle, The Rise and Fall of an Irish Nationalist, 1825-86* (Dublin, 1994).

— 'James Daly and the Rise and Fall of the Land League in the West of Ireland 1879-82', *Irish Historical Studies*, 29 114 (1994), pp189-207.

O'Brien, Cruise C., *Parnell and His Party, 1880-1890* (Oxford, 1957*)*.

Ó Broin, León, *Charles Gavan Duffy, Patriot and Statesman, the Story of Charles Gavan Duffy*, J. Duffy (1967).

— *The Chief Secretary, Augustine Birrell in Ireland* (London, 1969).

— *Fenian Fever, an Anglo-American Dilemma* (London, 1971).

— *Revolutionary Underground, the Story of the Irish Republican Brotherhood 1858-1924* (Dublin, 1976).

O'Day Alan, *Irish Home Rule 1867-1921* (Manchester, 1998).

Powell, Violet, *Margaret Countess of Jersey* (London, 1978.)

Quinlavin, Patrick and Paul Rose, *The Fenians in England* (London, 1982).

Spellissey, Sean, *The History of Galway* (The Celtic Bookshop, 1999).

Thornley, David, *Isaac Butt and Home Rule* (London, 1964).

Tóibín, Colm, *Lady Gregory's Toothbrush* (Dublin, 2002).

Tolkien, J. R. R., *The Notion Club papers, Sauron Defeated* (HarperCollins 1992).

Townend, Paul A, *Between Two Worlds, Irish Nationalists and Imperial Crisis 1878-1880*, Past and Present Society, Oxford, vol.194, Feb. 2007, pp139-174.

White, T. de Vere, *The Road of Excess* (Dublin,1946).